Lecture Notes in Computer Science 2262
Edited by G. Goos, J. Hartmanis, and J. van Leeuwen

T0223731

Springer
Berlin
Heidelberg
New York
Barcelona
Hong Kong
London
Milan
Paris
Tokyo

Peter Müller

Modular Specification and Verification of Object-Oriented Programs

Springer

Series Editors

Gerhard Goos, Karlsruhe University, Germany
Juris Hartmanis, Cornell University, NY, USA
Jan van Leeuwen, Utrecht University, The Netherlands

Author

Peter Müller
Staufenstraße 34
60323 Frankfurt, Germany
E-mail: p.mueller@web.de

Cataloging-in-Publication Data applied for

Die Deutsche Bibliothek - CIP-Einheitsaufnahme

Müller, Peter:
Modular specification and verification of object oriented programs / Peter Müller. - Berlin ; Heidelberg ; New York ; Barcelona ; Hong Kong ; London ; Milan ; Paris ; Tokyo : Springer, 2002
(Lecture notes in computer science ; Vol. 2262)
ISBN 3-540-43167-5

CR Subject Classification (1998):D.2, D.3, D.1.5, F.3

ISSN 0302-9743
ISBN 3-540-43167-5 Springer-Verlag Berlin Heidelberg New York

Springer-Verlag Berlin Heidelberg New York
a member of BertelsmannSpringer Science+Business Media GmbH

http://www.springer.de

Printed in Germany

Typesetting: Camera-ready by author, data conversion by PTP-Berlin, Stefan Sossna
Printed on acid-free paper SPIN 10846107 06/3142 5 4 3 2 1 0

Foreword

Software systems play an increasingly important role in modern societies. Smart cards for personal identification, e-banking, software-controlled medical tools, airbags in cars, and autopilots for aircraft control are only some examples that illustrate how everyday life depends on the good behavior of software. Consequently, techniques and methods for the development of high-quality, dependable software systems are a central research topic in computer science.

A fundamental approach to this area is to use formal specification and verification. Specification languages allow one to describe the crucial properties of software systems in an abstract, mathematically precise, and implementation-independent way. By formal verification, one can then prove that an implementation really has the desired, specified properties. Although this formal methods approach has been a research topic for more than 30 years, its practical success is still restricted to domains in which development costs are of minor importance. Two aspects are crucial to widen the application area of formal methods:

- Formal specification techniques have to be smoothly integrated into the software and program development process.
- The techniques have to be applicable to reusable software components. This way, the quality gain can be exploited for more than one system, thereby justifying the higher development costs.

Starting from these considerations, Peter Müller has developed new techniques for the formal specification and verification of object-oriented software. The specification techniques are declarative and implementation-independent. They can be used for object-oriented design and programming. To illustrate the techniques and to make them directly applicable, his book develops a detailed framework for the specification and verification of classes and interfaces written in a Java subset.

The main contributions of his work concern the modularity problem. In this context, modularity means that software modules can be specified and verified independently and that their specifications and proofs remain valid under composition. In addition, the specification techniques have to be sufficiently complete to verify a module based on the specifications of the imported modules. Modularity is of critical importance for reuse and the emerging paradigm of component-based programming, and yet something that is by far underdeveloped in the literature.

One of the difficult aspects of modular verification is the so-called frame problem, that is, the treatment of the modification behavior of methods and procedures. The frame problem is particularly interesting when software modules have an encapsulated state the implementation details of which should not be exposed to the public. Thus, the frame problem is not restricted to object-oriented programming, but is relevant for classical procedural modules as well. To handle encapsulation and modularity, state changes have to be specified in an abstract way, that is, without referring to the hidden variables. The main technique employed is to use so-called abstract variables. However, this approach leads to dependencies between abstract and concrete variables, which cause a major problem for modular verification.

The developed solution to the frame problem builds on and clearly goes beyond existing approaches. It supports very general and expressive dependencies which are important to increase the flexibility of frame property specification. In addition, the higher expressiveness allows one to apply the approach to class invariants by regarding them as abstract boolean variables. That simplifies the formal framework, because a special treatment of invariants becomes dispensable. The key to the developed solutions is a new, type-based technique for alias control. The so-called universe type system enforces a hierarchical structure in the object store and is a valuable contribution in its own right.

All presented concepts and techniques are well motivated and precisely described. In particular, the different aspects of modular programming are nicely explained so that their implications can be followed into the detailed formal framework. I can only wish that many readers take the time to dive into the deep waters of the following chapters. They will be rewarded by interesting and valuable insights and by the beauty of a coherent formal framework solving the sketched problems. I wish even more that the work encourages other researchers to further develop the theory, techniques, and tools for modular specification and verification.

October 2001 *Arnd Poetzsch-Heffter*

Preface

The paradigm shift from procedural to object-oriented programming has promoted modular software development. The reuse of prefabricated software modules has especially increased the demand for precise specifications and quality certification, and thus for *modular* specification and verification techniques. Such techniques must be capable of handling object-oriented language features such as subtyping, inheritance, and dynamic method binding, and have to support modular development of specifications and proofs. In particular, they should enable specifications and proofs to be reused along with implementations.

This book presents modular specification and verification techniques for the functional behavior, frame properties, and type invariants of OO-programs. The key idea underlying this work is the formal integration of state-of-the-art specification and verification techniques with a type system for alias control.

We present the universe type system that can be used to control aliasing statically. It combines strong type constraints for readwrite references with the flexibility of readonly references. This combination guarantees an invariant that enables modular verification while retaining enough flexibility to handle most common implementation patterns, especially patterns such as binary methods and iterators that are not supported by related approaches.

The declarative interface specification technique presented in this book provides pre-post-specifications, abstract fields with explicit dependencies, modifies-clauses, and type invariants. Functional method behavior can be covered by pre-post-specifications. Abstract fields are used to map object structures to values of an abstract domain. The dependencies of an abstract field on the concrete fields that represent it are explicitly declared. Together with modifies-clauses, these declarations are used to express frame properties. Frame properties are particularly difficult to verify in a modular way since they require one to prove that certain abstractions are not modified by a method even if these abstractions are declared in other modules. To cope with this problem, we exploit the invariant guaranteed by the universe type system to define a novel semantics for modifies-clauses and to restrict the permissible dependencies of abstract fields in a way that makes modular verification of frame properties possible. Regarding type invariants as special abstract fields allows us to apply the specification and verification technique for frame properties to invariants.

For verification, we use a Hoare-style programming logic that is capable of handling OO-features and modularity. In particular, it ensures that only those properties of a module can be proved that hold in all well-formed contexts in which the module might be reused. That is, the logic guarantees the modular soundness of our verification technique.

Our techniques are presented for a programming language similar to sequential Java, but can be adapted to procedural and other object-oriented languages as well.

This book is based on my dissertation which was accepted by FernUniversität Hagen, Germany, in April 2001. The underlying research was carried out at FernUniversität Hagen, Germany, Iowa State University, USA, and Technische Universität München, Germany, during the previous five years.

During that time, I was advised by Prof. Dr. Arnd Poetzsch-Heffter. His thoroughness and his focus on the essential semantics of the artifacts under consideration guided me during my work on my thesis. I'm especially grateful for his ample support, his confidence, numerous inspiring discussions, and for always taking my ideas and concerns seriously. Far beyond his guidance in professional matters, Arnd has substantially influenced my perspective on life, making the past five years such a valuable experience.

I would like to express my gratitude to Prof. Gary T. Leavens, Ph.D., for serving on my thesis committee. He raised my interest in the frame problem and pointed me to promising approaches to its solution. His valuable suggestions and several fruitful discussions had an important impact on my work. In particular, I would like to thank Gary and his wife Janet for being such great hosts during my stay at Iowa State University.

For the encouraging working atmosphere in our group as well as for continuous helpfulness, I am indebted to my team members Monika Lücke and Jörg Meyer. Jörg played an important role in my work on this book. I am thankful for the close collaboration, countless discussions, and Jörg's great sense of humor. Moreover, I would like to thank him and his wife Ilka for their friendship during the past years.

The contents of this book benefited from numerous discussions and joint work with my advisor and my fellow team members. To express my appreciation for this team work, I use the first person plural in the following, although I am the only author of this book.

Prof. Dr. Jürgen Eickel gave me the opportunity to work in his group at the Technical University of Munich before I moved to Hagen. I am especially grateful to him for making my frequent visits to Munich possible by hosting me as a guest at his chair.

This book benefited from the valuable comments of several proof readers. I highly appreciate the efforts of Marco Avitabile, Marcel Labeth, Volker

Markl, Jörg Meyer, David von Oheimb, Günther Rackl, and Christian Schiller. Furthermore, I thank those who have directly or indirectly contributed to my work.

Last, but not least, my special thanks go to my girlfriend Annette Boseck for her understanding and encouragement as well as to my sister Sabine Müller and my parents Josephine and Claus Müller for their ongoing support.

September 2001 *Peter Müller*

Contents

1. Introduction

"Life is like a box of chocolates... You never know what you're gonna get."
[Forrest Gump as played by Tom Hanks
in the movie *Forrest Gump*, 1994]

Building reliable computer systems is one of the central goals of computer science. The failure of Ariane 5's maiden flight and the Year 2000 Problem have brought to everybody's mind to which extent our economic system and even our lives depend on correctly working software.

To guarantee software quality levels beyond those that can be achieved by syntax checking, type checking, and testing, mathematical reasoning has been applied to computer programs. Formal specifications can be used to precisely describe the desired properties of a program, and verification techniques allow one to prove that a program meets its specification. Since specifications can still be flawed in the sense that they do not reflect the developer's intention, even verified programs might not behave like they are supposed to. Still, specifications are an important step towards more reliable software because they improve development methodology and abstract from implementation details, which simplifies reasoning about software systems and allows verifiers to rule out coding errors.

In this book, we investigate modular specification and verification of object-oriented programs. We focus on programs written in object-oriented languages since these languages are the state-of-the-art in commercial software development. By facilitating modular development, they form the basis for the component industry many experts expect to emerge. Furthermore, most procedural languages are essentially subsets of the common object-oriented languages. Thus, the techniques presented here can be adapted to this language family.

This introduction is structured as follows: In the next section, we motivate our work on modular specification and verification of object-oriented programs and present a typical application scenario for the techniques developed in this book. Section 1.2 introduces the basic formal specification and verification technique used in this book. To illustrate the main problems of modular specification and verification, we present a number of motivating examples in Section 1.3. In Section 1.4, we systematically analyze modula-

Peter Müller: Modular Specification ..., LNCS 2262, pp. 1–37, 2002.

rity aspects of programs, specifications, and correctness proofs. Based on this analysis, we summarize the technical problems tackled in this book, explain our approach to their solution, and present the structure of this book as well as a summary of its main contributions in Section 1.5. Section 1.6 contains an overview of general approaches to specification, verification, and program analysis.

1.1 Motivation

Techniques for formal specification and verification have been available for more than 30 years. Since the early work by Floyd and Hoare, researchers have invented new techniques and adapted the existing ones to new programming language features such as procedures, exception handling, pointers, and concurrency. In particular, specification and verification techniques have been developed that are capable of handling the new features of object-oriented languages such as subtyping, inheritance, and dynamic method binding. However, the step from procedural to object-oriented programming was more than the invention of new language features. It turned out to be a paradigm shift that affected the whole software life cycle from analysis over design and implementation to maintenance.

Modular Development. For implementation, one of the most prominent effects of this paradigm shift is that object-oriented languages lead to a breakthrough of code reuse. The large number of Java APIs bears witness to this development. Accordingly, OO-programs are usually not developed from scratch in a purely top-down manner like the functional decomposition methodology in procedural programming. Instead, large parts of OO-programs are implemented by reusing, adapting, and composing prefabricated classes or modules (often called *software components*). This form of bottom-up software development is called *modular* or *component-based software development.*

To be suitable for modular development, specification and verification techniques have to meet two requirements:

1. They must be capable of handling the language features for modular object-oriented programming such as module concepts, subtyping, and inheritance.
2. They must support modular development of specifications and proofs. For instance, specifications and proofs should be reusable together with program modules. In particular, correctness proofs for a module should stay valid when the module is reused. Furthermore, it should be possible to derive the correctness of composite programs from the correctness of their constituents.

Whereas many aspects of requirement 1 have already been solved, requirement 2 is not met in a satisfying way by existing specification and verification techniques. In particular, modular specification and verification of alias properties, the absence of certain side-effects (so-called *frame properties*), and invariants bear several open problems. It is the aim of this book to analyze and illustrate open problems related to both requirements and to present solutions to the most important ones.

Application Scenario. Although OO-languages provide powerful support for reuse, truly component-based software development has not become current practice yet. Instead of plugging together prefabricated components, OO-programs are typically implemented by writing significant portions of new code (so-called *client code*) based on reused classes from general-purpose class libraries. These libraries provide implementations for basic functionality such as container classes or GUI frameworks. Usually, libraries and client code are implemented by different development teams or companies.

Even though publicly-available class libraries such as the Java API are frequently used, commercial development of libraries is still uncommon. Besides economic reasons, a component industry is hampered by the following technical problems:

- Clients have to rely on documentation to properly reuse libraries. However, documentation tends to be imprecise and incomplete. Referring to the library implementation instead is not appropriate for several reasons: (1) To protect its intellectual property, a library vendor will usually sell binaries and won't give away source code. (2) Source code is not an appropriate abstraction level to describe library properties. (3) Implementations are in general subject to changes in future releases of the libraries, whereas explicitly documented properties are supposed to be stable.
- There is no quality certification for software components available yet. Therefore, clients have to trust the vendors that libraries meet certain quality standards and have the properties specified in their documentation. In particular for business-critical applications such as e-commerce products, this is extremely unsatisfactory.

In a nutshell, customers have no reliable basis for using class libraries from third parties: They don't know what they are going to get when they buy a library. In this sense, the quote at the top of this chapter characterizes the status-quo of component-based programming.

Techniques for formal specification and verification of object-oriented software modules can help to solve these problems: Formal specifications provide clients with precise documentations of libraries. They are a basis for contracts between clients and library vendors and make formal reasoning possible. Formal verification allows a component industry to define quality standards and certify libraries according to these standards.

Reusable libraries do not only lead to a strong demand for specification and verification techniques. They are also a particularly interesting application area for such techniques:

- To be suitable for class libraries, specification and verification techniques have to be both formal and modular. Formality guarantees the necessary precision and allows tools to be applied for the retrieval and analysis of software components as well as to check proofs. Modularity allows one to reuse specifications and proofs along with library classes.
- Since libraries focus on designated domains and usually provide basic functionality only, most of them have a simple structure, that is, rather flat class hierarchies and little interaction between different modules (see e.g., the Java API). This reduces complexity, which makes modular specification and verification feasible.
- Library classes are frequently reused which justifies the effort of formal specification and verification economically since bugs in libraries potentially affect thousands of client programs.

To sum up the previous paragraphs, the paradigm shift from procedural to object-oriented software development promoted modular development of reusable software components. In particular, class libraries lead to new challenges for formal specification and verification. Adequate techniques have to be modular in a sense that they support the OO-language features for modular programming and that they support modular development of specifications and proofs, especially reuse. We present such modular specification and verification techniques for object-oriented programs in this book.

1.2 Specification and Verification Technique

In this book, we build as much as possible on well-known languages and techniques, and enhance them to support modularity. For specification, we use an interface specification technique that is based on the two-tiered approach developed by the Larch project [GH93]. Specifications consist of two major parts:

1. A program-independent specification (*universal specification*[1]) that provides the mathematical vocabulary (e.g., definitions of abstract data types) used to formulate interface specifications. We use multisorted first-order logic and recursive data types to formalize universal specifications (see App. A.1).
2. Program-dependent *behavioral interface specifications* (or *interface specifications* for short) that describe properties of implementations in terms of the underlying universal specification. Interface specifications of OO-programs describe (1) the behavior of methods and (2) properties of data representations. We follow the classical way of specifying method behavior by pre- and postconditions. Frame properties of methods are

[1] sometimes called *auxiliary specification* [LG86]

captured by modifies-clauses. Properties of data structures are expressed by type invariants.

The formal meaning of interface specifications is defined by translating them into triples of a Hoare-style programming logic. To verify a program w.r.t. its interface specification, these triples have to be proved in the programming logic.

In combination with our programming logic, two-tiered interface specification techniques are well-suited for the verification of OO-programs:

1. The formal framework based on first-order logic provides a clean semantical foundation for specifications and proofs. Pre- and postconditions, modifies-clauses, and type invariants can be translated into proof obligations in terms of triples of the programming logic. Therefore, interface specifications have a precise formal meaning.
2. Specifications can be based on a formal data and state model of the programming language that allows one to specify both low-level implementation properties and abstract behavior. Thus, the specification technique is powerful enough to express all relevant program properties such as functional behavior, side-effects, frame properties, sharing properties, and invariants.
3. The data and state model enables us to explicitly specify abstraction of objects and object structures. A strong support for data abstraction is necessary (a) to handle subtyping; (b) to make implementation-independent specification of program properties possible, which is particularly important in the presence of information hiding; (c) to provide an abstract view to program elements for clients that are in general not interested in implementation details; (d) to enable the application of standard verification techniques for programs with complex data representations [Hoa72]; (e) to establish a connection to formal design specifications. See [LG86] for a detailed discussion on abstraction and specification in program development.

We illustrate these properties along with the discussion of the formal data and state model (Subsection 3.1.1) and the specification primitives (Chapters 4 to 6).

1.3 The Problem

In this section, we describe the core problems for modular specification and verification of OO-programs and illustrate them by examples. We sketch our approaches to these problems and compare them to nonmodular solutions. Based on a systematic analysis of modularity of programs, specifications, and proofs, we discuss these problems and our approaches on a more technical level in Sections 1.4 and 1.5.

As explained in Section 1.1, specification and verification techniques support modularity if they meet two requirements.

1. They must be capable of handling the language features for modular object-oriented programming such as subtyping, dynamic binding, and inheritance.
2. They must support modular development of specifications and proofs.

We consider the specification and verification of functional method behavior, frame properties, and type invariants. In these areas, the above requirements entail several problems, the most prominent of which are:

- *Modular correctness:* Due to dynamic method binding, a method invocation can lead to the execution of code that is declared outside the module that contains the invocation. Therefore, in a modular setting, the correctness of a module relies on properties of the context in which it can be reused. These properties have to be formally specified and then verified when the module is reused. Moreover, a precise definition of modular correctness has to take requirements for contexts into account.
- *The frame problem:* Frame properties describe which instance variables and abstractions of objects must not be modified by a method execution. Sophisticated techniques are necessary to modularly specify and verify the effects of a method execution on abstractions that are not visible in the method.
- *Modular verification of type invariants:* Type invariants lead to proof obligations for at least all public methods of a program. That is, invariants introduced by program extensions lead to proof obligations for imported public methods. Since re-verification of imported methods is prevented by information hiding, invariants have to be restricted such that these proof obligations can be proved based on the specifications of the imported methods.
- *The extended state problem:* Subclasses inherit from their superclasses and can introduce additional fields, so-called *extended state*. To be able to refine the behavior of inherited methods, their specifications of frame properties must be loose enough to allow subclasses to modify the extended state.

The above problems are inherently related to modular specification and verification of OO-programs (the second and third problem also occur in procedural programs). They are not due to a certain programming language, specification, or verification technique, but occur whenever functional method behavior, frame properties, and type invariants of OO-programs are specified and verified modularly.

Modular solutions to the frame problem and modular verification of invariants require alias control. Since alias control is very important for the techniques presented in this book, we discuss it here among the more fundamental problems:

- *Alias control:* Aliasing occurs when several local or instance variables hold references to the same object. Alias control is necessary for the modular verification of frame properties and invariants, but difficult to achieve in modular programs by means of classical interface specification and verification.

In the following subsections, we illustrate each of the above problems by an example. The examples are written in a Java-like language and use a fictitious Larch-style specification language. We abstract from technical details where appropriate. In particular, we are a bit sloppy about the difference between fields and instances of fields (instance variables). In the following, we assume that the reader is familiar with two-tiered interface specifications and their formal verification. If that is not the case, we recommend to continue with Section 1.4 and follow the references back to this section.

1.3.1 Modular Correctness

The first example illustrates a problem caused by dynamic method binding.

Example 1.3.1.

```
module COUNTER;
  public class Counter {
    int val;
    public void increment()
      ensures  val' = val^ + 1;
      { val++; }
    ...
  }
module CLIENT imports COUNTER;
  public class Client {
    public static void useCounter(Counter c)
      ensures  c.val' = c.val^ + 1;
      { c.increment(); }
  }
```

Class `Counter` implements a simple counter that can be incremented. The specification of `increment` ensures that the value of the counter in the post-state (denoted by `val'`) equals the value in the prestate (`val^`) incremented by 1 (we do not care about overflow here). Class `Client` uses `Counter`. At first sight, both modules seem to be correct, that is, the methods `increment` and `useCounter` seem to satisfy their specifications. However, this is not generally true in a modular setting as becomes clear when we add a further module:

```
module BADCOUNTER imports CLIENT;
  public class BadCounter extends Counter {
    public void increment()             { val--; }
    public void showIt(BadCounter bc)  { Client.useCounter(bc); }
  }
```

Class `BadCounter` extends `Counter` and overrides the `increment`-method in a way that does not satisfy the specification given in `Counter`. Obviously, method `useCounter` does not satisfy its specification if a `BadCounter`-object is passed as parameter as in method `showIt`: In this case, the invocation of `increment` is dynamically bound to the implementation given in class `BadCounter` that decrements the value of `c.val` instead of incrementing it. That is, extending a program by new modules can affect the behavior of reused methods and, thus, the correctness of reused modules.

Approach. To avoid the unsoundness described above, we require that subtype methods behave according to the specifications of corresponding supertype methods. In order to achieve that, our programming logic allows one to prove a property of a dynamically-bound method such as `Counter.increment` only if this property holds as well for all methods overriding the method, especially for methods declared in future program extensions such as `BadCounter.increment`. These requirements for program extensions are made explicit in our programming logic. Our definition of modular correctness describes precisely the properties a module may assume about the context it is reused in. According to this definition, modules `COUNTER` and `CLIENT` are modularly correct, but module `BADCOUNTER` does not meet the requirements imposed by method `Counter.increment`. That is, the context in which the other modules are reused is not well-formed.

Nonmodular Solution. In nonmodular settings, all method bodies that might be executed upon the invocation of a dynamically-bound method are available for verification. Therefore, the problem described in Example 1.3.1 does not occur, and a definition of correctness need not take program extensions into account.

1.3.2 The Frame Problem

Frame properties specify *all* instance variables and abstractions that may not be modified by a method execution. They are usually expressed by modifies-clauses that list the instance variables and abstractions of objects that may be modified by a method execution. All instance variables and abstractions that are not listed in the modifies-clause must remain unchanged, even if they are declared in program extensions and thus not visible in the method.

Example 1.3.2.

```
module BLIST;
  public class BoundedList {
    int next;
    Element[] elems;

    public void append(Element e)
      modifies next, elems[next];
      { if (next < elems.length) { elems[next] = e; next++; } }
    ... }
```

Class BoundedList implements bounded lists based on arrays. The modifies-clause of append grants the right to modify the next-field, the array elems at position next, and *nothing else*. However, append cannot be proved to satisfy its modifies-clause since program extensions can introduce new abstractions that might also be affected by an execution of append:

```
module BSET imports BLIST;
  public class BoundedSet {
    BoundedList list;
    abstract set value = { list.elems[i] | 0 <= i < list.next };

    public BoundedSet(BoundedList l)
      requires l.next=0;  // take an empty list
      { list = l; }

    public void insert(Element e)
      { list.append(e); }
    ...
  }
```

Class BoundedSet uses BoundedList to implement sets. The abstract value of a BoundedSet-object is formalized by a so-called *abstract field* value (often called specification variable). The abstract value of a BoundedSet-object is the set of all objects stored in the list. The abstract field value is represented in terms of several concrete fields such as list.next. Obviously, an invocation of method append such as in insert can modify value by updating these concrete fields, although its modifies-clause does not grant the right to modify value.

This example demonstrates that it is not possible to prove that a method leaves all instance variables and abstractions not listed in its modifies-clause unchanged if program extensions can introduce arbitrary abstractions since these abstractions are not available during verification of the method.

Approach. We say that an abstract field such as value *depends on* a concrete field if the modification of the concrete field can affect the value of the abstract field. Our approach to the modular verification of frame properties requires one to specify the dependencies of abstract fields explicitly as suggested in [Lei95b]. Appropriate modularity requirements guarantee that all abstract fields that might be affected by a method execution are visible in the method and can therefore be reasoned about. According to these rules, value is not an admissible abstraction. To support implementation patterns like the one above, we refine the semantics of modifies-clauses to allow the modification of abstractions in certain cases.

Nonmodular Solution. In nonmodular programs, all concrete and abstract fields are known. Thus, it is possible to reason about them in order to verify frame properties. In the example above, value could be listed in append's modifies-clause if it was visible in BoundedList.

1.3.3 Modular Verification of Type Invariants

Modular verification of type invariants leads to a problem that is similar to the one explained in the previous subsection. A public method of a program must preserve the invariants of *all* allocated objects even if these invariants are declared in program extensions. We illustrate this problem by adding an invariant to class BoundedSet:

```
  public class BoundedSet {
    invariant list != null /\ FORALL i,j. 0 <= i < j < list.next:
                                        list.elems[i] != list.elems[j];
    ...
  }
```

This invariant expresses that the list used to implement the set must not contain any element more than once. It depends on fields of BoundedList. Therefore, methods of BoundedList such as append can violate the invariant by modifying the fields it depends on (here, append allows one to add arbitrary elements to a list, which might violate the above invariant). Such violations can lead to unsoundness as illustrated in the following example:

```
module VIOLATOR imports BSET;
  public class Violator {
    public static void violate() {
      BoundedList l = new BoundedList();  // l is empty
      BoundedSet  s = new BoundedSet(l);  // invariant of s holds
      l.append(null);                     // invariant of s holds
      l.append(null);                     // invariant of s violated
    }
  }
```

Based on the assumption that the constructors establish the invariant of s and that append preserves this invariant, one can show that the invariant of s holds upon termination of method violate, which is obviously not sound.

The example shows that modular verification of invariants is not feasible if program extensions can introduce arbitrary invariants that depend on fields of imported classes: Imported methods can violate the invariants via these fields and thus lead to unsoundness.

Approach. We adapt the techniques for frame properties to the modular verification of invariants. That is, dependencies of invariants have to be declared explicitly and are restricted by the same modularity requirements. Theses requirements support two solutions to the above problem:

1. In general, invariants must not depend on fields declared in imported modules. Therefore, imported methods cannot violate invariants introduced in program extensions. In our example, the invariant of BoundedSet does not meet this requirement.

2. Since implementations like BoundedSet are common in practice, we provide an alternative solution: A refined semantics of invariants allows classes to introduce invariants that depend on fields of imported types, if (1) the objects of these types are not aliased and (2) the imported methods are only used in a way that preserves the invariant. This property has to be proved based on the specifications of the imported methods. With this solution, BoundedSet's invariant is admissible. However, the constructor of BoundedSet has to clone the list parameter in order to avoid the alias that allows method violate to break the invariant.

Nonmodular Solution. All invariants are known during nonmodular specification and verification. Thus, the problem described above can be circumvented by providing a suitable precondition for method append that states that the element to be added is not already contained in the list in case that the list is referenced by a BoundedSet-object:

```
public void append(Element e)
  requires  (EXISTS X: type(X)=BoundedSet /\ X.list=this) =>
            (FORALL i.0 <= i < next: elems[i] != e);
  ...
```

This precondition constrains invocations of append in a way that guarantees that the method preserves BoundedSet's invariant.

1.3.4 The Extended State Problem

The next example shows that specification of frame properties in a modular setting brings up the so-called *extended state problem* [Lei98, MPH00b] as illustrated by Example 1.3.3:

Example 1.3.3.

```
module M;
  public class Super {
    int state;
    public void set(int v)
      modifies state;
      { state = v; }
  }
```

```
module N imports M;
  public class Sub extends Super {
    int oldState;
    public void set(int v)
      { oldState = state;
        super.set(v);      }
    public void undo()
      { state = oldState; }
  }
```

Objects of class Super have an internal state that can be modified by invocations of set. Super's subclass Sub provides an undo-operation to restore the value of state to the value it had before the last invocation of set. Thus, it stores the most recent value of state in a field oldState and overrides the set-method. The modifies-clause of Super's set-method grants the right to modify the state-field of this and *nothing else*. This example illustrates two interesting aspects:

1. The specification of `set` is strong enough to prove the following property: *All instance variables except* `s.state` *are left unchanged by execution of the invocation* `s.set(n);` *where* `s` *is a variable of type* `Super` *that does not hold the null-value.* This property holds for programs that do not contain subclasses of `Super`, but it is not true for the composition of `M` and `N`: The invocation `s.set(n);` might modify the `oldState`-field of `s` in case that `s` holds a `Sub`-object.
   To avoid this unsoundness, we have to require that subtype methods behave according to the specifications of corresponding supertype methods. That is, the overriding `set`-method has to satisfy the modifies-clause of the overridden method as if it was textually repeated in the overriding method[2]. This requirement is not met in the above example: The overriding `set`-method modifies the `oldState`-field without having the explicit right to do so.
2. If we require `Sub`'s `set`-method to behave according to the modifies-clause of `Super`'s `set`-method, it must not modify the `oldState`-field and can thus not accomplish the desired behavior. That is, the specification in the superclass is too strong in this case.

To sum up, inheritance and specialization can lead to additional fields in subclasses (*extended state*). Since these fields are in general not known in superclasses, they cannot occur in the modifies-clauses of superclass methods. Hence, without further techniques, subclass methods are not allowed to modify the extended state because they have to fulfill the specifications of corresponding superclass methods. To support inheritance, these specifications must be loose enough to allow subclasses to refine implementations and especially to modify the extended state.

Approach. The state-of-the-art solution to the extended state problem is to use abstract fields with explicit dependencies as explained in Subsection 1.3.2. The extended state problem is then solved by the following rule: *The right to modify an abstract instance variable includes the right to modify all instance variables it depends on.* By this semantics, subtypes can gain the right to modify the extended state by introducing additional dependencies.

Nonmodular Solution. The extended state problem can easily be solved for nonmodular programs. Since all fields and methods are known in nonmodular programs, it is possible to include fields of the extended state in the modifies-clauses of the superclasses. In our example, we could add `this.oldState` to the modifies-clause of `Super.set`, possibly together with a formula that expresses that this extension does only apply if `this` is a `Sub`-object.

[2] This requirement ensures behavioral subtyping [LW94], which allows us to handle dynamically-bound method invocations.

1.3.5 Alias Control

In this subsection, we illustrate that uncontrolled aliasing of objects can lead to unwanted modifications of abstract fields. That is, alias control is necessary to enable modular verification of frame properties. Although our example focuses on frame properties, the same problem occurs for type invariants. Moreover, we show that classical interface specifications based on pre- and postconditions, modifies-clauses, and invariants are not sufficiently expressive to specify certain alias properties.

1.3.5.1 Co-dependencies. We say that a modifies-clause *covers* a concrete or abstract instance variable if it mentions the instance variable or an instance variable that is declared to depend on it. According to the usual semantics of modifies-clauses, all instance variables that are not covered by the modifies-clause of a method m have to stay unchanged when m is executed. In the following, we explain a problem that occurs when modifies-clauses are verified in a modular setting.

When abstractions depend on instance variables declared in reused modules, so-called *co-dependencies* [MPH00b, LN00] can lead to unwanted modification of abstractions and, thus, to unsoundness. We illustrate this by the following example[3]:

Example 1.3.4.

```
module M;
  public class C {
    int f;
    C(int p) { f = p; }
  }
```

```
module CM1 imports M;
  public class Client1 {
    C r1;
    abstract bool A1 = (r1.f > 0);
    Client1(C p) { r1 = p; }
    void m() modifies A1
      { r1.f = 1; }
  }
```

```
module CM2 imports M;
  public class Client2 {
    C r2;
    abstract bool A2 = (r2.f < 0);
    Client2(C p) { r2 = p; }
  }
```

```
module N imports CM1,CM2;
  public class BothClients {
    void useBoth() {
      C vc = new C(-1);
      Client1 cl1 = new Client1(vc);  // cl1.A1 = false
      Client2 cl2 = new Client2(vc);  // cl2.A2 = true
      cl1.m();                        // cl1.A1 = true, cl2.A2 = false
    }
  }
```

[3] For simplicity, we omit access protection here. However, using access modes for fields and methods does not change the general situation.

Two classes `Client1` and `Client2` declared in different modules contain abstract fields `A1` and `A2`. During execution of method `useBoth` of class `BothClients`, `cl1` and `cl2` hold instances of `Client1` and `Client2`, resp. `cl1.A1` yields whether the instance variable `f` of the `C`-object referenced by `cl1.r1` is greater than zero. Analogously, `cl2.A2` yields true if the instance variable `f` of the `C`-object referenced by `cl2.r2` is less than zero. That is, instances of `A1` and `A2` depend on instances of a field `f` declared in an imported class `C`. In method `useBoth`, `cl1` and `cl2` refer to the same `C`-object `vc`. Thus, `cl1.A1` and `cl2.A2` depend on the same instance of `f`, that is, are co-dependent.

In this situation, the method `m` of `Client1` with the permission to modify `A1` might also modify `A2` via the shared instance of `f`[4]. This side-effect cannot be detected during the verification of `m` since `A2` is not known in module `CM1`. However, such an undetected side-effect makes modular verification unsound: After the constructor invocations in method `useBoth`, `cl1.A1` yields false and `cl2.A2` yields true. From the modifies-clause of `Client1`'s `m`-method, we can conclude that `cl2.A2` still yields true after execution of `cl1.m()` since `cl2.A2` is not covered by `m`'s modifies-clause and is therefore supposed to be left unchanged. However, this is not the case in our example because `cl2.r2.f` is set to `1` such that `cl2.A2` yields false.

This unsoundness becomes even more clear if we look at the definitions of `cl1.A1` and `cl2.A2`: Since both abstract fields refer to the `f`-field of the same `C`-object in our example, they can never yield true in the same state (the value held by `f` cannot be both less and greater than zero). That is, we have proved a contradiction, or in other words, we have proved that false holds in the poststate of `m`! The reason for this unsoundness is that `Client1`'s `m`-method does not satisfy its modifies-clause due to the undetected modification of `A2`.

It is not feasible to avoid co-dependencies by generally preventing instances of `A2` from depending on an instance of `f` since this would obstruct reuse in an unbearable way (`Client2` would not be able to use `C` in any reasonable way). Therefore, such co-dependencies have to be prohibited by restricting aliasing: If `cl1` and `cl2` cannot share a common `C`-object, the harmful co-dependency described above cannot occur. More generally, objects of imported types must not be shared among objects of types declared in different modules [MPH99a, LN00].

1.3.5.2 Dynamic Aliasing. As illustrated in the previous paragraph, modular verification of frame properties requires restriction of aliasing. It is not sufficient to prevent object structures from sharing objects via heap-allocated instance variables (so called *static aliases* [HLW+92]). Sharing via variables on the stack (*dynamic aliases*) leads to serious problems for modular verification as well. Consider the following alternative implementation of class `Client1`:

[4] Recall that the right to modify an abstraction includes the right to modify the instance variables it depends on, in this case `r1.f` (see Subsection 1.3.4).

```
module CM1 imports M;
  public class Client1 {
    void m(C par) modifies par.f
      { par.f = 1; }
  }
```

Although objects of `Client1` do not contain references to C-objects (no static aliasing), method `m` can modify an instance of `A2` if this instance depends on the instance variable `f` of `m`'s actual parameter. Like in the first version of `Client1`, such modifications are not covered by `m`'s modifies-clause.

1.3.5.3 Alias Control by Specification and Verification. The above examples show that modular verification of frame properties requires one to control both static and dynamic aliasing. However, in a modular setting, it is not possible to control aliasing by classical interface specifications and verification.

Static aliasing properties can, in general, be expressed by type invariants such as the following invariant for class `Client2`:

```
invariant FORALL X,f: X.f=this.r2 => X=this /\ f=r2
```

This invariant expresses that the object referenced by `this.r2` is not referenced by any other instance variable `X.f`. However, such invariants can not be verified modularly. For instance the constructor of class `Client1` might violate the invariant, which cannot be detected during verification of `Client1` since the invariant is not visible in that class (see the problem described in Paragraph 1.3.3).

Neither classical specification and verification techniques nor restrictions of interfaces can control dynamic aliases: Although `Client2` does not contain a method that returns a reference to the C-object stored in `r2`, this does not guarantee that the object isn't aliased: Subclasses of `Client2` might introduce such methods[5]:

```
module CM3 imports CM2;
  public class SubClient2 extends Client2 {
    C    getReference()
      { return r2; }
    void setReference(C p)
      { r2 = p;     }
  }
```

Pre-post-specifications and invariants are not sufficiently expressive to prevent subtypes such as `SubClient2` from adding methods such as

[5] In this particular case, `r2` could be made private to prevent subclasses from accessing the field. However, in general it is necessary to make representations accessible for subclasses to facilitate efficient implementations.

`getReference` that introduce aliases by taking or passing out references to objects that are supposed not to be aliased. In particular, it is not sufficient to require that subclasses are behavioral subtypes.

1.3.5.4 Approach and Nonmodular Solution.

Approach. To control static and dynamic aliasing, we complement interface specifications by a sophisticated type system. Besides naming a type declaration, the types of this type system provide alias information which is used to control sharing. In the example above, `Client2` could use a special type to express that the `C`-objects referenced by `Client2`-objects are not supposed to be shared. That would prevent subclasses such as `SubClient2` from declaring methods that might introduce static or dynamic aliases. The type system allows one check alias properties statically.

Nonmodular Solution. In nonmodular programs, co-dependencies do not cause serious problems for verification. Whenever a field such as `f` in Example 1.3.4 is updated, all abstractions that depend on this field are visible. Thus, their declarations can be used to reason about the effects of the field update. Therefore, alias control is not crucial for verification in nonmodular settings. However, it is still an interesting feature to structure programs and to simplify verification.

Both static and dynamic aliasing can be controlled in nonmodular settings by specification and verification techniques. Invariants like the one presented in Paragraph 1.3.5.3 can be used to describe static aliasing; such invariants can be verified in nonmodular programs. Dynamic aliasing can be controlled by imposing appropriate restrictions on the parameters and result values of methods, which can be expressed by pre- and postconditions (possibly complemented by access modes for fields).

This concludes our discussion of the fundamental problems of modular specification and verification of OO-programs. In the next section, we present a systematic analysis of modular specification and verification. Based on this discussion, we re-visit the above problems on a more technical level and describe our approach to their solution in more detail in Section 1.5.

1.4 Modularity Aspects of Programs, Specifications, and Proofs

To develop a precise understanding of modularity of specifications and proofs, we give an overview of modular program development. Thereby, we explain four major objectives of the decomposition of programs into modules: Explicit structure, separate development, information hiding, and reuse. We analyze the status quo of modularity of universal specifications, interface specifications, and program proofs w.r.t. these objectives. This analysis improves our understanding of the problems illustrated in the previous section and explains which aspects of modularity are already supported in a satisfying way by state-of-the-art techniques.

1.4.1 Modularity of Programs

Modular program development has been an important research area for almost three decades [Ban95, BLO94, Bra92, Bud91, Cla93, Fai85, GP82, Par72, SMC74, Sny86, Sny87, Szy92]. In summary, this work identifies four reasons for the decomposition of programs into modules that are explained in the following.

1.4.1.1 Explicit Structure. Modules are used to decompose large software systems. Programs usually consist of a large number of *program elements* (such as classes, procedures, variables, etc.) The structure of such programs can be made explicit by grouping those elements that interact with each other closely into one module. Each module provides one or more interfaces that document how the elements of that module can be used by clients. Such interfaces make dependencies among modules explicit: A client module has to explicitly *import* a module to use its elements.

According to software engineering practice, the dependencies between modules (*coupling*) should be kept as small as possible to reduce complexity. Implicit dependencies, for instance introduced by undocumented information sharing, are error-prone [SMC74, GP82].

In good designs and implementations, modules are tailored such that the elements of each module are very closely associated with each other (*high cohesion*). Usually, they cooperate to implement a common *abstraction*, for instance an abstract data type [Fai85, Bud91]. The fact that elements of one module are closely related and therefore usually have access to the same data has impact on the design of encapsulation techniques (see Paragraph 2.1.2.2).

Many state-of-the-art programming languages provide module concepts that allow one to structure programs. Compare for instance Ada's packages [Ame83], modules in Modula-2 [WGSD89], structures in SML [Pau91], or modules in Miranda [Hol91]. In languages like C [KR88], modularization is applied by convention: Modules are associated with files, and interfaces are expressed by means of header files. In object-oriented languages, classes are used as units of modularization (see [Szy92] for the differences between modules and classes). Furthermore, some OO-languages provide additional module systems to group cooperating classes (see e.g., packages in Java [GJS96] and Ada 95 [Bar97]). Most languages provide only a flat structure of modules. However, some languages support hierarchical modularization (e.g., modules in Modula-2 and inner classes in Java [Ros97]). We will discuss Java's package concept and the interfaces of classes and packages in more detail in Subsection 2.1.2.

1.4.1.2 Separate Development. Besides the reduction of complexity, one of the most prominent motivations for modularization is separate development of modules. Since modules only interact with each other via explicit interfaces, modules can be implemented, compiled, and tested independently [BLO94, Kas90, Wir96].

Separate development is crucial for cost-effective software production: (1) It enables large numbers of programmers to work in parallel. (2) It reduces the time spent for compilation and program analysis since only new or modified modules have to be re-compiled or checked. (3) Separate development is a prerequisite for reuse.

The support for separate compilation varies. Languages like Ada, Modula-2, Modula-3, or Java guarantee syntactic and type correctness across module boundaries (presumed that modules are re-compiled when the interface of an imported module is changed). C compilers perform type checking local to a compilation unit, and types are not checked during linking.

1.4.1.3 Information Hiding. Information hiding is a technique for minimizing interdependencies among separately-written modules by defining strict external interfaces [Bud91, Par72, Sny86]. As long as clients of a module M *only* rely on M's interfaces, M can be re-implemented without affecting its clients as long as its interfaces stay unchanged. In other words, the support for information hiding can be characterized by the kinds of changes that can safely be made to the implementation of a module.

Many OO-languages combine information hiding with *encapsulation*. Encapsulation is a technique to prevent (parts of) the internal states of data structures from being accessed without using their interfaces (see e.g. [Szy98]). Restricting access to data allows modules to control data consistency (e.g., invariants) and prevents confidential information (e.g., passwords) from leaking. Encapsulation requires control of reference passing to prevent data manipulation via aliases. It plays an important role for modular verification and will be discussed in Section 2.2.

Most existing programming languages support information hiding. Implementors of modules describe the module interfaces by mentioning the elements that may be used by client modules in designated parts of the module declarations (such as packages in Ada [Ame83], export-clauses in Modula-2 [WGSD89, WE87], or signatures in SML [MTHM97, Pau91, Ull94]), or by marking elements with so-called *access modes* (such as in Java [GJS96], C++ [Str91], or Oberon [RW92]). Compilers guarantee that clients can only access the exported elements of other modules. Most OO-languages allow one to specify several interfaces for one module/class. Typically, there are different interfaces for users (*client interface*), implementors of subtypes (*specialization interface*), and so-called *friends*. We discuss information hiding techniques for OO-languages in Paragraph 2.1.2.2.

1.4.1.4 Reuse. Since the program elements of a module interact with each other closely and usually implement a common abstraction, modules are natural units of reuse and deployment (see e.g., the discussion of component software in [Szy98], where components are very similar to modules). Reusing software comprises three steps (see e.g., [Kru92]): (1) Retrieval and selection of suitable modules. This is done based on informal or formal module specifications [MZW97]. (2) Adaption of modules to the particular requirements of the context in which they will be reused. (3) Composition of various reused and newly built modules to composite programs. Besides explicit structure, separate development, and information hiding, which are prerequisites for reuse, module systems should thus support *adaptability* and *composability* of modules to make them reusable.

Some functional programming languages treat modules as first-class values. Thus, adaption and composition of modules can be expressed in the programming language in a very flexible way. In particular, adaption and composition can be done at runtime. In contrast, most OO-languages only provide means to statically adapt and compose modules. The following paragraphs give an overview of adaption and composition features of OO-languages.

Adaptability. In OO-languages, adaptability is achieved by[6]

- *Genericity (parametric polymorphism):* Languages such as Ada 95 [Bar97], C++ [Str91], Eiffel [Mey92b], Modula-3 [Nel91, Har92], Pizza [OW97], and Sather [SOM94] provide parametric modules/types that can be instantiated according to the requirements of the reuser.
- *Inheritance:* Classical OO-languages allow one to specialize inherited code by adding new variables/methods and by overriding inherited methods [Mey88, PH00]. More research-oriented OO-languages provide several variations of the classical inheritance mechanism. Sather [Omo94] separates code inheritance from subtyping. Name conflicts can be resolved by renaming inherited program elements. Instead of overriding, Beta [MMPN93, KMMPN83] allows one to specify the parts of a pattern that can be specialized by subpatterns. CLOS [Kee89] and Jigsaw [Bra92] provide so-called mixins (or abstract subclasses) to customize the behavior of a variety of superclasses, usually by introducing code that is executed before and after methods of superclasses [BC90]. [Pre97] generalizes inheritance and overriding to the combination of so-called features (which are quite similar to mixins) and the resolution of conflicts among them. [Ban95] and [BL91] give an interesting analysis of adaption and composition of modules. They unbundle different aspects of inheritance by introducing a set of operators for the adaption and composition of classes/modules (such as overriding, hiding, or renaming of elements).

Composability. To describe the nature of module composition, we use the taxonomy introduced for the composition of documents in OpenDoc [FM96]: Composition is done either by *combination* or by *synthesis* of components.

[6] In this book, we do not consider adaption by modification of reused code. See [RS93] for software verification in such a scenario.

With combination, the different components retain their own characteristics when composed (e.g., the components of a car are still recognizable in the resulting product). With synthesis, components are not recognizable after their composition (such as the ingredients in a loaf of bread).

Combination of modules results in a *set of modules* that interact with each other. That is, the code for each module occurs only once in the composite. Consequently, several clients of one module share the same code, which results in small binaries but can lead to an important problem with aliases: Let's assume that modules M_1 and M_2 both import a third module M. In the combination of M_1 and M_2, there is only a single instance of M. Thus, M_1 and M_2 share the program elements of M. For instance, they refer to the same global variables and types, which increases coupling. With synthesis, new and reused implementation parts are merged to a homogeneous composite. Usually, this means that reused code is duplicated. That avoids the problems of aliasing, but does on the other hand not permit mutual recursion among elements of different modules.

In programming languages, import, inclusion, inheritance, and instantiation of generic modules are means of module composition. They relate to combination and synthesis as follows:

- *Import:* Import of modules is the classical way of module combination. No actions are performed besides that the exported elements of the imported module are made available to the importing module.
- *Inclusion:* One way to compose modules by synthesis is *inclusion*, where the included code is textually copied into the including module (such as with `#include` in C [KR88] or `\input` in LaTeX [Lam86]).
- *Inheritance:* In most OO-languages, inheritance is realized as a form of combination (see e.g., [Szy98]): Inherited code is not copied to every subclass, but resides in the superclass and is shared by subclasses. This becomes, for instance, evident in the context of information hiding: Let e be a program element that is declared in class E and inherited by class D. The accessibility of e for a client C of D is determined by e's access mode and the relation of C to E (i.e., to the declaration class of e), and not by the relation of C to the inheriting class D. Therefore, the structure of inherited and new code is still observable after composition.
  However, there exist languages in which inheritance is based on synthesis. For instance in Sather, inherited code is textually copied to the inheriting class, and can thereby be adapted (e.g., by renaming routines). Thus, inherited code is duplicated and merged with the implementation of the inheriting class. Its origin is not recognizable in the inheriting class.
- *Instantiation:* As with inheritance, instantiation of generic modules is often done by combination: In languages such as Eiffel, Sather, or Pizza (with homogeneous translation, see [OW97]), all instances of a generic class share common code. That is, the generic module and its parameters are not merged to a new piece of code.

Languages such as C++, Ada [Ame83], or Pizza (with heterogeneous translation) implement genericity as synthesis. Each instantiation of a template or generic package leads to new code where the generic part and the actual parameters are merged.

OO-languages provide additional flexibility for class composition by the concept of substitutability [Bra92]: Objects of types that provide at least the same interface as a type T can be used wherever objects of type T are expected. Technically, *subtyping* or *matching* is used to determine whether objects of one type can be used in places where objects of another are expected (see [Boo94] for subtyping, [BPF97] for matching). Both subtyping and matching guarantee that substitution respects the syntactical constraints (e.g., well-typedness) of client code. Behavioral subtyping [LW94] in addition ensures that subtype objects behave according to the behavioral specifications of supertypes.

Substitutability allows one to express algorithms and data structures in a general way for all objects that provide a certain interface. This is used for variable and method declarations as well as for generic modules (constrained genericity [Mey86, DGLM95]). Thus, substitutability is one of the key concepts to make code sufficiently general to be reusable.

In the following subsections, we discuss the relevance of explicit structure, separate development, information hiding, and reuse for specifications and program proofs.

1.4.2 Modularity of Universal Specifications

In this subsection, we analyze the state-of-the-art in modular development of universal specifications w.r.t. the four objectives described in the last subsection. Due to our focus on two-tiered interface specifications as described in Section 1.2, we consider languages for logic-based specifications here. However, the situation is similar for other specification techniques (e.g., model-based specification languages such as Z or VDM [She95, Jon90]).

1.4.2.1 Explicit Structure. Many specification languages such as CLEAR, OBJ, KIV, the PVS Language, and the Larch Shared Language LSL allow specifications to be decomposed into *theories* [BG77, GH93, GWM+00, OSR93, Rei95]. Elements of a theory (such as function definitions or abstract data type definitions) can be used in other theories via import. As for program modules, hierarchical structuring of theories has been studied (see [WPP+83, GWM+00] and [Wir90, Section 5.4]).

1.4.2.2 Separate Development. Since languages for universal specifications are very similar to programming languages, the techniques developed for separate compilation of programs carry over to universal specifications: Theories can be written, syntax checked, and type checked separately. Theorems can be proved locally in a theory (and imported theories). Checks guarantee the validity of proofs across theory boundaries. For instance, PVS prevents two lemmas from being mutually used in each other's proof by establishing an order on lemmas based on the acyclic import relation on theories [OSR93]. The KIV system provides correctness management based on development graphs [RSSB98].

1.4.2.3 Information Hiding. Most specification languages support information hiding by hide or export features (e.g., CLEAR, PVS, and Isabelle [Pau94]).

1.4.2.4 Reuse. Like programming languages with their standard libraries (such as the Java API [GJS96]), specification languages often come with prelude theories containing specifications for natural numbers, strings, sets, lists, etc. For reusing these and other theories, specification languages provide sophisticated reuse features.

Adaptability is supported by parametric theories [TWW82]. So-called specification building operators combine ways to adapt and compose theories (see [Wir90, Sections 6.2–6.6] for an overview). For instance, such operators allow one to rename parts of theories and to extend theories. Both combination and synthesis can be found as composition techniques in specification languages. As in programming languages, subtyping can be used to make specifications more general (e.g., in PVS and OBJ2). There are specification languages with object-oriented flavor such as VDM++ [DK92] that provide inheritance.

To sum up, the modularization techniques for universal specifications developed so far are sufficient to support modular specification and verification of OO-programs. In fact, in this book, we will only use a small subset of the features described above, namely a simple formal language for multisorted first-order logic and recursive data types (see App. A.1) that allows one to declare sorts, functions, abstract data types, axioms, and lemmas. *Theories* are used to modularize specifications, that is, to group declarations and definitions. Therefore, we will not work on modularity aspects of universal specifications in this book.

1.4.3 Modularity of Interface Specifications

In contrast to programs and universal specifications, interface specifications are in general not self-contained: They depend heavily on both program interfaces and abstract specifications. Thus, modularity of interface specification relies on the modularization techniques for programs and universal specifications as described above.

1.4.3.1 Explicit Structure. The structure of interface specifications follows the module structure of the specified program. Interfaces of program modules are annotated by pre- and postconditions, modifies-clauses, invariants, history constraints[7], etc. (see e.g., [GH93, Lea96, Mey92a, MPH97a, PH97b]). Although some invariants act like global invariants (sometimes called system invariants), they are usually specified as module/class invariant of a designated module/class of the program [PH97b].

Besides their connection to program modules, interface specifications are based on theories of universal specifications. In some interface specification languages this connection is stated explicitly, for instance by uses-clauses in LCL [GH93] and Larch/C++ [Lea96], or by context-clauses in Larch/Ada [GMP90]. Others use implicit naming conventions (e.g., ANJA, the annotation language of the JIVE system [MMPH97]).

1.4.3.2 Separate Development. Interface specifications refer to elements of both programs (such as variable names) and universal specifications (e.g., abstract data types). Thus, syntax and sort checking of interface specifications are based on information about the program modules and theories that are referred to in the specification. Due to the modular structure of programs and specifications, the support for separate syntax and type checking carries over to interface specifications.

The functional behavior of methods as well as most class invariants and history constraints of a module M can in general be specified in terms of the modules used by M and the associated interface and universal specifications. Thus, these specifications can be developed in a modular way. However, the situation is different for the specification of frame properties: Although it is possible to specify the concrete instance variables that might be modified by a method in a modifies-clause [Lei98], techniques are required to describe the effects of a method m on abstractions of object structures that are not available for the specifier of m (due to information hiding or separate development of program modules). We will present a solution to this problem in Chapter 5.

1.4.3.3 Information Hiding. In programs and universal specifications, information hiding is used to provide clients with a restricted view of a module/class or theory. Thus, hidden parts can be modified (e.g., reimplemented) without affecting clients. This flexibility gets lost if hidden parts are revealed by interface specifications. Consider for instance the following fragment of a specification of a Java class:

```
public class Person {
  private int age;
  public void makeOneYearOlder()
    requires  true
    ensures   age' = age^ + 1
  ...
}
```

[7] History constraints are used to specify a property of the history of values which an instance variable may take [LW93, LW94].

If clients have access to the specification of the public method `makeOneYearOlder`, they can use the fact that class `Person` contains a field `age` (for instance in correctness proofs), although it is private. Therefore, the implementation of `Person` can no longer be modified without affecting clients.

Although such specifications obviously violate the principle of information hiding, most existing interface specification languages neglect this problem or suggest developers to express behavior without referring to hidden fields by introducing abstractions, but do not enforce this discipline (see e.g., [Lea97, Mey92b, PH97b]). Using abstractions instead of referring to concrete representations is appropriate in many situations (e.g., for the specification of frame properties with modifies-clauses [Lei95b, MPH00b]). However, especially in OO-programs, it is reasonable to provide certain clients (e.g., implementors of subclasses) with information about concrete representations as illustrated in the following example.

Example 1.4.1.

```
public class Fraction {
  protected int num,denom;
  ...
}
```

A normal client of a class `Fraction` only needs to know that the fraction has to be well-formed whenever it is passed to a method without further details (say, all operations take and return well-formed fractions). But a developer of a subclass who adds new operations needs to know the exact well-formedness conditions (e.g., that the representation as numerator and denominator is always reduced to lowest terms) in order to respect them.

The example demonstrates that interface specification languages for OO-languages should provide support for different views on specifications according to the access modes of the underlying programming language.

So far, JML [LBR99b, RL00] is the only interface specification language that provides access/visibility modes for specifications. In Chapter 4, we will discuss such visibility modes in detail and present a technique that allows us to statically check whether specifications respect information hiding.

1.4.3.4 Reuse. Behavioral interface specifications are reused in connection with program interfaces. Therefore, they have to be compatible with the reuse techniques for programs summarized above. In the following, we discuss the requirements that interface specifications should meet to support the adaption and composition techniques of modern OO-languages.

Genericity. To support genericity, interface specifications should (1) be sufficiently general to describe the behavior of all instances of a generic module, and (2) be able to express semantic constraints on the parameters of generic modules. For programming languages that support upper type bounds for module parameters such as Eiffel [Mey92b] or Pizza [OW97], this can be achieved by requiring that each actual type parameter is a behavioral subtype of the formal type parameter. If genericity is constrained by other techniques (such as the where-clauses in Theta [LCD+94]) or not constrained (such as in C++ [ES90] and Modula-3 [Nel91]), or if modules can also be parameterized with functions or values (like C++ templates), a specification primitive such as the where-clauses in Larch/C++ [Lea97] should be provided to specify suitable module parameters.

Inheritance. Interface specifications can be inherited along with code. In this case, subclass implementations must fulfill the specifications of their superclasses. In particular, inherited methods must behave according to their specifications in superclasses, no matter whether their implementations are inherited or overridden. As shown in [DL96], inheritance of interface specifications leads to behavioral subtyping. Behavioral subtyping is in turn a prerequisite for modular verification of OO-programs (see Paragraph 3.3.4.2).

Specifications of interfaces that are reused and specialized via inheritance and overriding must meet the following requirements:

- To allow subclasses to reuse inherited code effectively, abstract specification of behavior is in general not sufficient: As illustrated by Example 1.4.1, detailed specifications in terms of concrete data representations are required[8]. The need for specifications on a concrete level has in turn effects on information hiding in specifications (see above).
- Specifications must be loose enough to allow subclasses to refine implementations. This can easily be achieved for pre-post-pairs, invariants, and history constraints. However, for the specification of frame properties, the extended state problem (see Subsection 1.3.4) has to be solved. We tackle this problem in Chapter 5.

Subtyping. The concept of subtyping has two important consequences for interface specification languages:

(1) Abstraction: Supertypes represent common properties of their subtypes. Therefore, the specification of a type T describes the common behavior of all subtypes of T. Since each subtype can have a completely different — or even incomplete or missing — implementation, the behavior has to be specified in an implementation-independent way. Thus, interface specification languages must provide support for data abstraction (see Chapter 4). This requirement is met by most declarative state-of-the-art interface specification languages [DLNS98, GH93, GMP90, LBR99a, Lea96, Lei95b, MPH97a, PH97b].

(2) Behavioral Subtyping: Objects of subtypes can be used wherever objects of a supertype are expected. To enable modular verification, all subtypes must be behavioral subtypes (see Paragraph 3.3.4.2). However, to be able to

[8] Similar to subclasses that usually have direct access to concrete data representations of their superclasses, and that are thus not forced to manipulate the internal state via method invocations.

prove that a subtype meets the specifications of its supertypes, these specifications must be accessible to the verifier, which is not always the case in the presence of information hiding (see e.g., the discussion on the meaning of private pre-post-pairs on the JML mailing list [JML]). Therefore, interface specification languages have to take care that supertype specifications are either accessible for subtypes or automatically satisfied by subtypes. We will discuss this issue along with the presentation of our specification technique in Chapters 4, 5, and 6.

Import and Inclusion. Simple composition by import or inclusion causes problems for those specification primitives that lead to proof obligations for methods outside the module that contains the specification, such as class invariants and history constraints that have to be preserved by all nonprivate methods of a program [PH97b, Lea97]. To illustrate this problem, consider two modules M and N with M importing N. According to the invariant semantics used in [PH97b] and this book, this means that (1) all nonprivate methods in M have to preserve the invariants in N and (2) all nonprivate methods in N have to preserve the invariants in M. If the invariants of N are accessible in M, proof obligation (1) can be shown during verification of M. However, since the implementation of N is not accessible to the developer of M (due to information hiding), it cannot be used to prove the second obligation. Therefore, invariants have to be constrained such that they are automatically preserved by methods that are not available for re-verification (see [MPH97b] for such constraints). See Chapter 6 for the modular specification and verification of invariants.

In the paragraphs above, we focused on the features that are needed to make interface specifications suitable for reuse. So far, we have not discussed whether implementations do still satisfy their specifications when they are reused together. That is, if the corresponding correctness proofs can be reused as well. We explain such modularity aspects of proofs in the next subsection.

1.4.4 Modularity of Correctness Proofs

Separate verification of program modules has been an important research topic for a number of years (see e.g., [GMP90, Lei95b, MPH00b]). In this subsection, we discuss separate verification and other modularity aspects of correctness proofs.

1.4.4.1 Explicit Structure. Proofs in Hoare-style programming logics contain references to implementations (the program parts of triples), interface specifications (the pre- and postconditions), and to universal specifications, which are the formal context for pre- and postconditions and program-independent lemmas (introduced e.g., by the rule of consequence). Correctness proofs can be structured according to the modularization of implementations: Proofs for a module M need only refer to program parts that belong to

M or one of the modules used by M [Hoa69, PHM99]. Therefore, each proof can be associated with a program module. This program module determines the relevant interface specifications, which in turn make the references to theories of universal specifications explicit (see above). Therefore, correctness proofs have a clear structure following the program's decomposition.

1.4.4.2 Separate Development. Separate development of correctness proofs (separate verification) means that one can prove that a module M satisfies its specification based on the implementation of M, and the interface specifications, universal specifications, and proofs associated with M and the modules used by M. This means especially that the proofs for M stay valid when M is reused by any well-formed client (although the specification of M may lead to proof obligations for clients of M to guarantee this well-formedness). We have illustrated the problems for modular verification in the context of dynamic method binding, side-effects on objects or object structures, type invariants, and aliasing together with approaches to their solution in Section 1.3.

1.4.4.3 Information Hiding. Proofs in our Hoare-style programming logic directly refer to implementations. However, the correctness proofs of a module's implementation must not be accessible to its clients. Otherwise, hidden implementations would be exposed. But a client can be provided with the information that there is a proof for a certain property if all specifications and program elements (e.g., methods) of that property are accessible to the client.

In this book, we assume that the existence of certain program proofs can be expressed by *Hoare lemmas* [Mey02]. Hoare lemmas are Hoare triples (or sequents, see Subsection 3.1.2) that are used like lemmas in predicate logic. A lemma allows the verifier to use a program property without referring to its proof.

1.4.4.4 Reuse. Obviously, reuse of proofs requires proofs to stay valid when reused. In other words, a verification technique has to guarantee that proofs that are carried out in one context stay valid in any well-formed context they are reused in. This property is called *modular soundness*. It has to be proved for a verification technique, for instance by showing that the programming logic supports modular verification [PHM99] or by arguing about the way interface specifications are transformed into pre-post-specifications [Lei95b]. We discuss modular soundness in Subsection 3.3.4.

Due to the close connection of implementations and proofs, code reuse is a prerequisite for reusable proofs. Therefore, a verification technique should support the standard reuse techniques for implementations such as inheritance, subtyping, etc. (see above).

This concludes our discussion of modularity of programs, specifications, and proofs. In the next section, we summarize the open problems and our approach to their solution.

1.5 Approach, Outline, and Contributions

This section serves as an orientation for the reader. It summarizes the technical problems that are tackled in this book and sketches our approach to their solution. Moreover, it contains a summary of each chapter and enumerates the main contributions of this book.

1.5.1 Approach

In the previous sections, we have explained open problems for modular specification and verification of OO-programs and showed which aspects of modularity are already supported in a satisfying way by state-of-the-art techniques. To solve the remaining problems (especially the five fundamental problems described in Section 1.3), we have to develop solutions to the following technical problems:

- *Formal integration:* The existing modularization techniques for programs, universal specifications, interface specifications, and correctness proofs have to be integrated into a common formal framework.
- *Information hiding in interface specifications:* We need techniques to denote and check access modes for specifications.
- *Alias control:* We must develop techniques to control both static and dynamic aliasing. These techniques have to be strong enough to enable verification of frame properties and invariants, and flexible enough to handle most common implementation patterns.
- *Verification of frame properties:* We have to find suitable restrictions on the dependencies of abstractions that enable us to verify frame properties modularly. On the other hand, these restrictions have to be weak enough to allow us to handle realistic programs.
- *Verification of type invariants:* Like abstractions, the dependencies of invariants have to be restricted such that invariants can be introduced without re-verification of imported code.

In this subsection, we describe our approach to the solution of these problems.

Formal Integration. We build on the formal integration of specification and verification of OO-programs presented in [PH97b]: Interface specifications and proofs are based on a formal data and state model of the programming language, which is part of the universal specification. Poetzsch-Heffter showed how this model can be used, for instance, to make data abstraction explicit or to express reachability and sharing properties. We enhance the data and state model by formalizations of

- the module structure of programs, which is for example necessary to give a formal definition of modular correctness;

- the universe type system (see below); the type information with the associated alias properties is for instance necessary to prove well-formedness of specifications;
- dependencies of abstractions and invariants; this formalization is used to define the formal meaning of modifies-clauses and for verification of frame properties and type invariants.

Information Hiding in Specifications. Most OO-languages provide several interfaces for a module, for instance a client interface for normal users and a specialization interface for implementors of subclasses. Each interface consists of a syntactic description, a behavioral specification, and the underlying universal specifications. To support information hiding, the behavioral and universal specifications associated with an interface must not reveal information about implementation parts that do not belong to this interface.

Universal Specifications. To be able to use program properties such as type information in specifications and proofs, we formalize various aspects of implementations in program-dependent theories of the universal specification. These theories can be automatically generated by a verification system and contain for instance the names, types, and access modes of all fields of a program. Information hiding is achieved by decomposing the program-dependent universal specifications according to the modules of a program and their interfaces: We generate separate theories for each module/class and each of its interfaces. Therefore, different clients of a module can be provided with different theories.

Interface Specifications. Each syntactic interface of a module is associated with a behavioral interface specification. Following Java, we use access modes to determine the interface to which a part of a behavioral specification (e.g., a pre-post-pair) belongs. Thus, we can for instance provide a public method with several specifications: An abstract one for the client interface and a concrete one for the specialization interface.

Each behavioral interface specification is associated with the corresponding program-dependent theory of the universal specification. By requiring that all variables, functions, etc. mentioned in an interface specification must be declared in the underlying theory, we can enforce information hiding: For instance, a precondition of the client interface cannot refer to a field name of the specialization interface since this name is not declared in the universal specification generated for the client interface.

Alias Control. Since dynamic aliasing cannot be adequately restricted by means of classical interface specification and verification techniques, we use a type system to control aliasing. This type system enforces a hierarchical partitioning of the object store and controls references between the partitions.

The classes and interfaces of a program define a set of types together with a subtype relation. We call this set of types the *standard type universe* of the program. The basic idea of the universe type system is to use multiple "copies" of the standard universe (one could imagine copying the whole program text and adding a suitable postfix to the class names). Such a copy is called a *universe*. In each universe, there is a type for every class/interface of a program. But, although structurally identical, the types in different universes are considered to be distinct. Each object X is created for a type of a given universe U. That is, each object belongs to exactly one universe.

Since different types of one class are disjoint, references of one type cannot be assigned to variables of another, which allows us to control sharing. For instance, in Example 1.3.4, `Client1` and `Client2` could use different types of class `C` (i.e., different universes) to prevent aliasing of their `C`-objects and thus co-dependencies.

In addition to the standard universe, we assume a universe for every object (a so-called *object universe*) and a universe for every copy of a type (*type universe*) of a program's execution. This implies a hierarchical structuring of universes. The standard universe is the root of the universe hierarchy. Each type of the standard universe and each object that belongs to the standard universe has its own universe. The types and objects in these *child universes* are in turn associated with universes and so forth. We call the children, grandchildren, etc. of a universe U *descendants* of U. If V is a descendant of U, we call U *an ancestor* of V.

Besides type and object universes, the universe type system provides *readonly methods* and *readonly types*. Readonly methods are statically checked to be side-effect-free: They must not perform object creation, field updates, or invocations of readwrite (i.e., ordinary) methods. References of readonly types cannot be used to manipulate the referenced object structure: Neither field updates nor invocation of readwrite methods is allowed on readonly references. Therefore, readonly types can be used to grant restricted access to encapsulated representations.

Verification of Frame Properties. We specify frame properties by modifies-clauses. Information hiding and the extended state problem are handled by abstract fields with explicit dependencies. A dependency is called *static* if dependent and dependee belong to the same object in all execution states, and *dynamic* otherwise [LN00]. By incorporating dependencies into our formal framework, we achieve a uniform treatment of static and dynamic dependencies. This unification simplifies the semantics of modifies-clauses and the modularity requirements for dependencies. Besides that, our formal framework facilitates a semantic treatment of dependencies which is more accurate and more expressive than the rather syntactic treatment in existing approaches.

Example 1.3.4 illustrates that in a naïve approach clients of a module M must not introduce abstractions that depend on instance variables declared in M since this could allow methods of M to modify abstractions that are not covered by their modifies-clauses. To allow for such patterns, we exploit the hierarchic structure of universes to weaken the meaning of modifies-clauses. This refined semantics allows a client of module M to introduce an abstraction

X.f that depends on an instance variable Y.g declared in M if the universe to which Y belongs is a descendant of the universe to which X belongs. In connection with suitable restrictions on dependencies, this semantics is still strong enough for modular verification. The restrictions are essentially generalizations of the visibility requirement and the top-down requirement of [LN00]. We exploit the alias control of the universe type system to generalize these requirements for dynamic dependencies. Our constraints are sufficiently weak to be applicable to most implementations. On the other hand, they make modular verification possible; we proved modular soundness of our technique (see Section 5.2).

Verification of Type Invariants. For the specification and verification of type invariants, we apply the techniques developed for frame properties: We regard type invariants as boolean abstractions that (1) must yield true in the poststate of an execution of a nonprivate method if the object of the abstraction has not been alive in the corresponding prestate (i.e., the object was created during this execution), and (2) must not occur in modifies-clauses of nonprivate methods. These two requirements guarantee that a nonprivate method that is invoked on an object in universe U establishes/preserves the invariants of all objects in U and U's descendants (provided that the method respects its modifies-clause). In Chapter 6, we show that this semantics is strong enough for verification.

1.5.2 Outline

The rest of this book is structured into five main chapters, a conclusion, and appendices.

Chapter 2 introduces Mojave, the programming language that is used in this book. We describe Mojave's *universe* type system which allows one to express and statically check alias properties and the encapsulation of whole object structures. The chapter concludes with a discussion of related work on aliasing analysis and control.

A Hoare-style programming logic for Mojave is presented in Chapter 3. With this programming logic, we prove interesting language properties of Mojave such as type safety. The definition of modular correctness of OO-programs and a discussion of modular soundness of module composition prepare the presentation of our verification technique in the following chapters. Finally, the chapter summarizes related work on programming logics.

In Chapters 4 to 6, we present our specification and verification technique. Chapter 4 explains how information hiding can be preserved by interface specifications. Furthermore, it introduces abstract fields to express data abstraction and pre-post-specifications to describe functional method behavior. Chapter 4 concludes with an overview of related work.

Chapter 5 addresses modular specification and verification of frame properties. It contains the most important contributions of this book. In this chapter, we explain the role of explicit dependencies of abstract fields and the modularity rules that are necessary to make modular verification possible. Based on explicit dependencies and the hierarchic programming model of the universe type system, we define a novel semantics of modifies-clauses. Furthermore, we formalize and prove a modularity theorem that allows one to prove frame properties modularly. Besides other work on frame properties, the related work section contains a detailed comparison of our work to the approach taken by Leino and Nelson.

Chapter 6 shows that type invariants can be regarded as special abstract fields, which allows us to apply the techniques developed for the specification and verification of frame properties to type invariants. In particular, we can adapt ideas from the semantics of modifies-clauses to define an invariant semantics that is suitable for modular verification. The focus of the related work section is on invariant semantics.

Chapter 7 provides a summary of this book, sketches how the presented techniques can be implemented in our verification tool, and discusses several directions for future research.

Finally, the appendices present the formal background of our techniques and contain examples, auxiliary lemmas, and proofs from the main chapters.

1.5.3 Contributions

This book is mainly written for researchers in the area of specification and verification as well as in the area of object-oriented programming. For this audience, the main contribution of this book is solutions to four of the five fundamental problems described in Section 1.3 (the extended state problem has already been solved [Lei98]; we adapt these solutions).

To develop these solutions, we build as much as possible on well-known languages and techniques, and enhance them to support modularity. On a more technical level, we improve the state of the art in modular specification and verification by the following contributions:

1. a systematic analysis of modularity aspects of programs, specifications, and proofs;
2. a programming model and type system for flexible alias and dependency control;
3. a precise formal definition of modular correctness of programs and modules;
4. a uniform treatment of static and dynamic dependencies;
5. a novel semantics of modifies-clauses and invariants based on the hierarchic programming model of the universe type system;
6. a modular sound verification technique, especially for frame properties and invariants.

Besides these contributions for the main audience, there are several topics in this book that are interesting for designers of programming and specification languages, for developers of programming environments that support specification and verification as well as for programmers. We summarize the results for these groups in the conclusions.

1.6 Related Work

In this section, we discuss general approaches to specification, verification, and program analysis. Related work on the specific contributions of this book is discussed along with the presentation of our techniques in Chapters 2 to 6.

1.6.1 Specification Techniques

Specification techniques for object-oriented software have been investigated w.r.t. different development and abstraction levels ranging from requirement and design specification languages to executable assertions extending OO-programming languages.

1.6.1.1 Design Specifications. Design frameworks concentrate on design specifications and their refinement [Bac88, LH92]. Like in our approach, they usually apply declarative techniques to specify program properties. Design specifications are related to the universal specifications of two-tiered interface specifications which are also used to specify abstract models of software systems. In fact, most design specification languages could be used to express such specifications. However, design frameworks usually have a very abstract view of program semantics. In particular, they often neglect sharing, although it is essential in practice. Therefore, design specifications are in general not suitable for program verification since a formal connection between implementations and abstract specifications is missing. To avoid this problem, our universal specifications contain a formalization of the data and state model of our programming language that can be used to specify properties of concrete implementations.

There are numerous algebraic specifications languages such as CLEAR [BG77], OBJ [GWM+00], OBJ2 [FGJM85], ASL [Wir82, ST88], and LSL [GH93] and languages for higher-order logic that allow one to express algebraic specifications, for instance the PVS Language [OSR93] and the Isabelle language [Pau94]. All of these languages can be used to specify abstract designs of software systems. The reader is referred to [Wir90] for a discussion of this class of specification languages.

Among design specification languages, Z and VDM [She95, Jon90], and their object-oriented extensions Object-Z [CDD+89] and VDM++ [DK92] are the most widely used. In contrast to our logic-based universal specifications, these languages are model-based.

FOOPS [RS92] is an OO-specification language with an executable subset that is based on OBJ [GWM+00]. FOOPS uses abstract data types as unifying concept for the functional and object-oriented paradigm. The semantics is based on algebra and category theory. In contrast to our work, FOOPS is tailored towards top-down software development by refinement [BG94]. FOOPS provides a module system with parameterization, information hiding, and powerful composition techniques.

1.6.1.2 Interface Specifications. Interface specification languages (ISLs) are used to describe program behavior by annotations. Most languages provide invariants to express well-formedness criteria of object structures, pre-post-pairs to specify method behavior, and modifies-clauses to denote frame properties (see [LB99] for a discussion of additional specification primitives). ISLs can be classified in operational and declarative languages. Operational ISLs use boolean expressions of the underlying programming language in annotations. In contrast, annotations in declarative ISLs are based on a declarative specification framework (see above).

Operational Interface Specification Languages. Since operational ISLs are based on expressions of a programming language, they are easier to learn and simpler to use than declarative ISLs. Furthermore, operational interface specifications can in general be evaluated during program execution and provide therefore excellent support for testing and debugging. However, for the purpose of formal verification, operational interface specifications have several severe drawbacks:

- Operational ISLs often lack a clean semantics. Since expressions of the underlying programming language are used for annotations (in particular, methods can be invoked in interface specifications), it is possible that annotations do not terminate or that they have side-effects on the execution state. The meaning of such ill-formed specifications is unclear.
- They do not allow one to use functions and abstract data types that are defined in programming language-independent specification frameworks. Therefore, it is not possible to reason about abstractions of data structures in a purely declarative style, which makes verification more complex.
- Operational ISLs are not sufficiently expressive for verification. They do not provide free variables or quantification and their support for handling (recursive) object structures is in general weak: Most operational ISLs do not provide support for the specification of sharing or frame properties.

Meyer worked on software engineering aspects of interface specifications [Mey92a]. He incorporated an operational annotation mechanism into Eiffel [Mey92b] that is also used in Sather [Omo94]. Both ISLs suffer from the above shortcomings. [Mül95] presents an alternative ISL for Sather that statically checks that specifications are side-effect-free.

Among the numerous operational ISLs for Java (see e.g., JaWa [FM98] or iContract [Kra98]), JISL [MMPH99] is interesting since it overcomes some of the drawbacks of operational ISLs: It provides bounded quantification, an abstraction methodology based on the idea of observability in abstract data type theory (side-effect-free observer methods are used to inspect the internal state of objects without modifying it), and support for specifications of frame properties that can be checked at runtime. However, although these features increase the expressiveness of operational ISLs, they are still not sufficient for formal verification.

The Java Modeling Language JML [LBR99a, LBR99b] tries to bridge the gap between operational and declarative interface specification languages to combine the advantages of both. To improve expressiveness, JML enriches the expressions of Java by a set of operators that allow one to express/describe quantification, normal and abrupt termination of methods, object creation, and reachability of objects. As in our approach, frame properties are specified by modifies-clauses and abstract fields with explicit dependencies. JML imitates the two-tiered approach of declarative interface specifications by providing so-called pure types. Pure types are Java types that serve as abstract models for implementations and play therefore the role of abstract data types in declarative specifications. Methods of pure types are supposed not to have observable side-effects on program execution. The relation between concrete implementations and their abstract models is explicitly specified. The definition of a formal semantics for JML is still in progress [BPJ00]. So far, it is not clear how non-terminating specifications can be handled in Hoare-style programming logics, and whether JML's abstraction technique is appropriate for formal verification.

Declarative Interface Specification Languages. The two-tiered interface specification technique was introduced by the Larch project. The Larch family of languages consists of the Larch Shared Language LSL for universal specifications [GH93] and a set of ISLs tailored to specific programming languages, for example, Larch/Ada [GMP90], LCL (for C [GH93]), Larch/C++ [Lea96], LM3 (for Modula3 [GH93]), Larch/CLU [Win87], Larch/Smalltalk [CL94], etc. Besides pre-post-pairs, modifies-clauses, and invariants, some Larch ISLs provide additional specification primitives that make specifications more expressive and more convenient (see [LB99] for a discussion). For instance, so-called history constraints [LW93, LW94] are used to specify a property of the history of values which an instance variable may take. Many of these primitives such as case analysis or redundant specifications can be mapped to ordinary pre-post-specifications and are thus not considered in this book. From a verification point of view, history constraints behave similarly to invariants. Therefore, we omit an explicit treatment of history constraints and sketch how the specification and verification techniques for invariants can be applied to history constraints (see Subsection 6.4.2).

For verification, most Larch ISLs have major drawbacks: (1) Some of them lack a formal semantics in terms of proof obligations in a programming logic. A formal semantics is indispensable for verification. (2) Most Larch ISLs do not provide techniques for the modular specification of frame properties and sharing. (3) The abstraction of data structures to abstract values is kept implicit in the Larch ISLs except in Larch/Ada and Larch/C++. Thus, there is no explicit formal connection between the operational world of implementations and the abstract domain. However, such a formal connection is crucial for verification.

Poetzsch-Heffter presented techniques to overcome some of the shortcomings of the Larch ISLs [PH97b]: (1) The formal semantics of specifications is defined by transforming them into triples of a Hoare logic. (2) A formal model of the object store is used to describe sharing properties of object structures in a flexible way. (3) Based on this formalization of the object store, explicit abstraction functions can be defined. Instead of modifies-clauses, Poetzsch-Heffter's ISL specifies frame properties by relations on object stores. Such relations are useful to define a formal semantics for modifies-clauses, but are in general not appropriate for modular verification (see Section 5.5 for a discussion).

The ISL used in this book resembles Poetzsch-Heffter's ISL. Instead of abstraction functions, we use abstract fields to formally connect object structures to abstract specifications. Furthermore, we provide a technique for the specification of frame properties that makes modular verification possible. The semantics of type invariants used in this book is weaker than in [PH97b]. We discuss these specific differences along with the presentation of our ISL.

OCL [OMG, WK99] can be used to express constraints over object models. The semantics of OCL has not been formally defined so far [OCL], which makes OCL specifications inappropriate for formal verification. Anna [GMP90] contains both operational and declarative specification primitives. It has a rather complex semantics and is therefore not well-suited for verification.

1.6.2 Verification and Analysis Techniques

Since the end of the 1960s, an enormous effort has been taken to study software verification [Flo67, Apt81, CFR93]. In this subsection, we sketch the most important approaches. The reader is referred to [Cou90] for a comprehensive overview of verification techniques and representative work.

Since Hoare's seminal paper, programming logics are used for verification [Hoa69, Apt81, Cou90]. We use Hoare logic for verification since (1) it allows one to prove partial correctness of sequential programs w.r.t. their specifications; (2) it supports both systematic top-down program development from formal specifications and a-posteriori specification and verification of existing implementations (and hybrid development forms); (3) it is fairly simple to apply. Our verification technique is based on a Hoare-style programming logic for OO-languages [PHM99]. A discussion of programming logics is given in Section 3.4.

Based on a denotational semantics, [JBH+98] developed a technique that allows one to verify various properties of implementations written in a Java subset. Hoare logic provides an additional level of abstraction that simplifies the handling of subtyping and abstract methods, and makes proofs more intuitive. Consequently, Jacobs and his group are now using Hoare logic as well [HJ00].

The Extended Static Checking project [DLNS98] aims at the detection of certain frequent programming errors rather than at full verification of an implementation w.r.t. its specification. Instead of directly reasoning about source code, the ESC tool transforms Java or Modula-3 programs into a guarded command language and applies a predicate transformer semantics [LSS99]. Thereby, possible errors are detected and reported. The objective of ESC is to provide techniques and tools for fully automated program checking. Since human interaction during checking is not supported, ESC is limited by the capabilities of theorem provers.

2. Mojave and the Universe Type System

In this chapter, we introduce the programming language Mojave, a rich subset of sequential Java, enhanced by a type system for alias control. Mojave supports modular program development with a simple module concept. Since encapsulation of data representations is crucial for verification, it is discussed in detail. In particular, we describe and formalize the universe type system that supports encapsulation of whole object structures. The chapter concludes with a discussion of related work.

Beginning with the abstract syntax of Mojave, large parts of this book use formal notations based on multisorted first-order logic with recursive data types. The precise definitions and notations as well as naming and type setting conventions are explained in App. A. Frequently used notations are included in the index.

2.1 Mojave: The Language

In this section, we introduce the abstract syntax and static semantics of Mojave and explain its differences from Java. We illustrate several shortcomings of Java's package concept and information hiding techniques. To overcome these problems, we introduce a simple module concept for Mojave and refine Java's access modes.

2.1.1 The Language Core

Mojave (pronounced *Mohave* like the desert in southeastern California) stands for three of the keywords of this book: *modularity*, *Java*, and *verification*. It is essentially a large subset of sequential Java, enhanced by advanced encapsulation features. We chose a Java-like language since Java is a modern OO-language that provides all important object-oriented language features such as a class concept, strong typing, encapsulation, multiple subtyping, dynamic binding, and single inheritance. These features are supported in a way that is typical for a large family of OO-languages containing C++, Eiffel, Sather, Oberon, Modula-3, Simula, and Ada95. Therefore, the techniques presented in this book can be adapted for other languages of that family.

Peter Müller: Modular Specification ..., LNCS 2262, pp. 39–76, 2002.

2.1.1.1 Abstract Syntax and Static Semantics. Mojave is essentially sequential Java and contains all typical OO-features. To keep the language manageable, we omit abrupt completion, exception handling, user-defined constructors, several statements, complex expressions, most of Java's primitive types, inner classes, arrays, and dynamic class loading. For a detailed discussion of the language design, see the design rationale for SVENJA [MMPH97]. SVENJA is the Java subset used in the JIVE system and is very similar to Mojave.

In the following, we present and formalize the abstract syntax of Mojave. We assume that the reader is familiar with Java [GJS96]. Unless otherwise stated, all context conditions, type rules, etc. of Java apply to Mojave as well. The abstract syntax is formalized by the recursive data types presented in Figure 2.1. The concrete syntax of Mojave is almost identical to Java.

Modules. A Mojave program consists of a set of modules (see Subsection 2.1.2 for the differences between packages and modules and for a formalization of Mojave's module concept). Modules have an identifier of sort *ModId* that is unique in each program. A module can *import* other modules. The import relation is acyclic. Modules contain a list of type declarations, that is, class and interface declarations. All type declarations are public, that is, a type declaration in module M is accessible in all modules that import M.

Interfaces and Classes. We assume that class and interface identifiers (of sorts *ClassId* and *InterfaceId*) are unique in each program. This can easily be achieved by prefixing each class and interface name with the identifier of the module it is declared in[1]. Sort *TypeId* subsumes *ClassId* and *InterfaceId*.

As in Java, interfaces can extend superinterfaces. An interface contains a (possibly empty) list of abstract methods, which are either readwrite or readonly methods (indicated by the keyword `readonly`). For convenience, there is a predefined empty interface `Interface`.

The predefined class `Object` (see App. B for the definition) neither extends a class nor implements an interface. It is the root of the subtype hierarchy (see Paragraph 3.1.1.2 for a formalization). Each other class extends exactly one superclass and implements exactly one superinterface (`Interface` is used as default). To declare that a class C implements interfaces $I_1, \ldots, I_n$, an intermediate interface I has to be introduced that is implemented by C and that extends $I_1, \ldots, I_n$. Mojave does not provide abstract classes since we can demonstrate all interesting aspects either with interfaces or with concrete classes. An extension of our techniques to abstract classes is trivial. Each class declaration contains a list of class member declarations.

Class Members. Mojave provides methods and instance fields. Field declarations consist of an access mode, the range type of the field, and the field name of sort *SimpleCFieldId*. Field names are unique in each program. Final and static fields are not provided.

[1] We omit the module name in our examples when it is clear from the context.

```
data type
Module       = modu       ( ModId, list of ModId, list of TypeDecl)
TypeDecl     = class      ( ClassId, ClassId, InterfaceId, list of ClassMember)
             | interface  ( InterfaceId, list of InterfaceId, list of AbsMethDecl)
ClassMember  = field      ( AccessMode, Type, SimpleCFieldId )
             | method     ( AccessMode, Signature, MethBody )
             | smethod    ( AccessMode, Signature, MethBody )
             | romethod   ( AccessMode, Signature, MethBody )
             | sromethod  ( AccessMode, Signature, MethBody )
AbsMethDecl  = amethod    ( Signature )
             | aromethod  ( Signature )
Signature    = sig        ( Type, MethodId, list of FormPar)
MethBody     = mbody      ( list of VarDecl, Stmt )
FormPar      = formpar    ( Type, VarId )
AccessMode   = private
             | default
             | privprot
             | protected
             | public
TypeId       = ctid       ( cid : ClassId )
             | itid       ( iid : InterfaceId )
Type         = booleanT
             | intT
             | nullT
             | grndT      ( tid : TypeId )
             | orepT      ( tid : TypeId )
             | trepT      ( tid : TypeId, TypeId )
             | roT        ( tid : TypeId )
VarDecl      = locvar     ( Type, VarId )
Stmt         = emptyS
             | newS       ( VarId, Type )
             | seqS       ( Stmt, Stmt )
             | ifS        ( Expr, Stmt, Stmt )
             | whileS     ( Expr, Stmt )
             | freadS     ( VarId, VarId, SimpleCFieldId )
             | fwriteS    ( VarId, SimpleCFieldId, Expr )
             | castS      ( VarId, Type, Expr )
             | invocS     ( VarId, VarId, VirtualMethodId, list of Expr)
             | sinvocS    ( VarId, Type, ImplId, list of Expr)
             | callS      ( VarId, VarId, ImplId, list of Expr)
Expr         = varE       ( VarId )
             | nullE
             | intE       ( Int )
             | boolE      ( Bool )
end data type
```

Fig. 2.1. Abstract Syntax of Mojave

Each method in Mojave is either an instance method or a static method, and either a readwrite (i.e., ordinary) method or a readonly (i.e., side-effect-free) method. Method declarations consist of an access mode, the result type, a method identifier, a list of formal parameters, and a method body consisting of a list of local variable declarations and a statement. Default access is not allowed for instance methods (see Paragraph 2.1.2.2). In contrast to Java, each Mojave method returns a (dummy) value. Method identifiers are of sort *MethodId*, identifiers of formal parameters and local variables are of sort *VarId*. In Mojave, static methods are not inherited by subclasses.

To keep things simple, Mojave does not support static overloading. Since overloading can be resolved statically, it is not interesting for specification and verification. For overriding, we adopt the context conditions of Java (no co- and contravariance of the result and argument types). However, supporting co- and contravariance would only require a minor modification of the semantics of interface specifications.

Mojave does not provide user-defined constructors. Object creation is handled by the new-statement and static methods.

There are several context conditions for readonly methods: Since readonly methods are supposed to be side-effect-free, they must not contain field-write- and new-statements. Readonly methods must not invoke readwrite methods. To guarantee the absence of side-effects in the context of dynamic method binding, readonly methods can only be overridden by other readonly methods. In both the signature and the body of a readonly method, only primitive types and readonly types (see below) may be used to guarantee type safety.

Object creation neither affects the states of allocated objects nor their abstractions and invariants. Therefore, allowing readonly methods to create objects would not cause problems for our verification technique. However, excluding new-statements results in several technical simplifications.

Types. Mojave has a sophisticated type system that provides statically-checkable alias control. This *universe type system* and the respective context conditions are explained in detail in Section 2.2. Here, it suffices to know that it supports the primitive types *boolean* and *int* as well as four kinds of *reference types* (*ground types*, *orep types*, *trep types*, and *readonly types*). These reference types specify a type id and provide alias information. The *null type* is the type of the null-reference. It must not occur in program texts.

Statements. Mojave provides statements for reading and writing field access and method invocation as well as new-, if-, while-, skip-, and assign-/cast-statements, and sequential statement composition. That is, Mojave supports only a small subset of Java's statements to reduce the number of rules in the programming logic. In particular, all secondary statements (e.g., for- and do-statements), statements for abrupt completion (such as break-, continue-, and return-statements), and statements for exception handling (try- and throw-statements) are omitted.

Object creation, field access, cast, and method invocation is done by statements (and not by expressions as in Java), since Mojave provides only primitive expressions to make the programming logic simpler (see below). For the same reason, each if-statement must have an else-branch. The new-statement creates a fresh object of the specified type and initializes the instance fields with default values. That is, it behaves like the invocation of the predefined default constructor in Java. The type in a new-statement must be a ground, orep, or trep type. Objects of readonly types are not allowed. The assign-statement is combined with the cast-statement (the static type of the right-hand-side expression can be used as a default type for casting; we do not require to write down this default cast in the concrete syntax).

Since Mojave does not support abrupt completion, a return-statement is dispensable. Instead, Mojave has a predefined local variable `result` for every concrete method. The type of `result` is the result type of the enclosing method. Upon termination, a method returns the value of `result` (similar to functions in Pascal).

Method Invocations. For verification of OO-programs, it is reasonable to discern between *method implementations* and *virtual methods*. A method implementation is the implementation of a concrete method. Virtual methods are used to describe the common properties of all method implementations that might be invoked upon invocation of a dynamically-bound method (see Section 3.1). We assume two infinite sorts *ImplId* and *VirtualMethodId* for method implementations and virtual methods, resp. Every concrete method m declared in a class T introduces a constant of the form T@m of sort *ImplId*. Virtual methods are denoted by constants of the form T:m of sort *VirtualMethodId*. Each dynamically-bound (i.e., neither private nor static) concrete or abstract method m declared in type declaration T that does not override or implement a supertype method introduces virtual methods S:m for each subtype S of T (including T). For instance, for the following type declarations, we introduce T:m and S:m for the abstract method m in the interface T, S@m for the implementation of m in S, S@n for the statically-bound method n in S, and T:equals as well as S:equals for the dynamically-bound method equals that is inherited from Object.

```
public interface T {
  public int m();
}
```

```
public class S implements T {
  public  int m() { ... }
  private int n() { ... }
}
```

Whether a method implementation T@m is readonly is indicated by its declaration. The *declaration type* of a virtual method T:m is the least supertype of T (including T) that contains a declaration for m. This declaration determines whether T:m is a readwrite or readonly method.

To prepare for verification, we assume that the abstract syntax of method invocations is annotated with information from type analysis: Statically-bound method invocations (i.e., static-invocation-statements for invocations of static methods and call-statements for calls of private methods and calls via `super`) directly refer to the method implementation to be invoked. That is, an invocation with concrete syntax `v=w.m(...);` refers to T@m in the abstract syntax, where T is the compile-time type of `w`. Invocations of static methods of the form `v=T'.m(...);` refer to T@m in the abstract syntax, where T is the type id of type T′. In analogy to the target objects of invocations of instance methods, we call T′ the *target type* of the static invocation. Calls of the form `v=super.m(...);` correspond to v = this.T@m(...), where T is that superclass of the class enclosing the call-statement that contains the declaration of the method to be invoked. Dynamically-bound method invocations refer to virtual methods. That is, an invocation with concrete syntax `v=w.m(...);` refers to T:m in the abstract syntax, where T is the compile-time type of `w`.

Expressions. Mojave provides only primitive expressions: boolean and integer literals, the null-expression, and local variable and formal parameter access. Due to this restricted set of expressions, evaluation of expressions cannot cause side-effects. `this` is treated as a predefined formal parameter in all methods, which simplifies the syntax and the logic[2]. For simplicity, we also assume an implicit parameter `this` in static methods that holds the null-value. In formalizations, it is often convenient to denote the formal parameters of a method by indexed names such as v_i. Whenever we use this notation, the variable with index 0 denotes `this`.

Unary and binary operations are performed by static methods of a predefined class `Operator` (see App. B). This makes programs a bit more complicated, but simplifies the programming logic since all operations can be handled by the rules for static method invocations.

2.1.1.2 Open and Closed Programs. An ordinary program is a set of modules that meets certain syntactic criteria. However, the situation is more complex if we consider, for example, class libraries as (possibly incomplete) programs: For formal verification, a set of modules that can be imported by other modules must be treated fundamentally different from complete programs since the correctness of reusable modules relies on properties of the context in which they are reused (in particular on the behavior of overriding methods), whereas the correctness of a complete program is independent of any context. Furthermore, during verification of reusable modules, it is not possible to prove properties of *all* types, fields, etc. of a program since the program in which the modules might be reused is unknown at that point. To cope with these differences, we distinguish between so-called *open* and *closed programs*. Closed programs correspond to the usual notion of programs in imperative languages. They can be executed, but cannot be reused as parts of other programs. In contrast, open programs represent incomplete collections of modules that can be imported and extended like for instance a class library.

[2] However, assignments to `this` are still forbidden.

More precisely, a closed Mojave program consists of a designated *main module* named `Main` and all modules directly or indirectly imported by `Main`. `Main` cannot be imported by other modules. Thus, closed programs cannot be extended, which allows us (1) to define a notion of correctness that does not rely on the context in which a set of modules is reused (see Section 3.3), and (2) to prove properties of *all* types, fields, etc. of a program since closed programs are completely given (see Paragraph 3.1.1.4). A syntactically correct closed program can be executed by invoking a method `public static int main()` of one of the classes in `Main`[3].

An open program represents all closed programs that contain a given set of modules: Let S be a set of modules with the following properties: (1) S does not contain a main module. That is, S is not a closed program. (2) If S contains a module M, then all modules imported by M are also in S (i.e., S is closed under the import relation). An open program with *core* S is the set of all closed programs that contain S. An open program can be extended by adding modules to its core. By such extensions the open program itself (i.e., the set of closed programs) gets smaller. Since open programs can be extended, their correctness relies on the well-formedness of the extensions. Open programs cannot directly be executed. However, the core of an open program can be imported by a main module, which yields an executable closed program. Importing the core of an open program into a main module is called *closing an open program.* The act of closing an open program freezes the set of modules and adds certain axioms to its specification.

In this book, we focus on open programs since they are more interesting for modular verification. In particular, all examples presented in this book are parts of cores of open programs. However, we explain the additional axioms generated for closed programs in Paragraph 3.1.1.4 and define correctness of closed programs in Section 3.3.

2.1.2 Modularity

In Section 1.4 we have identified four important aspects of modularity: explicit structure, separate development, information hiding, and reuse. Mojave adopts the techniques for separate development and reuse (in particular, subtyping and inheritance) from Java. In this subsection, we focus on explicit structure and information hiding. We motivate the need for a module system, discuss why Java's package concept is not appropriate for modular verification, and present a simple module system for Mojave. Furthermore, we explain the difference between information hiding and encapsulation, and refine Java's access modes. Finally, we summarize which interfaces are provided by Mojave's modules, classes, and interface types.

[3] We omit command line arguments for simplicity.

2.1.2.1 The Module System of Mojave. Many OO-languages provide classes and interfaces as only means of modularization. However, even in the presence of nested classes, an additional module system is reasonable from a software engineering point of view:

- Very often, several classes are used to implement complex functionality. If this cooperation is asymmetric in a sense that some classes are auxiliary classes for others (e.g., the node class of a doubly linked list does usually not occur in the list's interface), nested classes are sufficient [HC97]. However, in the symmetric case (see for instance the `Component-Container-LayoutManager` cooperation in Java's AWT [Gea97]), modules should be used to group classes with high cohesion [BA96].
- Classes do not explicitly declare which other classes are used in their implementations (no explicit import [Szy92]). Thus, the structure of programs stays implicit.
- In many implementation patterns, classes should have access to hidden parts of the representation of other classes. For instance in C++, this can be achieved by so-called friends [ES90]. In combination with a dedicated access mode (such as default access in Java), modules are an appropriate means to group classes that have access to their mutual representations [BA96, Lak96, Szy92].

Besides these software engineering arguments, modular specification and verification relies on a module system for the following reasons:

- The explicit structure of programs is needed to determine visibility of declarations. Visibility is in turn a prerequisite for verification. (For instance, a developer cannot be required to prove the preservation of an invariant that is not even visible.)
- For the sake of information hiding, we cannot make the implicit uses-relation of classes explicit and determine visibility of declarations in the absence of modules.
- Access modes and encapsulation play an important role for modular reasoning. Thus, we want to develop verification techniques that work in the presence of friend mechanisms (see Subsection 5.4.3).

Modules vs. Packages. Both modules and packages are means to group type declarations. According to the terminology used in [Szy98], a *module* is *closed* in a sense that after development and deployment, it is not possible to add further program elements to the module. It can only be reused as a whole. In contrast, *packages* can be either open or closed. Open packages can be extended by clients. In this taxonomy, Java provides open packages (provided that the system environment allows one to add classes to a package, for instance, by storing files in a certain directory) and Ada's packages are closed (i.e., are modules).

For modular verification, it is absolutely necessary that packages are closed: (1) In particular the verification of frame properties and invariants requires one to prove properties of all fields/types that are visible to the verifier. However, an open package structure cannot be used to determine visibility: Although a package P is imported by package Q, a type declaration of P might not be present for the verification of Q if it is added after Q has been verified. Moreover, classes that are added to a package after verification can modify the import relation, especially by introducing recursive imports, and thus change the structure of the whole program. (2) In Java, default and protected access are used to realize a friend mechanism for classes in one package [GJS96, ES90]. However, Java allows clients to add new classes to an open package that are thus regarded as "friends" and have access to parts of the implementation that are supposed to be hidden ([Lak96] describes this problem as: "I'm leaving a hole, but please keep out!"). For these reasons, we replace Java's package concept by a proper module system in Mojave.

Mojave's Module System. To keep the results of this book as general as possible, we use a very simple module system for Mojave: Modules are named groups of type declarations with explicit import. In particular, we neither provide parametric modules nor modules as first-class values that can be manipulated by programs. Hierarchical structures by nested modules or inner classes are not supported. According to [Wir88] nested modules in Modula were not considered helpful and therefore omitted in Oberon. Although they are helpful for certain implementation patterns, we do not provide inner classes since the semantics of inner classes, in particular of local inner classes, is extremely complex [HC97, IP00, Ros97]. An extension of our techniques to inner classes is considered future work.

The import relation on modules is acyclic. That is, mutually recursive type declarations have to be placed in one module.

The *scope* of a program or specification element (such as an invariant or a method specification) consists of the module that contains the element and all imported modules.

2.1.2.2 Information Hiding and Encapsulation. In the literature about OO-programming, the terms information hiding and encapsulation are not used in a uniform way. Although the terms are often used synonymously, it is practical to separate the notions of information hiding and encapsulation, in particular since they should be supported by different language features.

Information hiding is a technique to minimize dependencies among separately-written classes. By restricting access to an implementation to explicit interfaces, hidden parts of implementations can be modified without affecting clients. That is, information hiding is a purely syntactical feature that eases separate development and maintenance of classes [Bud91]. In contrast, *encapsulation* is a technique to restrict access to the *internal representation* of an object or a whole object structure [Szy98]. The purpose of encapsulation is to guarantee data consistency, in particular, invariants. In general, encapsulation builds on information hiding techniques to enforce that clients can access a data structure only through designated interfaces. However, encapsulation requires additional techniques to control modification via references (aliases). This problem is discussed in Section 2.2.

Like Java, several OO-languages provide *access modes* as a means to achieve both information hiding and encapsulation. In the following paragraphs, we discuss shortcomings of Java's access modes and their solution in Mojave.

Access Modes in Java. Java provides access modes for four kinds of users of a class: (1) Clients in other packages that are not subclasses, (2) subclasses in other packages, (3) clients in the same package (friends), and (4) the class itself. Access modes allow one to specify the accessibility of a class member according to these groups. Thus, Java's access modes are well-suited to providing information hiding: They can be used to determine which clients of a class might be affected by the modification of a certain program element such as renaming a method. However, they do not provide proper support for encapsulation. For instance, they do not allow one to protect the instance variables of one object of type T from modifications by other T-objects. In particular, access modes do not allow one to protect representations of object structures from being modified when a reference to the representation is (accidently) passed to clients of the structure (see [BV99] for an example related to a security bug in Java).

As we have explained in [MPH98], there are two bugs in the cooperation of Java's access modes, overriding, and dynamic method binding. We briefly describe these bugs and a third shortcoming in the following since they have impact on the design of Mojave's access modes and on the semantics of method invocations:

1. *Overriding default access methods:* In Java, a class C can only declare a method that overrides an inherited method m if m is accessible in C. Otherwise, a new method is introduced that hides the inherited method [GJS96, §8.4.6.1]. That is, private methods are never overridden, protected and public method are always overridden, but default access methods are only overridden if the subclass belongs to the same package as the superclass.
   In [MPH98], we have illustrated an error in Java's algorithm for dynamic method selection [GJS96, §15.11.4]. The compiler associates a so-called compile-time declaration with each method invocation expression. This declaration is used for type checking, etc. Thus, only those methods may be selected at runtime that override the compile-time declaration. However, this is not the case in Java. Obviously, this is a flaw in the semantics that can be solved by a simple modification of the method selection algorithm: Only methods may be dynamically selected that override the compile-time declaration.
2. *Overriding protected methods:* According to the Java Language Specification, the access modifier of an overriding or hiding method must provide

at least as much access as the overridden or hidden method [GJS96, §8.4.6.3]. However, if a protected method declared in class C is overridden by another protected method in a different package (which is legal [GJS96, §8.4.6.3]), this rule is violated: Classes in C's package that are not subclasses of C have access to the overridden, but not to the overriding method[4].
3. *Semantics of protected access:* Protected access is supposed to make program elements accessible in subclasses of the declaration class. However, to achieve encapsulation, Java uses a more restrictive semantics, which we consider rather complicated: Let C and D be classes that are declared in different packages, where D is a subclass of C. D may only access a protected class member of C if it is guaranteed that the member is accessed on a D-object [GJS96, §6.6.2]. This rule guarantees that a class cannot access the protected representation of objects of supertypes or siblings in the subtype hierarchy.

Access Modes in Mojave. Access modes in Mojave are slightly different from Java to overcome the above shortcomings:

1. *Overriding default access methods:* The correct semantics of method invocations could easily be formalized in our programming logic. Since such a formalization does not reveal any interesting aspects for modular specification and verification, we simply forbid default access instance methods in Mojave, thereby circumventing the problem.
2. *Overriding protected methods:* The solution to this problem entails two steps: (1) We require that protected methods have to be overridden in other packages by public methods. However, this restriction is very strong: Implementations can hardly be distributed over several modules without loosening access protection. Thus, we make a second modification to Java's access modes: (2) We re-introduce the access mode *private protected* that existed in early versions of Java [CH96]. Private protected class members are accessible in subclasses only. A private protected method can be overridden by private protected, protected, or public methods. Therefore, private protected can be used to spread implementations over different packages without giving up information hiding.
3. *Semantics of protected access:* The specification and verification techniques presented in this book do not rely on the encapsulation provided by the restricted semantics of protected access in Java. Therefore, we use a weaker semantics: A class member of class C with protected or private protected access is accessible in all subclasses of C (and all classes in the module of C for protected access). This semantics is strong enough for information hiding.

[4] In [MPH98] we illustrated that this contradiction leads to protected methods that can be invoked by classes that do not have access to the methods.

To sum up the previous paragraphs, Mojave provides five different access modes: private, default access, private protected, protected, and public, where default access is not allowed for instance methods, and all type declarations are public. These modes are used for information hiding. Encapsulation is supported by access modes and the universe type system that allows one to control reference passing (see Section 2.2).

2.1.2.3 Interfaces and Views. A Mojave class provides five *interfaces*[5], one interface for each access mode. Since all methods of an interface type are public, interface types only have a public interface.

The public interface of a class or interface type consists of the class/interface name, the names of the direct superclass[6] and the direct superinterface(s), the names and types of public fields, and the names and signatures of public methods.

The protected interface of a class C consists of the names and types of the protected fields as well as the names and signatures of the protected methods declared in C (analogously for private, private protected, and default access). Modules provide only a public interface. A module interface consists of the module name, the names of imported modules, and the names of all types declared in this module.

A *client* of a type declaration or module E is a class, interface, or module that uses E. We discern between different groups of clients: normal users of E, subtypes of E, friends of E, and combinations of these roles. A *view* describes all information that is accessible to a group of clients. There is one view to a class for each access mode, one view to interface types, and two views to modules. These views contain the following information:

- The public view to a type declaration T consists of the public interfaces of all type declarations in the scope of T. This reflects that each client that has public access to T has also public access to the type declarations in the scope of T.
- The protected view to a class C consists of the public view to C and the protected interfaces of all superclasses of C.
- The private protected view to a class C consists of the protected view to C and the private protected interfaces of all superclasses of C.
- The default access view to a class C consists of the protected view to C and the default access interfaces of all classes in the module of C.

[5] Despite the name clash, we use the term *interface* to refer to the description of program elements that are exported by a class or module. We use *interface type* for the entities introduced by `interface`-declarations wherever the meaning of *interface* is ambiguous.

[6] It is often argued that information about inheritance should not be part of the public interface of a class since inheritance is regarded as an implementation technique [Bra92, Sny86, Sny87]. However, information about subtyping is definitely necessary for clients. Since inheritance is coupled with subtyping in Java and Mojave, we have to reveal information about inheritance, although this is not completely compatible with information hiding.

- The private view to a class C consists of the private protected view and the default access view to C, the private interface of C, and the implementation of C.
- The public view to a module M consists of the public views to the type declarations declared in M and the public interface of M.
- The default access view to a module M consists of the default access views to the type declarations declared in M.

The fact that the implementation of a class C belongs only to C's private view reflects the idea that only C itself has access to C's implementation. Neither classes in the same module nor subclasses may inspect C's implementation.

The notion of views is used to handle information hiding in specification and verification: The specification of an interface may only reveal implementation details that are contained in the corresponding view. The verifier of a class has knowledge about the private view of this class and nothing else (in particular, not about the implementation of other classes). We formalize views in Subsection 3.1.1.

This concludes the presentation of Mojave's language core. The reader is referred to App. C for examples of Mojave programs. In the next section, we explain Mojave's type system.

2.2 Universes: A Type System for Flexible Alias Control

Modular verification of frame properties and type invariants requires alias and dependency control [LN00]. In Subsection 1.3.5, we have illustrated that classical interface specifications based on pre-post-specifications and type invariants are not sufficiently expressive to control both static and dynamic aliasing. In particular, they cannot prevent subtypes from adding new methods that introduce aliases by taking or passing out references to objects that are supposed not to be aliased (see class `SubClient2` in Example 1.3.4). Therefore, we complement interface specifications by a sophisticated type system. Besides naming a type declaration, the types of this type system provide alias information which is used to control sharing.

In this section, we present a programming model that can be used to restrict aliasing. Its application to control dependencies of abstractions and type invariants is explained in Chapter 5. A sophisticated type system allows one to statically check whether a program respects this programming model. We formalize the type system and illustrate its application by several examples.

2.2.1 The Ownership Model

The universe type system builds on recently developed techniques for alias control (e.g., ownership types, see Section 2.3). The programming model underlying these approaches is based on the *ownership model.* The basic idea of the ownership model is that in general groups of one or more objects work closely together to realize a common functionality (e.g., an abstract data type). We call such groups *dynamic components.* Some objects (*interface objects*) of a dynamic component are used to interact with other dynamic components. The other objects are the internal *representation* of the dynamic component. The goal is to control references to representation objects.

There are different techniques to define which objects are interface objects and which are representation objects of a dynamic component. We explain one of them in Subsection 2.2.3. Dynamic components and their representations are defined based on a binary relation on objects, the so-called *ownership relation.* The idea underlying the ownership relation is that the interface objects of a dynamic component are the owners of all objects that are directly used to represent the dynamic component. For instance, the header of a doubly linked list is the owner of all node objects.

The ownership relation can be considered as a directed graph on the allocated objects in a program state where an edge goes from X to Y if X is the owner of Y. Figure 2.2 displays an object store with several objects (depicted by boxes) and their ownership relation (arrows). We say that a program *realizes the ownership model* if in all states there exists a partitioning of all allocated objects such that

- all objects of one partition (depicted by ellipses in Fig. 2.2) have the same (possibly empty) set of owners,
- the owners of the objects in a partition P are in one partition Q, and
- the ownership relation is acyclic.

Each partition P corresponds to exactly one dynamic component with the owners of P as interface objects. The representation of the dynamic component consists of the objects in P and all objects owned by objects in P (including transitive ownership). For instance in Fig. 2.2, the dynamic component corresponding to partition C (in the following called dynamic component C) consists of objects 2–7 with objects 2 and 3 as interface objects. At the roots of the ownership graph are the objects that have no owner. That is, objects that do not belong to any representation (object 1). This definition of the ownership relation implies the following facts:

- Interface objects of a dynamic component c do not belong to the representation of c.
- Representations of different dynamic components are either disjoint or one is contained in the other (*representation containment*). For instance, the representations of the dynamic components C and D (objects 4–7 and

object 8) are disjoint. The representation of dynamic component E (objects 5–7) is contained in the representation of dynamic component C (objects 4–7).

- An object can be an interface object of several dynamic components at the same time. For example, object 3 is interface object of the dynamic components C and D.

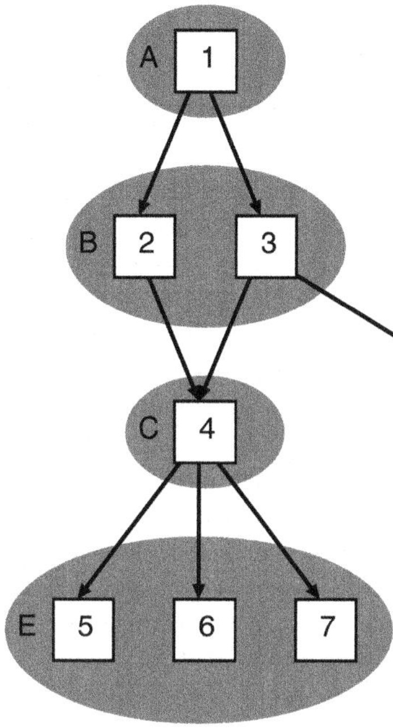

Fig. 2.2. Object Store with Ownership Relation

We say that an object Y is *inside* a dynamic component c if it belongs to the representation of c; Y is *outside* c if it is not inside. For modular verification, the distinction between inside and outside of dynamic components is used in two ways. First, it defines a boundary for incoming references (*alias control*). In particular, it provides a mechanism to specify which references to the representation may be passed to the outside by subclasses. Second, it defines the set of objects on which invariants and abstractions may depend (see Paragraph 5.1.3.1).

In the next subsection, we present the universe programming model which uses the ownership model to formulate restrictions on the permissible reference structures. This way, flexible alias control can be realized.

2.2.2 The Universe Programming Model

Mojave supports two variants of the ownership model: *Object universes* can be used to implement dynamic components that have exactly one interface object. They provide very strong alias control which is useful for many implementation patterns. Object universes can also be generalized to *type universes* which allow several objects of basically arbitrary classes to be interface objects of a dynamic component. Therefore, type universes provide alias control that is weaker than that of object universes; however, it is still strong enough to enable modular verification of frame properties and type invariants (see Chapters 5 and 6). Both variants of the ownership model are presented below. Furthermore, we describe how we can use typing mechanisms to delimit the world inside a dynamic component from the world outside.

2.2.2.1 Object Universes. With conventional type systems, a program $\mathcal{P}$ defines a set of types together with a subtype relation. We call this set of types the *standard universe* of $\mathcal{P}$. The basic idea of the universe type system is to use multiple "copies" of the standard universe (one could imagine copying the whole program text and adding a suitable postfix to the class and interface names). Such a copy is called a *universe.* In each universe, there is a type for each type declaration. Although structurally identical, the copies of a type in different universes are distinct. Each object is created for a copy of a type in a given universe. That is, each object *belongs to* exactly one universe.

As will be explained below, universes can be created dynamically during program execution (e.g., there is a universe for every object in a program execution). That is, the instances (copies) of a type are dynamic entities and therefore called *dynamic types* (not to be confused with the dynamic or runtime type of an object as opposed to the static type of a variable). In this respect, they are similar to value-dependent types, but dynamic types depend on a universe rather than a value (see Section 2.3). To clearly distinguish between the static and dynamic entities of the type system, we use the terms *type declaration*, *type*, and *dynamic type* to refer to classes/interfaces, the static type identifiers used in programs, and the copies of a type declaration in different universes, resp.

To realize dynamic components with exactly one interface object, we introduce a universe for each object X in a program execution (in addition to the standard universe and other universes, see Paragraph 2.2.2.2). We call X the *owner* of its universe. Note that this implies a hierarchical structuring of the universes. The standard universe is the root of the universe hierarchy. Each object in the standard universe has its own universe. Objects in these *child universes* are again owners of universes and so forth.

Universes can easily be used to implement the ownership model. Each object X is regarded as the only interface object of a dynamic component C. The objects directly used to represent C are put into the universe owned by X. Consequently, the whole representation of C is contained in X's universe and its descendants. The type rules of the universe type system enforce that

1. objects inside C can only be referenced (except for readonly references, see below) by C's interface objects or other objects of the representation. Thus, objects outside C can modify C's internal state only by accessing methods and fields of C's interface objects. We will exploit this *representation encapsulation* for verification of frame properties and type invariants (see Subsection 5.4.2).
2. objects inside C cannot have readwrite references to objects outside; we will use this property to control dependencies of abstractions and type invariants (see Paragraph 5.1.3.1).

The above restrictions control static aliases, that is, aliases via references stored in instance variables. However, the restrictions apply as well for local variables and formal parameters if they are considered as instance variables of the `this`-object. Thus, we can control static and dynamic aliasing. We will explain the universe invariant in more detail in Subsection 2.2.6.

Figure 2.3 illustrates how the node structure of a doubly linked list of integer values can be encapsulated to protect it from modifications (objects and references are depicted by boxes and arrows, resp.) The list header serves as interface object for the dynamic component; the nodes are stored in the header's object universe (objects belonging to that universe are encircled; boxes touching the ellipse stand for owner objects). Note that neither references from objects outside the dynamic component to the inside (except from the list header) nor references from inside to the outside are permitted.

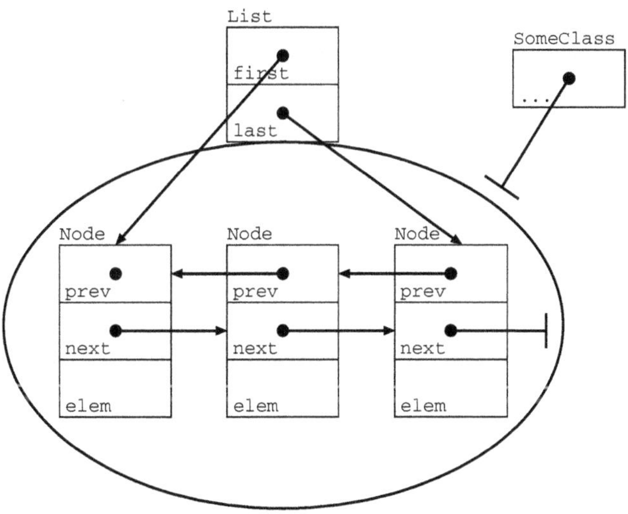

Fig. 2.3. Object Structure for a Doubly Linked Integer List

2.2.2.2 Type Universes. Object universes provide a very strong form of alias control. However, certain implementation patterns require dynamic components with several interface objects: (1) For efficiency, sharing should not be restricted more than necessary. For example if some doubly linked lists are modified very rarely, it is reasonable to allow several list headers to share a common node structure to save space. (2) In some scenarios, several objects must have read and write access to representations. For instance, list headers and iterators need access to the list structure. Some of these scenarios can be handled by object universes and readonly references (see Paragraph 2.2.2.3). However, other patterns such as the property editor example in Paragraph 2.2.4.2 require dynamic components with several interface objects.

To support such implementation patterns, we generalize object universes to *type universes*. That is, besides object universes, we introduce universes that are not exclusively associated with single objects but that can be owned by various objects. To explain the notion of type universes, we describe in the following a very general approach that allows programmers to declare universes. For simplicity, we do not follow this general approach here. Instead, Mojave only provides a restricted form of predefined type universes.

User-Defined Type Universes. In analogy to static fields that do not exclusively belong to an object and that can be accessed by several objects depending on their access modes, we could allow programmers to declare universes as static class members: If T_U is the dynamic type for a type declaration T in universe U then a universe declaration in T would introduce a child universe V of U. The access mode of the declaration could be used to determine the owner objects of this universe: An object X would be an owner of V if its dynamic type S was in U (i.e., X belonged to the parent universe of V) and the universe declaration was accessible in one of the supertypes of S. That is, such universe declarations could be used to provide universes that can be shared by all objects of one dynamic type (if the universe was declared private or private protected), by objects of dynamic types declared in one module (default or protected), or by objects of all dynamic types that had the declaration of the universe in their scope (public). These variants provide different strengths of alias control.

Type Universes in Mojave. In this book, we provide only a very restricted form of type universes: (1) We focus on public type universes since they are the weakest variant of type universes that is strong enough to enable modular verification. Please refer to [MPH00b] and [MPH00c] for the context conditions and invariants of private and default access type universes, resp. (2) Instead of allowing programmers to declare universes, we use a fixed set of predefined type universes to avoid syntactic overhead and to simplify formalizations. We introduce one type universe for each dynamic type in a program execution[7]. One could imagine that each type declaration in a Mojave program contains the declaration of one public type universe. This implies that the type universes for two different dynamic types S and T are disjoint, no matter whether S and T are subtypes or not. The extension to freely declared universes is straightforward, but not interesting for this book. The type universe U for dynamic type T is owned by all objects that belong to U's parent universe and the classes of which have T's declaration in their scope.

2.2.2.3 References across Representation Boundaries. The universe programming model as described in the previous paragraphs enables strong alias control and thus representation encapsulation. However, it is too restrictive for many applications: (1) One needs the capability of having references that point outside the representation of a dynamic component. For example, the representation of a list should not be forced to include the element objects of the list. In most cases, the list only stores references to its elements. The element objects are outside the list component. (2) Several common programming patterns such as iterators or binary methods require that the representation of a dynamic component can be accessed by several different objects. In cases where the representation can be exposed to several owners, type universes solve the problem. However, if both the strong alias control of object universes and several interface objects are needed, or if the objects that should have access to a representation do not belong to the same universe, then type universes are not sufficient. This is, for instance, the case for binary methods such as test for structural equality or for clone methods that copy an object structure from one universe to another. To support such idioms, we provide readonly references and readonly methods. Readonly references are allowed to point into arbitrary universes. Readonly methods enable one to observe aspects of the representation and are guaranteed not to make any modifications.

Readonly References. Readonly references cannot be used to perform field updates or invocations of readwrite methods. Readonly references allow objects to make part of their representation accessible without taking the risk that the representation is being modified.

Figure 2.4 shows how readonly references can be used to expose parts of a representation (here, the nodes of a doubly linked list) in a safe way (dashed arrows depict readonly references). Furthermore, they allow objects inside a dynamic component to reference objects outside (in this example the elements stored in the list).

Readonly Methods. Readonly references cannot be used to modify objects. To achieve that, methods that cause side-effects must not be invoked on readonly

[7] Note that this leads to an infinite proliferation of universes: Each universe contains a set of dynamic types; each dynamic type is in turn associated with a type universe and so forth.

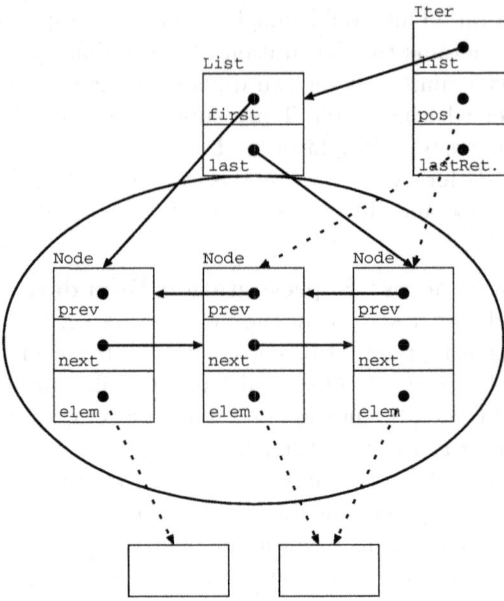

Fig. 2.4. Object Structure for a Doubly Linked Object List with Iterator

references. This property can be statically checked by either forbidding all method invocations on readonly references, or by introducing readonly methods that can be statically checked to be side-effect-free. Obviously, the former solution is not satisfactory since for example one would like to use a method `equals` to compare two objects referenced readonly. For this reason, Mojave provides readonly methods (see Subsection 2.1.1).

2.2.3 Programming with Universes

Mojave supports both object and type universes, which gives programmers the choice to use object universes with strong alias control — in cases where one owner object per representation is sufficient (e.g., many container implementations) — or type universes with weaker alias control in cases where the flexibility of type universes is required (such as the property editor in Paragraph 2.2.4.2). In this subsection, we explain how the ownership relation, and thus the application of object and type universes, can be specified by extended typing.

A closed Mojave program $\mathcal{P}$ defines the set of types that can be used in $\mathcal{P}$ together with the subtype relation. The set of types of an open program corresponds to the set of types of its core. However, both the set of types and the subtype relation are underspecified for open programs (see Subsection 3.1.1 for a formalization). We describe the types that can be used in programs in the following.

Readwrite Reference Types. In each execution state, there is a *current universe*. During execution of instance methods, the current universe is the universe to which the this-object belongs. The current universe for the execution of static methods is determined by the current universe in the state before the invocation and the target type of the invocation. Program execution starts in the standard universe. That is, the current universe of the initial program state is the standard universe.

The universe type system provides three kinds of readwrite reference types (see the syntax in Fig. 2.1). These types specify the dynamic type of a program element such as a variable *relative to the current universe*. More precisely, they provide information whether the dynamic type is in the current universe, the universe owned by this, or the universe associated with a dynamic type in the current universe. That is, the dynamic readwrite types that can be specified in a program always refer to the current universe or one of its child universes.

A ground type $\mathit{grndT}(\mathrm{T})$ (denoted by a plain type identifier T) refers to the dynamic type for T in the current universe. The types for child universes of the current universe are marked by the keyword **rep** and therefore called *rep types*: An object representation type (orep type for short) $\mathit{orepT}(\mathrm{T})$ (denoted by rep<this> T[8]) refers to the type for T in the object universe owned by **this**. The type for T in the child universe of the current universe that is associated with type id S is denoted by a type representation type (trep type) $\mathit{trepT}(\mathrm{T}, \mathrm{S})$ (denoted by rep<S> T).

Ground, orep, and trep types are disjoint types for the type checker. For instance, expressions of type rep<this> T cannot be assigned to variables of type T since T and rep<this> T correspond to different dynamic types. Since the type universes for different dynamic types are disjoint, rep<S> T and rep<R> T are different types. References of a type rep<this> T always point into the universe owned by this. To prevent them from leaking to other objects than this, fields having orep types and methods that have orep types as return or parameter types can only be accessed/invoked on this (we will relax this restriction for readonly references, see below; the precise rules are given in Subsection 2.2.5).

Readonly Types. We use the readonly type $\mathit{roT}(\mathrm{T})$ (denoted by readonly T) for readonly references to objects of class/interface T independent of the universe. Readonly types have three important properties:

1. They are supertypes of the corresponding readwrite types. That is, readonly T is a supertype of T, rep<this> T, and rep<S> T.
2. It is not possible to use an expression of a readonly type as target for a field update or an invocation of a readwrite method. This is checked by context conditions.

[8] Note that this serves as a keyword here, not an expression.

3. Reading fields or invoking readonly methods via readonly references yields again readonly references. Thus, it is not possible to gain a readwrite reference through a readonly reference. Consequently, we can allow fields of rep types to be accessed on readonly references without violating representation encapsulation.

We support downcasts to convert readonly references into readwrite references. As with conventional downcasts, such casts need runtime checks. If a readonly reference points into universe U, these checks guarantee that only the owners of U and objects belonging to U can successfully downcast the readonly reference into a readwrite reference. Technically, that is achieved by checking that the type mentioned in the cast-statement specifies a dynamic type of the universe to which the object in the right-hand-side variable belongs. See Subsection 2.2.5 for a formalization of these rules, and the following subsection for an example.

2.2.4 Examples

In this subsection, we present an example program which is used throughout this book. The program consists of two modules: Module `LIST` contains an implementation of a doubly linked lists of objects with iterators. The module `PROPERTY` implements a Java-Bean-like [Ham97] component that uses a list as internal representation. So-called property objects can be used to configure the internal state of the dynamic component with a property editor. This example contains applications of both object and type universes, methods that manipulate object structures by destructive updates, and interesting invariants. Thus, it illustrates the universe type system as well as our specification and verification techniques, in particular the handling of frame properties and invariants. In the text, we will only present small portions of the example to highlight certain aspects. The full example can be found in App. C.

2.2.4.1 Container Classes. Containers are interesting examples for alias control since (1) they usually work with internal representations (e.g., node structures or arrays) which have to be encapsulated; (2) they have to grant other objects restricted access to their representations, for instance to implement iterators; (3) the element objects do not, in general, belong to the representation, but are shared with other objects. As an example for a container class, we study a doubly linked list implementation.

Doubly Linked Lists. The node structure of a doubly linked list consists of a set of `Node`-objects. Since all nodes belong to the same universe (owned by the list header), we use ground types for the `prev`- and `next`-fields. The element objects stored in the list can belong to any universe. Thus, the only legal way to reference them is through a readonly type.

```
public class Node {
    public Node prev, next;
    public readonly Object elem;
}
```

The list header stores references to the first and last node of the node structure. To encapsulate the nodes, we put them into the header's object universe. This encapsulation allows us to make the fields of `Node` public to allow subclasses of `List` to directly manipulate their node structures.

```
public class List {
    protected rep<this> Node first, last;
    ...
}
```

This prevents the header from giving away a readwrite reference to a node. In particular, a subclass `BadList` of `List` cannot declare a method

```
    public Node getNode() { result = this.first; }  // type error
```

since the result type is not compatible with the type `rep<this> Node` of the `first`-field. On the other hand, if `getNode` had return type `rep<this> Node`, the method could only be invoked on `this`, which prevents the reference from leaking (see Subsection 2.2.3 and 2.2.5).

```
    public rep<this> Node getNode() { result = this.first; }  // safe
```

Turning Readonly References into Readwrite References. The following code fragment illustrates how the owner of an object X and objects that belong to the same universe as X can cast a readonly reference to X into a readwrite reference:

```
(1)   public int m(List l, Object rw) {
(2)       readonly  Object ro;
(3)       rep<this> Object rr;
(4)                 int dummy;
(5)       dummy = l.appFront(rw);
(6)       ro = l.getFirst();              // returns object in rw
(7)       rw = (Object) ro;               // legal
(8)       rr = (rep<this> Object) ro;     // runtime error
(9)     }
```

We assume that the list `l` is well-formed and `rw` references an object X upon invocation of `m`. Since the type of `rw` is a ground type, the `this`-object and X belong to the same universe. X is then stored in a list and retrieved again (lines 5 and 6), which yields a readonly reference to X (see property 3 of readonly types in Subsection 2.2.3). This reference is then downcast to a readwrite reference (line 7), which is legal since the ground type `Object` refers to the universe to which the `this`-object and X belong. However, the cast in line 8 leads to a runtime error since X does not belong to the object universe owned by `this`.

References into Representations. To illustrate the flexibility gained by readonly references, we explain how iterators and binary methods can be implemented. Both patterns are not supported by existing type systems for alias control such as ownership types or balloon types (see Section 2.3).

Positions and Iterators. For efficiency, an iterator has to store its current position in the data structure over which it iterates. For doubly linked lists, this means that an iterator has to hold a reference to a node object. As a basis for iterators, we introduce a simple class `ListPos` which is used to store positions in a list.

A `ListPos`-object references the list it is associated with (using a ground type) and a node of that list. Since the node belongs to the object universe owned solely be the list header, this reference has to be readonly[9].

```
public class ListPos {
    protected List list;
    protected readonly Node pos;
    ...
}
```

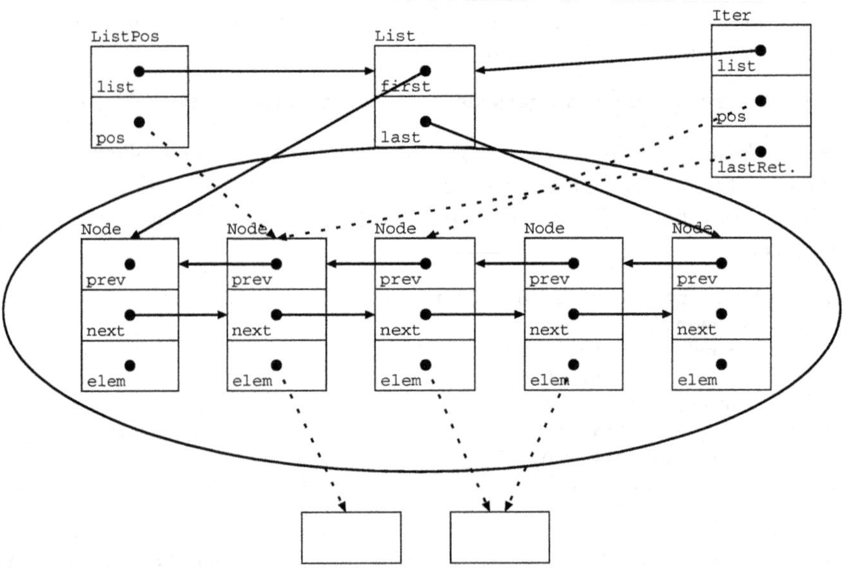

Fig. 2.5. Object Structure for a Doubly Linked List with Iterator and Position (dashed arrows depict readonly references)

[9] Using a type universe for the node structure would allow list positions to be owners of the node structure and thus to hold readwrite references to nodes. However, to achieve stronger alias control and to illustrate the flexibility of object universes, we use an object universe here. See the property editor example for a similar pattern using type universes.

ListPos can easily be extended to implement iterators (see App. C.1). Note that although the iterator has only a readonly reference to the node structure, it can remove elements from the list by invoking List's remove-method. (List's remove-method casts the readonly Node-reference into a readwrite reference.) The object structure of a doubly linked list with a ListPos-object and an iterator is illustrated by Figure 2.5 (the list implementation uses dummy nodes at both ends to simplify methods and invariants).

Binary Methods. Readonly references allow readonly methods to access several representations simultaneously. This is particularly useful to implement side-effect-free binary methods such as test for structural equality. The implementation of equalsList (see Fig. 2.6) demonstrates the concrete syntax of Mojave and the usage of Operator.

```
public class List {
    ...
    public boolean equalsList(readonly List l) readonly {
        readonly Node n1,n2,l1,l2;
        boolean  b, b1, b2, e;
        readonly Object o1,o2;

        result = true;
        n1 = this.first;
        n2 = l.first;
        n1 = n1.next;    // skip dummy node
        n2 = n2.next;    // skip dummy node
        l1 = this.last;
        l2 = l.last;
        b = true;
        b1 = true;

        while(b) {
            o1 = n1.elem;
            o2 = n2.elem;
            e  = Operator.equalO(o1,o2);
            if (e) {                     // elements are equal
                n1 = n1.next;
                n2 = n2.next;
                b1 = Operator.equalO(n1,l1);
                b2 = Operator.equalO(n2,l2);
                b1 = Operator.not(b1);
                b2 = Operator.not(b2);
                b  = Operator.condAnd(b1,b2);
            } else { result = false; b = false; }
        }
        b = Operator.condOr(b1,b2);
        if (b) result = false; else ;
    }
}
```

Fig. 2.6. Implementation of equalsList

2.2.4.2 Properties. A *property*[10] is a part of the state of a dynamic component that can be read and written (e.g., size and color are properties of a window). *Property editors* allow one to inspect and modify properties of dynamic components, similar to builder tools for Java Beans [Ham97]. Property editors read and manipulate properties via *property objects* that implement the following interface[11]:

```
public interface Property {
    public int setValue(readonly Object v);
    public readonly Object getValue() readonly;
}
```

Property objects provide very flexible control over access to properties: (1) They provide uniform access to all properties of a dynamic component; (2) A dynamic component can control what clients can get what kinds of and how many property objects; (3) Property objects can have state. Thus, property objects can be implemented that permit only one modification or that permit modifications only within a certain period of time. Such fine-grained control is difficult to achieve by ordinary get- and set-methods in a dynamic component's interface.

Properties are an interesting example with which to study dynamic components with several interface objects. Since property objects are used to manipulate the internal state of a dynamic component, they need readwrite access to the dynamic component's representation[12]. Therefore, we use type universes to realize dynamic components with property objects. To illustrate this pattern, we implement a very simple dynamic component with main class `MyBean` that uses a doubly linked list as internal representation (see Figure 2.7). Property objects (of class `ListProperty`) allow one to read and update certain elements of the list. `MyBean`, `Property`, and `ListProperty` are implemented in module `PROPERTY` which can be found in App. C.2. The implementation of class `MyBean` uses the type universe for `MyBean` for the representation. Thus, `ListProperty`-objects can hold readwrite references to the list of a `MyBean`-object and associated `ListPos`-objects. In particular, they can invoke the `setValue`-method of `ListPos` which is a readwrite method. Figure 2.8 illustrates the object and universe structure of a `MyBean`-object with one `ListProperty`-object.

The implementation of `ListProperty` reveals that type universes restrict reuse: In the absence of universes, `ListProperty` would only use the type declarations `ListPos` and `Property` and could therefore be implemented independently of `MyBean` and reused in different contexts. Even in the absence

[10] The example is taken from [HC97, pp. 216].

[11] In realistic applications, properties should also provide a name, a description, etc. We omit this information for brevity.

[12] It is not possible to manipulate the representation via methods of another interface object X (see the pattern used for the `remove`-method in class `Iter`) if property objects are implemented in different modules. That would require the set-methods of X to be public and thus allow one to circumvent access control.

```
public class MyBean {
    rep<MyBean> List beanRep;
    ...
}

public class ListProperty implements Property {
    protected rep<MyBean> ListPos lp;
    ...

    public int setValue(readonly Object v) {
        rep<MyBean> ListPos p;    p = this.lp;
        result = p.setValue(v);
    }
}
```

Fig. 2.7. Implementation of Property Pattern

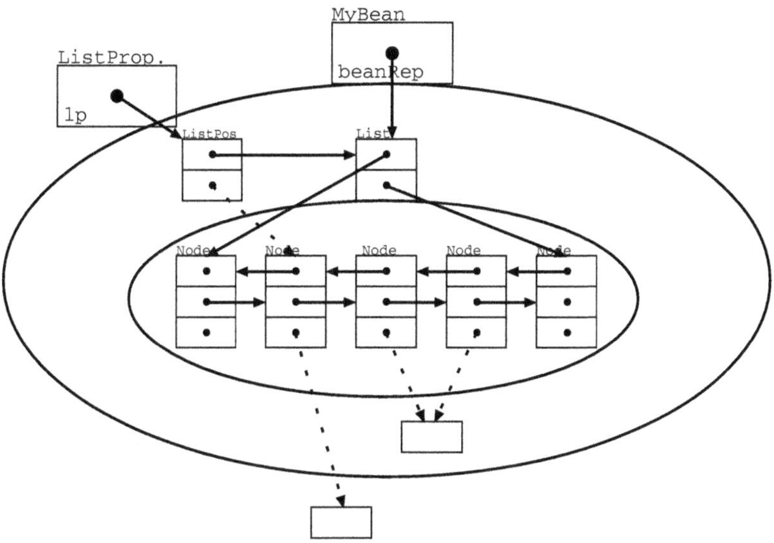

Fig. 2.8. Object Structure for a `MyBean`-Object

of universes, the same problem would occur if `ListProperty`-objects would contain a reference to the associated `MyBean`-object. In that scenario, the problem could be solved by using subtyping or genericity. We can apply the same solutions for universes: (1) We can use the type universe of a common superclass of all dynamic components that provide properties (if such a superclass exists); obviously, this weakens alias control since one universe is used for the representations of several dynamic components (analogously to losing type information when genericity is simulated by subtyping [Mey86]). (2) We could extend the type universes to support genericity. We consider such an extension further work (see Chapter 7).

2.2.5 Formalization of the Universe Type System

The universe type system can be used to statically check whether a program is compliant to the universe programming model described above. In this subsection, we formalize the universe type system and the relevant context conditions. A formal proof of type safety is contained in Subsection 3.2.1.

Types. The universe type system provides the primitive types boolean and int, four kinds of reference types (ground types, orep types, trep types, readonly types), and a type for the null-value (see Figure 2.1).

The subtype relation $\preceq_T$ on types follows the subtype relation in Java: Reference type S is a subtype of reference type S′ if (1) both types are of the same kind and (2) the class/interface of S extends or implements the class/interface of S′. In addition, every readonly type is a supertype of the ground and rep types for the same type declaration. A formalization of the subtype relation can be found in Paragraph 3.1.1.3.

The Type Combinator. Types describe the dynamic type of a program element (expression, field, method) relative to the current universe (see Subsection 2.2.3). Consequently, the type of a field access or of a method invocation has to be determined by combining the type of the target variable and the type of the field or method as illustrated by the following example.

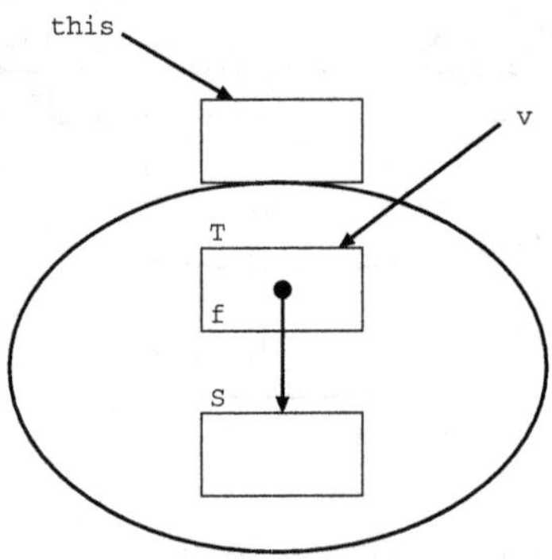

Fig. 2.9. Example for Type Combinator

Consider the field access `v.f`, where `v` is declared to be of type `rep<this> T` and class `T` contains a field `f` of type `S`. As illustrated in Figure 2.9, `v` holds a reference to an object that belongs to the universe owned by `this` (since `v` has an orep type), and the `S`-object referenced by `f` belongs to the same object as the object that contains `f` (since `f` has a ground type). Consequently, `v.f` holds a reference to an `S`-object that belongs to the universe owned by `this`. That is, relative to the current universe, `v.f` has the type `rep<this> S`. Such combinations of types are described by the *type combinator*

$\_ * \_ : \mathit{Type} \times \mathit{Type} \rightarrow \mathit{Type}$

If T and S are the types of `v` and `f`, then the type of `v.f` is $T * S$. This type combinator is partially defined by the following table (first argument: rows, second argument: columns):

	grndT(T)	*trepT*(T,T')	*orepT*(T)	*roT*(T)
grndT(S)	*grndT*(T)	*trepT*(T,T')	*orepT*(T)	*roT*(T)
trepT(S,S')	*trepT*(T,S')	undefined	undefined	*roT*(T)
orepT(S)	*orepT*(T)	undefined	undefined	*roT*(T)
roT(S)	*roT*(T)	*roT*(T)	*roT*(T)	*roT*(T)
booleanT	all undefined			
intT	all undefined			
nullT	all undefined			

	booleanT	*intT*	*nullT*
grndT(S)	*booleanT*	*intT*	*nullT*
trepT(S,S')	*booleanT*	*intT*	*nullT*
orepT(S)	*booleanT*	*intT*	*nullT*
roT(S)	*booleanT*	*intT*	*nullT*
booleanT	all undefined		
intT	all undefined		
nullT	all undefined		

The definition of the type combinator reveals four important aspects:

- The class/interface of the resulting type is the class/interface of the second argument. This is as in Java where the type of `v.f` is the type of `f`.
- The combination of two rep types is not defined to ensure that it is not possible to gain readwrite references to objects that belong to grandchildren of the current universe[13].
- If one of the arguments is a readonly type, the result is also a readonly type. This guarantees that readonly references are transitive. That is, it is not possible to gain a readwrite reference through a readonly reference.
- If the first argument is a primitive type, the result is undefined since such situations cannot occur in Mojave (e.g., it is not allowed to invoke methods on integer variables).

The definition of the type combinator affects the context conditions for readonly methods. In analogy to Java, the combination of the types of the target and the actual parameter of a method invocation has to be a subtype of the type of the formal parameter (see below for the type rules). In cases where the method is invoked on a readonly reference, this combination yields a readonly type. Therefore, we require that all formal parameters of readonly methods must have readonly or primitive types to meet the requirement above. This rule is no restriction since readonly methods must not modify their parameters anyway.

[13] It would be type safe if the combination of two rep types yielded a readonly type. However, we think that such a definition is rather unintuitive. If the readonly type is desired, it can be achieved by an additional assignment.

Type Rules. The type rules of Mojave follow the type rules of Java [GJS96, ON98]. Whereas most of Mojave's type rules are identical to Java (for instance, a while-statement is well-typed if the condition is of type `boolean` and if the body is well-typed), the rules for object creation, cast-statements, field access, and method invocations must be adapted, mainly w.r.t. the following aspects:

- We have to refine the requirements of Java's type rules for field accesses and method invocations. Java's requirements stay basically valid (e.g., the type of an actual method parameter must be a subtype of the type of the corresponding formal parameter). However, we have to apply the type combinator to determine the types of the field access and the return resp. the parameter types of method invocations.
- Field access and method invocation statements need additional requirements to guarantee that the object universes of different objects are kept apart. Therefore, fields having orep types and methods that have orep types as return or parameter types can only be accessed/invoked on `this` and variables of readonly types (see Subsection 2.2.3). The special treatment of the implicit parameter `this` is necessary for alias control on the object level in a statically-checkable type system.

The universe-specific rules are displayed below. Whenever we refer to a program element such as a variable or statement in a type rule, we assume that the program context of this element is implicitly given and that we can refer to declarations in this context[14]. We use $[e]$ to denote the type of an expression or field e. Note that we do not need type rules for expressions since Mojave provides only primitive expressions. Thus, the type of a literal, local variable, or formal parameter is directly defined by the program. In methods m declared in type T, [`this`][15] has $grndT(\mathrm{T})$ if m is a readwrite method, and $roT(\mathrm{T})$ if m is readonly (recall that all formal parameters of readonly methods are required to be readonly). We use $ret(m)$ and $par(m,i), 1 \leq i$ to refer to the result type and the type of the i-th explicit formal parameter of method m. `v` $\cong$ `w` expresses that `v` and `w` are identical variables.

The judgment $\vdash$ `stmt` expresses that statement `stmt` is well-typed in a given program. That is, each rule expresses that the statement below the line is well-typed in a closed program $\mathcal{P}$ or in the core M of an open program if the (comma-separated) requirements above the line are met by $\mathcal{P}$ resp. M. Note that all requirements can be checked modularly. That is, if the requirements are met by the core of an open program $\mathcal{P}$, they are also met by all closed programs in $\mathcal{P}$. If the type combinator occurs within a rule, the statement is only correctly typed if the application of the combinator is defined.

[14] Technically, this means that the rules are described for occurrences within a program context [PH97a].

[15] To distinguish expressions from the values they hold, we use `typewriter font` for the program elements and roman font for the values. For instance, `v` denotes a variable whereas v is the value held by `v`.

$$\frac{\mathrm{T} \preceq_T [\mathtt{v}],\, grndT?(\mathrm{T})^{16} \vee orepT?(\mathrm{T}) \vee trepT?(\mathrm{T})}{\vdash \mathtt{v=new\ T();}}$$

$$\frac{\mathrm{T} \preceq_T [\mathtt{v}],\, \mathrm{T} \preceq_T [\mathtt{e}],}{\vdash \mathtt{v=(T)e;}}$$

$$\frac{orepT?([\mathrm{S@f}]) \Rightarrow (\mathtt{w} \cong \mathtt{this} \vee roT?([\mathtt{w}])),\quad [\mathtt{w}] * [\mathrm{S@f}] \preceq_T [\mathtt{v}]}{\vdash \mathtt{v=w.S@f;}}$$

$$\frac{\neg roT?([\mathtt{w}]),\, orepT?([\mathrm{S@f}]) \Rightarrow \mathtt{w} \cong \mathtt{this},\quad [\mathtt{e}] \preceq_T [\mathtt{w}] * [\mathrm{S@f}]}{\vdash \mathtt{w.S@f=e;}}$$

$$\frac{\begin{array}{l}\forall i \in \{1,\ldots,n\} : orepT?(par(\mathrm{S{:}m}, i)) \Rightarrow \mathtt{w} \cong \mathtt{this},\\ orepT?(ret(\mathrm{S{:}m})) \Rightarrow \mathtt{w} \cong \mathtt{this},\\ \forall i \in \{1,\ldots,n\} : [\mathtt{e}_i] \preceq_T [\mathtt{w}] * par(\mathrm{S{:}m}, i),\\ [\mathtt{w}] * ret(\mathrm{S{:}m}) \preceq_T [\mathtt{v}]\end{array}}{\vdash \mathtt{v=w.S{:}m(e_1,\ldots,e_n);}}$$

$$\frac{\begin{array}{l}\neg roT?(\mathrm{S}'),\\ \forall i \in \{1,\ldots,n\} : \neg orepT?(par(\mathrm{S@m}, i)),\\ \neg orepT?(ret(\mathrm{S@m})),\\ \forall i \in \{1,\ldots,n\} : [\mathtt{e}_i] \preceq_T \mathrm{S}' * par(\mathrm{S@m}, i),\\ \mathrm{S}' * ret(\mathrm{S@m}) \preceq_T [\mathtt{v}]\end{array}}{\vdash \mathtt{v=S'.S@m(e_1,\ldots,e_n);}}$$

$$\frac{\begin{array}{l}\forall i \in \{1,\ldots,n\} : orepT?(par(\mathrm{S@m}, i)) \Rightarrow \mathtt{w} \cong \mathtt{this},\\ orepT?(ret(\mathrm{S@m})) \Rightarrow \mathtt{w} \cong \mathtt{this},\\ \forall i \in \{1,\ldots,n\} : [\mathtt{e}_i] \preceq_T [\mathtt{w}] * par(\mathrm{S@m}, i),\\ [\mathtt{w}] * ret(\mathrm{S@m}) \preceq_T [\mathtt{v}]\end{array}}{\vdash \mathtt{v=w.S@m(e_1,\ldots,e_n);}}$$

Four aspects of the universe type rules above need explanation:

- The rule for casts/assignments is like in Java. Note that it allows readonly references to be cast to readwrite references (see Subsection 2.2.3). The condition $\mathrm{T} \preceq_T [\mathtt{e}]$ is not necessary for type safety but prevents runtime errors.
- orep types indicate that a reference points to an object owned by `this`. Therefore, fields of orep types can only be accessed on `this` and readonly references. Methods with orep types as parameter or result types can only be invoked on `this` (readonly methods that could be invoked on readonly references have readonly or primitive types as parameter and result types). For example, if variable `v` is of a ground type (i.e., `v` and `this` belong to the same universe) and field `f` is of an orep type, `v.f` yields a reference to an object that belongs to the object universe owned by `v`. That corresponds

[16] Discriminator functions such as *grndT?* are automatically defined for each data type (see App. A.1).

only to the universe programming model if (a) the reference is readonly or (b) `v` and `this` hold the same object. To enforce the latter condition statically, we require that only the `this`-variable and variables of readonly types can be used to access fields of orep types. Methods with orep types as result types can only be invoked on the `this`-variable.
- orep types are not allowed in static methods since they don't have a `this`-object.
- Since readonly types do not specify a universe, it is neither possible to create objects of readonly types nor to invoke static methods with readonly target types. Otherwise, the universe the new object belongs to resp. the current universe for the execution of the static method would be undefined.
- Neither writing field access nor invocation of readwrite methods is allowed on readonly references.

We define and prove type safety of Mojave based on the above rules in Subsection 3.2.1.

2.2.6 Discussion

In this subsection, we present the informal universe invariant and discuss the expressiveness, limitations, and possible applications of the universe programming model. Furthermore, we explain the relation of type systems and interface specifications.

The Universe Invariant. In the description of the universe programming model, we focussed on references between objects, that is, static aliasing. However, as pointed out in Subsection 1.4.4, dynamic aliases are as problematic as static aliases since they can also be used to modify representations and to break invariants. We can control dynamic aliasing by treating local variables and formal parameters like instance variables of the `this`-object. More precisely: In instance methods, local variables and formal parameters behave like instance variables of the `this`-object. That is, they can hold readwrite references to objects belonging to the current universe, the type universes that are children of the current universe, and the object universe owned by `this`. Since orep types are not allowed in static methods, only the former two cases are possible in static methods.

Controlling both static and dynamic aliases leads to the following invariant that holds in all execution states: If there is a reference from object X to object Y (where local variables are treated as described above) then at least one of the following cases apply:

1. X and Y belong to the same universe;
2. Y belongs to a universe owned by X;
3. the reference is readonly.

We do not formally prove this invariant. However, it is easy to see that the invariant is a direct consequence of well-typedness: In a well-typed execution state, each instance variable X.f holds a value of a subtype of f's declared type. If the type of f is a ground type, this value is either the `null`-value or a reference to an object Y that belongs to the same universe as X (case 1 of the invariant); if the type is a rep type, Y belongs either to the object universe owned by X or to a type universe owned by X (case 2); if the type is a readonly type, Y can belong to an arbitrary universe (case 3). Therefore, type safety of the universe type system guarantees that the invariant holds in all interesting execution states (see Subsection 3.2.1 for our notion of type safety). During verification, we can assume that execution states are well-typed and can thus exploit the universe invariant (see Subsection 5.4.5 for an example).

Expressiveness and Limitations. The universe programming model allows one to realize dynamic components with encapsulated representations. By strong alias control and readonly references, whole object structures can be protected from unwanted modifications. Universes provide encapsulation that is far beyond what can be directly achieved by Java's access modes for fields, methods, and type declarations. In particular, object universes provide encapsulation on the object level, which cannot be directly expressed by access modes in Java.

On the other hand, the universe programming model is flexible enough to express many common implementation patterns including binary methods (such as `equals`), iterators, several objects sharing one representation, mutual recursive types, etc.[17]

We have developed type universes to enable modular verification of frame properties and invariants, and object universes to show the power of our approach and to simplify verification. Although universes provide a lot of flexibility, they are still too restrictive for certain programming patterns: (1) As presented here, universes do not support global data that can be read and written by objects that belong to different universes. For instance a global output stream that can be used by all objects of the program cannot be implemented (if the print method of the stream is not readonly). Such patterns could be supported by an additional global universe that can be accessed by all objects. To simplify the formalization of the universe type system and the restrictions on dependencies, we do not follow this approach here. (2) The universe programming model does not allow objects to migrate from one universe to another. Such patterns are for instance used in initialization methods (e.g., the initialization method of a lexer could take an input stream as parameter [DLN98]) or in the C++ Standard Template Library, where diffe-

[17] Strictly speaking, the universe programming model does not restrict programs at all: Each Java program can be modeled with universes by only using the standard universe and readwrite references. However, the modularity requirements for abstractions and invariants presented in Paragraph 5.1.3.2 forbid such programs.

rent components exchange whole implementations (see e.g., member function `swap` of class `vector` [MS96]). Possible work-arounds are cloning of object structures (thereby losing object identities) or readonly references (thereby losing the ability to modify objects). A promising approach to overcome these shortcomings is the combination of universes with unique variables. A unique variables guarantees that the referenced object is not aliased at all and can therefore easily be moved to another universe (personal communication with John Boyland)

Applications. The benefits of the universe programming model for modular specification and verification are discussed in detail in Chapters 5 and 6. Besides this application, the representation encapsulation provided by universes is helpful in various other areas:

- *Optimization:* The universe programming model provides additional information about the object store which can be used to improve memory allocation strategies (see e.g., sandwich types [GTZ98]) and garbage collectors.
- *Concurrent programming:* The centralized access to representations can be used to simplify synchronization in multithreaded programs: Access to the representation of a dynamic component could be synchronized on its interface objects instead of locking each single representation object.
- *Distributed programming:* The universe structure gives information about which objects should be copied/moved to a different process upon remote method invocations. For instance, it is reasonable to copy or move the whole component when an interface object has to be transferred. Readonly references are good candidates for references that should be turned into remote references instead of copying the referenced object.
- *Operational interface specifications:* One of the most prominent problems of operational interface specification languages is that execution of specifications should not lead to observable side-effects on program execution (see Paragraph 1.6.1.2). On the other hand, in languages like JML [LBR99a] it is not possible to completely forbid side-effects in specifications (i.e., object creation and location update) since object structures (so-called models) are used to represent abstractions. These models have to be created and initialized. Different universes could be used for model objects and objects of the normal program execution, where model objects can only have readonly references to non-model objects. This way, interface specification can be checked statically not to cause observable side-effects.

Implementation of the Universe Type System. To implement the universe type system, the type checker of a Java compiler has to be modified to check the above context conditions. Furthermore, the runtime environment must store for each object the universe it belongs to. This information is needed for dynamic checks when readonly references are cast to readwrite references. However, in theory, if only verified programs were executed on the virtual machine, these dynamic checks could be omitted since the correctness of all casts would have been proved during verification. An implementation of the universe type system is considered future work.

Type Systems vs. Interface Specifications. A variety of program properties can be both (1) formalized as interface specification and proved by means of formal verification and (2) expressed by programming language techniques such as type systems and checked statically. For instance in Mojave, alias control is realized by the universe type system, whereas other frameworks use invariants to describe static aliasing. Other type systems are for example used to assure that certain variables can never hold the null-value [JLMPH99], a property that has to be included in an interface specification in our approach.

Although type systems and interface specifications seem to be quite different at first glance, there are a number of similarities. In fact, type annotations of ordinary OO-programs can be regarded as a special form of interface specification. For instance, the parameter and result types of a method could be specified as pre- and post-conditions, and the types of fields could be expressed by type invariants; the co- and contravariance rules for overriding methods correspond to the rule that preconditions can be weakened and postconditions can be strengthened in overriding methods. Analogously, the universe type annotations can be regarded as specification which leads to proof obligations that essentially require one to prove that the universe invariant holds in every execution state.

When a specification and verification technique is developed, it is an important task to decide what program properties should be specified as interface specifications and verified, and what properties should be expressed and checked by means of a type system. For decidable properties, the application of type systems simplifies verification since they enable static checking. However, in contrast to verification, type systems often have to statically approximate the dynamic conditions to make static checking possible. For instance the universe type system requires that fields of an orep type can only be accessed on the `this`-parameter (and readonly references) although it would be suffcient to require that the target object is the `this`-object, which would be more precise, but cannot be checked statically. Thus, specification and verification provide in general more flexibility and accuracy than type systems. Furthermore, using interface specifications to express program properties allows one to clearly separate the specification technique from the semantics of the programming language.

Finding the right balance between specification and verification techniques on the one hand and type systems on the other hand is a non-trivial task. For Mojave, we decided to use the type system for alias control since especially dynamic aliasing cannot adequately be expressed by state-of-the-art interface specification techniques (see Subsection 1.3.5). To achieve a maximum of expressiveness and accuracy, and to focus on the essential semantics of Mojave, we require all other program properties to be expressed by means of interface specifications. To adapt the specification and verification techniques presented in this book to other programming languages, one can either transfer the universe type system to these languages or develop appropriate specification and verification techniques to guarantee the universe invariant without using the type system.

2.3 Related Work

In this section, we compare the universe type system to other approaches to alias analysis and control. Related work on the design of module systems is described in Subsection 1.4.1.

Aliasing has been studied to support optimization and reasoning. An overview of work on aliasing in OO-systems can be found in [NVLA99]. In the following, we discuss work on alias analysis, alias control, and readonly references that is relevant for this book.

Alias Analysis. Alias analysis is used to determine whether at a particular program point, two references refer to the same object. Interesting alias analyses can be obtained for instance by Steengaard's points-to analysis [Ste96] or Wilhelm's, Sagiv's, and Reps' shape analysis [WSR00]. Alias analysis can be used for compiler optimizations and reasoning, but not to control and restrict aliasing statically. To get reliable alias information in open programs, we have to apply techniques for alias control to make sure that program extensions cannot introduce new sources of aliasing.

Alias Control. Universes have been designed to meet the following objectives: They should (1) have simple semantics, (2) be easy to apply, (3) be statically-checkable (4) guarantee an invariant that is strong enough for modular reasoning, and (5) be flexible enough for many useful programming patterns. In this paragraph, we compare the universe type system to other approaches to alias control w.r.t. these objectives.

Type Systems. Ownership types [CPN98] provide a very flexible means for alias control. They realize the ownership model with strong alias control by a parametric type system. Like object universes, ownership types support only one owner per representation. So-called context parameters are used to provide references from inside a representation to the outside. Context parameters are similar to parametric polymorphism. Instead of parameterizing over types, they parameterize over owners. Context parameters allow objects of one context to hold readwrite references to enclosing contexts (which corresponds to readwrite references from an object belonging to universe U to an object belonging to an ancestor of U). Universes do not allow such references to guarantee that a method execution can only modify objects belonging to the current universe and its descendants. This property is crucial for our verification technique (see Subsection 5.4.2). Ownership types are statically-checkable. However, context parameters make ownership types rather difficult to apply [Bok99]. Readonly types can replace context parameters in many situations and lead to programs that are easier to read and reason about. Furthermore, they allow multiple objects to access one representation which is necessary to implement iterators or binary methods. Such patterns as well as several interface objects per representation are not supported by ownership types. In contrast to readonly references, context parameters support role separation. As presented in [CPN98], ownership types do not support subtyping and inheritance.

[NVP98] proposes alias modes to control aliasing. Similar to ownership types, each object is equipped with a context. Alias modes specify constraints on references. For example, the mode `rep` enforces representation containment (like our orep types). The mode `arg` provides references that can be freely passed around, but must not be used to manipulate the referenced object. Thus, they are similar to readonly references. The so-called roles for `arg` references are similar to context parameters. Like ownership types, alias modes have been presented for a language without subtyping and inheritance.

Balloon types [Alm97] aim at full representation encapsulation, that is, all objects reachable from an object are contained in its balloon (as if every field was declared as an orep type). This is too restrictive for many programs (e.g., singly linked lists). Balloon types require a rather complex checking algorithm based on abstract interpretation and cannot be checked modularly.

Like balloon types, Islands [Hog91] also provide only full encapsulation and suffer therefore from the same lack of expressiveness. Islands are based on a destructive read operation (see below). They permit dynamic aliases but restrict them to be readonly. Islands have not been formally validated.

Confined types [BV99] guarantee that objects of a confined type cannot be referenced in or accessed by code declared outside the confining package. Confined types have been designed for the development of secure systems. They do not support representation encapsulation on the object level, which makes some aspects of verification difficult. In [MPH00b, MPH99b, MPH00c], we show that access restrictions for trep types can be used to provide representation encapsulation on the type and package level. Such restrictions make trep types similar to confined types. However, we dropped these access restrictions in this book to use only the amount of alias control that is essential for verification. Therefore, the type universes here are more general than in [MPH00b] but provide less encapsulation.

We developed the universe type system systematically from the requirements of modular verification and formalized it similarly to ownership types [CPN98]. Since the universe type system provides one type universe for each object, it is closely related to value-dependent types [XP99]: Ground and rep types can be seen as types that depend on a value, namely an owner object (or a set of owner objects in case of type universes). Readonly types correspond to existentially quantified dependent types (there exists an owner for the referenced object). For future work, we plan to formalize the universe type system as a restriction of a type system with value-dependent types.

Uniqueness. Other approaches to alias control guarantee *uniqueness* of variables. The reference held by a unique variable is the only reference to the referenced object [Hog91, Min96, Wad90]. Unique variables are usually realized by a destructive read operation, which we consider rather unintuitive since it assigns a new value to the variable that is read. Uniqueness can also be achieved via reference counts and dynamic checks. Virginity [LS99] is similar to reference counts that can only be incremented. The application of the Extended Static Checker [DLNS98] avoids runtime checks to guarantee uniqueness. [DLN98] explains a discipline of alias control based on virginity. Instead of explicit declaration, the permissable aliases are determined purely based on the declaration of dependencies (see the absence of leaking requirement in Paragraph 5.5.1.3). In their pure form, unique variables are rather inflexible. In contrast to universes, alias control can only be achieved by completely forbidding sharing of objects referenced by a unique variable. However, combinations of uniqueness and other techniques such as universes are a promising approach for more flexible alias control.

Readonly Types and Methods. [KT99] realizes readonly types in Java by implicitly generating an interface for every type declaration. This interface contains only the signatures of readonly methods. To achieve transitive protection, readonly types are used as result types for these methods. This is a common technique, often proposed as a design pattern for write-protecting objects [Dav99, KT99]. Like in our approach, readonly types are supertypes of the user-defined types. Readonly types as described in [KT99] have three major drawbacks: (1) Since they are not directly supported by the type checker or runtime checks, inspection, reflection, or casts can be used to break the write-protection. (2) Java interfaces provide only public methods. Thus, they cannot be used to provide readonly access to the protected interface. (3) Readonly methods do not modify the state of `this`, but are not guaranteed to be side-effect-free. Thus, they are not *readonly* is our sense. This is also true for `const` member functions in C++: They only forbid the *direct* manipulation of the state of the *implicit* parameter. However, explicit parameters and global variables can be modified and thus, via aliasing, also the object referenced by `this` [Str91].

3. The Semantics of Mojave

This chapter presents a Hoare-style programming logic for Mojave. Based on this axiomatic semantics, we prove interesting language properties such as type safety. Moreover, we present a definition of modular correctness and discuss modular soundness. The chapter concludes with a discussion of related work.

3.1 Programming Logic

A programming logic provides the formal foundation for verification of program and language properties (such as type safety). It formalizes parts of the static and the dynamic semantics of a programming language. In this section, we present a programming logic for Mojave.

To be able to handle object structures with sharing and destructive updates, we formalize Mojave's data and state model. In particular, we specify object stores that enable us to express abstraction, which is a prerequisite for the specification and verification of abstract methods and interface types.

Our programming logic refines Hoare logics for procedural languages. To handle dynamic binding, the programming logic allows one to prove properties of virtual methods that capture the common properties of the corresponding methods in subtypes. The distinction between the virtual behavior of a method and the behavior of the associated implementations allows one to transfer verification techniques from procedural to OO-programming.

3.1.1 Formal Data and State Model

The formal data and state model describes the types, values, objects, and object states of a programming language. It is used

- as a formal foundation for the axiomatic semantics of the programming language, in particular for the field-access- and new-statements;
- to make properties of programs such as type information available for specifications and proofs;
- to specify abstraction functions of objects or object structures;
- to handle side-effects on the object store and sharing of object structures.

Peter Müller: Modular Specification ..., LNCS 2262, pp. 77–122, 2002.

The formal data and state model of Mojave is based on the model presented in [PH97b] which has been extended for Java-like languages in [PHM98]. It consists of a program-independent part that formalizes, for example, types and values, and a program-dependent part that contains information about the types, fields, etc. declared in a program.

In the following, we extend the data and state model of [PHM98] to support the universe type system. Furthermore, we decompose the specifications generated for a program to support modularity, especially information hiding. Thereby, we focus on those properties of Mojave's data and state model that are essential for the rest of this book. For a detailed discussion of formal data and state models, in particular of their use to specify sharing properties and relations on object stores, see [PH97b].

3.1.1.1 Modular Structure. To be able to use properties of programs such as type and field names or subtyping information in specifications, they have to be made available in universal specifications. Therefore, we generate program-dependent theories that contain formal descriptions of the interfaces of a program. However, due to information hiding, clients of a class or module must not be provided with all interfaces of that class or module. Thus, we generate different theories for different views to a class, interface type, or module. These theories are used to syntax check interface specifications and as part of the formal framework in which a class is verified (see Chapter 4).

Theories for Single Classes and Interface Types. A class has five different views. Conceptually, we provide one theory in the universal specification for each of these views (there is only one theory for interface types). These theories contain formalizations of the different interfaces of a class (see Paragraph 2.1.2.3) and of private information. For instance, the theory for the public view (the so-called *public theory*) contains the class name, subtype information, and the names and types of public fields, etc. (see below for details). The private theory contains information about private program elements such as the names and types of private fields.

Some views to a class include other views (for instance, every client that has protected view can also access the public interface). In the program-dependent theories, this is reflected by the import relation: If a view V includes view W, the theory for V imports the theory for W (see Figure 3.1, where theories are drawn as boxes and arrows depict the import relation).

Theories for Modules. Having public or default access view to one type declaration of a module includes public resp. default access view to all other type declarations of that module. To avoid cyclic imports of theories (which are forbidden in many languages for universal specifications), we replace the public and default access theories for all type declarations of one module by a single public and a single default access theory for the whole module.

Since access to the protected or the private protected interface of a class includes access to the protected resp. private protected interfaces of all su-

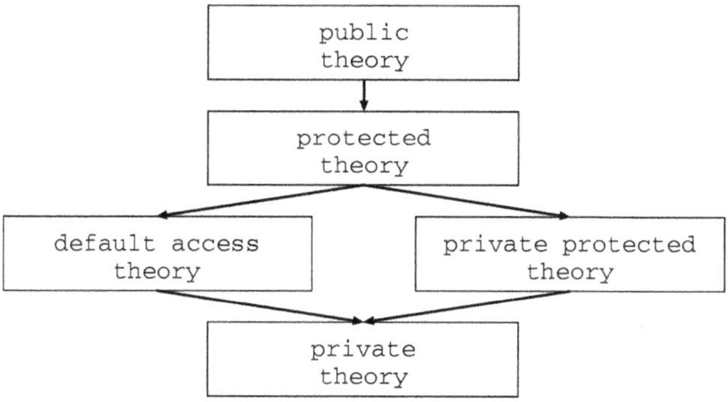

Fig. 3.1. Conceptual Theory Structure for One Class

perclasses, there is an import relation between the corresponding theories. The import relation is acyclic because the subtype relation is a partial order.

When a module N imports module M, the public interfaces of the class and interface types in M become accessible in N. Consequently, the public theory for M is imported by the public theory of N. Since the import of modules is acyclic, import of theories stays acyclic, too.

Figure 3.2 illustrates the theory structure for the following two modules. Each theory corresponds to one view to a module or class. Note that import of modules does not affect the theory structure of the imported modules. That is, the theories stay stable when a module is reused.

```
module M;
  public Interface Mi              { ... }
  public class M1 implements Mi    { ... }
  public class Mn extends M1       { ... }

module N imports M;
  public class N1 extends M1       { ... }
  public class Nn                  { ... }
  public interface Ni extends Mi { ... }
```

Properties of Closed and Open Programs. The universal specification of a closed program contains the program-dependent theories described above, the program-independent parts of the data and state model, the prelude theory, and user-defined theories. This specification allows one to prove properties of closed programs. To be suitable for modular verification, universal specifications for open programs must guarantee that properties proved for the core of an open program $\mathcal{P}$ stay valid in all extensions of $\mathcal{P}$. This is achieved as follows:

- Due to the theory structure described in the last paragraph, adding new modules to the core of an open program results in additional theories for

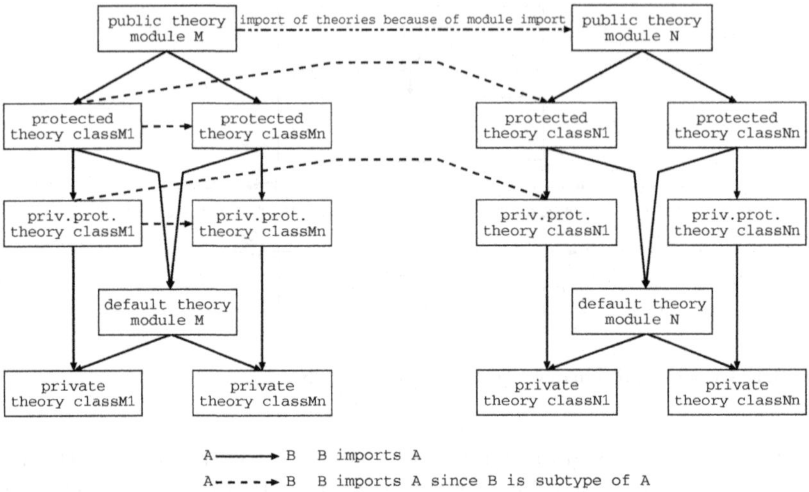

Fig. 3.2. Theory Structure for Two Modules

the universal specification of the extended core, but leaves existing theories unchanged. Therefore, extending an open program leads to a refinement of the universal specification. Consequently, all properties proved for the core of an open program $\mathcal{P}$ hold in all closed programs in $\mathcal{P}$. We say *a property holds in an open program* $\mathcal{P}$ if it holds in all closed programs in $\mathcal{P}$. Such properties can be used for the verification of $\mathcal{P}$. Unless otherwise stated, all lemmas presented in this book hold in all closed and, thus, in all open programs.

- To avoid contradictory specifications, we regard each module as part of an open program. The generated theories specify the interface information for that module and leave the types, fields, etc. not occurring in the scope of the module un(der)specified. In particular, inclusive axioms that allow one to reason about all types of a program (see Axiom **import6** in Paragraph 3.1.1.4) are only generated for main modules of closed programs.

3.1.1.2 Type Ids and Subtyping on Type Ids. As explained in Subsection 2.2.2, the universe type system distinguishes between type declarations, types, and dynamic types. We introduce one sort for each of these entities in the data and state model (see below for types and dynamic types). To formalize the type declarations of an open program, we assume infinite sorts *ClassId* and *InterfaceId* of type identifiers for classes and interfaces, resp. For each class or interface declared in a module, a constant of sort *ClassId* resp. *InterfaceId* is added to the public theory for that module. The fact that different constants denote different type ids is formalized by inequality axioms: For each pair of *TypeId* constants S, T in the scope of a module M, M's public theory contains an axiom of the form S $\neq$ T.

Subtype Relation on Type Ids. In Mojave, there are three kinds of subtype relations: (1) The subtype relation on type declarations (resp. their type ids) as defined by the Mojave program; (2) The subtype relation on types that is used to statically type check a program; (3) The subtype relation on dynamic types that is used for runtime type information (e.g., for cast-statements). The latter two relations are based on the former one, which is described in the following. Subtyping on type ids in Mojave follows the rules of Java. It is formalized as a relation $\_ \preceq_M \_$ on *TypeIds* (M stands for Mojave):

$$\_ \preceq_M \_ : \mathit{TypeId} \times \mathit{TypeId} \rightarrow \mathit{Bool}$$

If a module declares a class or interface S to be a subtype of T (by an extends- or implements-clause), an axiom of the form S $\preceq_M$ T is added to the public theory for that module. For the *TypeIds* declared in the core of an open program $\mathcal{P}$, $\preceq_M$ is the smallest reflexive, transitive closure of these axioms. That is, if S and T are declared in the scope of a module N, and S is not a subtype of T, an axiom of the form S $\not\preceq_M$ T is added to N's public theory. Thus, the subtype relation on *TypeIds* is completely specified for all *TypeIds* declared in a given core of an open program, and unspecified for all other *TypeIds*. Since Mojave does not allow one to introduce a subtype relation between two imported classes or interfaces (in contrast to Sather [SOM94]), program extensions lead to a refinement of the axiomatization of the subtype relation. The following properties of $\preceq_M$ are guaranteed by the context conditions of Mojave:

subM1 : $\preceq_M$ is a partial order

subM2 : $\mathit{ctid}(C) \preceq_M \mathit{ctid}(D) \wedge \mathit{ctid}(C) \preceq_M \mathit{ctid}(E) \Rightarrow$
$\mathit{ctid}(D) \preceq_M \mathit{ctid}(E) \vee \mathit{ctid}(E) \preceq_M \mathit{ctid}(D)$

$\preceq_M$ is antisymmetric since there are no cycles in the subtype hierarchy. Thus, $\preceq_M$ is a partial order (**subM1**). **subM2** formalizes single subtyping on classes. A more complete axiomatization of Java's subtype relation can be found in [Dip98].

We say S *is a subtype of* T if S $\preceq_M$ T holds. S *is a proper subtype of* T if S is a subtype of T and different from T.

3.1.1.3 Types and Subtyping on Types. Types have been formalized in Figure 2.1 and explained in Subsection 2.2.5. The subtype relation $\preceq_T$ on types

$$\_ \preceq_T \_ : \mathit{Type} \times \mathit{Type} \rightarrow \mathit{Bool}$$

is the smallest reflexive, transitive relation satisfying the following axioms. Note that this axiomatization is program-independent.

$$\begin{array}{rlrl}
\mathit{nullT} & \preceq_T \mathit{grndT}(T) & S \preceq_M T \Leftrightarrow & \mathit{grndT}(S) \preceq_T \mathit{grndT}(T) \\
\mathit{nullT} & \preceq_T \mathit{orepT}(T) & S \preceq_M T \Leftrightarrow & \mathit{orepT}(S) \preceq_T \mathit{orepT}(T) \\
\mathit{nullT} & \preceq_T \mathit{trepT}(T,R) & S \preceq_M T \Leftrightarrow & \mathit{trepT}(S,R) \preceq_T \mathit{trepT}(T,R) \\
\mathit{grndT}(T) & \preceq_T \mathit{roT}(T) & S \preceq_M T \Leftrightarrow & \mathit{roT}(S) \preceq_T \mathit{roT}(T) \\
\mathit{orepT}(T) & \preceq_T \mathit{roT}(T) & & \\
\mathit{trepT}(T,R) & \preceq_T \mathit{roT}(T) & &
\end{array}$$

Since subtyping on types resembles subtyping on type ids, $\preceq_T$ is also a partial order:

Lemma 3.1.1. *$\preceq_T$ is a partial order.*

See Appendix D.1 for the proof.

3.1.1.4 Modules. For each module, we add a constant of the infinite sort *ModId* and the corresponding inequality axioms (see above) to the public theory of that module. The function *module* yields the module that contains the type declaration for a given *TypeId*:

$$module : TypeId \to ModId$$

Since modules cannot be extended, we can provide a rather strong axiomatization of *module*. For each module M, we add an axiom of the form

$$module(T) = \mathrm{M} \Leftrightarrow T \in \{\mathrm{T}_1, \ldots, \mathrm{T}_n\}$$

to M's public theory, where $\mathrm{T}_1, \ldots, \mathrm{T}_n$ are the type identifiers of the classes and interfaces declared in M.

The Import Relation. The import relation is formalized by a function *imports*. *imports*(M, N) yields whether module M imports module N.

$$imports : ModId \times ModId \to Bool$$

For each module M directly importing modules $\mathrm{N}_1, \ldots, \mathrm{N}_n$, we add an axiom of the form

$$imports(\mathrm{M}, N) \Leftrightarrow \mathrm{M} = N \vee imports(\mathrm{N}_1, N) \vee \ldots \vee imports(\mathrm{N}_n, N)$$

The following properties are guaranteed by context conditions:

import1 : *imports* is a partial order

import2 : $\mathrm{S} \preceq_M \mathrm{T} \Rightarrow imports(module(\mathrm{S}), module(\mathrm{T}))$

import3 : T@m contains an invocation of S:n or S@n $\Rightarrow$ $imports(module(\mathrm{T}), module(\mathrm{S}))$

import4 : T@m contains a local variable (or a formal parameter) of type $grndT(\mathrm{S})$, $orepT(\mathrm{S})$, $trepT(\mathrm{S},\mathrm{R})$, or $roT(\mathrm{S})$ $\Rightarrow$ $imports(module(\mathrm{T}), module(\mathrm{S}))$

import5 : T@m contains a local variable (or a formal parameter) of type $trepT(\mathrm{S}, \mathrm{R}) \Rightarrow imports(module(\mathrm{T}), module(\mathrm{R}))$

The import relation is reflexive and transitive. Since it is acyclic, *imports* is a partial order (**import1**). Whenever a type name is used in a module M (as supertype, target of a method invocation, in a declaration of a local variable or method signature, etc.), M has to import the module that contains the corresponding type declaration (**import2**–**import5**). For closed programs with main module M, we add the following *inclusive axiom* to M's public theory. Together with the axioms generated for *module* and *imports*, this axiom allows one to reason about all types of a closed program.

import6 : $imports(\mathrm{M}, module(T))$

Accessibility. We formalize accessibility as defined in Subsection 2.1.2 by a function *accessible*. $accessible(M, T, S)$ yields whether a class member with access mode M declared in type declaration T is accessible in S:

$$
\begin{array}{lll}
\multicolumn{3}{l}{accessible : AccessMode \times TypeId \times TypeId \rightarrow Bool} \\
accessible(public, T, S) & \Leftrightarrow_{def} & imports(module(S), module(T)) \\
accessible(protected, T, S) & \Leftrightarrow_{def} & accessible(default, T, S) \vee \\
 & & accessible(privprot, T, S) \\
accessible(privprot, T, S) & \Leftrightarrow_{def} & S \preceq_M T \\
accessible(default, T, S) & \Leftrightarrow_{def} & module(T) = module(S) \\
accessible(private, T, S) & \Leftrightarrow_{def} & T = S
\end{array}
$$

Lemma 3.1.2. *A class member declared in* T *can only be accessible in* S *if* T *is in the scope of* S.

$$accessible(M, T, S) \Rightarrow imports(module(S), module(T))$$

The proof runs by case distinction on M and is straightforward.

3.1.1.5 Methods. For every method implementation, we add a constant of sort *ImplId* to the appropriate theory. *static* yields whether an implementation is a static method. It is defined by an axiom for each method implementation in a program.

$$static : ImplId \rightarrow Bool$$

3.1.1.6 Universes. The universe type system provides the standard universe, one universe for every object, and one universe for every dynamic type in a program execution. A type universe is characterized by a type id and the parent universe. An object universe is defined by the object id, class id, and universe of its owner object :

data type
Universe = *stdU*
  | *typeU*(*TypeId*, *Universe*)
  | *objU*(*ObjId*, *ClassId*, *Universe*)
end data type

The universes of a program execution form a hierarchy with the standard universe at the top. This hierarchy is formalized by the following functions. $U \lhd V$ yields whether U is a descendant of V. $\unlhd$ is the reflexive closure of $\lhd$.

$$
\begin{array}{lll}
\multicolumn{3}{l}{\_ \unlhd_{\_} \_ : Universe \times Universe \times Nat \rightarrow Bool} \\
U \unlhd_0 V & \Leftrightarrow_{def} & U = V \\
U \unlhd_{N+1} V & \Leftrightarrow_{def} & \exists W, T, O, C : \\
 & & (U = typeU(T, W) \vee U = objU(O, C, W)) \wedge W \unlhd_N V
\end{array}
$$

$$
\begin{array}{lll}
\multicolumn{3}{l}{\_ \unlhd \_ : Universe \times Universe \rightarrow Bool} \\
U \unlhd V & \Leftrightarrow_{def} & \exists N : U \unlhd_N V
\end{array}
$$

$$
\begin{array}{lll}
\multicolumn{3}{l}{\_ \lhd \_ : Universe \times Universe \rightarrow Bool} \\
U \lhd V & \Leftrightarrow_{def} & \exists N : N > 0 \wedge U \unlhd_N V
\end{array}
$$

Lemma 3.1.3. $\trianglelefteq$ *is a partial order.*

The proof is contained in Appendix D.1.

To be able to refer to the current universe in specifications and proofs, we introduce a global variable $\mathcal{U}$ that holds the current universe in every execution state. During execution of an instance method, $\mathcal{U}$ is identical to the universe to which the `this`-object belongs. In static methods, $\mathcal{U}$ is determined by the universe of the method incarnation that precedes the invocation, and the target of the invocation (see the static-invocation-rule in Subsection 3.1.2). Program execution begins in the standard universe.

3.1.1.7 Values. Values in Mojave are integers, booleans, the null-value, or references to objects. An object is characterized by its class, the universe it belongs to, and an identifier of the infinite sort *ObjId*. The class and the universe together determine the dynamic type of the object (see below). The identifier is used to distinguish different objects of the same dynamic type.

$$\begin{array}{l}\textbf{data type}\\ \quad \mathit{Value} = \mathit{bool}(\,\mathit{aB} : \mathit{Bool}\,)\\ \qquad\qquad \mid \mathit{int}(\,\mathit{aI} : \mathit{Int}\,)\\ \qquad\qquad \mid \mathit{null}\\ \qquad\qquad \mid \mathit{ref}(\mathit{cidV} : \mathit{ClassId}, \mathit{oid} : \mathit{ObjId}, \mathit{univV} : \mathit{Universe}\,)\\ \textbf{end data type}\end{array}$$

3.1.1.8 Dynamic Types and Subtyping on Dynamic Types. As explained in Subsection 2.2.2, a universe contains one *dynamic type* for every type declaration in a program. Consequently, we formalize dynamic readwrite reference types as tuples of type identifiers and universes. Besides dynamic readwrite reference types, we have dynamic types for readonly references and the primitive dynamic types:

$$\begin{array}{l}\textbf{data type}\\ \quad \mathit{DynType} = \mathit{booleanDT}\\ \qquad\qquad\quad \mid \mathit{intDT}\\ \qquad\qquad\quad \mid \mathit{nullDT}\\ \qquad\qquad\quad \mid \mathit{refDT}(\mathit{tidD} : \mathit{TypeId}, \mathit{univ} : \mathit{Universe}\,)\\ \qquad\qquad\quad \mid \mathit{roDT}(\mathit{tidD} : \mathit{TypeId})\\ \textbf{end data type}\end{array}$$

The dynamic types of variables on the stack, the dynamic types of instance variables, and the dynamic parameter and result types of method incarnations depend on (1) the corresponding types (of the variables, fields, methods), (2) the `this`-object (for local variables and formal parameters) resp. the target object (for instance variables and method incarnations), and (3) the current universe. The appropriate mapping of types, values, and the current universe to dynamic types is defined by *dyn*:

$$
\begin{array}{ll}
\multicolumn{2}{l}{dyn : Type \times Value \times Universe \rightarrow DynType} \\
dyn(grndT(T), X, U) & =_{def} refDT(T, U) \\
dyn(trepT(T_1, T_2), X, U) & =_{def} refDT(T_1, typeU(T_2, U)) \\
dyn(orepT(T), X, U) & =_{def} refDT(T, objU(oid(X), cidV(X), U)) \\
dyn(roT(T), X, U) & =_{def} roDT(T) \\
dyn(booleanT, X, U) & =_{def} booleanDT \\
dyn(intT, X, U) & =_{def} intDT \\
dyn(nullT, X, U) & =_{def} nullDT
\end{array}
$$

We call $dyn(\mathrm{T}, X, U)$ the *dynamization of* T *w.r.t.* X *and* U. The function *typeof* yields the dynamic type of a *Value*:

$$
\begin{array}{ll}
\multicolumn{2}{l}{typeof : Value \rightarrow DynType} \\
typeof(bool(B)) & =_{def} booleanDT \\
typeof(int(I)) & =_{def} intDT \\
typeof(null) & =_{def} nullDT \\
typeof(ref(C, OID, U)) & =_{def} refDT(ctid(C), U)
\end{array}
$$

init yields a designated default value for every dynamic type that is used to initialize instance variables and local variables:

$$
\begin{array}{ll}
\multicolumn{2}{l}{init : DynType \rightarrow Value} \\
init(booleanDT) & =_{def} bool(false) \\
init(intDT) & =_{def} int(0) \\
init(nullDT) & =_{def} null \\
init(refDT(T, U)) & =_{def} null \\
init(roDT(T)) & =_{def} null
\end{array}
$$

Lemma 3.1.4 relates *univ* to *univV*. It is a direct consequence of the definitions of *univV*, *univ*, and *typeof*.

Lemma 3.1.4. *The universe to which an object X belongs contains the dynamic type of X:*

$$ref?(X) \Rightarrow univV(X) = univ(typeof(X))$$

The Subtype Relation on Dynamic Types. The subtype relation on dynamic types

$$\_ \preceq \_ : DynType \times DynType \rightarrow Bool$$

follows the subtype relation on *TypeIds*. It is the smallest reflexive, transitive relation satisfying the following axioms:

$$
\begin{array}{llcll}
nullDT & \preceq refDT(T, U) & S \preceq_M T & \Leftrightarrow & refDT(S, U) \preceq refDT(T, U) \\
refDT(T, U) & \preceq roDT(T) & S \preceq_M T & \Leftrightarrow & roDT(S) \quad \preceq roDT(T)
\end{array}
$$

The irreflexive subtype relation is defined as follows:

$$
\begin{array}{l}
\_ \prec \_ : DynType \times DynType \rightarrow Bool \\
S \prec T \Leftrightarrow_{def} S \preceq T \wedge S \neq T
\end{array}
$$

The following lemmas formalize properties of $\preceq$. Lemma 3.1.6 follows directly from the definition of $\preceq$. The proofs of Lemmas 3.1.5 and 3.1.7 can be found in Appendix D.1.

Lemma 3.1.5. $\preceq$ *is a partial order.*

Lemma 3.1.6. *If two dynamic readwrite types are subtypes, then they are in the same universe:*

$$refDT?(S) \wedge refDT?(T) \wedge S \preceq T \Rightarrow univ(S) = univ(T)$$

Lemma 3.1.7. *If type S is a subtype of T, then the corresponding dynamic types w.r.t. value X and universe U are subtypes as well (in case that S or T is an orep type, X has to be an object reference to guarantee that dyn is welldefined):*

$$((orepT?(S) \vee orepT?(T)) \Rightarrow ref?(X)) \wedge S \preceq_T T \Rightarrow dyn(S, X, U) \preceq dyn(T, X, U)$$

3.1.1.9 Fields and Locations. As explained in Subsection 1.5.1, we use abstract fields to specify the abstract values of objects and object structures. For simplicity, we explain the formalization of abstract fields together with concrete fields (i.e., ordinary fields of the programming language). A detailed description of abstract fields can be found in Subsection 4.2.1.

Field Identifiers. We assume two infinite sorts *SimpleCFieldId* and *SimpleAFieldId* of simple field identifiers for concrete and abstract fields. Simple field identifiers have the form T@f for a field f declared in class or interface[1] T. For every field declared in a class or interface, a constant of sort *SimpleCFieldId* or *SimpleAFieldId* is added to the corresponding theory of the class (in case of protected, private protected, or private fields) or module (in case of public or default access fields).

To distinguish fields with the same simple field identifier in different classes, we use two infinite sorts *CFieldId* and *AFieldId* of the form C:T@f where T@f is a simple field identifier and C is a class that is a subtype of T (or T itself). C:T@f denotes the field f of class C that is declared in type declaration T. For each declared or inherited field T@f of class C, we introduce a constant of sort *CFieldId* or *AFieldId* in the appropriate theory of C or C's module. To preserve information hiding, such a constant is only generated if T@f is accessible in C. We use the sort *FieldId* as variant sort for *CFieldId* and *AFieldId*:

data type
FieldId = *cfield*(*cfid* : *CFieldId*)
| *afield*(*afid* : *AFieldId*)
end data type

The mapping of simple field ids to full field ids and vice versa is done by the following functions:

$$\begin{array}{lll} mkCFieldId: & SimpleCFieldId \times ClassId & \rightarrow CFieldId \\ mkAFieldId: & SimpleAFieldId \times ClassId & \rightarrow AFieldId \\ scfid: & CFieldId & \rightarrow SimpleCFieldId \\ safid: & AFieldId & \rightarrow SimpleAFieldId \end{array}$$

These functions are defined by enumeration. That is, for every field identifier C:T@f, axioms of the form

[1] Abstract fields can be declared in interface types (see Subsection 4.2.1).

$$\begin{array}{ll} \textit{mkCFieldId}(\mathrm{T@f, C}) = \mathrm{C{:}T@f} \text{ resp. } \textit{mkAFieldId}(\mathrm{T@f, C}) = \mathrm{C{:}T@f} \text{ and} \\ \textit{scfid}(\mathrm{C{:}T@f}) = \mathrm{T@f} \qquad\qquad \text{resp. } \textit{safid}(\mathrm{C{:}T@f}) = \mathrm{T@f} \end{array}$$

are added to the theory that contains the constant declaration for C:T@f.

We have to axiomatize the fact that two different constants for field ids or simple field ids denote different fields. However, due to information hiding, we can in general not generate appropriate inequality axioms as we do for module ids or type names: Assume that T@f and S@g are two private fields declared in different classes. Thus, there is no theory that could contain an axiom T@f $\neq$ S@g without breaking information hiding. Therefore, we generate inequality axioms only for those pairs of field ids or simple field ids for which there is at least one class that has access to both fields. That guarantees that there is always a suitable theory for the axiom. The inequality axioms for all other pairs are useless anyway since there is no client that has access to both fields. In addition, we can use the following axioms to show that two field ids are unequal, in particular for those fields for which we don't have constants of sort *CFieldId* or *AFieldId* (see above)[2]:

$$\begin{array}{l} \textbf{field1}: \textit{mkCFieldId}(f_C, D) = \textit{mkCFieldId}(g_C, C) \Leftrightarrow f_C = g_C \wedge D = C \\ \textbf{field2}: \textit{mkAFieldId}(f_A, D) = \textit{mkAFieldId}(g_A, C) \Leftrightarrow f_A = g_A \wedge D = C \end{array}$$

Access modes. The access mode of a field is returned by the following function:

$$\textit{accessMode} : \textit{FieldId} \rightarrow \textit{AccessMode}$$

accessMode(C:T@f) is defined by an appropriate axiom in the theory that contains the declaration of C:T@f.

Fields and Types. The relation between fields and types is defined by the following functions: *dtype* yields the id of the type declaration a field is declared in (the so-called *declaration type*). *otype* yields the id of the class a field belongs to (*object type*). *rtype* is the *range type* of a concrete field.

$$\begin{array}{lll} \textit{dtype} : \textit{FieldId} & \rightarrow & \textit{TypeId} \\ \textit{otype} : \textit{FieldId} & \rightarrow & \textit{ClassId} \\ \textit{rtype} : \textit{CFieldId} & \rightarrow & \textit{Type} \end{array}$$

For each field identifier C:T@f we generate axioms of the forms

$$\begin{array}{l} \textit{dtype}(\textit{cfield}(\mathrm{C{:}T@f})) = \mathrm{T} \text{ or } \textit{dtype}(\textit{afield}(\mathrm{C{:}T@f})) = \mathrm{T} \\ \textit{otype}(\textit{cfield}(\mathrm{C{:}T@f})) = \mathrm{C} \text{ or } \textit{otype}(\textit{afield}(\mathrm{C{:}T@f})) = \mathrm{C} \\ \textit{rtype}(\mathrm{C{:}T@f}) = [\mathrm{T@f}] \qquad \text{or no axiom} \end{array}$$

where [T@f] denotes the type of T@f as declared in the program. The axioms are added to the theory that contains the constant declaration for C:T@f. Note that the object type is always a subtype of the declaration type:

$$\textbf{field3}: \textit{ctid}(\textit{otype}(F)) \preceq_M \textit{dtype}(F)$$

[2] Please refer to App. A.2, p. 225 for the naming conventions used in the following axioms.

Field identifiers are very similar to tuples of a simple field identifier and a *ClassId*, with *scfid*/*safid* and *otype* as selectors. This behavior is expressed by the following axioms:

$$\begin{array}{l}\textbf{field4}: \mathit{scfid}(\mathit{mkCFieldId}(f,C)) = f\\ \textbf{field5}: \mathit{safid}(\mathit{mkAFieldId}(f,C)) = f\\ \textbf{field6}: \mathit{otype}(\mathit{cfield}(\mathit{mkCFieldId}(f,C))) = C\\ \textbf{field7}: \mathit{otype}(\mathit{afield}(\mathit{mkAFieldId}(f,C))) = C\\ \textbf{field8}: F_C = \mathit{mkCFieldId}(\mathit{scfid}(F_C), \mathit{otype}(\mathit{cfield}(F_C)))\\ \textbf{field9}: F_A = \mathit{mkAFieldId}(\mathit{safid}(F_A), \mathit{otype}(\mathit{afield}(F_A)))\end{array}$$

To reason about all (concrete and abstract) fields of a type declaration, we have to axiomatize the fact that classes and interfaces are closed in the sense that clients cannot add field declarations. However, due to information hiding, the axiomatization is not as simple as for modules. For each class T, we generate five axioms as follows (analogously for interfaces): Let $\mathrm{f}_1, \ldots, \mathrm{f}_{m-1}$ be the private, $\mathrm{f}_m, \ldots, \mathrm{f}_{n-1}$ the default access, $\mathrm{f}_n, \ldots, \mathrm{f}_{p-1}$ the private protected, $\mathrm{f}_p, \ldots, \mathrm{f}_{q-1}$ the protected, and $\mathrm{f}_q, \ldots, \mathrm{f}_r$ the simple field ids of the public fields declared in T. Then we add axioms of the following forms to the theories corresponding to the access modes of the mentioned field names (e.g., axiom (4) belongs to T's protected theory since only protected and public fields are mentioned). We use $\hat{\mathrm{f}}_i$ to denote $\mathit{cfield}(\mathrm{f}_i)$ resp. $\mathit{afield}(\mathrm{f}_i)$ in the axioms.

$$\begin{array}{lll}(1) & \mathit{dtype}(F) = \mathrm{T} \Rightarrow & F = \hat{\mathrm{f}}_1 \vee \ldots \vee F = \hat{\mathrm{f}}_r\\ (2) & \mathit{dtype}(F) = \mathrm{T} \Rightarrow & \mathit{accessMode}(F) = \mathit{private} \vee \mathit{accessMode}(F) = \mathit{privprot} \vee\\ & & F = \hat{\mathrm{f}}_m \vee \ldots \vee F = \hat{\mathrm{f}}_{n-1} \vee F = \hat{\mathrm{f}}_p \vee \ldots \vee F = \hat{\mathrm{f}}_r\\ (3) & \mathit{dtype}(F) = \mathrm{T} \Rightarrow & \mathit{accessMode}(F) = \mathit{private} \vee \mathit{accessMode}(F) = \mathit{default} \vee\\ & & F = \hat{\mathrm{f}}_n \vee \ldots \vee F = \hat{\mathrm{f}}_r\\ (4) & \mathit{dtype}(F) = \mathrm{T} \Rightarrow & \mathit{accessMode}(F) = \mathit{private} \vee \mathit{accessMode}(F) = \mathit{privprot} \vee\\ & & \mathit{accessMode}(F) = \mathit{default} \vee F = \hat{\mathrm{f}}_p \vee \ldots \vee F = \hat{\mathrm{f}}_r\\ (5) & \mathit{dtype}(F) = \mathrm{T} \Rightarrow & \mathit{accessMode}(F) \neq \mathit{public} \vee F = \hat{\mathrm{f}}_q \vee \ldots \vee F = \hat{\mathrm{f}}_r\end{array}$$

Locations. Object states are modeled via so-called *locations*. For each field of its class, an object has a location. Locations can be considered as anonymous variables, that is, variables that can only be referenced through the object they belong to. Similar to the formalization of fields, there are sorts for concrete and abstract locations, and the corresponding variant sort:

data type
CLocation = *cloc*(*CFieldId*, *ObjId*, *Universe*)
ALocation = *aloc*(*AFieldId*, *ObjId*, *Universe*)
Location = *mklc*(*CLocation*)
| *mkla*(*ALocation*)
end data type

A location is determined by the field identifier (which implicitly contains the class of the object), the object identifier, and the universe the object of the location belongs to. *lrtype* yields the dynamic range type of a concrete location, that is, the dynamization of the range type of the corresponding field w.r.t. the location's object. The identifier of this field can be obtained by *fid*. In programs and specifications, a location is usually specified by its object and its simple field identifier. The resulting location is returned by *locC* and *locA*, resp. For convenience we often write X.T@f or simply X.f for $locC(X, \mathrm{T@f})$, $mklc(locC(X, \mathrm{T@f}))$, $locA(X, \mathrm{T@f})$, and $mkla(locA(X, \mathrm{T@f}))$ where the meaning is clear from the context. *obj* yields the object a location belongs to. We say that a location *belongs to a universe* U if the location belongs to an object that belongs to U.

$$\begin{array}{lll}
lrtype : CLocation & \rightarrow & DynType \\
\quad lrtype(cloc(F_C, OID, U)) & =_{def} & dyn(rtype(F_C), \\
 & & \quad ref(otype(cfield(F_C)), OID, U), U)
\end{array}$$

$$\begin{array}{lll}
fid : Location & \rightarrow & FieldId \\
\quad fid(mklc(cloc(F_C, OID, U))) & =_{def} & cfield(F_C) \\
\quad fid(mkla(aloc(F_A, OID, U))) & =_{def} & afield(F_A)
\end{array}$$

$$\begin{array}{lll}
locC : Value \times SimpleCFieldId & \rightarrow & CLocation \\
\quad locC(ref(C, OID, U), f) & =_{def} & cloc(mkCFieldId(f, C), OID, U)
\end{array}$$

$$\begin{array}{lll}
locA : Value \times SimpleAFieldId & \rightarrow & ALocation \\
\quad locA(ref(C, OID, U), f) & =_{def} & aloc(mkAFieldId(f, C), OID, U)
\end{array}$$

$$\begin{array}{lll}
obj : Location & \rightarrow & Value \\
\quad obj(mklc(cloc(F_C, OID, U))) & =_{def} & ref(otype(cfield(F_C)), OID, U) \\
\quad obj(mkla(aloc(F_A, OID, U))) & =_{def} & ref(otype(afield(F_A)), OID, U)
\end{array}$$

For convenience, we define accessibility of locations:

$$\begin{array}{l}
accessibleL : Location \times TypeId \rightarrow Bool \\
\quad accessibleL(L, T) \Leftrightarrow_{def} \; accessible(accessMode(fid(L)), dtype(fid(L)), T)
\end{array}$$

We say that a location is *present* in a type declaration T if the declaration type of its field is in the scope of T's module:

$$\begin{array}{l}
presentL : Location \times TypeId \rightarrow Bool \\
\quad presentL(L, T) \Leftrightarrow_{def} \; imports(module(T), module(dtype(fid(L))))
\end{array}$$

Lemma 3.1.8. *If a location L is present in type declaration* S *and* S *is in the scope of* T*'s module, then L is also present in* T.

$$presentL(L, S) \wedge imports(module(T), module(S)) \Rightarrow presentL(L, T)$$

Lemma 3.1.9. *If a location is accessible in a type* T *then it is also present in* T.

$$accessibleL(L, T) \Rightarrow presentL(L, T)$$

Both proofs can be found in Appendix D.1.

3.1.1.10 Object Stores. An object store describes the states of all objects in a program at a certain point of execution. In particular, it describes how objects are linked via references and which objects are alive (i.e., allocated). A formalization of object stores is important as semantic foundation of program specifications and is central for the verification of OO-programs. The formalization presented in the following is based on [PH97b]. For a detailed explanation, the reader is referred to that thesis.

Object stores are modeled by an abstract data type with main sort *Store* and the following operations: $OS\langle L_C := X\rangle$ denotes updating the object store OS at concrete location L_C with value X. $OS(L_C)$ denotes reading concrete location L_C in store OS; $OS(L_C)$ is called the *value held by* L_C *in* OS. $new(OS, C, U)$ returns a reference to a new object (in store OS) of the dynamic type for class C in universe U. $OS\langle C, U\rangle$ denotes the store after allocating the object $new(OS, C, U)$. $alive(X, OS)$ yields true if and only if object X is allocated in OS:

$$
\begin{array}{lll}
\_\langle\_ := \_\rangle & : \mathit{Store} \times \mathit{CLocation} \times \mathit{Value} & \rightarrow \mathit{Store} \\
\_(\_) & : \mathit{Store} \times \mathit{CLocation} & \rightarrow \mathit{Value} \\
\mathit{new} & : \mathit{Store} \times \mathit{ClassId} \times \mathit{Universe} & \rightarrow \mathit{Value} \\
\_\langle\_,\_\rangle & : \mathit{Store} \times \mathit{ClassId} \times \mathit{Universe} & \rightarrow \mathit{Store} \\
\mathit{alive} & : \mathit{Value} \times \mathit{Store} & \rightarrow \mathit{Bool}
\end{array}
$$

In the following, we present and explain the axiomatization of these functions. Location update and object allocation construct new stores from given ones; location read and liveness test are used for the observation of stores. Axioms **store1**–**store5** specify the properties of stores observable by location reads, axioms **store6**–**store9** describe liveness properties, axioms **store10**–**store12** specify the properties of the *new*-operation, and **store13** is an extensionality axiom.

Axiom **store1** states that updating one location does not affect the values held by other locations. Axiom **store2** states that reading a location updated by a value X yields X, if the object of the location and X are both alive. We restrict this property to living objects in order to guarantee that locations never hold non-living objects and that locations of non-living objects are initialized as described by axiom **store3**. Axiom **store4** states that updates by non-living objects do not modify the store. The assumptions and requirements about the liveness of objects in axioms **store2**, **store3**, **store4** simplify the definition of equivalence properties on stores (see [PH97b]). Axiom **store5** states that allocation does not affect the values held by locations.

$$
\begin{array}{l}
\textbf{store1}: L_C \neq K_C \Rightarrow OS\langle L_C := X\rangle(K_C) = OS(K_C) \\
\textbf{store2}: \mathit{alive}(\mathit{obj}(\mathit{mklc}(L_C)), OS) \wedge \mathit{alive}(X, OS) \Rightarrow OS\langle L_C := X\rangle(L_C) = X \\
\textbf{store3}: \neg\mathit{alive}(\mathit{obj}(\mathit{mklc}(L_C)), OS) \Rightarrow OS(L_C) = \mathit{init}(\mathit{lrtype}(L_C)) \\
\textbf{store4}: \neg\mathit{alive}(X, OS) \Rightarrow OS\langle L_C := X\rangle = OS \\
\textbf{store5}: OS\langle C, U\rangle(L_C) = OS(L_C)
\end{array}
$$

Once an object has been allocated, it stays alive until the executed program terminates. In particular, there is no garbage collection in Mojave. Thus, Axiom **store6** states that location updates do not influence liveness of objects. Axiom **store7** specifies that an object is alive after allocation if and only if it was alive before allocation or it is the newly allocated object. Axiom **store8** ensures that objects held by locations are alive. Together with **store2**, **store3**, and **store4**, this simplifies proofs. Finally, values that are not references to objects, are considered to be alive.

store6 : $alive(X, OS\langle L_C := Y\rangle) \Leftrightarrow alive(X, OS)$
store7 : $alive(X, OS\langle C, U\rangle) \Leftrightarrow alive(X, OS) \vee X = new(OS, C, U)$
store8 : $alive(OS(L_C), OS)$
store9 : $\neg ref?(X) \Rightarrow alive(X, OS)$

The following three axioms specify properties of the *new*-operation. A newly created object is not alive in the store from which it was created (**store10**) and it has the correct type (**store11**). The creation of an object of the dynamic type for class C and universe U yields the same result in two stores if and only if liveness for all objects of that dynamic type is equivalent in these stores (**store12**).

store10 : $\neg alive(new(OS, C, U), OS)$
store11 : $typeof(new(OS, C, U)) = refDT(ctid(C), U)$
store12 : $new(OS_1, C, U) = new(OS_2, C, U) \Leftrightarrow$
$\Big(\forall X : typeof(X) = refDT(ctid(C), U) \Rightarrow$
$(alive(X, OS_1) \Leftrightarrow alive(X, OS_2))\Big)$

Finally, we guarantee that two stores are equal if we cannot distinguish them by the observer functions.

store13 : $(\forall X : alive(X, OS_1) \Leftrightarrow alive(X, OS_2)) \wedge$
$(\forall L_C : OS_1(L_C) = OS_2(L_C)) \Rightarrow OS_1 = OS_2$

A model for a very similar axiomatization of object stores can be found in [PH97b]. Since the formalization of Mojave's objects stores is very close to the one presented in [PH97b], almost all of the properties shown for that formalization carry over to Mojave and are not repeated here.

3.1.1.11 Properties of Object Stores. To illustrate how the formal data and state model can be used to express properties of object stores, we formalize reachability of objects. Object X *reaches* object Y in store OS if there is a chain of references from X to Y in OS [PH97b]. For specifications it is often useful to have a restricted form of reachability that requires all references of such a chain to be stored in locations with a given field id (see Paragraph 4.2.1.3 for an example). This form of reachability can be formalized as follows:

$\rho_{\_} : Nat \times Value \times Value \times Store \times SimpleCFieldId \rightarrow Bool$
$\rho_0(X, Y, OS, f) \quad \Leftrightarrow_{def} X = Y$
$\rho_{N+1}(X, Y, OS, f) \Leftrightarrow_{def} \exists Z : OS(locC(X, f)) = Z \wedge \rho_N(Z, Y, OS, f)$

$\rho : Value \times Value \times Store \times SimpleCFieldId \rightarrow Bool$
$\rho(X, Y, OS, f) \quad \Leftrightarrow_{def} \exists N : \rho_N(X, Y, OS, f)$

Poetzsch-Heffter discusses reachability intensely [PH97b]. For this book, we only need two properties:

Lemma 3.1.10. *Reachability is not affected by object creation (part (i) below). If the f-locations of all objects reachable via f from object X hold the same value in two stores, then reachability from X via f is equivalent in these stores (part (ii) below).*

$$(i)\ \rho(X,Y,OS,f) \Leftrightarrow \rho(X,Y,OS\langle C,U\rangle,f)$$

$$(ii)\ \Big(\rho(X,obj(mklc(L_C)),OS,f) \wedge scfid(cfid(fid(mklc(L_C)))) = f \Rightarrow OS(L_C) = OS'(L_C)\Big) \Rightarrow (\rho(X,Y,OS,f) \Leftrightarrow \rho(X,Y,OS',f))$$

The proofs run by induction on the length of the reference chain. They are straightforward and therefore omitted here.

3.1.1.12 Program-Specific Aspects of Signatures and States. To specify properties of a program, we have to refer to variables, fields, and types in formulas. This is enabled by introducing constant symbols for all these entities as described above. $\Sigma_{general}$ denotes a signature that includes the signature of the data and state model as introduced above without the program-dependent constants. We assume that the constant symbols of $\Sigma_{general}$ and the identifiers occurring in a Mojave program are distinct. For an open program $\mathcal{P}$, $\Sigma(\mathcal{P})$ (or simply Σ if $\mathcal{P}$ is clear from the context) is the signature that is obtained from $\Sigma_{general}$ by adding the constant symbols for module, class, interface, simple field and field identifiers declared in $\mathcal{P}$'s core (analogously for closed programs).

To refer to the current object store the constant symbol \$ of sort *Store* is used, and Γ denotes $\Sigma \cup \{\$\}$. The current object store \$ can be considered as a global variable (like the current universe $\mathcal{U}$). In programs, \$ can only be accessed and modified through the read and write operations of fields, and the new-operation. Specifications may directly refer to \$. Furthermore, we introduce three signatures for each method m occurring in the core of $\mathcal{P}$: (1) The extension of Γ by constant symbols of sort *Value* for each parameter (in particular, `this`) and a constant symbol $\mathcal{U}$ of sort *Universe* for the current universe is denoted by $\Gamma_{pre(\mathrm{m})}$. (2) The extension of Γ by constant symbols of sort *Value* for each parameter and local variable, and the constant symbol $\mathcal{U}$ of sort *Universe* is denoted by $\Gamma_{body(\mathrm{m})}$. (3) The extension of Γ by the constant symbol result of sort *Value* is denoted by Γ_{post}.

Informally, an *execution point* is a position before or after a statement or method. A *state* is characterized by the current execution point and by the interpretation of the constant symbols representing variables. In particular, a *prestate* is a state before the execution of a method and provides interpretations for the parameters, the object store \$, and the current universe $\mathcal{U}$; a *poststate* is a state after the execution of a method and provides interpretations for the local variable result, for \$, and for $\mathcal{U}$.

3.1.2 Axiomatic Semantics

In this subsection, we present an axiomatic semantics for Mojave. The axioms and rules of this semantics are the language-dependent part of a programming logic for Mojave. The language-independent axioms and rules can be found in Subsection 3.1.3. The semantics presented here emerged from the programming logics presented in [PH97b, PHM98, PHM99].

3.1.2.1 Triples and Sequents. A *program component* is a method signature occurrence[3] or a statement occurrence within a given program. We assume that the program context of a statement or method is always implicitly given and that we can refer to method declarations in this context[4].

For each method implementation, we can obtain the statement constituting its body by the function *body*. The method implementation associated with a virtual method is returned by *impl*. Note that the implementation can be inherited from a superclass. For abstract methods, *impl* is undefined.

A *Hoare triple* or simply *triple* has the form $\{ \mathbf{P} \}$ COMP $\{ \mathbf{Q} \}$ where COMP is a program component and **P** and **Q** are first-order formulas, called *pre-* and *postconditions*, resp. If the component in a triple **A** is a method, we call **A** a *method annotation*; otherwise **A** is called a *statement annotation*. Pre- and postconditions of statement annotations are formulas over $\Gamma_{body(\mathrm{m})}$ where m is the enclosing method; pre- and postconditions in annotations of method m are $\Gamma_{pre(\mathrm{m})}$-formulas and Γ_{post}-formulas, resp.

A triple $\{ \mathbf{P} \}$ COMP $\{ \mathbf{Q} \}$ specifies the following *refined* partial correctness property: If **P** holds in a state before executing COMP, then execution of COMP either

1. terminates and **Q** holds in the state after execution or
2. aborts because of errors or actions that are beyond the semantics of the programming language (e.g., memory allocation problems, stack overflow, external interrupts from the execution environment), or
3. runs forever.

In particular, execution of COMP does not abort because of dereferencing of null-references or illegal casts. Thus, this refined partial correctness logic can be used to prove that a program does not produce such runtime errors (see [PH97b] for a discussion of this semantics).

A *sequent* has the form $\mathcal{A} \rhd \mathbf{A}$ where $\mathcal{A}$ is a set of method annotations and **A** is a triple. Triples in $\mathcal{A}$ are called *assumptions* of the sequent and **A** is called the *consequent* of the sequent. A sequent expresses the fact that we can prove a triple based on some assumptions about methods. Sequents are necessary to handle recursive procedures and subtyping in open programs (see Subsection 3.3.2).

3.1.2.2 Axioms and Rules. The semantics of statements and methods is specified by a set of *axioms* and *rules*. A rule consists of a number of antecedents and a sequent as *succedent*. The *antecedents* are first-order formulas or sequents. Rules may contain metavariables for formulas and assumptions. A rule allows one to prove the succedent from the antecedents. Axioms are like rules that do not have antecedents.

---

[3] We omit the formal parameters in case they are not needed.

[4] Technically, this means that the semantics is described for method and statement occurrences within a program context [PH97a].

3.1.2.3 Statement Semantics. In this paragraph, we present the axioms and rules for Mojave's statements. To keep the rules readable, we use the concrete statement syntax instead of terms of the abstract syntax and abbreviate $dyn(\mathrm{T}, \mathrm{this}, \mathcal{U})$ by $\tau(\mathrm{T})$.

The cast-axiom is very similar to Hoare's classical assignment-axiom [Hoa69]. However, to prevent runtime errors, a stronger precondition assures that the type conversion is legal:

cast-axiom:

$$\rhd \{\ typeof(\mathrm{e}) \preceq \tau(\mathrm{T}) \wedge \mathbf{P}[\mathrm{e}/\mathrm{v}]\ \}\ \ \mathrm{v} = (\mathrm{T})\ \mathrm{e};\ \ \{\ \mathbf{P}\ \}$$

The new-axiom works like an assignment axiom: The new object is substituted for the left-hand-side variable and the modified object store for the initial store.

new-axiom:

$$\begin{array}{l}\rhd\ \{\ \mathbf{P}[new(\$, cid(tid(\mathrm{T})), univ(\tau(\mathrm{T})))/\mathrm{v}\ ,\ \$\langle cid(tid(\mathrm{T})), univ(\tau(\mathrm{T}))\rangle/\$]\ \}\\ \quad \mathrm{v} = \mathrm{new\ T}();\\ \quad \{\ \mathbf{P}\ \}\end{array}$$

Reading a field substitutes the value held by the addressed instance variable for the left-hand-side variable. Writing field access replaces the initial object store by the updated store:

field-read-axiom:

$$\rhd \{\ \mathrm{w} \neq null \wedge \mathbf{P}[\$(locC(\mathrm{w}, \mathrm{S@f}))/\mathrm{v}]\ \}\ \ \mathrm{v} = \mathrm{w.S@f};\ \ \{\ \mathbf{P}\ \}$$

field-write-axiom:

$$\rhd \{\ \mathrm{w} \neq null \wedge \mathbf{P}[\$\langle locC(\mathrm{w}, \mathrm{S@f}) := \mathrm{e}\rangle/\$]\ \}\ \ \mathrm{w.S@f} = \mathrm{e};\ \ \{\ \mathbf{P}\ \}$$

The axioms and rules for the empty, while-, if-, and sequential-statement are canonical except that we have to map the boolean expressions to values of sort *Bool* by using the selector function *aB* of data type *Value*:

skip-axiom:

$$\rhd \{\ \mathbf{P}\ \}\ \ ;\ \ \{\ \mathbf{P}\ \}$$

while-rule:

$$\frac{\mathcal{A} \rhd \{\ aB(\mathrm{e}) \wedge \mathbf{P}\ \}\ \mathrm{STMT}\ \{\ \mathbf{P}\ \}}{\mathcal{A} \rhd \{\ \mathbf{P}\ \}\ \mathrm{while\ (e)}\ \{\ \mathrm{STMT}\ \}\ \ \{\ \neg aB(\mathrm{e}) \wedge \mathbf{P}\ \}}$$

if-rule:

$$\frac{\begin{array}{l}\mathcal{A} \rhd \{\ aB(\mathrm{e}) \wedge \mathbf{P}\ \}\ \mathrm{STMT1}\ \{\ \mathbf{Q}\ \}\\ \mathcal{A} \rhd \{\ \neg aB(\mathrm{e}) \wedge \mathbf{P}\ \}\ \mathrm{STMT2}\ \{\ \mathbf{Q}\ \}\end{array}}{\mathcal{A} \rhd \{\ \mathbf{P}\ \}\ \mathrm{if\ (e)}\ \{\ \mathrm{STMT1}\ \}\ \mathrm{else}\ \{\ \mathrm{STMT2}\ \}\ \ \{\ \mathbf{Q}\ \}}$$

seq-rule:

$$\frac{\begin{array}{l}\mathcal{A} \rhd \{\ \mathbf{P}\ \}\ \mathrm{STMT1}\ \{\ \mathbf{Q}\ \}\\ \mathcal{A} \rhd \{\ \mathbf{Q}\ \}\ \mathrm{STMT2}\ \{\ \mathbf{R}\ \}\end{array}}{\mathcal{A} \rhd \{\ \mathbf{P}\ \}\ \ \mathrm{STMT1\ STMT2}\ \ \{\ \mathbf{R}\ \}}$$

The invocation-rule uses properties of virtual methods to verify invocations of dynamically-bound methods and is very intuitive: Formal parameters are substituted by the actual parameter expressions and the result variable is substituted by the left-hand-side variable. The universe to which the target object belongs becomes the current universe for the invoked method. The fact that local variables different from the left-hand-side variable are not modified by an invocation is expressed by the *invocation-var-rule* that allows one to substitute logical variables Z in pre- and postconditions by local variables `x` (`x` different from `v`). In this context, the current universe $\mathcal{U}$ behaves like a program variable since control flow returns to the universe of the invocation site after termination. Thus, $\mathcal{U}$ can also be substituted for logical variables[5].

invocation-rule:

$$\frac{\mathcal{A} \triangleright \{\, \mathbf{P} \,\}\;\; \mathrm{T{:}m}(\mathrm{p}_1,\ldots,\mathrm{p}_n)\;\; \{\, \mathbf{Q} \,\}}{\begin{array}{l}\mathcal{A} \triangleright \{\; \mathrm{w} \neq \mathit{null} \wedge \mathbf{P}[\mathrm{w}/\mathrm{this}, \mathrm{e}_1/\mathrm{p}_1, \ldots, \mathrm{e}_n/\mathrm{p}_n, \mathit{univV}(\mathrm{w})/\mathcal{U}] \;\}\\ \qquad \mathrm{v} = \mathrm{w.T{:}m}(\mathrm{e}_1,\ldots,\mathrm{e}_n);\\ \quad\; \{\; \mathbf{Q}[\mathrm{v}/\mathrm{result}] \;\}\end{array}}$$

invocation-var-rule:

$$\frac{\mathcal{A} \triangleright \{\, \mathbf{P} \,\}\; \mathrm{v} = \mathrm{w.T{:}m}(\mathrm{e}_1,\ldots,\mathrm{e}_n);\; \{\, \mathbf{Q} \,\}}{\mathcal{A} \triangleright \{\, \mathbf{P}[\mathrm{x}/Z] \,\}\; \mathrm{v} = \mathrm{w.T{:}m}(\mathrm{e}_1,\ldots,\mathrm{e}_n);\; \{\, \mathbf{Q}[\mathrm{x}/Z] \,\}}$$

Static methods are bound statically. Therefore, method implementations are used instead of virtual methods to verify invocations. The new current universe is the universe of the dynamic type on which the static method is invoked. It is determined by the target type of the invocation and the current universe. Note that *null* is passed to the `this`-parameter of static methods.

static-invocation-rule:

$$\frac{\mathcal{A} \triangleright \{\, \mathbf{P} \,\}\;\; \mathrm{T@m}(\mathrm{p}_1,\ldots,\mathrm{p}_n)\;\{\, \mathbf{Q} \,\}}{\begin{array}{l}\mathcal{A} \triangleright \{\; \mathbf{P}[\mathit{null}/\mathrm{this}, \mathrm{e}_1/\mathrm{p}_1, \ldots, \mathrm{e}_n/\mathrm{p}_n, \mathit{univ}(\tau(\mathrm{T}'))/\mathcal{U}] \;\}\\ \qquad \mathrm{v} = \mathrm{T'.T@m}(\mathrm{e}_1,\ldots,\mathrm{e}_n);\\ \quad\; \{\; \mathbf{Q}[\mathrm{v}/\mathrm{result}] \;\}\end{array}}$$

static-invocation-var-rule:

$$\frac{\mathcal{A} \triangleright \{\, \mathbf{P} \,\}\; \mathrm{v} = \mathrm{T'.T@m}(\mathrm{e}_1,\ldots,\mathrm{e}_n);\; \{\, \mathbf{Q} \,\}}{\mathcal{A} \triangleright \{\, \mathbf{P}[\mathrm{x}/Z] \,\}\; \mathrm{v} = \mathrm{T'.T@m}(\mathrm{e}_1,\ldots,\mathrm{e}_n);\; \{\, \mathbf{Q}[\mathrm{x}/Z] \,\}}$$

Like static methods, calls of private methods and calls via `super` are statically bound:

call-rule:

$$\frac{\mathcal{A} \triangleright \{\, \mathbf{P} \,\}\;\; \mathrm{T@m}(\mathrm{p}_1,\ldots,\mathrm{p}_n)\;\{\, \mathbf{Q} \,\}}{\begin{array}{l}\mathcal{A} \triangleright \{\; \mathrm{w} \neq \mathit{null} \wedge \mathbf{P}[\mathrm{w}/\mathrm{this}, \mathrm{e}_1/\mathrm{p}_1, \ldots, \mathrm{e}_n/\mathrm{p}_n, \mathit{univV}(\mathrm{w})/\mathcal{U}] \;\}\\ \qquad \mathrm{v} = \mathrm{w.T@m}(\mathrm{e}_1,\ldots,\mathrm{e}_n);\\ \quad\; \{\; \mathbf{Q}[\mathrm{v}/\mathrm{result}] \;\}\end{array}}$$

[5] For simplicity, we use indices $1, \ldots, n$ for the explicit parameters of a method T@m or T:m. It would be more precise to use $1, \ldots, n_{\mathrm{T:m}}$.

call-var-rule:

$$\frac{\mathcal{A} \triangleright \{ \mathbf{P} \}\ \mathrm{v} = \mathrm{w.T@m}(\mathrm{e}_1, \ldots, \mathrm{e}_n);\ \{ \mathbf{Q} \}}{\mathcal{A} \triangleright \{ \mathbf{P}[\mathrm{x}/Z] \}\ \mathrm{v} = \mathrm{w.T@m}(\mathrm{e}_1, \ldots, \mathrm{e}_n);\ \{ \mathbf{Q}[\mathrm{x}/Z] \}}$$

3.1.2.4 Method Semantics. The behavior of the predefined methods is given by their specifications (see App. B) and their translation into Hoare triples (see Subsection 4.2.2). This paragraph presents the semantics of user-defined method implementations and virtual methods.

Essentially, an annotation of a method implementation holds if it holds for its body. In order to handle recursion, the method annotation may be assumed for the proof of the body. Informally, this is sound, because in any terminating execution, the last incarnation does not contain a recursive invocation of the method. In Mojave, all local variables are initialized with default values ($\mathrm{v}_{n+1}, \ldots, \mathrm{v}_k$ are the local variables of the method):

implementation-rule:

$$\frac{\begin{array}{l} \mathcal{A},\ \{\mathbf{P}\}\ \mathrm{T@m}(\mathrm{p}_1, \ldots, \mathrm{p}_n)\ \{\mathbf{Q}\} \triangleright \\ \quad \{\mathbf{P} \wedge (\mathit{static}(\mathrm{T@m}) \Leftrightarrow \mathrm{this} = \mathit{null}) \wedge \bigwedge_{i=n+1}^{k} (\mathrm{v}_i = \mathit{init}(\tau([\mathrm{v}_i])))\} \\ \quad \mathit{body}(\mathrm{T@m}) \\ \quad \{\mathbf{Q}\} \end{array}}{\mathcal{A} \triangleright \{\mathbf{P}\}\ \ \mathrm{T@m}(\mathrm{p}_1, \ldots, \mathrm{p}_n)\ \ \{\mathbf{Q}\}}$$

Virtual methods have been introduced to model dynamically-bound methods. That is, a method annotation for T:m reflects the common properties of all implementations that might be executed on invocation of T:m. If T is a class, there are two obligations to prove an annotation **A** of a virtual method T:m: (1) Show that the corresponding implementation satisfies **A** if invoked for objects of type T. (2) Show that **A** holds for objects of proper subtypes of T. The second obligation and annotations of abstract methods can be proved by the *subtype-rule*: If S is a subtype of T, an invocation of T:m on an S-object is equivalent to an invocation of S:m. Thus, all properties of S:m carry over to T:m[6]:

subtype-rule:

$$\frac{\begin{array}{l} \mathrm{S} \preceq_M \mathrm{T} \\ \mathcal{A} \triangleright \{\ \mathit{typeof}(\mathrm{this}) \preceq \mathit{refDT}(\mathrm{S}, \mathcal{U}) \wedge \mathbf{P}\ \}\ \mathrm{S{:}m}(\mathrm{p}_1, \ldots, \mathrm{p}_n)\ \{\ \mathbf{Q}\ \} \end{array}}{\mathcal{A} \triangleright \{\ \mathit{typeof}(\mathrm{this}) \preceq \mathit{refDT}(\mathrm{S}, \mathcal{U}) \wedge \mathbf{P}\ \}\ \mathrm{T{:}m}(\mathrm{p}_1, \ldots, \mathrm{p}_n)\ \{\ \mathbf{Q}\ \}}$$

If T denotes an interface, it is sufficient to prove that an annotation for T:m holds in all cases where T:m is invoked on subtype objects. If T denotes a class, we have to show in addition that the desired annotation holds for the implementation of m in T if T:m is invoked on a T-object:

class-rule:

$$\frac{\begin{array}{l} \mathcal{A} \triangleright \{\ \mathit{typeof}(\mathrm{this}) = \mathit{refDT}(\mathrm{T}, \mathcal{U}) \wedge \mathbf{P}\ \}\mathit{impl}(\ \mathrm{T{:}m}\ )\{\ \mathbf{Q}\ \} \\ \mathcal{A} \triangleright \{\ \mathit{typeof}(\mathrm{this}) \prec \mathit{refDT}(\mathrm{T}, \mathcal{U}) \wedge \mathbf{P}\ \}\ \mathrm{T{:}m}(\mathrm{p}_1, \ldots, \mathrm{p}_n)\ \{\ \mathbf{Q}\ \} \end{array}}{\mathcal{A} \triangleright \{\ \mathit{typeof}(\mathrm{this}) \preceq \mathit{refDT}(\mathrm{T}, \mathcal{U}) \wedge \mathbf{P}\ \}\ \mathrm{T{:}m}(\mathrm{p}_1, \ldots, \mathrm{p}_n)\ \{\ \mathbf{Q}\ \}}$$

[6] For simplicity, we assume here that formal parameters have the same names in sub- and supertype methods. Otherwise, a substitution would be necessary.

3.1.3 Programming Logic

Besides the axiomatic semantics, the programming logic for Mojave contains language-independent axioms and rules to handle assumptions and to establish a connection between the predicate logic of pre- and postconditions and triples of the programming logic. The logic for Mojave is based on the programming logic presented in [PH97b]. For brevity, we refer to that thesis for a detailed discussion of the logic.

Language-Independent Rules. The language-independent axioms and rules of the programming logic are summarized in Figure 3.3. The *assumpt-axiom* states that the trivial sequence is true. Assumptions can be introduced at any point of a derivation (*assumpt-intro-rule*) and eliminated if they can be derived from other assumptions (*assumpt-elim-rule*). The *false-axiom* together with the *weak-rule* allows one to prove any postcondition if the precondition is *false*. The *inv-rule* expresses that logical variables and the program variables `this` and $\mathcal{U}$ cannot be modified by executing a statement or method. This is not true for other program variables, especially for $. The remaining rules are used to apply conjunction, disjunction, implication, substitution, and binding of free variables to pre- and postconditions.

Soundness and Completeness. In [PHM99], we have proved soundness for a very similar programming logic w.r.t. an operational semantics. The main difference between Mojave and the language in [PHM99] is the universe type system. However, almost all modifications for the universe type system concern the data and state model rather than the axioms and rules. Since the operational semantics builds on this model as well, we are confident that the soundness proof of [PHM99] carries over to the Mojave logic.

As presented here, the logic for Mojave is obviously not complete. For instance, it does not allow one to prove properties about method invocations or field accesses on the `null`-reference. To solve this problem, one can either change the meaning of triples (see Paragraph 3.1.2.1) such that all exceptions are treated in the same way as memory errors (i.e., a triple holds if the program component aborts), or one can extend Mojave and its logic by exception handling. However, although our logic is incomplete, it can be used to verify interesting programs as illustrated by the nontrivial case study presented in [LMMPH00]. Extending the Java subset by exceptions and proving completeness for the refined logic is considered future work.

3.2 Language Properties

In this section, we specify and prove properties that hold for all Mojave programs: We show that Mojave is a type safe language, prove that execution of statements and methods leaves living objects alive, and show that readonly methods are side-effect-free. The proofs illustrate an interesting proof technique that is frequently used in this book.

assumpt-axiom:

$$\mathbf{A} \triangleright \mathbf{A}$$

false-axiom:

$$\triangleright \{\, \mathit{false} \,\}\ \mathrm{COMP}\ \{\, \mathit{false} \,\}$$

assumpt-intro-rule:

$$\frac{\mathcal{A} \triangleright \mathbf{A}}{\mathbf{A}_0\,,\mathcal{A} \triangleright \mathbf{A}}$$

assumpt-elim-rule:

$$\frac{\mathcal{A} \triangleright \mathbf{A}_0 \qquad \mathbf{A}_0\,,\mathcal{A} \triangleright \mathbf{A}}{\mathcal{A} \triangleright \mathbf{A}}$$

conjunct-rule:

$$\frac{\mathcal{A} \triangleright \{\, \mathbf{P}_1 \,\}\ \mathrm{COMP}\ \{\, \mathbf{Q}_1 \,\} \qquad \mathcal{A} \triangleright \{\, \mathbf{P}_2 \,\}\ \mathrm{COMP}\ \{\, \mathbf{Q}_2 \,\}}{\mathcal{A} \triangleright \{\, \mathbf{P}_1 \wedge \mathbf{P}_2 \,\}\ \mathrm{COMP}\ \{\, \mathbf{Q}_1 \wedge \mathbf{Q}_2 \,\}}$$

disjunct-rule:

$$\frac{\mathcal{A} \triangleright \{\, \mathbf{P}_1 \,\}\ \mathrm{COMP}\ \{\, \mathbf{Q}_1 \,\} \qquad \mathcal{A} \triangleright \{\, \mathbf{P}_2 \,\}\ \mathrm{COMP}\ \{\, \mathbf{Q}_2 \,\}}{\mathcal{A} \triangleright \{\, \mathbf{P}_1 \vee \mathbf{P}_2 \,\}\ \mathrm{COMP}\ \{\, \mathbf{Q}_1 \vee \mathbf{Q}_2 \,\}}$$

strength-rule:

$$\frac{\mathbf{P}' \Rightarrow \mathbf{P} \qquad \mathcal{A} \triangleright \{\, \mathbf{P} \,\}\ \mathrm{COMP}\ \{\, \mathbf{Q} \,\}}{\mathcal{A} \triangleright \{\, \mathbf{P}' \,\}\ \mathrm{COMP}\ \{\, \mathbf{Q} \,\}}$$

weak-rule:

$$\frac{\mathcal{A} \triangleright \{\, \mathbf{P} \,\}\ \mathrm{COMP}\ \{\, \mathbf{Q} \,\} \qquad \mathbf{Q} \Rightarrow \mathbf{Q}'}{\mathcal{A} \triangleright \{\, \mathbf{P} \,\}\ \mathrm{COMP}\ \{\, \mathbf{Q}' \,\}}$$

inv-rule:

$$\frac{\mathcal{A} \triangleright \{\, \mathbf{P} \,\}\ \mathrm{COMP}\ \{\, \mathbf{Q} \,\}}{\mathcal{A} \triangleright \{\, \mathbf{P} \wedge \mathbf{R} \,\}\ \mathrm{COMP}\ \{\, \mathbf{Q} \wedge \mathbf{R} \,\}}$$

where $\mathbf{R}$ is a $\Sigma \cup \{\mathrm{this}, \mathcal{U}\}$-formula in case that COMP is a statement and a Σ-formula otherwise.

subst-rule:

$$\frac{\mathcal{A} \triangleright \{\, \mathbf{P} \,\}\ \mathrm{COMP}\ \{\, \mathbf{Q} \,\}}{\mathcal{A} \triangleright \{\, \mathbf{P}[t/Z] \,\}\ \mathrm{COMP}\ \{\, \mathbf{Q}[t/Z] \,\}}$$

where Z is an arbitrary logical variable and t a Σ-term.

all-rule:

$$\frac{\mathcal{A} \triangleright \{\, \mathbf{P}[Y/Z] \,\}\ \mathrm{COMP}\ \{\, \mathbf{Q} \,\}}{\mathcal{A} \triangleright \{\, \mathbf{P}[Y/Z] \,\}\ \mathrm{COMP}\ \{\, \forall Z : \mathbf{Q} \,\}}$$

where Z, Y are arbitrary, but distinct logical variables.

ex-rule:

$$\frac{\mathcal{A} \triangleright \{\, \mathbf{P} \,\}\ \mathrm{COMP}\ \{\, \mathbf{Q}[Y/Z] \,\}}{\mathcal{A} \triangleright \{\, \exists Z : \mathbf{P} \,\}\ \mathrm{COMP}\ \{\, \mathbf{Q}[Y/Z] \,\}}$$

where Z, Y are arbitrary, but distinct logical variables.

Fig. 3.3. Language-Independent Axioms and Rules

A programming language guarantees a big variety of properties that hold for all implementations. For instance, Mojave guarantees type safety, that a readonly method does not cause side-effects, that a method can only update locations that are reachable from one of the parameter objects, etc. To use such properties for reasoning, one can either directly incorporate them as rules in the programming logic, or one can prove appropriate lemmas within the programming logic. The former approach makes the application of such properties very easy. However, it makes the programming logic and its soundness proof more complex. Furthermore, the selection of language properties that are incorporated into the logic is rather arbitrary and depends on the intended applications of the programming logic. For instance the local update property (see Definition 5.4.1) is a very specific property that only makes sense in combination with our specification technique for dependencies of abstract fields.

Therefore, we follow the latter approach: Language properties are formalized by *language property operators* for triples that add conjuncts to the pre- and postconditions of the triples. These conjuncts describe the language properties. We assume that there is a fixed finite set of language property operators for our programming language and a partial ordering on these operators. The set of operators can for instance be defined by the implementation of a verification tool.

Definition 3.2.1 (Language Properties). *An operator l for triples and sets of triples is an admissible language property if the following properties hold:*

- *If* $\mathbf{A}$ *is a triple of the form* $\{\, \mathbf{P} \,\}\ \mathrm{COMP}\ \{\, \mathbf{Q} \,\}$ *then* $l(\mathbf{A})$ *has the form* $\{\, \mathbf{P} \wedge \mathbf{P}' \,\}\ \mathrm{COMP}\ \{\, \mathbf{Q} \wedge \mathbf{Q}' \,\}$. *$l$ is extended pointwise to sets of triples.*
- *If there is a proof for a sequent* $\mathcal{A} \mathrel{|\!\!\!>} \mathbf{A}$ *then there is a proof for* $l(\mathcal{A}), l_1(\mathcal{A}), \ldots, l_n(\mathcal{A}) \mathrel{|\!\!\!>} l(\mathbf{A})$, *where the* l_i *are language property operators that are less than* l *in the ordering of operators.*

3.2.1 Type Safety

In this subsection, we formalize and prove type safety of Mojave. This is interesting for the following reasons:

- Due to the universe type system, type safety of Java [ON98] does not automatically carry over to Mojave.
- The type safety proof provides insight to and motivates the exact context conditions for the universe type system.
- The type safety invariant will be used intensely for the verification of frame properties and invariants.
- The type safety proof illustrates a proof technique that is frequently used in this book.

Usually, a language is called type safe if each syntactically and type correct program component that is executed in a well-typed state leads to a well-typed state upon termination [NO98, ON98]. However, to be able to use our partial correctness logic to prove type safety, we have to use a weaker notion of type safety here. We require type safety only for program components that do not terminate abnormally, since we cannot prove anything otherwise. We call a language type safe if every program component COMP for which there is a proof of the triple $\{\, \mathbf{R} \,\}$ COMP $\{\, \mathit{true} \,\}$[7] either runs forever or terminates in a well-typed state if execution starts in a well-typed state satisfying $\mathbf{R}$ (see [PH97b]). To prove type safety, we have to show $\{\, \mathbf{R} \wedge \mathrm{TA}_{pre} \,\}$ COMP $\{\, \mathrm{TA}_{post} \,\}$ for such program components where TA_{pre} and TA_{post} express well-typedness of pre- and poststates, resp. In the following, we formalize this notion of type safety.

Definition 3.2.2 (Well-Typed States). *A parameter or variable* v *is called well-typed in a state if* $\mathit{typeof}(\mathrm{v}) \preceq \tau([\mathrm{v}])$ *where* [v] *is the type declared for* v. *A state is called well-typed if all variables and parameters are well-typed and the object store is well-typed. An object store is called well-typed if all concrete locations are well-typed in the following sense:*

$$\begin{array}{l} \mathit{wt} : \mathit{Store} \rightarrow \mathit{Bool} \\ \mathit{wt}(OS) \Leftrightarrow_{def} \forall L_C : \mathit{typeof}(OS(L_C)) \preceq \mathit{lrtype}(L_C) \end{array}$$

Definition 3.2.3 (Type Annotations). *Well-typedness of pre- and post-states of program components is expressed by type annotations.* Adding type annotations *to a triple* **A** *means to add type information about the parameters and variables to the pre- and postcondition of* **A** *and to require that the store is well-typed. The resulting triple is denoted by typed(***A***); it depends on the kind of* **A***:*

- *Let* m *be a virtual method* T:m *or a method implementation* T@m. *For method annotations,* $\mathit{typed}(\{\, \mathbf{P} \,\}\ \mathrm{m}\ \{\, \mathbf{Q} \,\})$ *yields*

  $$\begin{array}{l} \{\, \mathbf{P} \wedge \bigwedge_{i=0}^{k} \mathit{typeof}(\mathrm{v}_i) \preceq \tau([\mathrm{v}_i]) \wedge \mathit{wt}(\$) \wedge R = \tau(\mathit{ret}(\mathrm{m})) \,\} \\ \mathrm{m} \\ \{\, \mathbf{Q} \wedge \mathit{typeof}(\mathrm{result}) \preceq R \wedge \mathit{wt}(\$) \,\} \end{array}$$

  where $\mathrm{v}_0,\ldots,\mathrm{v}_k$ *are the formal parameters of* m[8]*; recall from Paragraph 2.1.1.1 that we refer to* `this` *as* v_0. *R is a fresh logical variable that neither occurs in any specification nor in any proof.*
- *For statement annotations,* $\mathit{typed}(\{\, \mathbf{P} \,\}\ \mathrm{STMT}\ \{\, \mathbf{Q} \,\})$ *yields*

  $$\begin{array}{l} \{\, \mathbf{P} \wedge \bigwedge_{i=0}^{n} \mathit{typeof}(\mathrm{v}_i) \preceq \tau([\mathrm{v}_i]) \wedge \mathit{wt}(\$) \wedge (\mathit{static}(\mathrm{T@m}) \Leftrightarrow \mathrm{this} = \mathit{null}) \,\} \\ \mathrm{STMT} \\ \{\, \mathbf{Q} \wedge \bigwedge_{i=0}^{n} \mathit{typeof}(\mathrm{v}_i) \preceq \tau([\mathrm{v}_i]) \wedge \mathit{wt}(\$) \,\} \end{array}$$

[7] We have to require the existence of such a proof since our programming logic is incomplete and we can thus not assume that the property can be shown for all program components that do not terminate abnormally.

[8] That is, $[\mathrm{v}_i] = \mathit{par}(\mathrm{m}, i)$ for $1 \leq i \leq k$.

where T@m *is the method implementation enclosing* STMT, $\mathrm{v}_0, \ldots, \mathrm{v}_k$ *are the formal parameters, and* $\mathrm{v}_{k+1}, \ldots, \mathrm{v}_n$ *are the local variables of* T@m.

The typed-operator is extended pointwise to sets of triples.

Lemma 3.2.1 (Type Safety). *If there is a proof for* $\mathcal{A} \models \mathbf{A}$ *then there is a proof for* $typed(\mathcal{A}) \models typed(\mathbf{A})$

According to Definition 3.2.1, type safety is a language property (*typed* is a minimal element in the ordering of operators for language properties). The proof of type safety is based on the following auxiliary lemmas about the type combinator $*$. The proofs for these lemmas can be found in App. D.1.

The type combinator $*$ is used to determine the type of a field access, or the parameter or result types of a method invocation. In most cases, the dynamization of a type combination $S*T$ w.r.t. a universe U yields the same result as the dynamization of T w.r.t. the universe of the dynamization of S w.r.t. U. For instance for a field access `v.f`, $\tau([\mathrm{v}] * [\mathtt{f}]) = dyn([\mathtt{f}], \mathrm{this}, univ(\tau([\mathrm{v}])))$ holds if $[\mathtt{f}]$ is not a readonly type $(\neg roT?([\mathtt{f}]))$. We formalize this property by the following lemma:

Lemma 3.2.2. *The dynamization of a type combination* $S * T$ *w.r.t. object* X *and universe* U *yields the same dynamic type as the dynamization of* T *w.r.t. an object* Y *and the universe of the dynamization of* S *w.r.t.* X *and* U*, provided that* $S * T$ *is defined, that* S *is not a readonly type, and that* $X = Y$ *if* T *is an orep type. That is, if* $S * T$ *is defined, the following property holds:*

$$\neg roT?(S) \wedge (orepT?(T) \Rightarrow X = Y) \Rightarrow$$
$$dyn(T, Y, univ(dyn(S, X, U))) = dyn(S * T, X, U)$$

Lemma 3.2.2 requires that S is not a readonly type. Otherwise, we have to use the following lemma:

Lemma 3.2.3. *If* S *is a readonly type, the dynamization of a type* T *is a subtype of the dynamization of the combination* $S * T$*:*

$$roT?(S) \Rightarrow dyn(T, Y, V) \preceq dyn(S * T, X, U)$$

We can now prove type safety of Mojave. Most cases of the proof are presented as proof outlines. See App. A.2 for a brief explanation of this notation.

To understand the proof, it is helpful to have the type rules of the universe type system (see Subsection 2.2.5, p. 68) and the intuition behind these rules in mind. We mention the properties used in a proof step (in particular, those that are guaranteed by the type system) in comments.

Proof of Lemma 3.2.1:

The proof of this lemma runs by rule induction, that is, induction on the depth of the proof for $\mathcal{A} \models \mathbf{A}$. For each axiom or rule application in that proof, we show that the type annotations can be added.

Induction Basis. For the induction base, we have to show that the type annotations can be added for all proof trees of depth 1. Proof trees of depth 1 are either applications of axioms or specifications of predefined method implementations (however, properties of Object:equals are not axioms since they do not hold in all programs). That is, the induction base runs by case distinction over all possible axiom applications and predefined methods.

assumpt-axiom: $typed(\mathbf{A}) \triangleright typed(\mathbf{A})$ is an instance of the assumpt-axiom.

false-axiom: Let $\mathbf{TA}_{pre}$ and $\mathbf{TA}_{post}$ denote the type annotation for the pre- and poststate of COMP:

$$\{\, false \wedge \mathbf{TA}_{pre} \,\}$$
$$\Rightarrow$$
$$\{\, false \,\}$$
$$\text{COMP} \quad [\![\text{ false-axiom }]\!]$$
$$\{\, false \,\}$$
$$\Rightarrow$$
$$\{\, false \wedge \mathbf{TA}_{post} \,\}$$

new-axiom:

$$\{\, \mathbf{P}[new(\$, cid(tidD(\tau(\text{T}))), univ(\tau(\text{T})))/\text{v}, \$\langle cid(tidD(\tau(\text{T}))), univ(\tau(\text{T}))\rangle/\$] \wedge$$
$$\textstyle\bigwedge_{i=0}^{n} typeof(\text{v}_i) \preceq \tau([\text{v}_i]) \wedge wt(\$) \wedge (static(\text{T@m}) \Leftrightarrow \text{this} = null) \,\}$$
$$\Rightarrow \quad [\![\, \text{T} \preceq_T [\text{v}], \text{Lemma 3.1.7} \,]\!]$$
$$\{\, \mathbf{P}[new(\$, cid(tidD(\tau(\text{T}))), univ(\tau(\text{T})))/\text{v}, \$\langle cid(tidD(\tau(\text{T}))), univ(\tau(\text{T}))\rangle/\$] \wedge$$
$$\textstyle\bigwedge_{i=0}^{n} typeof(\text{v}_i) \preceq \tau([\text{v}_i]) \wedge \tau(\text{T}) \preceq \tau([\text{v}]) \wedge wt(\$) \wedge (orepT?(T) \Rightarrow \text{this} \neq null) \,\}$$
$$\Rightarrow \quad [\![\, \textbf{store11}, \textbf{store5}, grndT?(\text{T}) \vee orepT?(\text{T}) \vee trepT?(\text{T}) \,]\!]$$
$$\{\, \mathbf{P}[new(\$, cid(tidD(\tau(\text{T}))), univ(\tau(\text{T})))/\text{v}, \$\langle cid(tidD(\tau(\text{T}))), univ(\tau(\text{T}))\rangle/\$] \wedge$$
$$\textstyle\bigwedge_{i=0}^{n} typeof(\text{v}_i) \preceq \tau([\text{v}_i]) \wedge wt(\$\langle cid(tidD(\tau(\text{T}))), univ(\tau(\text{T}))\rangle) \wedge$$
$$typeof(new(\$, cid(tidD(\tau(\text{T}))), univ(\tau(\text{T})))) \preceq \tau(\text{T}) \wedge \tau(\text{T}) \preceq \tau([\text{v}]) \,\}$$
$$\Rightarrow \quad [\![\, \text{v} \not\equiv \textbf{this} \,]\!]$$
$$\{\, (\mathbf{P} \wedge \textstyle\bigwedge_{i=0}^{n} typeof(\text{v}_i) \preceq \tau([\text{v}_i]) \wedge wt(\$))[new(\$, cid(tidD(\tau(\text{T}))), univ(\tau(\text{T})))/$$
$$\text{v}, \$\langle cid(tidD(\tau(\text{T}))), univ(\tau(\text{T}))\rangle/\$] \,\}$$
$$\text{v} = \text{new T();} \quad [\![\text{ new-axiom }]\!]$$
$$\{\, \mathbf{P} \wedge \textstyle\bigwedge_{i=0}^{n} typeof(\text{v}_i) \preceq \tau([\text{v}_i]) \wedge wt(\$) \,\}$$

cast-axiom:

$$\{\, typeof(\text{e}) \preceq \tau(\text{T}) \wedge \mathbf{P}[\text{e}/\text{v}] \wedge \textstyle\bigwedge_{i=0}^{n} typeof(\text{v}_i) \preceq \tau([\text{v}_i]) \wedge wt(\$) \wedge$$
$$(static(\text{T@m}) \Leftrightarrow \text{this} = null) \,\}$$
$$\Rightarrow \quad [\![\, \text{T} \preceq_T [\text{v}], \text{Lemma 3.1.7} \,]\!]$$
$$\{\, typeof(\text{e}) \preceq \tau(\text{T}) \wedge \mathbf{P}[\text{e}/\text{v}] \wedge \textstyle\bigwedge_{i=0}^{n} typeof(\text{v}_i) \preceq \tau([\text{v}_i]) \wedge$$
$$typeof(\text{e}) \preceq \tau([\text{v}]) \wedge wt(\$) \,\}$$
$$\Rightarrow \quad [\![\, \text{v} \not\equiv \textbf{this} \,]\!]$$
$$\{\, typeof(\text{e}) \preceq \tau(\text{T}) \wedge (\mathbf{P} \wedge \textstyle\bigwedge_{i=0}^{n} typeof(\text{v}_i) \preceq \tau([\text{v}_i]) \wedge wt(\$))[\text{e}/\text{v}] \,\}$$
$$\text{v} = \text{(T) e;} \quad [\![\text{ cast-axiom }]\!]$$
$$\{\, \mathbf{P} \wedge \textstyle\bigwedge_{i=0}^{n} typeof(\text{v}_i) \preceq \tau([\text{v}_i]) \wedge wt(\$) \,\}$$

skip-axiom:

$\{\ \mathbf{P} \wedge \bigwedge_{i=0}^{n} \mathit{typeof}(\mathrm{v}_i) \preceq \tau([\mathtt{v}_i]) \wedge \mathit{wt}(\$) \wedge (\mathit{static}(\mathrm{T@m}) \Leftrightarrow \mathrm{this} = \mathit{null})\ \}$

$\Rightarrow$

$\{\ \mathbf{P} \wedge \bigwedge_{i=0}^{n} \mathit{typeof}(\mathrm{v}_i) \preceq \tau([\mathtt{v}_i]) \wedge \mathit{wt}(\$)\ \}$

; ⟦ skip-axiom ⟧

$\{\ \mathbf{P} \wedge \bigwedge_{i=0}^{n} \mathit{typeof}(\mathrm{v}_i) \preceq \tau([\mathtt{v}_i]) \wedge \mathit{wt}(\$)\ \}$

field-read-axiom:

$\{\ \mathrm{w} \neq \mathit{null} \wedge \mathbf{P}[\$(\mathit{locC}(\mathrm{w}, \mathrm{S@f}))/\mathrm{v}] \wedge \bigwedge_{i=0}^{n} \mathit{typeof}(\mathrm{v}_i) \preceq \tau([\mathtt{v}_i]) \wedge \mathit{wt}(\$) \wedge$
$(\mathit{static}(\mathrm{T@m}) \Leftrightarrow \mathrm{this} = \mathit{null})\ \}$

$\Rightarrow$ ⟦ $\mathit{lrtype}(\mathit{locC}(\mathrm{w}, \mathrm{S@f})) = \mathit{dyn}([\mathrm{S@f}], \mathrm{w}, \mathit{univV}(\mathrm{w}))$ ⟧

$\{\ \mathrm{w} \neq \mathit{null} \wedge \mathbf{P}[\$(\mathit{locC}(\mathrm{w}, \mathrm{S@f}))/\mathrm{v}] \wedge \bigwedge_{i=0}^{n} \mathit{typeof}(\mathrm{v}_i) \preceq \tau([\mathtt{v}_i]) \wedge$
$\mathit{typeof}(\$(\mathit{locC}(\mathrm{w}, \mathrm{S@f}))) \preceq \mathit{dyn}([\mathrm{S@f}], \mathrm{w}, \mathit{univV}(\mathrm{w})) \wedge$
$\mathit{wt}(\$) \wedge (\mathit{orepT?}([\mathtt{w}]) \Rightarrow \mathrm{this} \neq \mathit{null})\ \}$

$\Rightarrow$ ⟦ Case 1: $\mathit{roT?}([\mathtt{w}])$: Lemma 3.2.3
Case 2: $\neg \mathit{roT?}([\mathtt{w}]) \wedge (\mathit{orepT?}([\mathrm{S@f}]) \Rightarrow \mathtt{w} \cong \mathtt{this} \cong \mathrm{v}_0 \vee \mathit{roT?}([\mathtt{w}]))$
$\Rightarrow \mathit{dyn}([\mathrm{S@f}], \mathrm{w}, \mathit{univV}(\mathrm{w})) = \tau([\mathtt{w}] * [\mathrm{S@f}])$
(Lemmas 3.2.2, 3.1.6, 3.1.4) ⟧

$\{\ \mathrm{w} \neq \mathit{null} \wedge \mathbf{P}[\$(\mathit{locC}(\mathrm{w}, \mathrm{S@f}))/\mathrm{v}] \wedge \bigwedge_{i=0}^{n} \mathit{typeof}(\mathrm{v}_i) \preceq \tau([\mathtt{v}_i]) \wedge$
$\mathit{typeof}(\$(\mathit{locC}(\mathrm{w}, \mathrm{S@f}))) \preceq \tau([\mathtt{w}] * [\mathrm{S@f}]) \wedge \mathit{wt}(\$)\ \}$

$\Rightarrow$ ⟦ $[\mathtt{w}] * [\mathrm{S@f}] \preceq_T [\mathrm{v}]$, Lemma 3.1.7 ⟧

$\{\ \mathrm{w} \neq \mathit{null} \wedge \mathbf{P}[\$(\mathit{locC}(\mathrm{w}, \mathrm{S@f}))/\mathrm{v}] \wedge \bigwedge_{i=0}^{n} \mathit{typeof}(\mathrm{v}_i) \preceq \tau([\mathtt{v}_i]) \wedge$
$\mathit{typeof}(\$(\mathit{locC}(\mathrm{w}, \mathrm{S@f}))) \preceq \tau([\mathrm{v}]) \wedge \mathit{wt}(\$)\ \}$

$\Rightarrow$ ⟦ $\mathtt{v} \not\cong \mathtt{this}$ ⟧

$\{\ \mathrm{w} \neq \mathit{null} \wedge (\mathbf{P} \wedge \bigwedge_{i=0}^{n} \mathit{typeof}(\mathrm{v}_i) \preceq \tau([\mathtt{v}_i]) \wedge \mathit{wt}(\$))[\$(\mathit{locC}(\mathrm{w}, \mathrm{S@f}))/\mathrm{v}]\ \}$

v = w.S@f; ⟦ field-read-axiom ⟧

$\{\ \mathbf{P} \wedge \bigwedge_{i=0}^{n} \mathit{typeof}(\mathrm{v}_i) \preceq \tau([\mathtt{v}_i]) \wedge \mathit{wt}(\$)\ \}$

field-write-axiom:

$\{\ \mathrm{w} \neq \mathit{null} \wedge \mathbf{P}[\$\langle \mathit{locC}(\mathrm{w}, \mathrm{S@f}) := \mathrm{e}\rangle/\$] \wedge \bigwedge_{i=0}^{n} \mathit{typeof}(\mathrm{v}_i) \preceq \tau([\mathtt{v}_i]) \wedge \mathit{wt}(\$) \wedge$
$(\mathit{static}(\mathrm{T@m}) \Leftrightarrow \mathrm{this} = \mathit{null})\ \}$

$\Rightarrow$ ⟦ $\mathit{typeof}(\mathrm{e}) \preceq \tau([\mathtt{e}]), [\mathtt{e}] \preceq_T [\mathtt{w}] * [\mathrm{S@f}]$, Lemma 3.1.7 ⟧

$\{\ \mathrm{w} \neq \mathit{null} \wedge \mathbf{P}[\$\langle \mathit{locC}(\mathrm{w}, \mathrm{S@f}) := \mathrm{e}\rangle/\$] \wedge \bigwedge_{i=0}^{n} \mathit{typeof}(\mathrm{v}_i) \preceq \tau([\mathtt{v}_i]) \wedge \mathit{wt}(\$) \wedge$
$(\mathit{orepT?}([\mathtt{w}]) \Rightarrow \mathrm{this} \neq \mathit{null}) \wedge \mathit{typeof}(\mathrm{e}) \preceq \tau([\mathtt{w}] * [\mathrm{S@f}])\ \}$

$\Rightarrow$ ⟦ $\neg \mathit{roT?}([\mathtt{w}]), \mathit{orepT?}([\mathrm{S@f}]) \Rightarrow \mathtt{w} \cong \mathtt{this}$, Lemmas 3.2.2, 3.1.6, 3.1.4 ⟧

$\{\ \mathrm{w} \neq \mathit{null} \wedge \mathbf{P}[\$\langle \mathit{locC}(\mathrm{w}, \mathrm{S@f}) := \mathrm{e}\rangle/\$] \wedge \bigwedge_{i=0}^{n} \mathit{typeof}(\mathrm{v}_i) \preceq \tau([\mathtt{v}_i]) \wedge \mathit{wt}(\$) \wedge$
$\mathit{typeof}(\$\langle \mathit{locC}(\mathrm{w}, \mathrm{S@f}) := \mathrm{e}\rangle(\mathit{locC}(\mathrm{w}, \mathrm{S@f}))) \preceq \mathit{dyn}([\mathrm{S@f}], \mathrm{w}, \mathit{univV}(\mathrm{w}))\ \}$

$\Rightarrow$ ⟦ $\mathit{lrtype}(\mathit{locC}(\mathrm{w}, \mathrm{S@f})) = \mathit{dyn}([\mathrm{S@f}], \mathrm{w}, \mathit{univV}(\mathrm{w}))$ ⟧

$\{\ \mathrm{w} \neq \mathit{null} \wedge \mathbf{P}[\$\langle \mathit{locC}(\mathrm{w}, \mathrm{S@f}) := \mathrm{e}\rangle/\$] \wedge \bigwedge_{i=0}^{n} \mathit{typeof}(\mathrm{v}_i) \preceq \tau([\mathtt{v}_i]) \wedge$
$\mathit{wt}(\$\langle \mathit{locC}(\mathrm{w}, \mathrm{S@f}) := \mathrm{e}\rangle)\ \}$

$\Rightarrow$

$\{\ \mathrm{w} \neq \mathit{null} \wedge (\mathbf{P} \wedge \bigwedge_{i=0}^{n} \mathit{typeof}(\mathrm{v}_i) \preceq \tau([\mathtt{v}_i]) \wedge \mathit{wt}(\$))[\$\langle \mathit{locC}(\mathrm{w}, \mathrm{S@f}) := \mathrm{e}\rangle/\$]\ \}$

w.S@f = e; ⟦ field-write-axiom ⟧

$\{\ \mathbf{P} \wedge \bigwedge_{i=0}^{n} \mathit{typeof}(\mathrm{v}_i) \preceq \tau([\mathtt{v}_i]) \wedge \mathit{wt}(\$)\ \}$

Predefined method implementations: All predefined methods are readonly and have a specification of their result. So the type safety proof is analogous for all methods. Here, we show the proof for Object@equals:

$$\{\, \mathrm{p} = O \wedge \mathrm{this} = T \wedge tidD(typeof(\mathrm{this})) = ctid(\mathrm{Object}) \wedge \$ = OS \wedge \mathbf{P} \wedge \\ typeof(\mathrm{this}) \preceq \tau(roT(ctid(\mathrm{Object}))) \wedge typeof(\mathrm{p}) \preceq \tau(roT(ctid(\mathrm{Object}))) \wedge \\ wt(\$) \wedge R = \tau(booleanT) \,\}$$

$$\Rightarrow \quad [\![\, \text{Definition of } \tau \text{ and } dyn \,]\!]$$

$$\{\, \mathrm{p} = O \wedge \mathrm{this} = T \wedge tidD(typeof(\mathrm{this})) = ctid(\mathrm{Object}) \wedge \$ = OS \wedge \mathbf{P} \wedge \\ R = booleanDT \wedge wt(OS) \,\}$$

$$\overline{\hspace{20em}} \downarrow \quad [\![\, \text{inv-rule} \,]\!]$$

$$\{\, \mathrm{p} = O \wedge \mathrm{this} = T \wedge tidD(typeof(\mathrm{this})) = ctid(\mathrm{Object}) \wedge \$ = OS \wedge \mathbf{P} \,\}$$

Object@equals $[\![$ Semantics of pre-post-specifications for a suitable $\mathbf{P}$ $]\!]$

$$\{\, \mathrm{result} = bool(O = T) \wedge \$ = OS \,\}$$

$$\overline{\hspace{20em}} \uparrow \quad [\![\, \text{inv-rule} \,]\!]$$

$$\{\, \mathrm{result} = bool(O = T) \wedge \$ = OS \wedge R = booleanDT \wedge wt(OS) \,\}$$

$$\Rightarrow \quad [\![\, \text{Definition of } typeof \,]\!]$$

$$\{\, \mathrm{result} = bool(O = T) \wedge \$ = OS \wedge typeof(\mathrm{result}) \preceq R \wedge wt(\$) \,\}$$

Induction Step. For the induction step, we can assume that type annotations are added to all proof trees up to depth N. We show now, that the annotations can be added to proof trees of depth $N+1$ by case distinction on the possible rule applications that lead to proof trees of depth $N+1$. That is, we can assume the induction hypothesis for the antecedents of the rule applications and have to prove it for the succedents. The induction step is trivial for many rules. We present only the interesting cases here.

assumpt-intro-rule:

$$\frac{typed(\mathcal{A}) \triangleright typed(\mathbf{A})}{typed(\mathbf{A}_0)\ ,\ typed(\mathcal{A}) \triangleright typed(\mathbf{A})} \quad [\![\, \text{assumpt-intro-rule} \,]\!]$$

Invocation-rule: In the following cases, each sequent has $typed(\mathcal{A})$ as assumptions. Note that (1) $\mathrm{p}_0, \ldots, \mathrm{p}_l$ are the formal parameters of S:n (i.e., $\mathrm{p}_i = par(\mathrm{S{:}n}, i), 1 \leq i$); (2) $\mathrm{v}_0, \ldots, \mathrm{v}_n$ are the local variables and formal parameters of T@m (the enclosing method implementation); (3) $[\mathrm{v}]$ is a logical constant and therefore a Σ-formula (in contrast to v which is a program variable). Recall that $\mathcal{U}$ behaves like a program variable that can be substituted for a logical variable by the invocation-var-rule.

$\{\ \mathrm{w} \neq \mathit{null} \wedge \mathbf{P}[\mathrm{w}/\mathrm{this}, \mathrm{e}_1/\mathrm{p}_1, \ldots, \mathrm{e}_l/\mathrm{p}_l, \mathit{univV}(\mathrm{w})/\mathcal{U}] \wedge$
$\bigwedge_{i=0}^{n} \mathit{typeof}(\mathrm{v}_i) \preceq \tau([\mathrm{v}_i]) \wedge \mathit{wt}(\$) \wedge (\mathit{static}(\mathrm{T@m}) \Leftrightarrow \mathrm{this} = \mathit{null})\ \}$

$\Rightarrow$ ⟦ if variables are well-typed then primitive expressions are, too ⟧

$\{\ \mathrm{w} \neq \mathit{null} \wedge \mathbf{P}[\mathrm{w}/\mathrm{this}, \mathrm{e}_1/\mathrm{p}_1, \ldots, \mathrm{e}_l/\mathrm{p}_l, \mathit{univV}(\mathrm{w})/\mathcal{U}] \wedge \bigwedge_{i=0}^{l} \mathit{typeof}(\mathrm{e}_i) \preceq \tau([\mathtt{e}_i]) \wedge$
$\mathit{wt}(\$) \wedge \bigwedge_{i=0}^{n} \mathit{typeof}(\mathrm{v}_i) \preceq \tau([\mathrm{v}_i]) \wedge (\mathit{orepT?}([\mathtt{w}]) \Rightarrow \mathrm{this} \neq \mathit{null})\ \}$

$\Rightarrow$ ⟦ $[\mathtt{e}_i] \preceq_T [\mathtt{w}] * [\mathtt{p}_i]$, Lemma 3.1.7 ⟧

$\{\ \mathrm{w} \neq \mathit{null} \wedge \mathbf{P}[\mathrm{w}/\mathrm{this}, \mathrm{e}_1/\mathrm{p}_1, \ldots, \mathrm{e}_l/\mathrm{p}_l, \mathit{univV}(\mathrm{w})/\mathcal{U}] \wedge$
$\bigwedge_{i=0}^{l} \mathit{typeof}(\mathrm{e}_i) \preceq \tau([\mathtt{w}] * [\mathtt{p}_i]) \wedge \mathit{wt}(\$) \wedge$
$\bigwedge_{i=0}^{n} \mathit{typeof}(\mathrm{v}_i) \preceq \tau([\mathrm{v}_i]) \wedge (\mathit{orepT?}([\mathtt{w}]) \Rightarrow \mathrm{this} \neq \mathit{null})\ \}$

$\Rightarrow$ ⟦ Case 1: $\mathit{roT?}([\mathtt{w}]) \Rightarrow \mathit{roT?}([\mathtt{p}_i]) \vee \mathit{booleanT?}([\mathtt{p}_i]) \vee \mathit{intT?}([\mathtt{p}_i])$
(Context condition for readonly methods, Paragraph 2.1.1.1)
Case 2: $\neg \mathit{roT?}([\mathtt{w}])$, $(\mathit{orepT?}([\mathtt{p}_i]) \Rightarrow \mathtt{w} \cong \mathtt{this})$,
Lemmas 3.2.2, 3.1.6, 3.1.4 ⟧

$\{\ \mathrm{w} \neq \mathit{null} \wedge \mathbf{P}[\mathrm{w}/\mathrm{this}, \mathrm{e}_1/\mathrm{p}_1, \ldots, \mathrm{e}_l/\mathrm{p}_l, \mathit{univV}(\mathrm{w})/\mathcal{U}] \wedge \bigwedge_{i=0}^{n} \mathit{typeof}(\mathrm{v}_i) \preceq \tau([\mathrm{v}_i]) \wedge$
$\bigwedge_{i=0}^{l} \mathit{typeof}(\mathrm{e}_i) \preceq \mathit{dyn}([\mathtt{p}_i], \mathrm{w}, \mathit{univV}(\mathrm{w})) \wedge \mathit{wt}(\$) \wedge (\mathit{orepT?}([\mathtt{w}]) \Rightarrow \mathrm{this} \neq \mathit{null})\ \}$

$\Rightarrow$ ⟦ Case 1: $\mathit{roT?}([\mathtt{w}])$, Lemma 3.2.3
Case 2: $\neg \mathit{roT?}([\mathtt{w}])$, $\mathit{orepT?}(\mathit{ret}(\mathrm{S{:}n})) \Rightarrow \mathtt{w} \cong \mathtt{this}$,
Lemmas 3.2.2, 3.1.6, 3.1.4 ⟧

$\{\ \mathrm{w} \neq \mathit{null} \wedge \mathbf{P}[\mathrm{w}/\mathrm{this}, \mathrm{e}_1/\mathrm{p}_1, \ldots, \mathrm{e}_l/\mathrm{p}_l, \mathit{univV}(\mathrm{w})/\mathcal{U}] \wedge$
$\bigwedge_{i=0}^{l} \mathit{typeof}(\mathrm{e}_i) \preceq \mathit{dyn}([\mathtt{p}_i], \mathrm{w}, \mathit{univV}(\mathrm{w})) \wedge \mathit{wt}(\$) \wedge$
$\bigwedge_{i=0}^{n} \mathit{typeof}(\mathrm{v}_i) \preceq \mathit{dyn}([\mathrm{v}_i], \mathrm{this}, \mathcal{U}) \wedge$
$\mathit{dyn}(\mathit{ret}(\mathrm{S{:}n}), \mathrm{w}, \mathit{univV}(\mathrm{w})) \preceq \mathit{dyn}([\mathtt{w}] * \mathit{ret}(\mathrm{S{:}n}), \mathrm{this}, \mathcal{U})\ \}$

$\Rightarrow$

$\{\ \exists R : \mathrm{w} \neq \mathit{null} \wedge (\mathbf{P} \wedge \bigwedge_{i=0}^{l} \mathit{typeof}(\mathrm{p}_i) \preceq \tau([\mathtt{p}_i]) \wedge \mathit{wt}(\$) \wedge$
$R = \tau(\mathit{ret}(\mathrm{S{:}n})))[\mathrm{w}/\mathrm{this}, \mathrm{e}_1/\mathrm{p}_1, \ldots, \mathrm{e}_l/\mathrm{p}_l, \mathit{univV}(\mathrm{w})/\mathcal{U}] \wedge$
$R \preceq \mathit{dyn}([\mathtt{w}] * \mathit{ret}(\mathrm{S{:}n}), \mathrm{this}, \mathcal{U}) \wedge \bigwedge_{i=0, \mathrm{v}_i \not\cong \mathrm{v}}^{n} \mathit{typeof}(\mathrm{v}_i) \preceq \mathit{dyn}([\mathrm{v}_i], \mathrm{this}, \mathcal{U})\ \}$

———————————————————— $\downarrow$ ⟦ ex-rule ⟧

$\{\ \mathrm{w} \neq \mathit{null} \wedge (\mathbf{P} \wedge \bigwedge_{i=0}^{l} \mathit{typeof}(\mathrm{p}_i) \preceq \tau([\mathtt{p}_i]) \wedge \mathit{wt}(\$) \wedge$
$R = \tau(\mathit{ret}(\mathrm{S{:}n})))[\mathrm{w}/\mathrm{this}, \mathrm{e}_1/\mathrm{p}_1, \ldots, \mathrm{e}_l/\mathrm{p}_l, \mathit{univV}(\mathrm{w})/\mathcal{U}] \wedge$
$R \preceq \mathit{dyn}([\mathtt{w}] * \mathit{ret}(\mathrm{S{:}n}), \mathrm{this}, \mathcal{U}) \wedge \bigwedge_{i=0, \mathrm{v}_i \not\cong \mathrm{v}}^{n} \mathit{typeof}(\mathrm{v}_i) \preceq \mathit{dyn}([\mathrm{v}_i], \mathrm{this}, \mathcal{U})\ \}$

———————————————————— $\downarrow$ ⟦ var-rule ⟧

$\{\ \mathrm{w} \neq \mathit{null} \wedge (\mathbf{P} \wedge \bigwedge_{i=0}^{l} \mathit{typeof}(\mathrm{p}_i) \preceq \tau([\mathtt{p}_i]) \wedge \mathit{wt}(\$) \wedge$
$R = \tau(\mathit{ret}(\mathrm{S{:}n})))[\mathrm{w}/\mathrm{this}, \mathrm{e}_1/\mathrm{p}_1, \ldots, \mathrm{e}_l/\mathrm{p}_l, \mathit{univV}(\mathrm{w})/\mathcal{U}] \wedge$
$R \preceq \mathit{dyn}([\mathtt{w}] * \mathit{ret}(\mathrm{S{:}n}), R0, U) \wedge \bigwedge_{i=0, \mathrm{v}_i \not\cong \mathrm{v}}^{n} \mathit{typeof}(R_i) \preceq \mathit{dyn}([\mathrm{v}_i], R0, U)\ \}$

———————————————————— $\downarrow$ ⟦ inv-rule ⟧

$\{\ \mathrm{w} \neq \mathit{null} \wedge (\mathbf{P} \wedge \bigwedge_{i=0}^{l} \mathit{typeof}(\mathrm{p}_i) \preceq \tau([\mathtt{p}_i]) \wedge \mathit{wt}(\$) \wedge$
$R = \tau(\mathit{ret}(\mathrm{S{:}n})))[\mathrm{w}/\mathrm{this}, \mathrm{e}_1/\mathrm{p}_1, \ldots, \mathrm{e}_l/\mathrm{p}_l, \mathit{univV}(\mathrm{w})/\mathcal{U}]\ \}$

$\mathrm{v} = \mathrm{w.S{:}n}(\mathrm{e}_1, \ldots, \mathrm{e}_l);$ ⟦ applying the invocation-rule to the ind. hypothesis ⟧

$\{\ (\mathbf{Q} \wedge \mathit{typeof}(\mathrm{result}) \preceq R \wedge \mathit{wt}(\$))[\mathrm{v}/\mathrm{result}]\ \}$

$\Rightarrow$

$\{\ \mathbf{Q}[\mathrm{v}/\mathrm{result}] \wedge \mathit{typeof}(\mathrm{v}) \preceq R \wedge \mathit{wt}(\$)\ \}$

———————————————————— $\uparrow$ ⟦ inv-rule ⟧

$$\{\ \mathbf{Q}[\mathrm{v}/\mathrm{result}] \wedge \mathit{typeof}(\mathrm{v}) \preceq R \wedge \mathit{wt}(\$)\wedge$$
$$R \preceq \mathit{dyn}([\mathtt{w}] * \mathit{ret}(\mathrm{S{:}n}), R0, U) \wedge \textstyle\bigwedge_{i=0,\mathrm{v}_i \not\equiv \mathrm{v}}^{n} \mathit{typeof}(R_i) \preceq \mathit{dyn}([\mathrm{v}_i], R0, U)\ \}$$

$$\overline{\hspace{20em}}\uparrow\ [\![\ \text{var-rule}\ ]\!]$$

$$\{\ \mathbf{Q}[\mathrm{v}/\mathrm{result}] \wedge \mathit{typeof}(\mathrm{v}) \preceq R \wedge \mathit{wt}(\$)\wedge$$
$$R \preceq \mathit{dyn}([\mathtt{w}] * \mathit{ret}(\mathrm{S{:}n}), \mathrm{this}, \mathcal{U}) \wedge \textstyle\bigwedge_{i=0,\mathrm{v}_i \not\equiv \mathrm{v}}^{n} \mathit{typeof}(\mathrm{v}_i) \preceq \mathit{dyn}([\mathrm{v}_i], \mathrm{this}, \mathcal{U})\ \}$$
$$\Rightarrow\quad [\![\ [\mathtt{w}] * \mathit{ret}(\mathrm{S{:}n}) \preceq_T [\mathrm{v}],\ \text{Lemma 3.1.7}\ ]\!]$$
$$\{\ \mathbf{Q}[\mathrm{v}/\mathrm{result}] \wedge \mathit{typeof}(\mathrm{v}) \preceq \tau([\mathrm{v}]) \wedge \mathit{wt}(\$) \wedge \textstyle\bigwedge_{i=0,\mathrm{v}_i \not\equiv \mathrm{v}}^{n} \mathit{typeof}(\mathrm{v}_i) \preceq \tau([\mathrm{v}_i])\ \}$$
$$\Rightarrow$$
$$\{\ \mathbf{Q}[\mathrm{v}/\mathrm{result}] \wedge \textstyle\bigwedge_{i=0}^{n} \mathit{typeof}(\mathrm{v}_i) \preceq \tau([\mathrm{v}_i]) \wedge \mathit{wt}(\$)\ \}$$

$$\overline{\hspace{20em}}\uparrow\ [\![\ \text{ex-rule}\ ]\!]$$

$$\{\ \mathbf{Q}[\mathrm{v}/\mathrm{result}] \wedge \textstyle\bigwedge_{i=0}^{n} \mathit{typeof}(\mathrm{v}_i) \preceq \tau([\mathrm{v}_i]) \wedge \mathit{wt}(\$)\ \}$$

invocation-var-rule:

$$\{\ \mathbf{P}[\mathrm{x}/Z] \wedge \textstyle\bigwedge_{i=0}^{n} \mathit{typeof}(\mathrm{v}_i) \preceq \tau([\mathrm{v}_i]) \wedge \mathit{wt}(\$)\ \}$$
$$\Rightarrow$$
$$\{\ (\mathbf{P} \wedge \textstyle\bigwedge_{i=0}^{n} \mathit{typeof}(\mathrm{v}_i) \preceq \tau([\mathrm{v}_i]) \wedge \mathit{wt}(\$))[\mathrm{x}/Z]\ \}$$
$\mathrm{v} = \mathrm{w.S{:}n}(\mathrm{e}_1, \ldots, \mathrm{e}_l);$ [[applying the invocation-var-rule to the ind. hypothesis]]
$$\{\ (\mathbf{Q} \wedge \textstyle\bigwedge_{i=0}^{n} \mathit{typeof}(\mathrm{v}_i) \preceq \tau([\mathrm{v}_i]) \wedge \mathit{wt}(\$))[\mathrm{x}/Z]\ \}$$
$$\Rightarrow$$
$$\{\ \mathbf{Q}[\mathrm{x}/Z] \wedge \textstyle\bigwedge_{i=0}^{n} \mathit{typeof}(\mathrm{v}_i) \preceq \tau([\mathrm{v}_i]) \wedge \mathit{wt}(\$)\ \}$$

static-invocation-rule:

$$\{\ \mathbf{P}[\mathit{null}/\mathrm{this}, \mathrm{e}_1/\mathrm{p}_1, \ldots, \mathrm{e}_l/\mathrm{p}_l, \mathit{univ}(\tau(\mathrm{S}'))/\mathcal{U}] \wedge \textstyle\bigwedge_{i=0}^{n} \mathit{typeof}(\mathrm{v}_i) \preceq \tau([\mathrm{v}_i])\wedge$$
$$\mathit{wt}(\$) \wedge (\mathit{static}(\mathrm{T@m}) \Leftrightarrow \mathrm{this} = \mathit{null})\ \}$$
$$\Rightarrow\quad [\![\ \text{if variables are well-typed then primitive expressions are, too}\ ]\!]$$
$$\{\ \mathbf{P}[\mathit{null}/\mathrm{this}, \mathrm{e}_1/\mathrm{p}_1, \ldots, \mathrm{e}_l/\mathrm{p}_l, \mathit{univ}(\tau(\mathrm{S}'))/\mathcal{U}] \wedge \textstyle\bigwedge_{i=0}^{l} \mathit{typeof}(\mathrm{e}_i) \preceq \tau([\mathrm{e}_i])\wedge$$
$$\mathit{wt}(\$) \wedge \textstyle\bigwedge_{i=0}^{n} \mathit{typeof}(\mathrm{v}_i) \preceq \tau([\mathrm{v}_i]) \wedge (\mathit{orepT?}(\mathrm{S}') \Rightarrow \mathrm{this} \neq \mathit{null})\ \}$$
$$\Rightarrow\quad [\![\ [\mathrm{e}_i] \preceq_T \mathrm{S}' * [\mathrm{p}_i],\ \text{Lemma 3.1.7}\ ]\!]$$
$$\{\ \mathbf{P}[\mathit{null}/\mathrm{this}, \mathrm{e}_1/\mathrm{p}_1, \ldots, \mathrm{e}_l/\mathrm{p}_l, \mathit{univ}(\tau(\mathrm{S}'))/\mathcal{U}] \wedge \textstyle\bigwedge_{i=0}^{l} \mathit{typeof}(\mathrm{e}_i) \preceq \tau(\mathrm{S}' * [\mathrm{p}_i])\wedge$$
$$\mathit{wt}(\$) \wedge \textstyle\bigwedge_{i=0}^{n} \mathit{typeof}(\mathrm{v}_i) \preceq \tau([\mathrm{v}_i]) \wedge (\mathit{orepT?}(\mathrm{S}') \Rightarrow \mathrm{this} \neq \mathit{null})\ \}$$
$$\Rightarrow\quad [\![\ \neg\mathit{roT?}(\mathrm{S}'),\ \neg\mathit{orepT?}([\mathrm{p}_i]),\ \text{Lemma 3.2.2}\ ]\!]$$
$$\{\ \mathbf{P}[\mathit{null}/\mathrm{this}, \mathrm{e}_1/\mathrm{p}_1, \ldots, \mathrm{e}_l/\mathrm{p}_l, \mathit{univ}(\tau(\mathrm{S}'))/\mathcal{U}] \wedge \textstyle\bigwedge_{i=0}^{n} \mathit{typeof}(\mathrm{v}_i) \preceq \tau([\mathrm{v}_i])\wedge$$
$$\mathit{wt}(\$) \wedge \textstyle\bigwedge_{i=0}^{l} \mathit{typeof}(\mathrm{e}_i) \preceq \mathit{dyn}([\mathrm{p}_i], \mathit{null}, \mathit{univ}(\tau(\mathrm{S}')))\wedge$$
$$(\mathit{orepT?}(\mathrm{S}') \Rightarrow \mathrm{this} \neq \mathit{null})\ \}$$
$$\Rightarrow\quad [\![\ \neg\mathit{roT?}(\mathrm{S}'),\ \neg\mathit{orepT?}(\mathit{ret}(\mathrm{S@n})),\ \text{Lemma 3.2.2}\ ]\!]$$
$$\{\ \mathbf{P}[\mathit{null}/\mathrm{this}, \mathrm{e}_1/\mathrm{p}_1, \ldots, \mathrm{e}_l/\mathrm{p}_l, \mathit{univ}(\tau(\mathrm{S}'))/\mathcal{U}]\wedge$$
$$\textstyle\bigwedge_{i=0}^{l} \mathit{typeof}(\mathrm{e}_i) \preceq \mathit{dyn}([\mathrm{p}_i], \mathit{null}, \mathit{univ}(\tau(\mathrm{S}'))) \wedge \mathit{wt}(\$)\wedge$$
$$\textstyle\bigwedge_{i=0}^{n} \mathit{typeof}(\mathrm{v}_i) \preceq \mathit{dyn}([\mathrm{v}_i], \mathrm{this}, \mathcal{U})\wedge$$
$$\mathit{dyn}(\mathit{ret}(\mathrm{S@n}), \mathit{null}, \mathit{univ}(\tau(\mathrm{S}'))) \preceq \mathit{dyn}(\mathrm{S}' * \mathit{ret}(\mathrm{S@n}), \mathrm{this}, \mathcal{U})\ \}$$
$$\Rightarrow$$

$\{ \exists R : (\mathbf{P} \wedge \bigwedge_{i=0}^{l} \mathit{typeof}(\mathrm{p}_i) \preceq \tau([\mathrm{p}_i]) \wedge \mathit{wt}(\$) \wedge$
$R = \tau(\mathit{ret}(\mathrm{S@n})))[\mathit{null}/\mathrm{this}, \mathrm{e}_1/\mathrm{p}_1, \ldots, \mathrm{e}_l/\mathrm{p}_l, \mathit{univ}(\tau(\mathrm{S}'))/\mathcal{U}] \wedge$
$R \preceq \mathit{dyn}(\mathrm{S}' * \mathit{ret}(\mathrm{S@n}), \mathrm{this}, \mathcal{U}) \wedge \bigwedge_{i=0,\mathrm{v}_i \not\equiv \mathrm{v}}^{n} \mathit{typeof}(\mathrm{v}_i) \preceq \mathit{dyn}([\mathrm{v}_i], \mathrm{this}, \mathcal{U}) \}$

———————————————————— ↓ ⟦ ex-rule ⟧

$\{ (\mathbf{P} \wedge \bigwedge_{i=0}^{l} \mathit{typeof}(\mathrm{p}_i) \preceq \tau([\mathrm{p}_i]) \wedge \mathit{wt}(\$) \wedge$
$R = \tau(\mathit{ret}(\mathrm{S@n})))[\mathit{null}/\mathrm{this}, \mathrm{e}_1/\mathrm{p}_1, \ldots, \mathrm{e}_l/\mathrm{p}_l, \mathit{univ}(\tau(\mathrm{S}'))/\mathcal{U}] \wedge$
$R \preceq \mathit{dyn}(\mathrm{S}' * \mathit{ret}(\mathrm{S@n}), \mathrm{this}, \mathcal{U}) \wedge \bigwedge_{i=0,\mathrm{v}_i \not\equiv \mathrm{v}}^{n} \mathit{typeof}(\mathrm{v}_i) \preceq \mathit{dyn}([\mathrm{v}_i], \mathrm{this}, \mathcal{U}) \}$

———————————————————— ↓ ⟦ var-rule ⟧

$\{ (\mathbf{P} \wedge \bigwedge_{i=0}^{l} \mathit{typeof}(\mathrm{p}_i) \preceq \tau([\mathrm{p}_i]) \wedge \mathit{wt}(\$) \wedge$
$R = \tau(\mathit{ret}(\mathrm{S@n})))[\mathit{null}/\mathrm{this}, \mathrm{e}_1/\mathrm{p}_1, \ldots, \mathrm{e}_l/\mathrm{p}_l, \mathit{univ}(\tau(\mathrm{S}'))/\mathcal{U}] \wedge$
$R \preceq \mathit{dyn}(\mathrm{S}' * \mathit{ret}(\mathrm{S@n}), R0, U) \wedge \bigwedge_{i=0,\mathrm{v}_i \not\equiv \mathrm{v}}^{n} \mathit{typeof}(R_i) \preceq \mathit{dyn}([\mathrm{v}_i], R0, U) \}$

———————————————————— ↓ ⟦ inv-rule ⟧

$\{ (\mathbf{P} \wedge \bigwedge_{i=0}^{l} \mathit{typeof}(\mathrm{p}_i) \preceq \tau([\mathrm{p}_i]) \wedge \mathit{wt}(\$) \wedge$
$R = \tau(\mathit{ret}(\mathrm{S@n})))[\mathit{null}/\mathrm{this}, \mathrm{e}_1/\mathrm{p}_1, \ldots, \mathrm{e}_l/\mathrm{p}_l, \mathit{univ}(\tau(\mathrm{S}'))/\mathcal{U}] \}$
v = S'.S@n($\mathrm{e}_1, \ldots, \mathrm{e}_l$); ⟦ applying the static-invocation-rule to the ind. hyp. ⟧
$\{ (\mathbf{Q} \wedge \mathit{typeof}(\mathrm{result}) \preceq R \wedge \mathit{wt}(\$))[\mathrm{v}/\mathrm{result}] \}$
$\Rightarrow$
$\{ \mathbf{Q}[\mathrm{v}/\mathrm{result}] \wedge \mathit{typeof}(\mathrm{v}) \preceq R \wedge \mathit{wt}(\$) \}$

———————————————————— ↑ ⟦ inv-rule ⟧

$\{ \mathbf{Q}[\mathrm{v}/\mathrm{result}] \wedge \mathit{typeof}(\mathrm{v}) \preceq R \wedge \mathit{wt}(\$) \wedge$
$R \preceq \mathit{dyn}(\mathrm{S}' * \mathit{ret}(\mathrm{S@n}), R0, U) \wedge \bigwedge_{i=0,\mathrm{v}_i \not\equiv \mathrm{v}}^{n} \mathit{typeof}(R_i) \preceq \mathit{dyn}([\mathrm{v}_i], R0, U) \}$

———————————————————— ↑ ⟦ var-rule ⟧

$\{ \mathbf{Q}[\mathrm{v}/\mathrm{result}] \wedge \mathit{typeof}(\mathrm{v}) \preceq R \wedge \mathit{wt}(\$) \wedge$
$R \preceq \mathit{dyn}(\mathrm{S}' * \mathit{ret}(\mathrm{S@n}), \mathrm{this}, \mathcal{U}) \wedge \bigwedge_{i=0,\mathrm{v}_i \not\equiv \mathrm{v}}^{n} \mathit{typeof}(\mathrm{v}_i) \preceq \mathit{dyn}([\mathrm{v}_i], \mathrm{this}, \mathcal{U}) \}$
$\Rightarrow$ ⟦ $\mathrm{S}' * \mathit{ret}(\mathrm{S@n}) \preceq_T [\mathrm{v}]$, Lemma 3.1.7 ⟧
$\{ \mathbf{Q}[\mathrm{v}/\mathrm{result}] \wedge \mathit{typeof}(\mathrm{v}) \preceq \tau([\mathrm{v}]) \wedge \mathit{wt}(\$) \wedge \bigwedge_{i=0,\mathrm{v}_i \not\equiv \mathrm{v}}^{n} \mathit{typeof}(\mathrm{v}_i) \preceq \tau([\mathrm{v}_i]) \}$
$\Rightarrow$
$\{ \mathbf{Q}[\mathrm{v}/\mathrm{result}] \wedge \bigwedge_{i=0}^{n} \mathit{typeof}(\mathrm{v}_i) \preceq \tau([\mathrm{v}_i]) \wedge \mathit{wt}(\$) \}$

———————————————————— ↑ ⟦ ex-rule ⟧

$\{ \mathbf{Q}[\mathrm{v}/\mathrm{result}] \wedge \bigwedge_{i=0}^{n} \mathit{typeof}(\mathrm{v}_i) \preceq \tau([\mathrm{v}_i]) \wedge \mathit{wt}(\$) \}$

Implementation-rule: Since assumptions are important in the case for the implementation-rule, we do not display it as proof outline. Instead, we use the usual notation for subsequent rule applications, which can easily be seen by the missing arrows at the end of the horizontal lines. In the proof, we use the equality [`result`] = *ret*(T@m).

$$\mathcal{A}, \{\, \mathbf{P} \wedge \bigwedge_{i=0}^{k} \mathit{typeof}(\mathrm{v}_i) \preceq \tau([\mathrm{v}_i]) \wedge \mathit{wt}(\$) \wedge R = \tau(\mathit{ret}(\mathrm{T@m}))\,\}$$
$$\mathrm{T@m}\ \{\, \mathbf{Q} \wedge \mathit{typeof}(\mathrm{result}) \preceq R \wedge \mathit{wt}(\$)\,\} \triangleright$$
$$\{\, \mathbf{P} \wedge (\mathit{staticM}(\mathrm{T@m}) \Leftrightarrow \mathrm{this} = \mathit{null}) \wedge \bigwedge_{i=k+1}^{n} \mathrm{v}_i = \mathit{init}(\tau([\mathrm{v}_i])) \wedge$$
$$\bigwedge_{i=0}^{n} \mathit{typeof}(\mathrm{v}_i) \preceq \tau([\mathrm{v}_i]) \wedge \mathit{wt}(\$) \wedge (\mathit{staticM}(\mathrm{T@m}) \Leftrightarrow \mathrm{this} = \mathit{null})\,\}$$
$$\mathit{body}(\mathrm{T@m})\ \{\, \mathbf{Q} \wedge \bigwedge_{i=0}^{n} \mathit{typeof}(\mathrm{v}_i) \preceq \tau([\mathrm{v}_i]) \wedge \mathit{wt}(\$)\,\}$$

[[inv-rule]]

$$\mathcal{A}, \{\, \mathbf{P} \wedge \bigwedge_{i=0}^{k} \mathit{typeof}(\mathrm{v}_i) \preceq \tau([\mathrm{v}_i]) \wedge \mathit{wt}(\$) \wedge R = \tau(\mathit{ret}(\mathrm{T@m}))\,\}$$
$$\mathrm{T@m}\ \{\, \mathbf{Q} \wedge \mathit{typeof}(\mathrm{result}) \preceq R \wedge \mathit{wt}(\$)\,\} \triangleright$$
$$\{\, \mathbf{P} \wedge (\mathit{staticM}(\mathrm{T@m}) \Leftrightarrow \mathrm{this} = \mathit{null}) \wedge \bigwedge_{i=k+1}^{n} \mathrm{v}_i = \mathit{init}(\tau([\mathrm{v}_i])) \wedge \mathit{wt}(\$) \wedge$$
$$\bigwedge_{i=0}^{n} \mathit{typeof}(\mathrm{v}_i) \preceq \tau([\mathrm{v}_i]) \wedge (\mathit{staticM}(\mathrm{T@m}) \Leftrightarrow \mathrm{this} = \mathit{null}) \wedge R = \tau(\mathit{ret}(\mathrm{T@m}))\,\}$$
$$\mathit{body}(\mathrm{T@m})\ \{\, \mathbf{Q} \wedge \bigwedge_{i=0}^{n} \mathit{typeof}(\mathrm{v}_i) \preceq \tau([\mathrm{v}_i]) \wedge \mathit{wt}(\$) \wedge R = \tau(\mathit{ret}(\mathrm{T@m}))\,\}$$

[[strength-rule]]

$$\mathcal{A}, \{\, \mathbf{P} \wedge \bigwedge_{i=0}^{k} \mathit{typeof}(\mathrm{v}_i) \preceq \tau([\mathrm{v}_i]) \wedge \mathit{wt}(\$) \wedge R = \tau(\mathit{ret}(\mathrm{T@m}))\,\}$$
$$\mathrm{T@m}\ \{\, \mathbf{Q} \wedge \mathit{typeof}(\mathrm{result}) \preceq R \wedge \mathit{wt}(\$)\,\} \triangleright$$
$$\{\, \mathbf{P} \wedge (\mathit{staticM}(\mathrm{T@m}) \Leftrightarrow \mathrm{this} = \mathit{null}) \wedge \bigwedge_{i=k+1}^{n} \mathrm{v}_i = \mathit{init}(\tau([\mathrm{v}_i])) \wedge$$
$$\bigwedge_{i=0}^{k} \mathit{typeof}(\mathrm{v}_i) \preceq \tau([\mathrm{v}_i]) \wedge \mathit{wt}(\$) \wedge R = \tau(\mathit{ret}(\mathrm{T@m}))\,\}$$
$$\mathit{body}(\mathrm{T@m})\ \{\, \mathbf{Q} \wedge \bigwedge_{i=0}^{n} \mathit{typeof}(\mathrm{v}_i) \preceq \tau([\mathrm{v}_i]) \wedge \mathit{wt}(\$) \wedge R = \tau(\mathit{ret}(\mathrm{T@m}))\,\}$$

[[weak-rule]]

$$\mathcal{A}, \{\, \mathbf{P} \wedge \bigwedge_{i=0}^{k} \mathit{typeof}(\mathrm{v}_i) \preceq \tau([\mathrm{v}_i]) \wedge \mathit{wt}(\$) \wedge R = \tau(\mathit{ret}(\mathrm{T@m}))\,\}$$
$$\mathrm{T@m}\ \{\, \mathbf{Q} \wedge \mathit{typeof}(\mathrm{result}) \preceq R \wedge \mathit{wt}(\$)\,\} \triangleright$$
$$\{\, \mathbf{P} \wedge (\mathit{staticM}(\mathrm{T@m}) \Leftrightarrow \mathrm{this} = \mathit{null}) \wedge \bigwedge_{i=k+1}^{n} \mathrm{v}_i = \mathit{init}(\tau([\mathrm{v}_i])) \wedge$$
$$\bigwedge_{i=0}^{k} \mathit{typeof}(\mathrm{v}_i) \preceq \tau([\mathrm{v}_i]) \wedge \mathit{wt}(\$) \wedge R = \tau(\mathit{ret}(\mathrm{T@m}))\,\}$$
$$\mathit{body}(\mathrm{T@m})\ \{\, \mathbf{Q} \wedge \mathit{typeof}(\mathrm{result}) \preceq R \wedge \mathit{wt}(\$)\,\}$$

[[implementation-rule]]

$$\mathcal{A} \triangleright \{\, \mathbf{P} \wedge \bigwedge_{i=0}^{k} \mathit{typeof}(\mathrm{v}_i) \preceq \tau([\mathrm{v}_i]) \wedge \mathit{wt}(\$) \wedge R = \tau(\mathit{ret}(\mathrm{T@m}))\,\}$$
$$\mathrm{T@m}\ \{\, \mathbf{Q} \wedge \mathit{typeof}(\mathrm{result}) \preceq R \wedge \mathit{wt}(\$)\,\}$$

□

3.2.2 Liveness Properties

Mojave guarantees that all objects held by local variables or formal parameters are alive. Since objects can be referenced in programs only through program variables, and since locations can only hold living objects (see Axiom **store8**), all objects reachable in a program state are alive. Furthermore, Mojave does not allow objects to be deleted. That is, all operations on object stores leave living objects alive. We formalize these properties as follows:

Definition 3.2.4 (Liveness Annotations). *Like for type annotations (see Def. 3.2.3), we use the operators lal and oal to add liveness annotations about local variables and formal parameters resp. about all living objects to a triple. The operator lal expresses that all objects held by local variables or formal parameters are alive. Its definition depends on the kind of triple it is applied to:*

- *Let* m *be a virtual method* T:m *or a method implementation* T@m. *For method annotations, lal*({ **P** } m { **Q** }) *yields*

  $\{ \mathbf{P} \wedge \bigwedge_{i=0}^{k} \mathit{alive}(\mathrm{v}_i, \$) \}$ m $\{ \mathbf{Q} \wedge \mathit{alive}(\mathrm{result}, \$) \}$

  where $\mathrm{v}_0, \ldots, \mathrm{v}_k$ *are the formal parameters of* m.
- *For statement annotations, lal*({ **P** } STMT { **Q** }) *yields*

  $\{ \mathbf{P} \wedge \bigwedge_{i=0}^{n} \mathit{alive}(\mathrm{v}_i, \$) \}$ STMT $\{ \mathbf{Q} \wedge \bigwedge_{i=0}^{n} \mathit{alive}(\mathrm{v}_i, \$) \}$

  where $\mathrm{v}_0, \ldots, \mathrm{v}_k$ *are the formal parameters, and* $\mathrm{v}_{k+1}, \ldots, \mathrm{v}_n$ *are the local variables of the enclosing method.*

The fact that living objects stay alive is expressed by the operator oal. oal({ **P** } COMP { **Q** }) *is defined as*

$$\{ \mathbf{P} \wedge \mathit{alive}(X, \$) \} \text{ COMP } \{ \mathbf{Q} \wedge \mathit{alive}(X, \$) \} .$$

The lal- and oal-operators are extended pointwise to sets of triples.

Lemma 3.2.4 (Adding Liveness Annotations). *If there is a proof for* $\mathcal{A} \mathrel{|\!\!\triangleright} \mathbf{A}$ *then there are proofs for* $\mathit{lal}(\mathcal{A}) \mathrel{|\!\!\triangleright} \mathit{lal}(\mathbf{A})$ *and* $\mathit{oal}(\mathcal{A}) \mathrel{|\!\!\triangleright} \mathit{oal}(\mathbf{A})$.

Like the type safety proof, the proof of this lemma runs by induction on the depth of the proof for $\mathcal{A} \mathrel{|\!\!\triangleright} \mathbf{A}$. It is straightforward and therefore omitted. According to Definition 3.2.1, both liveness properties are language properties (*lal* and *oal* are minimal elements in the ordering of operators for language properties).

3.2.3 Properties of Readonly Methods

Readonly methods are syntactically checked to be side-effect-free. That is, they do not modify the object store. To be able to exploit this property in proofs, we formalize and prove it in the programming logic:

Definition 3.2.5 (Readonly Annotations). *We use an operator ro to add the readonly-property to a triple. The definition of ro*({ **P** } COMP { **Q** }) *depends on the method enclosing COMP:*

- *Annotations of readwrite methods and statements in readwrite methods:*

  { **P** } COMP { **Q** }
- *Annotations of readonly methods and statements in readonly methods:*

  $\{ \mathbf{P} \wedge \$ = \mathit{OS} \}$ COMP $\{ \mathbf{Q} \wedge \$ = \mathit{OS} \}$

OS is a fresh logical variable that neither occurs in any specification nor in any proof.

Lemma 3.2.5. *If there is a proof for* $\mathcal{A} \mathrel{|\!\!\triangleright} \mathbf{A}$ *then there is a proof for* $\mathit{ro}(\mathcal{A}) \mathrel{|\!\!\triangleright} \mathit{ro}(\mathbf{A})$

The proof can be found in App. D.1. Note that the readonly property is a language property (*ro* is a minimal element in the ordering of operators for language properties, see Definition 3.2.1).

3.3 Correctness

To verify a program w.r.t. an interface specification, the specification is transformed into a set of proof obligations that have to be shown in the programming logic. The proof obligations stemming from an interface specification are defined by the semantics of the interface specification language and will be explained in Chapters 4 to 6. As discussed in Subsection 1.3.1, correctness of open programs relies on certain assumptions about further program extensions, whereas closed programs can be completely verified based on the knowledge of the given program. Thus, we present different notions of correctness for open and closed programs in this section and explain how they are related to each other. Furthermore, we discuss modular soundness and show that our notion of correctness of open programs is compatible with composition: The combination of correct open programs leads in turn to a correct open program.

3.3.1 Correctness of Closed Programs

Correctness of a closed program w.r.t. its specification is defined as follows:

Definition 3.3.1 (Correctness of Closed Programs). *A closed program $\mathcal{P}$ is* correct *w.r.t. its specification if*

1. *$\mathcal{P}$ is syntactically correct (which includes type correctness);*
2. *the interface specification of $\mathcal{P}$ is well-formed (which includes syntactical and sort correctness of the associated universal specification, see Section 4.1);*
3. *there is a proof for each sequent $\rhd \mathbf{A}$ generated from the specification of $\mathcal{P}$[9].*

Instead of the third requirement, we could also require the sequents $\rhd \mathbf{A}$ *to hold.* With an incomplete logic, the stronger, syntactic requirement is more appropriate, in particular for reuse of verified programs (see Subsection 3.3.4).

3.3.2 Correctness of Open Programs: Modular Correctness

For open programs, we have to assume that all extensions to the program are well-formed. This means (1) that all inherited or overridden virtual methods meet the specifications of the corresponding supertype methods (behavioral subtyping) and (2) that methods of program extensions have certain properties such as well-typedness that are guaranteed by the programming language (see Section 3.2). Properties of program extensions can be formalized as assumptions in the programming logic.

[9] We assume that interface specifications lead to sequents with empty assumption sets as proof obligations, which corresponds to the usual semantics of interface specifications.

Definition 3.3.2 (Modular Correctness). *An open program $\mathcal{P}$ with core* M *or a closed program $\mathcal{P}$ with set of modules* M *is* modularly correct *w.r.t. its specification if*

1. M *is syntactically correct;*
2. *the interface specification of* M *is well-formed;*
3. *for each sequent* $\rhd$ **A** *generated from the specification of* M*, there is a proof of* $\mathcal{A}, \mathcal{B} \rhd \mathbf{A}$*, where*
   - $\mathcal{A}$ *contains the assumptions that subtype methods in program extensions meet the specifications of the corresponding supertype methods. That is,* $\mathcal{A}$ *contains a triple of the form*
     $\{\ \mathit{module}(\mathit{tidD}(\mathit{typeof}(\text{this}))) \notin \text{M} \wedge \mathbf{P}\ \}\ \text{T:m}\ \{\ \mathbf{Q}\ \}$
     for each proof obligation $\rhd \{\ \mathbf{P}\ \}\ \text{T:m}\ \{\ \mathbf{Q}\ \}$ *generated for* M.
   - $\mathcal{B}$ *contains the assumptions that program extensions have all properties guaranteed by the programming language. That is,* $\mathcal{B}$ *contains triples of the form* $l(\mathbf{B})$ *for each triple* **B** *in* $\mathcal{A}$ *and each language property operator* l[10]*.*

Note that each module M_0 together with imported modules $\text{M}_1, \ldots, \text{M}_n$ defines a closed program in case that M_0 is a main module or an open program with core $\bigcup_{i=0}^{n} \text{M}_i$ otherwise. Therefore, we say that a module is modularly correct, if the open or closed program defined by that module is modularly correct. The definitions of correctness and modular correctness imply that each modularly correct closed program is correct according to Def. 3.3.1:

Lemma 3.3.1. *Every modular correct closed program is correct.*

Proof of Lemma 3.3.1:

Let $\mathcal{P}$ be a modularly correct closed program $\mathcal{P}$ with set of modules M. From Def. 3.3.2, we know that for each proof obligation $\rhd$ **A** that is generated from the specification of M, there is a proof of $\mathcal{A}, \mathcal{B} \rhd \mathbf{A}$. To prove that $\mathcal{P}$ is correct according to Def. 3.3.1, we have to eliminate the assumption sets $\mathcal{A}$ and $\mathcal{B}$ of these sequents.

For closed programs, the axiom **import6** and the axiomatization of *module* allow us to derive $\forall T : \mathit{module}(T) \in \text{M}$. We can use this property to eliminate the assumptions: For each assumption of the form

$$\{\ \mathit{module}(\mathit{tidD}(\mathit{typeof}(\text{this}))) \notin \text{M} \wedge \mathbf{P}\ \}\ \text{T:m}\ \{\ \mathbf{Q}\ \}$$

(i.e., for each assumption in $\mathcal{A} \cup \mathcal{B}$), we derive:

---

[10] $\mathcal{B}$ contains $n \times m$ triples where n is the number of language properties (see Section 3.2) and m is the number of proof obligations for virtual methods in M. Due to the clear structure of $\mathcal{B}$, a verification tool can provide the verifier with a structured view to this large number of assumptions and thus keep the complexity manageable.

$$\dfrac{\dfrac{\begin{array}{l}\triangleright \{\ \mathit{false}\ \}\ \text{T:m}\ \{\ \mathit{false}\ \} \\ \mathit{module}(\mathit{tidD}(\mathit{typeof}(\text{this}))) \notin \text{M} \wedge \mathbf{P} \Rightarrow \mathit{false}\quad [\![\ \text{property above}\ ]\!]\end{array}}{\triangleright \{\ \mathit{module}(\mathit{tidD}(\mathit{typeof}(\text{this}))) \notin \text{M} \wedge \mathbf{P}\ \}\ \text{T:m}\ \{\ \mathit{false}\ \}}\ [\![\ \text{strength-rule}\ ]\!]}{\triangleright \{\ \mathit{module}(\mathit{tidD}(\mathit{typeof}(\text{this}))) \notin \text{M} \wedge \mathbf{P}\ \}\ \text{T:m}\ \{\ \mathbf{Q}\ \}}\ [\![\ \text{weak-rule}\ ]\!]$$

Now we can apply the assumpt-elim-rule to discard the assumptions and show that $\mathcal{P}$ is a correct closed program. □

3.3.3 Modular Soundness

A programming logic is usually applied to reason about one given program. However, to verify an open program $\mathcal{P}$, we have to prove properties that hold in all closed programs contained in $\mathcal{P}$. In our programming logic, each proof for the core of an open program $\mathcal{P}$ is also a proof for the core of each extension $\mathcal{P}'$ of $\mathcal{P}$ since

1. each valid application of an axiom or rule in a proof for the core of $\mathcal{P}$ is also a valid axiom/rule application for the core of $\mathcal{P}'$. This is due to the handling of dynamic method binding [PHM99].
2. the program-dependent universal specification for the core of $\mathcal{P}'$ is a refinement of the generated specification for the core of $\mathcal{P}$ (see Paragraph 3.1.1.1). That is, all proofs in predicate logic based on the universal specification for the core of $\mathcal{P}$ stay valid in the specification for the core of $\mathcal{P}'$.

Therefore, if a property can be proved for the core of an open program $\mathcal{P}$, it holds for the cores of all extensions of $\mathcal{P}$ and in all closed programs contained in $\mathcal{P}$. Hence, such proofs can be reused when an open program is extended or closed[11]. We say that a sequent holds in an open program $\mathcal{P}$ if it holds in all closed programs in $\mathcal{P}$.

The property that proofs stay valid when an open program is extended is often called *modular soundness* in the literature [Lei95b, LN00]. The above considerations show that our programming logic and the way universal specifications are generated guarantee modular soundness of our verification technique.

3.3.4 Composition of Modular Correct Open Programs

The composition of open programs $\mathcal{P}_1, \ldots, \mathcal{P}_n$ with cores $\text{M}_1, \ldots, \text{M}_n$ is the open program with core $\bigcup_{i=1}^{n} \text{M}_i$. In Mojave, open programs can be composed by import of modules. That is, a module M that imports modules $\text{M}_1, \ldots, \text{M}_n$ composes the open programs defined by $\text{M}_1, \ldots, \text{M}_n$ and adds further type

[11] Proofs that require well-formedness of interface specifications can only be reused in programs with well-formed interface specifications. See Section 4.1.

declarations. In this subsection, we present a proof strategy that allows one to compose reused proofs of individual open programs and yields the correctness proofs for the composite program.

3.3.4.1 Composition of Proofs. A complete logic allows one to prove every property in the logic that holds. However, even in a complete logic, it is not guaranteed that correctness can be proved *modularly*, that is, based on reused proofs. One would need a notion of *modular completeness* of a logic which means that every property that holds in a composite program can be proved without re-verification of the constituents. To our knowledge, this issue has not been discussed in the literature so far.

Our programming logic is not modular complete: It is not possible to modularly prove all properties that can be proved for an open program in a nonmodular way. The reason for that is the rather complex handling of recursion. Assumptions about recursive methods can only be discarded by the implementation-rule. In OO-programs it is possible that two virtual methods are mutually recursive even if they are defined in different open programs as illustrated by Example 3.3.1: Let $\mathcal{P}_1$ and $\mathcal{P}_2$ be the open programs defined by M1 and M2, resp., and $\mathcal{P}$ the composition of $\mathcal{P}_1$ and $\mathcal{P}_2$. In $\mathcal{P}$, the virtual methods C1:m and C2:m mutually depend on each other's behavior: For the verification of C1:m, we need properties of I:m which in turn depend on the subtype methods C1:m and C2:m. Thus, there is mutual recursion across the boundaries of the open programs $\mathcal{P}_1$ and $\mathcal{P}_2$[12]. Consequently, the proofs for $\mathcal{P}$ require a quite complex handling of assumptions about C1@m and C2@m and cannot simply be composed from the (reused) proofs of C1:m and C2:m in $\mathcal{P}_1$ and $\mathcal{P}_2$.

Example 3.3.1.

```
module M;
public interface I extends Interface {
  public int m();
}
```

```
module M1 imports M;
public class C1 implements I {
  public int m() {
    I v;
    ...
    result = v.m();
}
```

```
module M2 imports M;
public class C2 implements I {
  public int m() {
    I v;
    ...
    result = v.m();
}
```

To solve this problem, we could modify the handling of recursion in our programming logic. However, the implementation-rule is the classical approach to recursion. It is one of the crucial parts of the logic since it contains the

[12] Note that this kind of mutual recursion cannot occur in languages with statically-bound procedures only.

inductive argument to handle recursion. Thus, its soundness proof is not trivial. There is no obvious alternative way to handle recursion. Replacing the classical implementation-rule would raise many questions about soundness, completeness, and application of the new logic. A detailed discussion of modular completeness is beyond the scope of this book since we want to focus on specification and verification techniques rather than on logical foundations. Thus, we decided to keep the classical rule and follow an alternative approach to proof composition: We use a proof strategy that allows us to combine proofs for method bodies instead of virtual methods. This way, we can use the implementation-rule to eliminate the assumptions for recursive methods.

3.3.4.2 Proof Strategy for Program Composition. In this paragraph, we show how modular correctness of a composite program can be derived from the reused correctness proofs of its constituents. We describe the requirements an interface specification language has to meet to support proof composition and present a proof strategy for proof composition.

Requirements. Compositionality of correct programs relies on four properties of the interface specification language that are assumed in this paragraph:

1. A legal composition of well-formed specifications leads to a well-formed specification.
2. The set of proof obligations for the composition of open programs $\mathcal{P}_z$ $(z = 1, \ldots, s)$ is the union of the sets of proof obligations for the single open programs $\mathcal{P}_z$. In particular, specifications of modules do not lead to proof obligations for imported modules.
3. All proof obligations about virtual methods contain the typing of `this` and the fact that `this` does not hold the null-value in the precondition. That is, they have the form

   $$\{\ \mathit{tidD}(\mathit{typeof}(\mathrm{this})) \preceq_M \mathrm{T} \land \mathrm{this} \neq \mathit{null} \land \mathbf{P}\ \}\ \mathrm{T{:}m}\ \{\ \mathbf{Q}\ \}$$

4. Interface specifications are inherited. That is, if

   $$\rhd \{\ \mathit{tidD}(\mathit{typeof}(\mathrm{this})) \preceq_M \mathrm{T} \land \mathrm{this} \neq \mathit{null} \land \mathbf{P}\ \}\ \mathrm{T{:}m}\ \{\ \mathbf{Q}\ \}$$

   is a proof obligation for $\mathcal{P}$'s core then

   $$\rhd \{\ \mathit{tidD}(\mathit{typeof}(\mathrm{this})) \preceq_M \mathrm{S} \land \mathrm{this} \neq \mathit{null} \land \mathbf{P}\ \}\ \mathrm{S{:}m}\ \{\ \mathbf{Q}\ \}$$

   is also a proof obligation for all S in the core of $\mathcal{P}$ that are subtypes of T[13].

We will show that the interface specification language used in this book meets these requirements in Chapters 4 to 6.

[13] Inheritance of interface specifications leads automatically to behavioral subtyping [DL96]. For this strategy, it would also be sufficient to require a weaker notion of behavioral subtyping [Dha97].

Correctness Proofs of Reused Programs. Let $\mathcal{P}_z$ ($z = 1, \ldots, s$) be modularly correct open programs and $\mathcal{P}_0$ the syntactically correct[14] composition of the $\mathcal{P}_z$. For $t = 0, \ldots, s$, let

- $l_1, \ldots, l_n$ be the language property operators defined for our programming language, where l_i is less than or equal to l_{i+1} in the ordering of language property operators (see Definition 3.2.1); l_0 denotes the identity operator (i.e., $l_0(\mathbf{A}) = \mathbf{A}$);
- $\mathbf{A}_{1,t}, \ldots, \mathbf{A}_{p,t}$ be the consequents of the proof obligations for the concrete (i.e., implemented) virtual methods in the core of $\mathcal{P}_t$ of the form
  $\{\ tidD(typeof(\text{this})) \preceq_M \text{T} \wedge \text{this} \neq null \wedge \mathbf{P}\ \}\ \text{T:m}\ \{\ \mathbf{Q}\ \}$
- $\mathbf{A}_{p+1,t}, \ldots, \mathbf{A}_{q,t}$ be the consequents of the proof obligations for the abstract virtual methods in the core of $\mathcal{P}_t$;
- $\mathbf{A}_{q+1,t}, \ldots, \mathbf{A}_{r,t}$ be the consequents of the proof obligations for the other program components in the core of $\mathcal{P}_t$, especially for implementations of statically-bound methods;
- $\mathbf{I}_{1,t}, \ldots, \mathbf{I}_{p,t}$ be like the triples $\mathbf{A}_{1,t}, \ldots, \mathbf{A}_{p,t}$ with the virtual methods T:m replaced by their implementations S@m[15]:
  $\{\ tidD(typeof(\text{this})) \preceq_M \text{S} \wedge \text{this} \neq null \wedge \mathbf{P}\ \}\ \text{S@m}\ \{\ \mathbf{Q}\ \}$
- $\mathbf{B}_{1,t}, \ldots, \mathbf{B}_{p,t}$ be the corresponding triples for the bodies of these implementations:

  $$\begin{array}{l}\{\ tidD(typeof(\text{this})) \preceq_M \text{S} \wedge \text{this} \neq null \wedge \mathbf{P} \wedge \bigwedge_i(\ \text{v}_i = init(\tau([\text{v}_i]))\ )\ \} \\ \quad body(\text{S@m}) \\ \{\ \mathbf{Q}\ \}\end{array}$$

- $\mathbf{T}^h_{i,t}, h = 0, \ldots, n$ be $l_h(\mathbf{T}_{i,t})$. That is, the superscript indicates which language property has been applied to the triple.

Modular correctness of composite programs is proved as follows: Instead of requiring the verifier to directly show the proof obligations $\models \mathbf{A}_{j,z}$ for the cores of each $\mathcal{P}_z$, we require him to show

1. that the properties specified for concrete virtual methods hold for the bodies of their implementations, and
2. the proof obligations with program parts that are not virtual methods.

For both kinds of proof obligations, the verifier can assume that all virtual methods of $\mathcal{P}_z$'s core have all specified and language properties (see below for a formalization). Note that the verifier is not required to prove properties of abstract methods. The above proof obligations do not put additional burden on the verifier. The triples for the method bodies have to be proved anyway to show modular correctness of the $\mathcal{P}_z$. The verifier can prove these

---

[14] That means in particular that there are no name clashes between the module names of the $\mathcal{P}_z$.

[15] Several virtual methods can have common implementations. Thus, some of the $\mathbf{I}_{i,t}$ can be identical.

obligations modularly since all specified properties and language properties for virtual methods are given as assumptions. Therefore, the assumptions already contain well-formedness of program extensions.

A verification tool can then carry out a proof strategy to derive modular correctness of $\mathcal{P}_0$ from the above proof obligations (see below). To preserve information hiding, the verifier would actually be forced to use a smaller assumption set, namely only those triples that are generated from accessible parts of the interface specification (see Subsection 4.2.2). However, since a verification tool can apply the assumpt-intro-rule to add the missing assumptions before the strategy is carried out, we present the proof strategy for the full assumption set.

Correctness of the Composite Program. The composition of several modularly correct open programs leads to a modularly correct open program:

Lemma 3.3.2. *If the interface specification language meets the above requirements, and the following sequents can be proved for the cores of each open program* $\mathcal{P}_z, z = 1, \ldots, s$

$$(1) \quad \bigcup_{h=0}^{n} \bigcup_{i=1}^{q} \mathbf{A}_{i,z}^{h} \rhd \mathbf{B}_{j,z} \quad \textit{for } j = 1, \ldots, p$$

and

$$(2) \quad \bigcup_{h=0}^{n} \bigcup_{i=1}^{q} \mathbf{A}_{i,z}^{h} \rhd \mathbf{A}_{j,z} \quad \textit{for } j = q+1, \ldots, r$$

then the syntactically correct composition of the $\mathcal{P}_z, z = 1, \ldots, s$ *is modularly correct.*

Proof of Lemma 3.3.2:

We can assume that the composition of the $\mathcal{P}_z, z = 1, \ldots, s$ (called $\mathcal{P}_0$ in the following) is syntactically correct. According to requirement 1 for interface specifications, the composition of the well-formed specifications of the $\mathcal{P}_z$ leads to a well-formed specification for $\mathcal{P}_0$. Thus, it remains to show that the proof obligations for $\mathcal{P}_0$ can be proved (see Definition 3.3.2). According to requirement 2 for interface specifications, the proof obligations for $\mathcal{P}_0$ are the union of the proof obligations for the $\mathcal{P}_z, z = 1, \ldots, s$. In the following we describe a strategy that generates proofs for these obligations and thus shows that Lemma 3.3.2 holds.

The intuition behind this strategy is as follows: According to Lemma 3.3.2, method bodies are verified based on the assumption that all virtual methods of the individual programs $\mathcal{P}_z$ meet their specifications and have the admissible language properties. To prove that the composition is correct, we have (1) to replace these assumptions by the assumptions about program extensions described in Definition 3.3.2 and (2) to show correctness of virtual methods and method implementations based on the proofs for the method bodies. The central idea of the strategy is that a property holds for a virtual method T:m if the corresponding property holds (a) for all implementations in $\mathcal{P}_0$ that might be executed when T:m is invoked, and (b) for all virtual methods of subtypes of T that might be added to $\mathcal{P}_0$ later on. Besides this idea and the application of language property operators, the strategy consists mainly of manipulations of assumption sets.

Step 1: Reuse of Existing Proofs. We know that we can reuse the proofs for (1) and (2) (see above and Subsection 3.3.3) for the verification of $\mathcal{P}_0$. By requirement 2 for interface specification languages and the assumpt-intro-rule, we get from (1) and (2):

$$(3)\quad \bigcup_{h=0}^{n}\bigcup_{i=1}^{q} \mathbf{A}_{i,0}^{h} \triangleright \mathbf{B}_{j,0} \;\text{ for } j = 1,\ldots,p$$

and

$$(4)\quad \bigcup_{h=0}^{n}\bigcup_{i=1}^{q} \mathbf{A}_{i,0}^{h} \triangleright \mathbf{A}_{j,0} \;\text{ for } j = q+1,\ldots,r$$

In the following, we will only talk about triples for $\mathcal{P}_0$. Thus, we drop the second subscript of the triples.

Step 2: Application of the Language Property Operators. In this step, we add the language properties to the triples for method bodies. To do that, we apply every language property operator l_k to each triple of (3) which yields:

$$\bigcup_{m=0}^{k}\bigcup_{h=0}^{n}\bigcup_{i=1}^{q} l_m(\mathbf{A}_i^h) \triangleright \mathbf{B}_j^k \;\text{ for } j = 1,\ldots,p; k = 0,\ldots,n$$

Since the language property operators only add conjuncts to pre- and post-conditions, we can derive:

$$\frac{\begin{array}{ll} l_a(\mathbf{A}) \triangleright l_a(\mathbf{A}) & [\![\text{ assumpt-axiom }]\!] \\ l_b(\mathbf{A}) \triangleright l_b(\mathbf{A}) & [\![\text{ assumpt-axiom }]\!] \end{array}}{l_a(\mathbf{A}), l_b(\mathbf{A}) \triangleright l_b(l_a(\mathbf{A}))} \quad [\![\text{ assumpt-intro-rule, conjunct-rule }]\!]$$

We use this property, the assumpt-elim-rule, and the assumpt-intro-rule to derive

$$(5)\quad \bigcup_{h=0}^{n}\bigcup_{i=1}^{q} \mathbf{A}_{i}^{h} \triangleright \mathbf{B}_{j}^{k} \;\text{ for } j = 1,\ldots,p; k = 0,\ldots,n$$

Step 3: Replacing Virtual Methods by their Implementations. Now, we replace the $\mathbf{A}_i^h$ in the assumptions of (5) by the corresponding triples for method implementations and triples about further program extensions. For each triple $\mathbf{A} \equiv \{\, \mathbf{P} \,\}$ COMP $\{\, \mathbf{Q} \,\}$, $\hat{\mathbf{A}}$ is defined as

$$\{\, \mathit{module}(\mathit{tidD}(\mathit{typeof}(\text{this}))) \notin \text{M} \wedge \mathbf{P} \,\}\ \text{COMP}\ \{\, \mathbf{Q} \,\},$$

where M denotes the core of $\mathcal{P}_0$. First, we introduce assumptions and get

$$(6)\quad \bigcup_{h=0}^{n}\bigcup_{i=1}^{q} \mathbf{A}_i^h \cup \bigcup_{h=0}^{n}\bigcup_{i=1}^{q} \hat{\mathbf{A}}_i^h \cup \bigcup_{h=0}^{n}\bigcup_{i=1}^{p} \mathbf{I}_i^h \rhd \mathbf{B}_j^k \text{ for } j=1,\dots,p; k=0,\dots,n$$

Now we eliminate the $\mathbf{A}_i^h$ by the following strategy: Let $\mathbf{A}_1, \dots, \mathbf{A}_{q\cdot(n+1)}$ be the triples in $\bigcup_{h=0}^{n}\bigcup_{i=1}^{q} \mathbf{A}_i^h$ in the following order: All triples for supertype methods have lower indices than the triples for the corresponding subtype methods. In the strategy, we abbreviate *tidD*(*typeof*(this)) by ϕ.

for $g = 1$ **to** $q \cdot (n+1)$ **do**

Let $\mathbf{A}_g \equiv \{\ \phi \preceq_M \mathrm{T} \wedge \text{this} \neq \mathit{null} \wedge \mathbf{P}\ \}\ \mathrm{T{:}m}\ \{\ \mathbf{Q}\ \}$.

if M contains proper subtypes of T **then**

For each of T's direct subtypes in M, we know from requirement 4 for interface specifications that there is a corresponding triple for the subtype method in $\mathbf{A}_{g+1}, \dots, \mathbf{A}_{q\cdot(n+1)}$. For each of these triples, we instantiate the assumpt-axiom and the subtype-rule which yields

$$\{\ \phi \prec_M \mathrm{S} \wedge \text{this} \neq \mathit{null} \wedge \mathbf{P}\ \}\ \mathrm{S{:}m}\ \{\ \mathbf{Q}\ \} \rhd$$
$$\{\ \phi \prec_M \mathrm{S} \wedge \text{this} \neq \mathit{null} \wedge \mathbf{P}\ \}\ \mathrm{T{:}m}\ \{\ \mathbf{Q}\ \}$$

Now, we use the assumpt-intro-rule, the disjunct-rule, and the strength-rule to derive

$$\bigcup_{f=g+1}^{q\cdot(n+1)} \mathbf{A}_f \rhd \{\ \phi \prec_M \mathrm{T} \wedge \text{this} \neq \mathit{null} \wedge \mathit{module}(\phi) \in \mathrm{M} \wedge \mathbf{P}\ \}\ \mathrm{T{:}m}\ \{\ \mathbf{Q}\ \}$$

else

The sequent derived in the if-branch follows from the false-axiom, the strength-rule, the weak-rule, and the assumpt-intro-rule.

end if

We use the assumpt-axiom and the disjunct-rule to derive

$$\{\hat{\mathbf{A}}_g\} \cup \bigcup_{f=g+1}^{q\cdot(n+1)} \mathbf{A}_f \rhd \{\ \phi \prec_M \mathrm{T} \wedge \text{this} \neq \mathit{null} \wedge \mathbf{P}\ \}\ \mathrm{T{:}m}\ \{\ \mathbf{Q}\ \}$$

if T:m is an abstract method **then**

We know that T is an interface and thus $\phi \neq \mathrm{T}$. Using the strength-rule and the assumpt-intro-rule yields

$$\{\mathbf{I}, \hat{\mathbf{A}}_g\} \cup \bigcup_{f=g+1}^{q\cdot(n+1)} \mathbf{A}_f \rhd \{\ \phi \preceq_M \mathrm{T} \wedge \text{this} \neq \mathit{null} \wedge \mathbf{P}\ \}\ \mathrm{T{:}m}\ \{\ \mathbf{Q}\ \}$$

else

We use the corresponding triple **I** for the implementation of T:m and apply the assumpt-axiom for **I**, the assumpt-intro-rule, and the strength-rule to derive

$$\frac{\begin{array}{l}\{\mathbf{I}, \hat{\mathbf{A}}_g\} \cup \bigcup_{f=g+1}^{q\cdot(n+1)} \mathbf{A}_f \rhd \{\ \phi = \mathrm{T} \wedge \text{this} \neq \mathit{null} \wedge \mathbf{P}\ \}\mathit{impl}(\ \mathrm{T{:}m}\ )\{\ \mathbf{Q}\ \} \\ \{\mathbf{I}, \hat{\mathbf{A}}_g\} \cup \bigcup_{f=g+1}^{q\cdot(n+1)} \mathbf{A}_f \rhd \{\ \phi \prec_M \mathrm{T} \wedge \text{this} \neq \mathit{null} \wedge \mathbf{P}\ \}\ \mathrm{T{:}m}\ \{\ \mathbf{Q}\ \}\end{array}}{\{\mathbf{I}, \hat{\mathbf{A}}_g\} \cup \bigcup_{f=g+1}^{q\cdot(n+1)} \mathbf{A}_f \rhd \{\ \phi \preceq_M \mathrm{T} \wedge \text{this} \neq \mathit{null} \wedge \mathbf{P}\ \}\ \mathrm{T{:}m}\ \{\ \mathbf{Q}\ \}}\ [\![\text{ class-rule }]\!]$$

end if

Eliminate the assumption $\mathbf{A}_g$ in all triples of (6)

end for

By applying this strategy, we get

$$(7)\quad \bigcup_{h=0}^{n}\bigcup_{i=1}^{q}\hat{\mathbf{A}}_i^h \cup \bigcup_{h=0}^{n}\bigcup_{i=1}^{p}\mathbf{I}_i^h \rhd \mathbf{B}_j^k \quad \text{for } j=1,\ldots,p; k=0,\ldots,n$$

Step 4: Elimination of Implementations from Assumptions. In this step, we use the triples for method bodies to discard the method implementations from the assumptions in (7). Let $\mathbf{I}_i$ and $\mathbf{B}_i, i = 1,\ldots,p\cdot(n+1)$ denote the $\mathbf{I}_j^k$ and $\mathbf{B}_j^k, j = 1,\ldots,p; k = 0,\ldots,n$ in any order. Thus, we can write (7) as

$$(8)\quad \bigcup_{h=0}^{n}\bigcup_{i=1}^{q}\hat{\mathbf{A}}_i^h \cup \bigcup_{i=1}^{p\cdot(n+1)}\mathbf{I}_i \rhd \mathbf{B}_j \quad \text{for } j=1,\ldots,p\cdot(n+1)$$

We eliminate the $\mathbf{I}_i$ in (8) by the following strategy:

for $g = 1$ **to** $p\cdot(n+1)$ **do**
  apply implementation-rule to sequent with consequent $\mathbf{B}_g$
  for $f = g+1$ **to** $p\cdot(n+1)$ **do**
    eliminate assumption $\mathbf{I}_g$ in the sequent with consequent $\mathbf{B}_f$
  end for
end for

After running this loop, we get

$$\bigcup_{h=0}^{n}\bigcup_{i=1}^{q}\hat{\mathbf{A}}_i^h \cup \bigcup_{i=j+1}^{p\cdot(n+1)}\mathbf{I}_i \rhd \mathbf{I}_j \quad \text{for } j=1,\ldots,p\cdot(n+1)$$

Now we eliminate the remaining assumptions $\mathbf{I}_i$ by the following loop:

for $g = p\cdot(n+1)$ **to** 2 **do**
  for $f = g-1$ **to** 1 **do**
    eliminate assumption $\mathbf{I}_g$ in the sequent with consequent $\mathbf{I}_f$
  end for
end for

This yields

$$\bigcup_{h=0}^{n}\bigcup_{i=1}^{q}\hat{\mathbf{A}}_i^h \rhd \mathbf{I}_j \quad \text{for } j=1,\ldots,p\cdot(n+1)$$

or equivalently

$$(9)\quad \bigcup_{h=0}^{n}\bigcup_{i=1}^{q}\hat{\mathbf{A}}_i^h \rhd \mathbf{I}_j^k \quad \text{for } j=1,\ldots,p; k=0,\ldots,n$$

Step 5: Proving Virtual Methods. In step 3, we have already shown how properties of virtual methods can be proved based on the properties of their implementations. We run an almost identical strategy to prove the sequents

$$(10)\quad \bigcup_{h=0}^{n}\bigcup_{i=1}^{q}\hat{\mathbf{A}}_i^h \rhd \mathbf{A}_j^k \quad \text{for } j=1,\ldots,q; k=0,\ldots,n$$

The sequent with consequent $\mathbf{A}_j^k$ is derived as follows. Let T:m be the program component of $\mathbf{A}_j^k$. First, we show that the property holds for all direct subtypes of T. If there are proper subtypes of T in the core of $\mathcal{P}_0$, this can be done by applying the subtype-rule to the corresponding sequents of subtype methods (see requirement 4 for interface specifications) and by building the disjunction of the resulting triples and the assumption $\hat{\mathbf{A}}_j^k$ (assumpt-axiom). Otherwise, the false-axiom, the strength-rule, the weak-rule, and then the assumpt-intro-rule are applied. Then, $\mathbf{A}_j^k$ can be derived by the strength-rule, if T is an interface or by the class-rule and the sequent for T:m's implementation in (9) if T is a class.

Step 6: Elimination of Remaining Assumptions. Finally, we replace the assumptions in (4) by assumptions about program extensions by using the triples in (10).

In summary, we have proved

$$\bigcup_{h=0}^{n} \bigcup_{i=1}^{q} \hat{\mathbf{A}}_i^h \triangleright \mathbf{A}_j \quad \text{for } j = 1, \ldots, r$$

That is, we have derived all proof obligations for $\mathcal{P}_0$ based on assumptions about extensions of $\mathcal{P}_0$ (the $\hat{\mathbf{A}}_i^h$ are exactly the admitted assumptions in Definition 3.3.2). Consequently, $\mathcal{P}_0$ is modularly correct. □

3.4 Related Work

In this section, we give an overview of programming logics for OO-languages.

In [Lei97], a wlp-calculus for an OO-language similar to our Java subset is presented. In contrast to our work, method specifications are part of the programs. The approach in [Lei97] can be considered as restricting our approach to a certain program development strategy (see [PHM98]). Thereby, it becomes simpler and more appropriate for automatic checking, but gives up flexibility that seems important to us for interactive program development and verification. In addition to that, we consider it as an advantage to clearly separate the axioms for the object store from the programming logic, as it is done in our approach.

A different logic for OO-programs that is related to type systems is presented and proved sound in [AL97]. It is developed for an OO-language in the style of the lambda calculus whereas we aim at directly supporting the verification of an existing language. In particular, our language provides inheritance and dynamic method binding in the form they occur in widely-used OO-languages.

A programming logic for a concurrent OO-language without methods and subtyping is presented in [AdB94]. Based on this work, [Boe99] presents a wp-calculus, also for a language without subtyping and dynamic method binding. Since this calculus does not have an explicit object store, data abstraction cannot be expressed. Therefore, an extension towards realistic OO-languages with subtyping and inheritance seems difficult.

Von Oheimb presents a programming logic for a programming language with recursive methods, but without subtyping or dynamic method binding in [Ohe99]. The logic is formally proved sound and complete w.r.t. an operational semantics using Isabelle. In [Ohe00], this logic is extended to support subtyping and dynamic binding. Instead of using virtual methods, the rule for method invocations requires one to show a property for the bodies of all methods that might be executed by the invocation. This has two important disadvantages compared to our logic: (1) Since the implementations of all methods that might be invoked have to be present for verification of the invocation statement, open programs cannot be handled. (2) The rule for method invocations is fairly complex and not easy to apply.

The programming logic presented in [HJ99, HJ00] supports subtyping, dynamic binding, and abrupt termination. Dynamically-bound methods are handled by requiring behavioral subtyping which makes virtual methods dispensable. To deal with abrupt termination, there are several rules for most statements that capture the different cases of termination. Soundness and completeness have not been proved for this logic, and are not obvious due to the large number of rules.

The programming logic in this book has been inspired by the partial correctness logic described in [Apt81]. The extension to object-orientation profited from other papers about verification of imperative languages with complex data structures, especially [Suz80], [HW73], and [Bij89]. The logic presented here extends the foundations developed in [PHM98] by covering encapsulation and subclassing. A very simliar logic was presented and proved sound w.r.t. an operational semantics in [PHM99].

Dynamic logics [KT90] allow programs to occur in formulas. Therefore, dynamic logic is more expressive than Hoare logic (e.g., it can express equivalence of programs), but also more difficult to apply.

The assuption-commitment (or rely-guarantee) paradigm [XS98, XdRH97] provides a compositional specification and verification technique for concurrent and real time programs. It has been studied as an extension to Hoare logic. Besides pre- and postconditions, an assumption-commitment specification for a program component COMP consists of an assumption that describes the state transitions other program components (that can be executed concurrently) are allowed to perform in a global environment, in particular, the modifications of shared variables. A commitment specifies the state transitions of COMP, provided that all other components meet the assumptions of COMP. Assumption-commitment logics do not contribute to the modular verification of sequential programs. Since control flow is passed from one program component to another by method invocations, assumptions about state transitions caused by other components can be formulated as pre-post-specifications of invoked methods. Analogously, the commitment of a program component corresponds to its pre-post-specification in the sequential case.

Behavioral subtyping [Ame87, Ame89, Dha97, LD00, LW93, LW94] is essential for understanding and verifying OO-programs. It facilitates modular verification in the presence of subtyping and dynamic method binding [Lea88, LW90] by relating subtype specifications to supertype specifications. Therefore, it is a key concept of most verification techniques for OO-languages. However, behavioral subtyping alone does not provide solutions for three major problems addressed in this book: (1) Modular verification of frame properties, (2) alias control, and (3) modular verification of type invariants. We discuss the impact of behavioral subtyping on our interface specification technique in Chapters 4 to 6.

4. Modular Specification and Verification of Functional Behavior

In the following three chapters, we present our modular specification and verification technique for Mojave programs, beginning with the so-called *functional behavior* of methods. Under functional behavior, we subsume the deliberate effects of a method: the computation of a result value and modifications to the object store. That is, "functional" does not mean "side-effect-free". We describe our specification technique for functional behavior based on abstract fields and pre-post-pairs, illustrate modular verification of functional behavior, and discuss related work.

4.1 Foundations of Interface Specifications

In this section, we explain some general aspects of all specification primitives of the Mojave interface specification language. We explain how the different interfaces of a class or interface type can be annotated with specifications and show how information hiding is preserved in interface specifications. Furthermore, we introduce well-formedness of interface specifications and explain how their formal meaning is defined.

Specifying the Interfaces of a Class or Interface Type. In our specification language, there are two groups of specification primitives: primitives for method specifications (such as pre-post-pairs or modifies-clauses) and primitives for the specification of data representations (such as type invariants and abstract fields). That is, we specify the interfaces of class and interface types, but do not provide specification primitives for modules. Since abstract fields and invariants are not limited to expressing properties of one object, they can be used to specify properties of object structures declared in a module or scope and make thereby special module specifications dispensable for most applications[1].

A class provides five different interfaces (see Paragraph 2.1.2.3). Our specification language allows one to specify each of these interfaces. Elements of the private interface can only be accessed from within the enclosing class. Although the verifier of that class has access to the implementation and is

[1] However, in Subsection 6.4.1, we discuss module invariants that can be used to specify sharing properties of several object structures.

Peter Müller: Modular Specification ..., LNCS 2262, pp. 123–141, 2002.

therefore not required to refer to an interface specification, specifications of the private interface are necessary (1) for the specification of dependencies, (2) to describe the effects of methods on locations with private fields, and (3) to define abstraction functions. To specify the different interfaces of a class, each specification primitive is equipped with one of Mojave's access modes that determines to which interface the specification element belongs. Since interface types have only a public interface, specifications of interface types have to be public.

Information Hiding. The specification of an interface must not reveal implementation details that should be hidden from clients of that interface (for instance, a public precondition must not refer to a private field). Technically, this is checked as follows: Every interface is associated with a theory of the universal specification (see Paragraph 3.1.1.1). We require that every constant symbol used in the specification of an interface is present (i.e., declared or imported) in the corresponding theory. This can be enforced by type checking all formulas of an interface specification in this theory. Thus, the theory structure explained in Paragraph 3.1.1.1 guarantees that no hidden information is exposed. For instance, the occurrence of a private field T@f in a public precondition in module M would be detected since T@f is not declared in M's public theory and would thus lead to an error such as *undeclared symbol* during type checking M's public theory.

More formally, each theory for a class or module determines signatures corresponding to Σ, Γ, etc. (see Paragraph 3.1.1.12). Formulas in interface specifications must fit to the signatures introduced by the corresponding universal specification.

Well-Formed Interface Specifications. As with programs, there are a number of context conditions for interface specifications that will be explained along with the specification primitives. In particular, all formulas occurring in the specification of an interface must be sort correct w.r.t. the associated theory of that interface.

In addition to these statically-checkable rules, interface specifications have to meet several semantic conditions, in particular requirements that enable modular verification. These so-called *well-formedness conditions* are formalized as proof obligations for interface specifications. That is, these are proof obligations about the specification itself, not about the specified program. We call an interface specification of a closed program *well-formed* if (1) the interface specification and the associated universal specification are syntactically and sort correct, and (2) all well-formedness conditions for the interface specification are met. The interface specification of an open program $\mathcal{P}$ is called well-formed, if the interface specifications of all closed programs in $\mathcal{P}$ are well-formed.

In the following, we assume that each open or closed program $\mathcal{P}$ to which the programming logic is applied has a well-formed interface specification. That is, we assume that the specification of each closed program in an open program $\mathcal{P}$ meets the well-formedness criteria, not only the specification of $\mathcal{P}$'s core. This is sound because every open program is closed before execution. For the closed program, the well-formedness criteria are required to hold. Since they will hold for every closed program in an open program $\mathcal{P}$, we can assume well-formedness already during verification of $\mathcal{P}$'s core. Using properties that hold for an open program $\mathcal{P}$ with well-formed specification only (such as Lemma 5.2.1) during verification of $\mathcal{P}$'s core is similar to raising a mortgage that has to be amortized by program extensions. Technically, a verification tool can assure well-formedness of the specification of a closed program (i.e., that the mortgage is completely amortized) or of the core of an open program (i.e., that the respective portion of the mortgage is amortized) before proofs in the programming logic can be reused or newly constructed.

Meaning of Interface Specifications. The formal meaning of an interface specification is defined by translating the specification into a set of proof obligations in the programming logic. In the following section, we define the meaning of pre-post-specifications. Modifies-clauses and invariants are transformed into pre-post-pairs (see Chapter 5 and 6). So the semantics of pre-post-specifications applies as well to the transformed modifies-clauses and invariants.

4.2 Specification of Functional Behavior

Pre-post-specifications are the standard technique for the specification of functional behavior [Jon91b]. They are very intuitive, have an obvious connection to software engineering [Mey92a], and are well integrated with Hoare-style verification techniques [PH97b]. In the context of object structures and subtyping, *data abstraction* is another key concept for the description of functional properties [GH93, Hoa72, Lea88, LG86]: Abstraction functions map object structures to values of an abstract domain. Modifications of object structures can be described in terms of their abstract values which makes implementation-independent specifications possible. In this section, we introduce abstract fields to provide data abstraction and present the syntax and semantics of pre-post-specifications.

4.2.1 Abstract Fields

Data abstraction is used to map object structures to abstract values and can therefore be found in all two-tiered interface specification languages. However, different abstraction techniques have been developed for different applications:

- *Implicit vs. explicit abstraction:* For formal verification, it is indispensable to have a formal connection between the operational world and declarative specifications [PH97b]. If this connection is formally defined, for instance by conventions or by declarations in the interface specification, we call the mapping from object structures to values *explicit abstraction*, and *implicit abstraction* otherwise.

- *Abstraction functions vs. abstract fields:* Abstraction functions/relations can be specified as part of the universal specifications. For instance, our formal data and state model allows one to define abstraction functions with signature $Value \times Store \rightarrow Sort$, where *Sort* is an appropriate sort of the abstract domain [PH97b]. Alternatively, abstraction can be expressed by so-called *abstract fields* (often called specification variables). Abstract fields are part of the interface of a class, but have no correspondence in the state space of an object. The range type of an abstract field is a sort of the universal specification (and not a type of the program). The value of an abstract location (i.e., the instance of an abstract field) is determined by the values of a set of concrete locations, the abstract location *depends on*. Thus, abstract fields express a mapping from concrete object states to abstract values.
  Abstract fields can be regarded as syntactically restricted abstraction functions. Abstract fields map one object or object structure to a value of the abstract domain whereas abstraction functions can have an arbitrary number of arguments and can thus, for instance, express that two object structures are disjoint, that is, have no objects in common (see [PH97b] for examples of abstraction functions that take several arguments). However, although almost identical in their formalizations, abstract fields have an important advantage over abstraction functions: Since they are declared as member of a class or interface type (in contrast to abstraction functions that can usually be defined in any theory of a universal specification), it is possible to generate axioms that allow one to reason about *all* abstract fields of a class, interface, module, or scope (see Paragraph 3.1.1.9). As pointed out by Leino [Lei95b], this kind of reasoning is crucial for the specification and verification of frame properties (see Subsection 5.4.1), where one has to prove that all abstract locations not covered by the modifies-clause of a method m stay unchanged when m is executed.
- *Abstraction functions vs. abstraction relations:* As explained in [SWO95], there are applications where object states should be related to several abstract values. We simulate such abstraction relations by set-valued abstraction functions.

To sum up, our interface specification language provides explicit abstraction functions, encoded by abstract fields.

4.2.1.1 Declaration of Abstract Fields. An abstract field f with range sort *Sort* is introduced by a declaration of the following form

`public abstract` *Sort* `f;`

where *Sort* is a sort of the universal specification. Since abstract fields are in particular necessary to specify the behavior of abstract methods of interface types (there is no implementation specifications could refer to), the declaration of an abstract field can occur in class *and* interface bodies.

Our verification technique for frame properties requires abstract fields to be public (see Section 5.4.3). Although it might be convenient to hide abstract fields from some kinds of clients (e.g., it is reasonable to provide certain abstractions for the protected interface only), public abstract fields do not violate information hiding: The declaration of an abstract field only reveals the name of an abstract field, but not its representation in terms of concrete fields. Thus, if an implementation is changed, one can provide a different representation for the abstract field.

The formalization of abstract fields has already been presented in Paragraph 3.1.1.9. Since there is no "supersort" of all possible range sorts of abstract fields, we cannot define the location read function $\_(\_)$ for abstract locations (see Paragraph 3.1.1.10). Therefore, for each abstract field declared as above, we introduce a function signature $rep_{\mathrm{f}} : Value \times Store \to Sort$ to denote the abstraction function that corresponds to abstract field f. The abstract location to be read is determined by the field name f and the value passed to rep_{f}; that is, $rep_{\mathrm{f}}(X, OS)$ for abstract fields f corresponds to $OS(X.\mathrm{f})$ for concrete fields f. Consequently, we abbreviate $rep_{\mathrm{f}}(X, OS)$ by $OS(X.\mathrm{f})$, where the meaning is clear from the context, .

To have a convenient notation for comparing the value of a location in two stores, we introduce so-called *L-equivalence*. In particular, L-equivalence allows us to quantify over the values held by abstract locations.

$$\_ \equiv_{\_} \_ : Store \times Location \times Store \to Bool$$

For concrete locations, this function is defined as follows:

$$OS \equiv_{mklc(L_C)} OS' \Leftrightarrow_{def} OS(L_C) = OS'(L_C)$$

For abstract locations, each field declaration of the form above adds an axiom to the universal specification:

$$OS \equiv_{X.\mathrm{f}} OS' \Leftrightarrow_{def} rep_{\mathrm{f}}(X, OS) = rep_{\mathrm{f}}(X, OS')$$

Lemma 4.2.1. $\_ \equiv_L \_$ *is an equivalence relation.*

Proof of Lemma 4.2.1:

For closed programs $\mathcal{P}$, we prove the lemma as follows: The lemma is trivial if L is a concrete location. If L is an abstract location with simple field id f, we know that there is a declaration of f in $\mathcal{P}$ (axiom **import6**, axiomatization of *module*, axiomatization of fields). For this declaration, an axiom for $\_ \equiv_{X.\mathrm{f}} \_$ is generated as described above. Since this axiom is based on equality, $\_ \equiv_{X.\mathrm{f}} \_$ is an equivalence relation.

Since $\_ \equiv_L \_$ is an equivalence relation in each closed program, it is also an equivalence relation in each open program. □

4.2.1.2 Representations of Abstract Fields. Abstract locations are not part of an object's state. The value of an abstract location is determined by the values held by a set of concrete locations, called the *representation* of the abstract location. The mapping of values of concrete locations to the value of an abstract location is specified by a so-called *defines-clause* or briefly *def-clause*[2]. Def-clauses have the form

mode **def f by** *t*;

where *mode* is one of Mojave's access modes, f is the name of an abstract field, and t is a $\Gamma \cup \{\text{this}\}$-term of f's range sort that does not contain free variables. Roughly speaking, t specifies the value of this.f in \$ (see Paragraph 4.2.1.3 for several examples of abstract fields and their def-clauses). For def-clauses, the following context conditions apply:

1. Def-clauses are declared in bodies of class or interface declarations. The def-clauses for an abstract field T@f have to be declared in T or subtypes of T.
2. Each subtype S of T (including T) may contain at most one def-clause for T@f; this clause can be either declared in S or inherited from a supertype. This implies that
   - inherited def-clauses cannot by overridden in subtypes. Since subtypes inherit implementations of supertypes, it is natural that they represent an abstraction in the same way.
   - two subtypes of T that are not subtypes of each other can contain different def-clauses for T@f. Thus, an abstract field can have different representations in different type declarations that are not subtypes.
   - multiple subtyping of interfaces must not lead to multiple inheritance of def-clauses. That is, when an interface I extends several interfaces $I_1, \ldots, I_n$, at most one I_i may contain a def-clause for each abstract field inherited by I.
3. Each class C must contain a def-clause for each of its abstract fields, which can be either declared in C or inherited. This restriction guarantees that there is a representation for each abstract location, which simplifies well-formedness proofs for interface specifications.
4. To guarantee information hiding, a def-clause may only exhibit implementation details that are accessible in every client that has access to the def-clause (see Section 4.1).

A def-clause of the above form declared in type declaration S specifies the representation of instances of field f in allocated S-objects. More precisely, such a def-clause adds an axiom for the specification of rep_{f} of the form

$$X \neq null \wedge tidD(typeof(X)) \preceq_M \mathrm{S} \wedge alive(X, OS) \Rightarrow$$
$$rep_{\mathrm{f}}(X, OS) = t[X/\text{this}, OS/\$]$$

[2] Def-clauses are called *represents-clause* or *rep declaration* in [Lei95b, LBR99a]. We changed the name and the keyword to avoid ambiguities with rep types.

to the universal specification. The theory of this axiom is determined by S and the access mode of the def-clause.

4.2.1.3 Example. To demonstrate the declaration of abstract fields and def-clauses, we revisit the list example introduced in Subsection 2.2.4 (see also App. C.1). Abstract fields are used to represent the abstract values of data structures and to express well-formedness conditions of data representations. We illustrate these applications in the following paragraphs.

Lists. We use lists of references (sort *list of Value*) to represent the abstract value of lists. Consequently, we declare an abstract field

public abstract *list of Value* `val;`

in class `List`. Since well-formedness of list representations is expressed by an invariant (see Subsection 6.2.2), we do not need an abstract field to specify validity of lists.

The mapping of node structures to lists of values is performed by a function *col* (in the following, [ ], [_], and _ + _ denote the empty list, the list with one element, and list concatenation):

$$\begin{array}{l} col : Value \times Store \rightarrow list\ of\ Value \\ X \neq null \wedge \ \rho(X, null, OS, \mathrm{next}) \Rightarrow \\ \qquad\qquad col(X, OS) =_{def} [OS(X.\mathrm{elem})] + col(OS(X.\mathrm{next}), OS) \\ X = null \vee \neg\rho(X, null, OS, \mathrm{next}) \Rightarrow col(X, OS) =_{def} [\,] \end{array}$$

To be able to show certain well-formedness criteria (see Obligation 5.1), we use a total definition for *col* that is well-defined even in states in which invariants don't hold: In case that the list structure is acyclic (i.e., the chain of `next`-references reaches the null-value; this property is implied by the invariant for `Node`), the node structure is mapped to the list of stored references. Otherwise, *col* yields the empty list.

col is defined in the public theory for the `LIST` module. We assume that this theory also contains appropriate lemmas about *col* to simplify verification, for instance:

Lemma 4.2.2. *The abstract value of a node structure is not affected by object creation.*

$$col(X, OS) = col(X, OS\langle T, U\rangle)$$

The proof of this lemma is based on Lemma 3.1.10 (i) and Axiom **store5**. It is straightforward and therefore omitted here.

A function *cut* is used to remove the first and last element of a list (*cut* yields the empty list if its argument has less than two elements). By *col* and *cut*, we can express the representation of `val` in class `List`:

protected def val by *cut*(*col*(\$(this.first), \$));

Recall from Subsection 2.2.4 that our list representation uses a dummy node at each end of the node structure. Thus, the abstract value of the list is obtained by removing the dummy elements from the list of references. The def-clause has protected access since it refers to `List`'s `first`-field.

List Positions. Objects of class `ListPos` store positions in doubly linked lists as references to `Node`-objects. On the abstract level, the position of the ith node of a list can be represented by the natural number i. Since nodes can be removed from a list, a list position can become invalid. Therefore, we introduce an additional abstract field for `ListPos` that indicates whether the position is valid[3]:

```
public abstract Nat position;
public abstract Bool valid;
```

To be a valid list position, the node referenced by `pos` has to belong to the node structure of the list referenced by `list`. That can be expressed by the following formula: $\rho(\$(\$(\text{this.list}).\text{first}), \$(\text{this.pos}), \$, \text{next})$. However, using this formula in the def-clause for `valid` requires the def-clause to have private or default access since `List`'s `first`-field is not accessible in subclasses of `ListPos`.

To avoid this obstruction for `ListPos`' subclasses, we introduce a public abstract field `anchor`. An `anchor`-location holds a reference to the first node of the associated list. Therefore, it makes this reference available in public interface specifications while the `list`- and `first`-fields are not exposed:

```
public abstract Value anchor;
def anchor by $($(this.list).first);
```

The pattern of introducing an abstract field that is represented by a single concrete field is sometimes called "readonly by specification pattern" since it allows one to loosen information hiding (the value of the abstract location can be referred to in public specifications) without breaking encapsulation (the concrete fields are still hidden and not accessible to all clients). The abstract field in this pattern is called "spec_public variable" in ESC/Java and JML.

Based on `anchor`, we can specify the def-clause for `valid`[4]. To be valid, the referenced node must belong to the list's node structure and be different from the dummy nodes:

```
protected def valid by ρ($(this.anchor), $(this.pos), $, next)∧
                       $(this.anchor) ≠ $(this.pos)∧
                       $($(this.pos).next) ≠ null;
```

Although the representation of `anchor` is not visible for subclasses of `ListPos`, the above def-clause provides enough information to verify subclasses such as `Iter` that modify the `pos`-field.

The abstraction of list positions to natural numbers is based on a function *index*. $index(X, Y, OS)$ yields the distance from node X to node Y in a node

---

[3] Validity cannot be expressed by an invariant since it is violated by `List`'s `remove`-method.

[4] `anchor` is an example of an abstract field that could be declared private protected or protected. However, we only provide public abstract fields (see Paragraph 4.2.1.1).

structure. It is defined in the public theory for `LIST`. $\{X \mid P(X)\}$ is the set of all X for which $P(X)$ holds. *min* yields the minimum of a set of natural numbers.

$$\begin{array}{rl} \mathit{index} : \mathit{Value} \times \mathit{Value} \times \mathit{Store} & \rightarrow \ \mathit{Nat} \\ \rho(X, Y, OS, \text{next}) \Rightarrow \mathit{index}(X, Y, OS) & =_{def} \ \mathit{min}(\{N \mid \rho_N(X, Y, OS, \text{next})\}) \\ \neg\rho(X, Y, OS, \text{next}) \Rightarrow \mathit{index}(X, Y, OS) & =_{def} \ 0 \end{array}$$

The abstract value of a valid list position is the distance from the first node. It lies between 1 and the number of elements in the list (position 0 would be the first dummy node):

protected def position by $\mathit{index}(\$(\text{this.anchor}), \$(\text{this.pos}), \$)$;

4.2.2 Pre-post-specifications

In this subsection, we present the syntax of pre-post-specifications and their semantics in terms of proof obligations of the underlying programming logic.

4.2.2.1 Syntax. As suggested in [LB99, PH97b, Win83], we provide several pre-post-pairs for each method. This allows one to structure specifications and to separate for instance the specification of the result value, modifications of the object store, and sharing properties. Common properties of all preconditions, especially properties that protect subsequent pre-post-pairs from undefinedness [LW97], can be specified in a so-called *requires-clause* or briefly *req-clause*. In particular, the req-clause of a method must be strong enough to guarantee that execution of the method does not abort because of null-pointer dereferencing, etc. Besides its use as notational abbreviation, the req-clause is necessary to define the meaning of modifies-clauses and invariants (see Section 5.3 and Subsection 6.2.3). A *pre-post-specification* consists of a requires-clause and an arbitrary number of pre-post-pairs.

Notation. A pre-post-specification can occur in declarations of abstract or concrete methods following the method signature. Furthermore, specifications of inherited methods can be refined without overriding the inherited method by repeating the method signature in the subclass and adding pre-post-pairs. However, in case the subclass does not override the inherited method, it must not specify an additional req-clause for this method[5]. Pre-post-specifications have the form

[5] If a subclass would provide a weaker req-clause without overriding the method implementation, it is no longer guaranteed that the new req-clause is sufficiently strong to guarantee that the inherited method implementation does not abort. That is, the method implementation would have to be reverified which is not possible in a modular setting. If a stronger req-clause is provided, behavioral subtyping is violated.

```
        req  R;
mode_1  pre  P_1;
        post Q_1;
        ...
mode_n  pre  P_n;
        post Q_n;
```

where each $mode_i$ is one of Mojave's access modes, $\mathbf{R}$ and the $\mathbf{P}_i$ are Γ_{pre}-formulas and the $\mathbf{Q}_i$ are Γ_{post}-formulas. That is, req-clauses and preconditions may refer to formal parameters, the object store, and the current universe, whereas the postcondition may only refer to the object store and `result`. Logical variables can be used to refer in postconditions to values held by formal parameters in the prestate (see below for an example).

Information Hiding. The access modes of pre-post-pairs have to guarantee that the method is accessible wherever its specification is. Otherwise, the method specification would reveal hidden information about the method signature. Req-clauses play a vital role for the meaning of pre-post-specifications, modifies-clauses, and invariants (see below). Therefore, the req-clause is involved whenever a property of a method invocation is proved. Consequently, a req-clause should not be hidden from clients. It has implicitly the same access mode as the method it belongs to. Req-clauses and pre-post-pairs must not refer to implementation parts that are less accessible than the req-clause/pre-post-pair to preserve information hiding (see Section 4.1).

Example. Since pre-post-specifications are a well-known means to express functional behavior, it is not necessary to discuss several examples here. (Thus, the pre-post-specifications are omitted for most methods in our example, see App. C.) [PH97b] contains a functional specification of two list implementations in a similar specification language. Here, we give a short example to show the syntax and highlight some specialties of our specification technique.

The method `setValue` of class `ListPos` updates the list element at the current list position. We specify this functional behavior as follows (see App. C.1 for the implementation). $update(S, N, V)$ yields the list S with the Nth element replaced by V.

```
public int setValue(readonly Object v)
 req         $(this.valid);
 public pre  $(this.theList) = L ∧ $(L.val) = S ∧ v = V ∧ $(this.position) = N;
        post $(L.val) = update(S, N, V);
```

If the list position is valid in the prestate, the abstract value of the associated list is updated at the designated position. `theList` is an abstract field that yields the list header that corresponds to the list position. It is necessary to refer to the list associated with a position in public specifications (`theList` is another example for the "readonly by specification" pattern). The logical variables L, N, and V are bound to values of the prestate such that they can be referred to in the postcondition. They are necessary since program variables such as `this` or `v` must not appear in postconditions. Note that the functional behavior of `setValue` is achieved by a destructive update of the list structure. There is no meaningful result value and thus no specification for the result. The proof for the above specification is presented in Section 4.3.

4.2.2.2 Meaning of Pre-post-specifications. The semantics of interface specifications is defined by translating them into proof obligations of the underlying programming logic.

Informal Meaning. To fit our programming logic, our pre-post-specifications express partial correctness. Although their meaning seems to be straightforward, there are some subtle questions we have to answer:

1. *How can behavioral subtyping be enforced in the context of information hiding?* To prove a property for a virtual method, one has to show that the corresponding property holds for all subtype methods, that is, that subtypes are behavioral subtypes. For this task, specifications of the supertype methods have to be accessible to implementors of subtypes.
2. *Should pre-post-specifications be inherited?* Pre-post-specifications can either only lead to proof obligations for the specified method or also for inherited or overriding methods in subtypes. To prove a property for a supertype method, the corresponding property has to hold for all subtype methods (see subtype-rule). Thus, both alternatives are semantically equivalent. However, inheriting specifications has some minor advantages: (1) It directly leads to proof obligations for inherited virtual methods. These triples simplify verification of invocations of inherited methods. (2) Specification inheritance leads to behavioral subtyping [DL96] which makes the treatment of open programs easier (see Subsection 3.3.4).
3. *Which invariants can be assumed to hold in preconditions?* The behavior of method implementations, in general, relies on the validity of type invariants. Therefore, it should be possible to assume that certain type invariants hold in the prestate (see Chapter 6 for details on type invariants).

For our specification language, we answer these questions as follows:

1. Private and default access specifications are used to document properties of methods for internal use by the developer of a module only. That is, private and default access specifications describe properties of a certain *method implementation* rather than of a virtual method (neither users nor implementors of subclasses have access to such specifications, see discussion on the JML interest list [JML]). Thus, private and default access specifications lead to proof obligations for method implementations whereas specifications with other access modes lead to proof obligations for virtual methods or implementations for dynamically or statically-bound methods, resp.

2. Pre-post-specifications of a dynamically-bound method T:m that do not have private or default access are inherited by subtypes. That is, they lead to proof obligations for all virtual subtype methods S:m where S is a subtype of T.
3. According to the semantics of type invariants (see Paragraph 6.1.3.2), we require that the invariants of all allocated objects that belong to $\mathcal{U}$ or one of its descendants hold upon invocation of a nonprivate readwrite method or a nonprivate static readonly method. If a private method or a readonly instance method must rely on certain invariants, they have to be repeated in the req-clause or a precondition, which is possible but limits the application of the method[6] (see specification of `List`'s `isEmpty`-method in App. C.1).

Furthermore, we can assume that the store is well-typed and all actual parameters are alive and well-typed in the prestate.

Formal Meaning. We formalize the above considerations as follows: Assume that $(\mathbf{P}_i, \mathbf{Q}_i)$ are the pre-post-pairs and $\mathbf{R}$ is the req-clause specified for a method m of type declaration T in a closed program $\mathcal{P}$ or the core of an program $\mathcal{P}$. Such a specification leads to proof obligation(s) of the forms:

$$(1)\ \{\ \mathbf{R}'\ \}\ \mathrm{COMP}\ \{\ \mathit{true}\ \} \qquad\qquad (2)\ \{\ \mathbf{R}' \wedge \mathbf{P}_i\ \}\ \mathrm{COMP}\ \{\ \mathbf{Q}_i\ \}$$

where

- COMP is T@m in case, that the method is private or static (i.e., statically-bound) or that the pre-post-pair has private or default access. In all other cases, the proof obligation is generated for each virtual method S:m in $\mathcal{P}$ resp. $\mathcal{P}$'s core where S is a subtype of T.
- $\mathbf{R}'$ abbreviates $\mathbf{R}\wedge$TA for private methods and readonly instance methods, and $\mathbf{R} \wedge \mathrm{TA} \wedge \mathit{inv}(\$,\mathcal{U})$ for all other methods. $\mathit{inv}(\$,\mathcal{U})$ expresses that the invariants of all living objects that belong to $\mathcal{U}$ or a descendant of $\mathcal{U}$ hold (see Subsection 6.2.3 for a formal definition). TA denotes the type and liveness annotations for the prestate of COMP ($\mathrm{v}_0,\ldots,\mathrm{v}_k$ are the formal parameters of COMP):

$$\begin{aligned}\mathrm{TA} \Leftrightarrow_{def}\ & \mathit{wt}(\$) \wedge (\mathit{static}(\mathrm{COMP}) \Leftrightarrow \mathrm{this} = \mathit{null})\wedge \\ & \textstyle\bigwedge_{i=0}^{k}(\mathit{typeof}(\mathrm{v}_i) \preceq \tau([\mathrm{v}_i]) \wedge \mathit{alive}(\mathrm{v}_i, \$))\end{aligned}$$

Proof obligations of the first form define the semantics of the req-clause: In conjunction with type and liveness annotations (and possibly invariants), it must be strong enough to guarantee that the method does not abort. Obligations of the second form formalize the meaning of pre-post-pairs.

Note that on the level of triples, inheritance of interface specifications does not mean that triples with identical formulas are generated for supertype and subtype methods. The precise type annotations lead to stronger preconditions for subtype methods since `this` is known to be an object of the subtype.

[6] One can in general invoke such methods only on targets belonging to $\mathcal{U}$ or a descendant of $\mathcal{U}$.

4.3 Verification of Functional Behavior

Modular verification of a module M means to prove modular correctness of the open program defined by M based on the modular correctness of the modules directly imported by M. We prove modular correctness of an open program $\mathcal{P}$ in two steps:

1. We verify method bodies based on the assumption that all methods in $\mathcal{P}$ behave according to their specifications. These proofs can be reused for imported methods.
2. We combine the proofs of step 1 and discard the assumptions to get the correctness proof for $\mathcal{P}$.

We discuss these steps in the following subsections and illustrate them by an example.

4.3.1 Verification of Method Bodies

The verifier of a method body has private view to the implementation and specification of the enclosing class. That is, she has access to the private theory for that class and to all imported theories. However, the verifier has only incomplete knowledge about the (open) program to be verified for two reasons:

- *Information hiding:* The verifier of a class C does not have access to hidden parts (in particular, the implementation) of type declarations used by C.
- *Open programs:* The verifier does not know about the context in which the verified method might be reused (except that the context is well-formed).

However, modular verification of functional behavior is possible despite these forms of incomplete knowledge:

- As defined above, functional behavior of a method m consists of the computation of a result value and modifications of the object store. That is, verification of functional behavior is mainly concerned with *changes* to the object store, not with the absence of modifications like frame properties and invariants (see Chapters 5 and 6). These changes are specified in terms of concrete and abstract fields that are accessible in m (see e.g., the specification of `setValue` above).
- To achieve its functional behavior, an implementation of method m can
  1. perform operations on local variables, formal parameters, and literals (such as assignment). Such operations are not affected by incomplete knowledge.
  2. access the object store by field-read- and field-write-statements. m can update concrete fields only if they are accessible in m. To reason about the effects of field updates on accessible abstract locations, the relevant

def-clauses have to be accessible in m, which has to be guaranteed by a good specification (i.e., it is a matter of specification methodology, not of the verification technique). The effects on abstract locations declared outside the scope of m need not be taken into account during verification of functional behavior[7]. Instead, the caller of m must reason about these effects. Thus, field access does not lead to problems for modular verification.

3. invoke methods. m can directly invoke methods only if they are declared in the scope of m. Thus, the specifications of the invoked methods can be used to reason about the invocations. That is, if we assume that all invoked methods behave according to their specifications, we can reason about method invocations modularly. It remains to the specifier to provide method specifications that are sufficiently complete for the verification of invocations.

Consequently, functional properties about method bodies can be proved modularly based on assumptions about the invoked methods. We illustrate such a proof in Subsection 4.3.3.

4.3.2 Proofs for Virtual Methods

Due to dynamic binding, method invocations in module M can lead to the execution of code that is declared outside the scope of M. To be able to verify M modularly, we have to guarantee that subtype methods behave according to the specifications of the corresponding supertype methods such that we can use the supertype specification to reason about the invocations. This problem of *behavioral subtyping* has been studied intensely [Ame87, Ame89, Dha97, LD00, LW93, LW94]. We achieve behavioral subtyping by specification inheritance [DL96], which is exploited by the proof strategy presented in Paragraph 3.3.4.2.

This strategy allows one to automatically combine the proofs of step 1 and discard the assumptions which yields the correctness proof for the open program. Thus, the verifier does not have to struggle with the effects of dynamic binding.

Meeting the Requirements. The specification primitives introduced so far meet the requirements of the proof strategy:

1. All context conditions for pre-post-specifications and abstract fields can be checked locally in a type declaration and the declarations of its supertypes. Thus, a legal composition of well-formed specifications consisting of abstract fields with def-clauses and pre-post-specifications yields a well-formed specification.

[7] This is exactly the point that makes modular verification of frame properties and type invariants much harder than verification of functional behavior (see Subsection 5.1.1).

2. The specification of static and private methods only leads to proof obligations for the corresponding implementations. Thus, the composition of programs cannot lead to new proof obligations for these specifications. The specification of a virtual method T:m leads to proof obligations for T:m and the corresponding subtype methods. Assume two open programs $\mathcal{P}_1$ and $\mathcal{P}_2$ with cores M_1 and M_2. Let M_1 contain the declaration of T. If M_2 declares a subtype S of T, then T must also be contained in M_2 (Axiom **import2**). Thus, the proof obligations for S:m in $M_1 \cup M_2$ have already been generated for M_2. If M_2 does not declare subtypes of T, then the specification of T:m does not lead to proof obligations for methods of types declared in M_2. In this case, the proof obligations stemming from the specification of T:m in $M_1 \cup M_2$ are exactly the proof obligations in M_1.
3. Type annotations are part of every proof obligation for a pre-post-specification.
4. Pre-post-specifications for virtual methods are inherited (see Paragraph 4.2.2.2).

Application of the Proof Strategy. For the modular verification of a module M, we require:

- the verifiers of the modules M_i imported by M to prove the properties about method implementations and bodies of virtual methods declared in M_i as required by Lemma 3.3.2;
- the verifier of M to provide proofs for the corresponding sequents about the methods declared in M.

We can now use the assumpt-intro-rule to get all sequents required by Lemma 3.3.2 and run this strategy to prove modular correctness of M.

For the rest of this book, we assume that all proofs are constructed as described above. This means in particular, that neither the subtype- nor the class-rule have to be used to prove the input for the proof strategy since all specified properties about virtual methods are contained in the assumption set. This restriction simplifies verification of frame properties and type invariants (see Subsection 5.4.4).

4.3.3 Example

As explained above, a verifier only shows proof obligations for method implementations, and — for each proof obligation for a concrete virtual method — the corresponding property for the body of its implementation. The remaining proof steps are automatically carried out according to Lemma 3.3.2 by a verification tool. We illustrate this methodology by verifying that ListPos:setValue meets the specification presented in Subsection 4.2.2. This specification leads to the following proof obligation:

$\{\ \$(\text{this.valid}) \wedge \$(\text{this.theList}) = L \wedge \$(L.\text{val}) = S \wedge \text{v} = V \wedge$
$\$(\text{this.position}) = N \wedge wt(\$) \wedge typeof(\text{this}) \preceq \tau(grndT(ctid(\text{ListPos})))\wedge$
$typeof(\text{v}) \preceq \tau(roT(ctid(\text{Object}))) \wedge alive(\text{this}, \$) \wedge alive(\text{v}, \$)\wedge$
$(static(\text{ListPos@setValue}) \Leftrightarrow \text{this} = null) \wedge inv(\$, \mathcal{U})\ \}$

ListPos:setValue(readonly Object v)

$\{\ \$(L.\text{val}) = update(S, N, V)\ \}$

From Lemma 3.3.2, we know that it is sufficient to show the corresponding property for the body of ListPos@setValue, based on the assumption that all virtual methods (in particular, List:setAtPos) meet their specifications. Thus, we derive:

$\{\ \$(\text{this.valid}) \wedge \$(\text{this.theList}) = L \wedge \$(L.\text{val}) = S \wedge \text{v} = V \wedge$
$\$(\text{this.position}) = N \wedge wt(\$) \wedge typeof(\text{this}) \preceq \tau(grndT(ctid(\text{ListPos})))\wedge$
$typeof(\text{v}) \preceq \tau(roT(ctid(\text{Object}))) \wedge alive(\text{this}, \$) \wedge alive(\text{v}, \$) \wedge inv(\$, \mathcal{U})\wedge$
$(static(\text{ListPos@setValue}) \Leftrightarrow \text{this} = null) \wedge \text{l} = init(\tau(grndT(ctid(\text{List}))))\wedge$
$\text{n} = init(\tau(roT(ctid(\text{Node}))))\ \}$

$\Rightarrow$ ⟦ $\text{this} \neq null \wedge typeof(\text{this}) \preceq \tau(grndT(ctid(\text{ListPos}))) \wedge alive(\text{this}, \$)\wedge$
$inv(\$, \mathcal{U}) \Rightarrow \$(\text{this.list}) \neq null \wedge \$(\text{this.pos}) \neq null$
(see App. C.1 and Chapter 6);
Axiom **store8**; unfolding representations of abstract fields ⟧

$\{\ \text{this} \neq null \wedge \$(\text{this.list}) \neq null \wedge \$(\text{this.pos}) \neq null\wedge$
$index(\$(\$(\text{this.list}).\text{first}), \$(\text{this.pos}), \$) = N \wedge N > 0\wedge$
$\$(\$(\text{this.pos}).\text{next}) \neq null \wedge \text{v} = V \wedge \$(\text{this.list}) = L \wedge \$(L.\text{val}) = S \wedge wt(\$)\wedge$
$typeof(\$(\text{this.list})) \preceq \tau(grndT(ctid(\text{List}))) \wedge inv(\$, univV(\$(\text{this.list})))\wedge$
$typeof(\$(\text{this.pos})) \preceq \tau(roT(ctid(\text{Node}))) \wedge typeof(\text{v}) \preceq \tau(roT(ctid(\text{Object})))\wedge$
$alive(\$(\text{this.list}), \$) \wedge alive(\$(\text{this.pos}), \$) \wedge alive(\text{v}, \$)\ \}$

l = this.list;

$\{\ \text{this} \neq null \wedge \text{l} \neq null \wedge \$(\text{this.pos}) \neq null \wedge index(\$(\text{l.first}), \$(\text{this.pos}), \$) = N\wedge$
$N > 0 \wedge \$(\$(\text{this.pos}).\text{next}) \neq null \wedge \text{v} = V \wedge \text{l} = L \wedge \$(L.\text{val}) = S \wedge wt(\$)\wedge$
$inv(\$, univV(\text{l})) \wedge typeof(\text{l}) \preceq \tau(grndT(ctid(\text{List})))\wedge$
$typeof(\$(\text{this.pos})) \preceq \tau(roT(ctid(\text{Node}))) \wedge typeof(\text{v}) \preceq \tau(roT(ctid(\text{Object})))\wedge$
$alive(\text{l}, \$) \wedge alive(\$(\text{this.pos}), \$) \wedge alive(\text{v}, \$)\ \}$

n = this.pos;

$\{\ \text{l} \neq null \wedge \text{n} \neq null \wedge index(\$(\text{l.first}), \text{n}, \$) = N \wedge N > 0 \wedge \$(\text{n.next}) \neq null\wedge$
$\text{v} = V \wedge \text{l} = L \wedge \$(L.\text{val}) = S \wedge wt(\$) \wedge typeof(\text{l}) \preceq \tau(grndT(ctid(\text{List})))\wedge$
$typeof(\text{n}) \preceq \tau(roT(ctid(\text{Node}))) \wedge typeof(\text{v}) \preceq \tau(roT(ctid(\text{Object})))\wedge$
$alive(\text{l}, \$) \wedge alive(\text{n}, \$) \wedge alive(\text{v}, \$) \wedge inv(\$, univV(\text{l}))\ \}$

result = l.List:setAtPos(n,v); ⟦ assumpt-axiom, invocation-rule ⟧

$\{\ \$(L.\text{val}) = update(S, N, V)\ \}$

By the assumpt-intro-rule, we get the property that is required for the application of Lemma 3.3.2. In a similar way, we can prove properties about the method implementations and the bodies of the implementations of the other virtual methods in `LIST`. We can then apply Lemma 3.3.2 which yields the correctness proofs of functional behavior for module `LIST`.

Compared to the size of the method, the above proof is very complex. However, most of the complexity stems from the treatment of type and liveness properties. Due to Lemmas 3.2.1 and 3.2.4, these properties can be automatically carried around in proofs by a verification tool, and can therefore be hidden from the user. For instance, the JIVE system keeps type and liveness properties implicit during proofs in the programming logic, but adds them whenever a program-independent lemma is generated (e.g., by applications of the strength- and weak-rules). For this book, we decided to keep typing and liveness properties explicit for two reasons: (1) Type properties are often needed in proofs since they also contain universe information. Therefore, explicit type information makes proofs easier to follow. (2) A formalization of the behavior of the JIVE system results in a rather complex programming logic in which correctness of some rules is based on the type safety proof, which is in turn formalized in the programming logic. Although such a logic can be formalized, we want to avoid this complexity.

4.4 Related Work

The specification and verification technique presented in this chapter is mainly adapted from [Lei95b] and [PH97b]. In this section, we discuss this and other related work on modular specification and verification of functional method behavior.

4.4.1 Specification of Functional Behavior

In the following, we give an overview of relevant work on data abstraction and pre-post-specifications.

Data Abstraction. The idea of using data abstraction to reason about complex data structures goes back to Hoare [Hoa72]. The abstract fields of our specification language are mainly influenced by Poetzsch-Heffter's and Leino's work. Poetzsch-Heffter explains how explicit abstraction functions can be formally founded by a data and state model of the programming language [PH97b]. In particular, he illustrates how abstraction functions can be used to describe object sharing in an abstract way. In contrast to our work, Poetzsch-Heffter's abstraction functions are defined as part of the universal specification, not of the interface specification. There is no support for information hiding or reasoning about all abstractions of a class, module, etc. in [PH97b].

Besides the missing support for information hiding, Leino's abstract fields and rep declarations are very similar to ours [Lei95b, LN00].

Larch/C++ [Lea97] also uses abstract fields and represents-clauses. The represents-clauses allow one to specify the representations of abstract fields by arbitrary axioms which is very convenient (in particular, for the specification of abstraction relations). These axioms are not part of the universal specification. Instead, they are conjoined to the pre- and postconditions of public member functions, which requires the verifier to carry around the conjuncts in proofs.

As already explained in Paragraph 1.6.1.2, abstract fields in JML (so-called model fields) map object structures to objects of so-called pure Java types, not to values of a declarative universal specification [LBR99a]. Pure types allow programmers to use Java to provide abstractions for their implementations. Thus, they are a promising approach to bring formal methods to practice. However, to use pure types for reasoning in our programming logic, they have to be translated into universal specifications of our formal system. Although it is usually feasible to use our data type definitions to imitate the data structures specified by pure types, the translation of methods of pure types is in general not trivial. For this book, we decided to simplify verification by putting the burden on the specifier to provide abstractions formalized in our logic system. Combining the verification techniques presented in this book with specification languages in the style of JML is an interesting direction for future work.

Data abstraction is kept implicit in most Larch interface specification languages. Thus, there is no explicit formal connection between object structures and values of the universal specification. However, such a formal connection is crucial for verification.

Pre-post-specifications. The idea of annotating programs by pre- and postconditions was first mentioned by Floyd [Flo67] and Hoare [Hoa69]. Pre-post-specifications are widely used to specify contracts between the caller and the implementor of a method [Jon91b, Mey92a, Mor94]. We discussed the operational and declarative techniques for interface specifications in Paragraph 1.6.1.2.

The syntax and formal meaning of pre-post-specifications used in this book was adapted from [PH97b] and enhanced by access modes for specifications. [LB99] presents several variations of pre-post-specifications such as informal, liberal, and redundant specifications as well as specification by examples. These variations are interesting to make specifications more expressive and easier to understand. We do not provide them in this book since we do not need the additional expressiveness here and since we want to avoid the additional complexity. Many of these variations are implemented in JML and Larch/C++. Like our specification language, JML provides access modes for pre-post-specifications.

Ruby and Leavens present an extension of pre-post-specifications that allows developers to implement subclasses without looking at inherited code [RL00]. So-called callable-clauses are used to determine which methods have to be overridden to specialize the behavior of an inherited method. Although such specifications improve adaptability and reusability, we do not support them since there is no adequate verification technique so far.

Standard pre-post-specifications can express relations between the pre- and poststate of a method, but fail to specify actions that do not affect the result value or the object store. Therefore, they are not capable of specifying event-driven systems or callbacks (the task of an event dispatcher is to invoke certain methods, no matter what actions are performed by these methods). An extension of pre-post-specifications by so-called model programs to handle such behavior is presented in [LD00]. To keep things simple, we do not treat event communication in this book.

Inheritance of interface specifications is discussed in [DL96]. According to this work, relating supertype to subtype abstractions is the most prominent problem for assigning a semantics to inherited specifications. This is due to implicit abstraction. In specification languages with explicit abstraction, the meaning of inherited interface specifications is clear since abstractions for supertypes are also defined for subtypes (abstract fields and def-clauses are inherited). To cover the extended state of subtypes, additional abstract fields have to be introduced, and the behavior of subtype methods has to be specified in terms of the new abstract fields (in addition to the inherited specifications). The relation between the new and the inherited abstract fields can be specified by the def-clauses for the new fields or by coercion functions or coercion relations in the universal specification [Ame91, LW93].

4.4.2 Verification of Functional Behavior

Modular reasoning about functional properties of OO-programs has been studied intensely. Existing work focuses on handling subtyping and dynamic binding [Lea88, LW90, UR93] and lead to/exploits the concept of behavioral subtyping [Ame87, Ame89, Dha97, LD00, LW93, LW94]. Behavioral subtyping is a relation between specified type declarations. It guarantees that subtype objects behave according to the supertype specification when used in place of a supertype object.

In this book, we enforce behavioral subtyping by inheritance of interface specifications (see [DL96] for a discussion). Behavioral subtyping allows us to apply a proof strategy (Lemma 3.3.2) to construct proofs for virtual methods from proofs for method bodies. (Technically, behavioral subtyping is needed to apply the subtype- and class-rule in the strategy.) As described and illustrated in Section 4.3, this strategy releases the verifier from struggling with subtyping and dynamic method binding.

Poetzsch-Heffter [PH97b] discusses modular verification based on a module system with linear import (i.e., each module directly imports at most one module). Such a restricted module system simplifies verification significantly. In particular, the mutual dependencies between imported methods described in Paragraph 3.3.4.1 cannot occur, which make a complex proof strategy for program composition dispensable. However, linear import is too restrictive for practical applications. For instance, it does not allow one to reuse modules from different sources.

5. Modular Specification and Verification of Frame Properties

In the last chapter, we explained how the functional behavior of methods can be specified and verified. Specification of functional method behavior describes the result value and modifications of the object store, but not the *absence of modifications*. However, precise information about what is left unchanged by a method execution is crucial for verification. We illustrate that by a small example. Consider the following method that takes a list and a mutable string (we call it `StringBuffer` as in Java), modifies the string, and appends it to the list. We assume that `List` and `StringBuffer` are implemented in different modules that do not import each other.

```
int m(List l, StringBuffer sb)
 req  l ≠ null ∧ sb ≠ null;
 pre  $(l.val) = L ∧ $(sb.theString) = S;
 post $(l.val) = [uppercase(S)] + L;
 {
   result = sb.toUpperCase();
   result = l.appFront(sb);
 }
```

Without going into details, one can see that for the verification of the method implementation, it is necessary to know that method `toUpperCase` does not modify the abstract value of the list[1]. However, the absence of side-effects is in general not specified in a method's functional specification (in particular, the absence of side-effects on structures declared outside the scope of the method like in this case). In a modular setting, it is not a matter of course that `toUpperCase` leaves the list unchanged although `StringBuffer` and `List` are declared in different modules: There could be a subtype of `StringBuffer` that overrides `toUpperCase` such that it modifies the list via a reference (alias) from a location of the `StringBuffer`-object.

This example demonstrates that verification of functional properties relies on information about what is left unchanged by method executions. Such aspects of method behavior that concern the absence of side-effects are called the *frame properties* of a method. The problem of specifying frame properties is called the *frame problem* [BMR95]. Although the frame problem is crucial

[1] After the invocation of `toUpperCase` the following property has to hold: $\$(\text{l.val}) = L \wedge \$(\text{sb.theString}) = uppercase(S)$.

Peter Müller: Modular Specification ..., LNCS 2262, pp. 143–194, 2002.

for verification, it has not been solved in a satisfying way for modular settings so far. In the next paragraph, we explain the particular difficulties for the modular specification of frame properties.

Modularity Requirements. If the entire program is known, the specification of frame properties is relatively simple since the developer has complete knowledge about all types and fields. Thus, it is possible to directly specify all locations that are modified by a method execution (this approach is for instance taken in LCL [GH93] and in [Heh93]). Within a modular setting, the frame problem is more complicated for the following reasons:

1. *Information hiding:* Hidden fields must not be contained in interface specifications. Thus, abstraction techniques have to be used to specify frame properties.
2. *Extended state:* The specification of frame properties must be loose enough to allow overriding methods to modify the extended state (see Subsection 1.3.4 and [Lei98]). On the other hand, they have to be rigorous enough to guarantee behavioral subtyping.
3. *Open programs:* It is never possible to know all types and fields of an open program. Therefore, frame properties cannot be specified by listing *all* modified locations.

In this chapter, we present a modularly sound solution to the frame problem that meets the requirements above. It is organized as follows: Section 5.1 describes informally how the modifies-clause technique can be enhanced by explicit dependencies to cope with the above modularity requirements. A formalization of dependencies and modifies-clauses is contained in Sections 5.2 and 5.3. Modular verification of frame properties is addressed in Section 5.4, and related work is presented in Section 5.5.

5.1 Approach

As explained in Subsection 1.5.1, we use modifies-clauses and abstract fields with explicit dependencies to specify frame properties. An abstract location L depends on a concrete or abstract location K in a store OS if modification of K in OS can affect the value of L. We require such dependencies to be declared explicitly in the interface specification. If L depends on K, we call L a *dependent* of K and K a *dependee* of L.

In this section, we explain informally our approach to specification and verification of frame properties. We present an informal semantics of modifies-clauses, introduce the depends-relation, and motivate the modularity rules that make modular verification of frame properties possible and guarantee modular soundness. The depends-relation, in general, is a function of the object store (i.e., a location can have different dependees in different stores). However, we neglect this fact throughout this informal description of our technique for clarity.

5.1.1 Meaning of Modifies-Clauses

Modifies-clauses specify sets of concrete or abstract locations. A method is allowed to modify the locations mentioned in its modifies-clause and their dependees (see Subsection 1.3.4). That is, the license to modify an abstract location L includes the license to modify L's dependees. It is intuitive that the license to modify the abstract value of an object structure includes the license to modify the concrete representation. (How could the modification of the abstract value be achieved otherwise?) However, the license to modify a location K does certainly not include the license to modify all locations that depend on K!

If a method is *only* allowed to modify locations mentioned in its modifies-clause and their dependees, code cannot be reused effectively. Consider the following example:

Example 5.1.1.

```
module ADDRESSBOOK imports LIST;

public class AddressBook {
 protected List data;
 public abstract AddressBookSort absValue;
 protected def absValue by map($($(this.data).val), $)

 public int insert(Address a) { result = data.appFront(a); }
}
```

The address book uses a list to store its entries. Consequently, the abstract value of the address book is obtained from the abstract list value by an appropriate mapping. As illustrated by method `insert`, `List`'s `appFront` method is used to insert entries into the address book. Therefore, invocations of List:appFront potentially modify the abstract value of an address book. However, in a modular setting, the modifies-clause of List:appFront only contains the abstract location this.val (and possibly some locations of objects associated with the list such as iterators), but no `absValue`-locations since class `AddressBook` is declared outside the scope of `List`. Thus, according to the above semantics, List:appFront is allowed to modify this.val and its dependees, but not the abstract value of the address book (we assume that the abstract value of the list does not depend on the abstract value of the address book). That is, the abstract value of the address book must not depend on the abstract list value to enable modular verification of List:appFront. Obviously, this is an unbearable restriction since lists, or imported classes in general, could in fact not be used to implement other data structures.

To permit implementations as described above, we have to loosen up the semantics of modifies-clauses. In the context of the universe programming model, this can be achieved in three ways:

Approach 1. We can generally allow a method m to modify abstract locations with fields declared outside the scope of m. However, this results in an extremely weak semantics that puts the burden completely on the verifier of invocations of m. She has to show that certain abstract locations are not modified by m for every invocation of m instead of proving this property once for the method m. In particular for methods that are frequently re-used, this approach is very inefficient.

Approach 2. We can use a scope-dependent semantics for modifies-clauses: A method m is allowed to modify certain abstract locations with fields declared outside m's scope. The set of potentially modifiable locations is determined by m's modifies-clause and the dependencies declared in the scope in which the modifies-clause is desugared. When an open program is extended, the additional dependency-declarations lead to a smaller set of modifiable locations. Thus, the semantics of the modifies-clause in the scope of an invocation is in general stronger than the semantics proved for the method implementation. Appropriate modularity requirements have to guarantee the soundness of this technique.

This approach is taken in the ESC Project [LN00]. It seems to have certain advantages for static checking. However scope-dependent semantics are difficult to handle by Hoare-style programming logics since the sequent proved about a method implementation is different from the sequent used to verify an invocation of the method. Furthermore, it is very difficult to find the appropriate modularity requirements to guarantee soundness of the technique. In fact, Leino and Nelson have not proved modular soundness for dynamic dependencies so far.

Approach 3. We can use the hierarchic universe programming model to define the semantics of modifies-clauses: We say that a location is *relevant for a method execution* if and only if it belongs to the current universe of this execution or a descendant thereof. An execution of a method m may modify relevant locations only if they are covered by m's modifies-clause. Modification of other locations is not restricted.

This semantics allows one to represent an object X in terms of objects of imported types as long as these objects belong to descendants of the universe to which X belongs. In the example above, the list that represents an `AddressBook`-object X has to be placed in an object or type universe owned by X. Thereby, `appFront` is allowed to modify the abstract locations of the `AddressBook`-object.

Let L be a location that is not modified by an execution of a method m. The actual proof that L stays unchanged by the execution of m is done (1) by the verifier of m if L is relevant for the execution of m, and (2) by the verifier of the invocation otherwise[2]. That is, this approach puts part of the burden

[2] As will be explained in Paragraph 5.1.3.2, this case only occurs when a readwrite method is invoked in a child universe of the current universe.

on the verifier of invocations of m, which allows her in return to handle the kind of implementations illustrated in Example 5.1.1. This semantics is weak enough for modular verification of methods (see Section 5.4). On the other hand, it is strong enough to reason about invocations: Modularity rules guarantee that the caller of a method m can decide whether a location might be changed by execution of m based on m's modifies-clause and the dependency-declarations in the scope of the caller (see below).

For the reasons described along with the three approaches, we follow variant 3 in this book.

Meeting the Requirements. The semantics of modifies-clauses described above meets the modularity requirements for frame properties:

1. *Information hiding:* Instead of mentioning a location L which is supposed to be hidden in modifies-clauses, one can use a public dependent of L. Therefore, the permission to modify L is granted without violating information hiding.
2. *Extended state:* Subclasses are allowed to introduce new dependencies for inherited abstract fields. Thereby, inherited methods get the permission to modify the extended state.
3. *Open programs:* By imposing appropriate restrictions on the permissible dependencies, we can enforce that all locations that are relevant for an execution of method implementation T@m have fields declared in the scope of T (see Subsection 5.1.3). Therefore, it is possible to specify these locations in T@m's modifies-clause.

5.1.2 Explicit Dependencies

We require dependencies to be declared explicitly as part of the interface of a type declaration. For verification, these declarations are used to generate axioms specifying the *depends-relation* on locations. Since each program extension may declare further dependencies, the depends-relation in an open program is underspecified. For modular verification, the (under-)specification of the depends-relation must guarantee four properties:

1. *Consistency with representation:* Explicit dependencies reveal information about the locations that represent the value of an abstract location without giving away its actual representation. To be useful to decide which modifications of the object store might change the value of an abstract location and which definitely will not, the value of an abstract location may only depend on locations it is declared to depend on. This is achieved by a proof obligation for every def-clause (see Obligation 5.1, p. 157).

2. *Expressiveness:* To prove that a location cannot be modified by a method, it is crucial to know which locations do not depend on each other. Since the depends-relation is underspecified, this information cannot directly be concluded from the specification of the depends-relation. We have to generate axioms expressing that certain locations do not depend on each other. We present the axiomatization of the depends-relation and its negation (in the following called *notdepends-relation*) in Section 5.2.
3. *Modular soundness:* As explained in Paragraph 3.1.1.1, we achieve modular soundness by using underspecification: The programming logic can only verify properties of a program that hold in all program extensions (provided that the specification of the core of the extended program is well-formed). However, program extensions lead to additional axioms for the depends-relation and its negation. To be reasonable, our technique has to ensure that the new axioms are consistent with the existing specification. That is, there must be a model for the axiomatization of the depends-relation for each program. We present such a model in App. D.4.
4. *Separate verification:* With open programs and arbitrary dependencies it is neither possible to verify a method m w.r.t. its modifies-clause nor can the notdepends-relation be specified. Therefore, dependencies have to be restricted to make modular verification possible. We present the appropriate modularity rules in the next subsection.

5.1.3 Modularity Rules

As pointed out in the last subsection, dependencies have to be restricted such that (1) they facilitate the modular verification of frame properties and (2) they enable a consistent axiomatization of the depends-relation. In this subsection, we informally explain the modularity rules that guarantee these properties. A formalization of the rules can be found in Subsection 5.2.4.

5.1.3.1 Locality Rule. The key idea for modular verification of frame properties is to exploit the hierarchic structure of the universe programming model. Universes provide *locality* in a sense that methods can only interact with objects belonging to the current universe (in instance methods, the universe to which the `this`-object belongs) or its descendants (except for objects referenced readonly, which are not relevant for the verification of frame properties since they cannot be modified). Locality has two important consequences: (1) Frame properties of a method can be verified without regarding objects, locations, and dynamic types that do not belong to the current universe or its descendants. (2) Callers of a method are only interested in modifications of locations belonging to the current universe or its descendants. Locality is supported by

– *the semantics of modifies-clauses:* The semantics of modifies-clauses requires only relevant locations to stay unchanged. We have motivated this semantics in Subsection 5.1.1.

– *the local update property of methods:* Methods can only modify concrete locations belonging to the current universe or its descendants. This is a consequence of the universe invariant (see Subsection 2.2.6): A method can only update locations or invoke readwrite methods of objects belonging to the current universe or its child universes. A formal proof of the local update property can be found in Subsection 5.4.2.
  The necessity for this property follows from the semantics of the modifies-clause: If a method m could get hold of a readwrite reference to an object that does not belong to the current universe or its descendants, it could use this reference for modifications. However according to the semantics of modifies-clauses, it would not be necessary to specify such modifications in m's modifies-clause. Thus, the modification would not be documented for callers of m.

To enable modular verification of frame properties, we require *locality of dependencies*: *A location that belongs to universe U may only depend on locations belonging to U or U's descendants.* We call this property *locality requirement.* It is enforced by the *locality rule* (see Obligation 5.2).

To see why the locality rule is necessary, we consider a small example that is illustrated in Figure 5.1. Three locations L_U, L_V, L_W belong to different universes U, V, W, resp. V and W are different child universes of U. Abstract location L_U depends on L_W (depicted by the dashed line). If abstract location L_V could depend on L_U (i.e., disregard the locality rule), L_V would transitively depend on L_W. Thus, a method m executed in universe W could modify L_V by updating L_W. Since L_V is not relevant for the execution of m (the shaded area contains the relevant locations), this modification would again not necessarily be specified in m's modifies-clause and could therefore stay undetected by callers of m. Thus, dependees of L_V must not belong to other universes than V and its descendants.

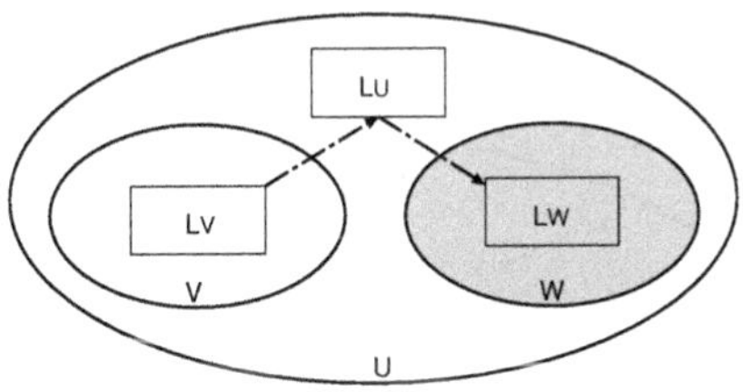

Fig. 5.1. Non-local Dependency

5.1.3.2 Authenticity Rule. The frame properties of a method cannot be verified modularly if program extensions are allowed to introduce arbitrary dependencies: For each statement in the body of a method implementation m that modifies the object store, the verifier of m must be able to determine which relevant locations might be affected by this modification.

A method can modify locations either directly by field-write-statements or indirectly by invoking readwrite methods. In the following paragraphs, we discuss the restrictions of dependencies that are necessary to determine the effects of these operations. Afterwards, we present a unifying formulation of these restrictions.

Field Updates. According to the type rules of the universe type system, a method m can directly update a concrete location Y.g belonging to a universe U if U is the current universe or U is a child universe of the current universe. Due to the locality rule, an abstract location X.f that might be affected by such a modification (i.e., that depends on Y.g) belongs to U, the current universe, or ancestors of the current universe. However, because of the semantics of modifies-clauses, abstract locations of the last kind are not relevant for the execution of m. Thus, we have to consider two cases: (1) X.f and Y.g belong to the same universe, namely U. (2) X.f belongs to the current universe, which is the parent universe of U. These cases are illustrated by Figures 5.2 and 5.3.

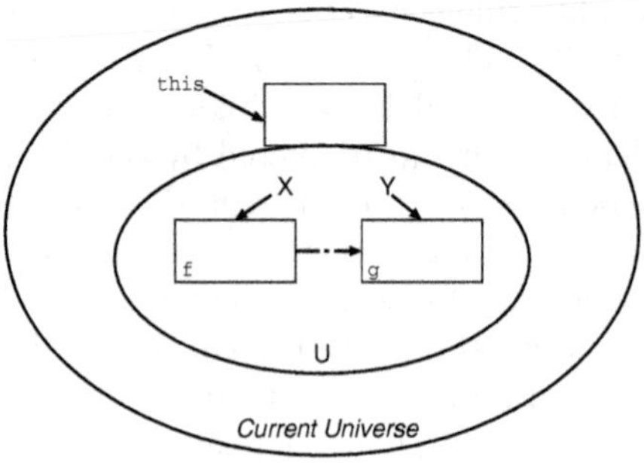

Fig. 5.2. Case 1 for Field Updates

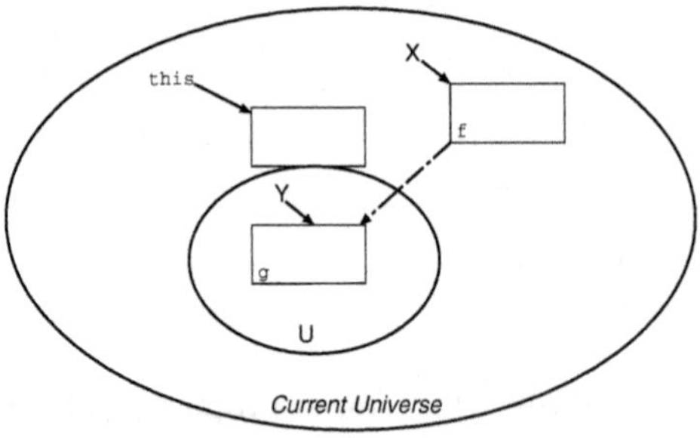

Fig. 5.3. Case 2 for Field Updates

Case 1: To determine the effects of an update of Y.g on X.f, f must be accessible in every type declaration that might contain an update of g. These type declarations are characterized by the fact that they have access to the declaration of g. Therefore, we have to require that the declaration of f is accessible in the declaration type of g, and thus in all type declarations that can update g. Recall that abstract fields are public. By having access to both f and g, the verifier of m can determine whether an update of Y.g effects the value of X.f by referring to the axiomatization of the depends-relation (see below).

Case 2: In this case, we could use the same requirement as for case 1. However, an alternative requirement is easier to integrate with the requirements needed for method invocations (see below). For the alternative requirement, we exploit the encapsulation provided by universes: If we neglect static methods for a moment, m can modify Y.g only if m is an instance method of an owner object of U.

If U is a type universe associated with a dynamic type T, all owner objects of U have in common that their classes have the declaration of T in their scope (see Paragraph 2.2.2.2). Thus, we require that f is accessible in T and thus in the classes of all owner objects of U and in the implementation of m.

If U is an object universe, the situation is somewhat complicated: m could be declared in any superclass C of the class of U's owner. Therefore, a first guess would be to require f to be accessible in `Object` and thus in C. However, this requirement would only be met by abstract fields declared in the predefined type declarations and is therefore inappropriate. Thus, we weaken this requirement by exploiting two properties of `Object`:

- Instances of `Object` do not make use of their object universes (`Object` does not contain field declarations). Therefore, the class of U's owner must be of a proper subclass of `Object`.
- `Object` does not contain readwrite methods. Thus, m must be implemented in a proper subclass of `Object`.

Due to these limitations of `Object`, it is sufficient that f is accessible in that superclass of the class of U's owner that is a direct subclass of `Object`[3]. Although this requirement is rather restrictive, object universes can be applied in many implementations as we explain in Paragraph 5.2.7.4

We can use the same restrictions for static methods: If U is the type universe associated with a dynamic type T, a static method m executed in the current universe can access Y.g only if the declaration of T is present in the declaration of m. If U is an object universe, Y.g cannot be accessed by static methods executed in U's parent universe since these methods do not have a `this`-object which is necessary to access an object universe.

[3] These limitations essentially also hold for Java's `Object`-class. It does not contain field declarations. There are method in Java's `Object` that are not side-effect-free, but these methods do not modify the state of existing object structures and can therefore be treated like our readonly methods here.

Method Invocations. Analogously to field updates, a readwrite method m can invoke a readwrite method n on an object resp. dynamic type (for static methods) belonging to the current universe or one of its child universes. The first case is trivial since all modifications that are relevant for m are specified in n's modifies-clause. If n is invoked in a child universe U of the current universe, we have to look at three groups of relevant locations that could be affected by the execution of n: (1) abstract locations that belong to the current universe; (2) abstract locations that belong to U or its descendants; (3) abstract locations that belong to descendants of the current universe, but not to U or its descendents. For an invocation `v=w.n();` the three cases are illustrated by Figures 5.4 to 5.6. The shaded areas depict the universes to which the locations of the three cases belong.

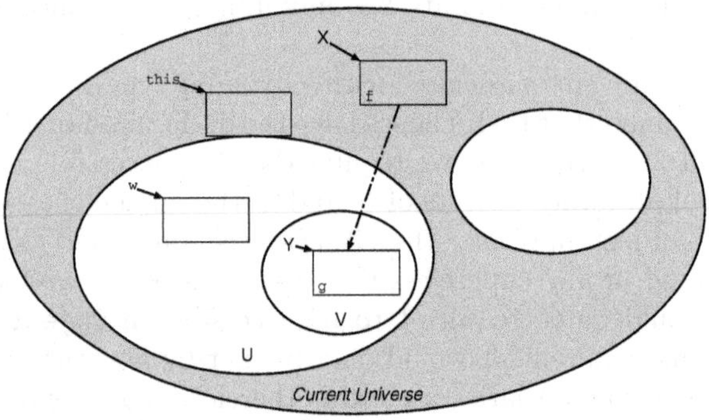

Fig. 5.4. Case 1 for Method Invocations

Case 1: This case is analogous to case 2 for field updates: m can invoke n only if m is an instance method of an owner of U (again neglecting static methods for a moment). That is, if a location X.f belonging to the current universe depends on a concrete location Y.g that might be modified by execution of n (i.e., Y.g belongs to a universe V, which equals U or is a descendent of U), f must be accessible in the implementations of all owners of U (see above). Note that U is the child universe of the current universe that is an ancestor of V (or V itself). We can apply the requirements described in case 2 for field updates to guarantee accessibility of f in the implementations of owners of U, and therefore in the implementation of m. Again, the same restrictions are appropriate if m is a static method.

Case 2: This case is trivial since modification of locations of this group is specified by n's modifies-clause.

Case 3: Due to the local update property, the locality rule (see Paragraph 5.1.3.1), and the tree structure of the universe hierarchy, locations of the third group cannot be modified by execution of n.

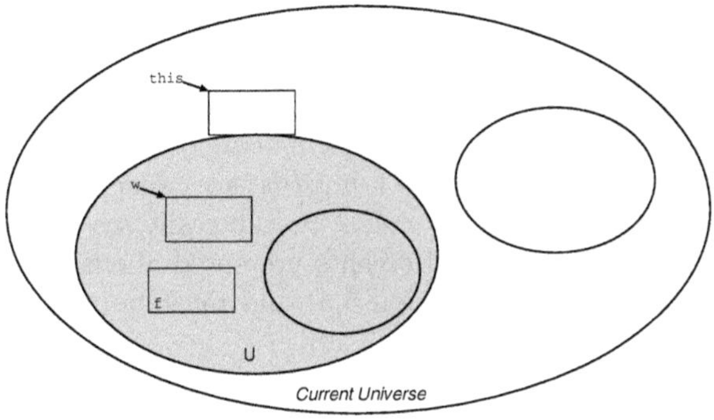

Fig. 5.5. Case 2 for Method Invocations

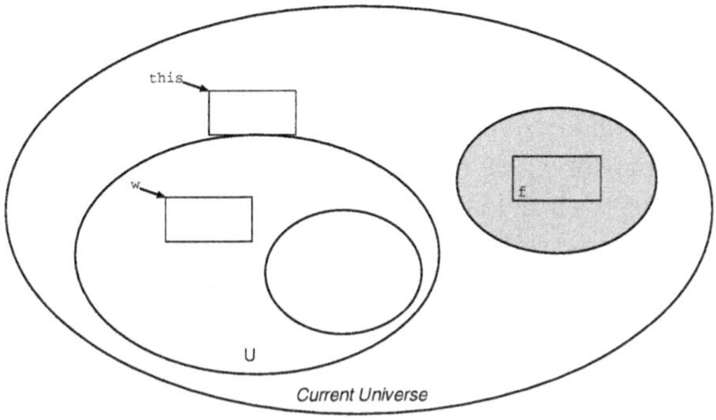

Fig. 5.6. Case 3 for Method Invocations

Guards and Authenticity. In the previous paragraphs, we presented a number of requirements for dependencies and motivated their necessity for modular verification. In the following, we unify the different requirements by the *authenticity requirement*[4].

All requirements presented in the last paragraphs have in common that — if a location X.f depends on Y.g — they require f to be accessible in a certain type declaration T that is determined by Y.g and the universe U_X to which X belongs. Since T is used to guard modifications of Y.g and to determine their effects on locations belonging to U_X, we call T the *guard of* Y.g *w.r.t.* U_X.

The guard is defined as follows: Let Y.g belong to universe U_Y. If U_Y equals U_X, the guard of Y.g w.r.t. U_X is the type id of the declaration type of g. Otherwise, there is a universe V that is a child universe of U_X and an ancestor of U_Y (or U_Y itself). If V is the type universe associated with dynamic type S then the guard of Y.g w.r.t. U_X is the type id of S. If V is an object universe then the guard of Y.g w.r.t. U_X is the type id of that

[4] The name stems from the authenticity rule for static dependencies in [Lei95b]. Our rule is a generalization of Leino's rule. See Section 5.5 for a comparison.

superclass of the class of V's owner that is a direct subclass of `Object`. We formalize guards in Subsection 5.2.4.

By the definition of guards, we can summarize the requirements presented above by the following *authenticity requirement*: *If location X.*f *depends on location Y.*g *then the declaration of* f *must be accessible in the guard of Y.*g *w.r.t. the universe to which X belongs.* One can easily see that the authenticity requirement unifies the requirements presented above. It is enforced by the authenticity rule (see Obligation 5.3) and must be met in well-formed specifications.

Roughly speaking, the locality and authenticity rules guarantee that a method m can only modify relevant locations with fields declared in the scope of m. This *modularity theorem* is the central property for the modular verification of frame properties. We formalize and prove it in Subsection 5.4.4.

5.1.3.3 Visibility Rule. As explained in Subsection 5.1.2 (point 2), an axiomatization of the notdepends-relation is necessary to prove that a location cannot be modified by a method invocation or location update. Thus, we generate axioms for each module M that specify the conditions under which two locations with fields declared in the scope of M do not depend on each other. This axiomatization must be consistent with program extensions: Clients of M must not introduce dependencies that contradict the axioms generated for M. Therefore, the placement of dependency declarations has to be constrained.

In the following, we consider two locations X.f and Y.g, where f and g are declared in the scope of module M. To be able to decide whether X.f depends on Y.g based on the information available in M, we could require that the declaration of a dependency of X.f on Y.g must be contained in every scope that contains both the declarations of f and g. Thus, if no dependency of X.f on Y.g is declared in the scope of M, we can generate an axiom that states that X.f does not depend on Y.g. This rule works fine in most situations since dependencies are usually declared together with either the field of the dependent or the field of the dependee. However, it rules out one important programming pattern that is illustrated by Example 5.1.2.

Example 5.1.2.

```
module M1;

public class C {
  public abstract Value f;
}
```

```
module M2;

public class D {
  public int g;
}
```

```
module N imports M1,M2;

public class CS extends C {
  protected rep<CS> D d; // rep type because of authenticity
  def f by $($(this.d).g);
}
```

In the example, X.f depends on Y.g if X is a CS-object and $Y = \$(X.\mathrm{d})$. This dependency can only be declared in module N. However, according to the above rule, this is not allowed since there are scopes that contain the declarations of f and g, but not module N (think of a module that imports M1 and M2 and nothing else). Therefore, placing the dependency declaration in module N would violate the above rule.

To support the implementation patterns illustrated by Example 5.1.2, we use the following weaker *visibility requirement*: *The declaration of a dependency of* X.f *on* Y.g *must be contained in every scope that contains the declarations of* f *and of the guard of* Y.g *w.r.t. the universe to which* X *belongs.* The visibility requirement is enforced by the visibility rule (see Obligation 5.4) and must be met in well-formed specifications.

If X and Y belong to the same universe, the refined requirement is identical to the above version (recall that the guard of Y.g w.r.t. the universe to which Y belongs is the declaration type of g). If Y belongs to a descendant of the universe to which X belongs, the visibility requirement allows one to declare dependencies of X.f on Y.g in the module that contains the declaration of the guard of Y.g w.r.t. the universe to which X belongs. Therefore, implementations like in Example 5.1.2 meet this requirement.

The visibility requirement guarantees the consistency of the axiomatization of the depends-relation and its negation when programs are extended. For each pair of fields f and g declared in the scope of module M, we can generate an axiom that states that X.f does not depend on Y.g if no according dependency is declared in the scope of M and if certain requirements about the guards of Y.g are met (see Subsection 5.2.4 for a formalization). The visibility requirement assures that extensions of M cannot declare dependencies that contradict the axioms generated for M.

The above modularity rules facilitate modular specification and verification of frame properties. We present a formalization of the rules and discuss their impact on the class of programs that can be handled by our specification and verification technique in the next section.

5.2 Formalization of Explicit Dependencies

In this section, we formalize the depends-relation that was introduced in Subsection 5.1.2. We drop the simplification used there and make explicit that the depends-relation has to depend on the store to be able to handle abstractions of object structures.

5.2.1 Declaration of Dependencies

Dependencies are declared by *depends-clauses* of the form

mode `depends f on` $\{Y.\mathrm{g} \mid P\}$;

where *mode* is one of Mojave's access modes, `f` is the name of an abstract field, `g` is the name of an abstract or concrete field, Y is a logical variable of sort *Value*, and P is a $\Gamma \cup \{\text{this}\}$-formula with Y as only free variable. Both `f` and `g` must be accessible in the type declaration that contains the depends-clause. Informally, such a depends-clause states that abstract location this.f depends in store \$ on all locations Y.g for which P holds (see below for a formalization).

To illustrate the declaration of dependencies, we show a depends-clause of class `List` here. It declares abstract `val`-locations of `List`-objects to depend on all `elem`-locations of the nodes in the list. See Subsection 5.2.6 for more examples.

`protected depends val on` $\{Y.\mathrm{elem} \mid \rho(\$(\text{this.first}), Y, \$, \text{next})\}$;

Depends-clauses are declared in bodies of class or interface declarations. There can be none, one, or several depends-clauses for each abstract field. All depends-clauses for a field T@f must be declared in T or subtypes of T. To guarantee information hiding, a depends-clause may only exhibit implementation details that are accessible to every client that has access to the depends-clause (see Section 4.1). We discuss expressiveness and limitations of our depends-clauses in Subsection 5.2.7

5.2.2 Axiomatization of the Depends-Relation

For each depends-clause in a program, we automatically introduce an identifier of sort *DepId* that is unique in the program and its extensions. Such an identifier can for instance be a combination of the type id of the type declaration that contains the depends-clause and a number.

A depends-clause of the above form declared in a type declaration with type id T introduces a dependency of X.f on Y.g in OS if X and Y are non-null, X is an instance of a subtype of T, X and Y are alive in OS, and the condition P is met. Since these requirements are used in various axioms and lemmas, we formalize them by a function dc:

$$dc : \mathit{DepId} \times \mathit{Value} \times \mathit{Value} \times \mathit{Store} \rightarrow \mathit{Bool}$$

For the definition of dc, each depends-clause d of the above form contributes an axiom of the form

$$\begin{aligned} dc(\mathrm{d}, X, Y, OS) \;\Leftrightarrow\;\; & X \neq \mathit{null} \wedge Y \neq \mathit{null} \wedge \mathit{tidD}(\mathit{typeof}(X)) \preceq_M \mathrm{T} \wedge \\ & \mathit{alive}(X, OS) \wedge \mathit{alive}(Y, OS) \wedge P[X/\text{this}, OS/\$] \end{aligned}$$

The theory for the identifiers and axioms is determined by the type declaration and the access mode of the depends-clause. The depends-relation is formalized by the function

$$\_ \xrightarrow{-} \_ : \mathit{Location} \times \mathit{Store} \times \mathit{Location} \to \mathit{Bool}$$

that is axiomatized as follows: For each depends-clause $\mathrm{d} \equiv \mathit{mode}$ `depends f on` $\{Y.\mathrm{g} \mid P\}$`;` we introduce an axiom of the form

$$dc(\mathrm{d}, X, Y, OS) \Rightarrow X.\mathrm{f} \xrightarrow{OS} Y.\mathrm{g}$$

The theories for these axioms are determined by the type declarations and the access modes of the depends-clauses. The depends-relation is reflexive and transitive. These properties and the fact that concrete locations depend only on themselves are expressed by the following axioms:

$$\begin{array}{ll} \textbf{dep1}: & L \xrightarrow{OS} L \\ \textbf{dep2}: & L \xrightarrow{OS} K \wedge K \xrightarrow{OS} J \Rightarrow L \xrightarrow{OS} J \\ \textbf{dep3}: & \mathit{mklc}(L_C) \xrightarrow{OS} K \Rightarrow \mathit{mklc}(L_C) = K \end{array}$$

For a closed program $\mathcal{P}$, $\_ \xrightarrow{OS} \_$ is the smallest relation satisfying **dep1**, **dep2**, and the axioms generated for the depends-clauses declared in $\mathcal{P}$. For an open program $\mathcal{P}$, $\_ \xrightarrow{OS} \_$ is underspecified. It satisfies **dep1**–**dep3** as well as the axioms generated for the depends-clauses declared in $\mathcal{P}$'s core and the axioms generated for the notdepends-relation for $\mathcal{P}$'s core (see Subsection 5.2.5).

5.2.3 Consistency with Representation

Based on $\_ \xrightarrow{-} \_$, we can formalize the proof obligation that guarantees that the declaration of the dependencies of a location L is consistent with L's representation (see Subsection 5.1.2, point 1). A consistent declaration of dependencies means that only modifications of explicitly declared dependees may affect the value held by an abstract location. In other words, if the values of all declared concrete dependees of a location L hold the same values in two stores then L must also hold the same value in these stores:

Proof Obligation 5.1 (Consistency with Representation) *Every def-clause for an abstract field* f *in a class or interface with TypeId* T *leads to the following proof obligation that has to be met in well-formed specifications:*

$$X \neq \mathit{null} \wedge \mathit{tidD}(\mathit{typeof}(X)) \preceq_M \mathrm{T} \wedge \mathit{alive}(X, OS) \wedge \mathit{alive}(X, OS') \wedge \mathit{wt}(OS) \wedge \\ \mathit{wt}(OS') \wedge \left(\forall K_C : \mathit{mkla}(\mathit{locA}(X, \mathrm{f})) \xrightarrow{OS} \mathit{mklc}(K_C) \Rightarrow OS(K_C) = OS'(K_C)\right) \Rightarrow \\ OS \equiv_{\mathit{mkla}(\mathit{locA}(X,\mathrm{f}))} OS'$$

As can be seen from this formalization, we require that an abstract location L must hold the same value in two object stores if all declared concrete dependees of L *in one of these stores* hold the same values in both stores. The reason for this asymmetry is as follows: Obligation 5.1 is necessary to conclude that certain modifications of the object store do not change the value held by an abstract location, which is in particular necessary to prove frame properties (see Section 5.4). To be applicable for such proofs, the formalization of dependencies must suit the semantics of modifies-clauses, which requires a method m to leave all locations unchanged that belong to objects allocated *in the prestate* and that are not dependees of locations in m's modifies-clause *in the prestate* (see Section 5.3).

This asymmetry between pre- and poststates in the semantics of modifies-clauses has to be reflected by Obligation 5.1 as illustrated by the following example: Let OS_1 and OS_2 be the pre- and poststates of the execution of a method m, and let L be an abstract location that is not relevant for this execution of m. Suppose m is specified to modify nothing. That is, all dependees of L in OS_1 are left unchanged by m. If we allowed L to have additional or different dependees in OS_2 (i.e., if for instance object creation could introduce new dependencies), then m could change the value of L although it does not modify any of L's dependees. Therefore, the frame properties of m would be too weak to allow callers of m to conclude whether L is modified by m.

Consequently, we have to require that if all dependees of an abstract location L in store OS_1 hold the same values in stores OS_1 and OS_2 then each dependee of L in OS_2 is also a dependee of L in OS_1. This property is enforced by the above asymmetric formalization of Obligation 5.1 that applies to all pairs of stores, not only to the pre- and poststates of a method execution. We discuss the impact of this formalization on the expressiveness of our technique in Paragraph 5.2.7.1.

The following lemmas simplify the application of Obligation 5.1 in proofs. Their proofs can be found in App. D.2.

Lemma 5.2.1. *For all open or closed programs with well-formed interface specifications, the following property holds:*

$$alive(obj(L), OS) \wedge alive(obj(L), OS') \wedge wt(OS) \wedge wt(OS') \wedge \\ \left(\forall K_C : L \xrightarrow{OS} mklc(K_C) \wedge alive(obj(mklc(K_C)), OS) \Rightarrow OS(K_C) = OS'(K_C)\right) \Rightarrow \\ OS \equiv_L OS'$$

Abstract fields specify the abstract value of an object or object structure. Intuitively, the abstract value of an existing object structure must not be changed by allocating new objects. Such ill-formed abstractions are prevented by the above proof obligation:

Lemma 5.2.2. *For all open or closed programs with well-formed interface specifications, the following property holds:*

$$alive(obj(L), OS) \wedge wt(OS) \Rightarrow OS \equiv_L OS\langle S, U\rangle$$

5.2.4 Formalization of the Modularity Rules

In this paragraph, we formalize the definition of guards and the modularity rules described in Subsection 5.1.3.

5.2.4.1 Guards. The guard G of a location L w.r.t. a universe U is defined as follows:

1. If L belongs to U, G is the type id of the declaration type of L's field.
2. If L belongs to a descendant of U then G depends on that child universe V of U that is an ancestor of or equal to the universe to which L belongs.
   a) If V is the type universe associated with dynamic type T then G is T's type id.
   b) If V is an object universe owned by an instance of class C then G is the type id of that superclass of C that is a direct subclass of `Object`.
3. G is undefined otherwise.

The function *guard* yields the guard of a location w.r.t. a universe:

$$\begin{array}{ll}
\mathit{guard} : \mathit{Location} \times \mathit{Universe} \rightarrow \mathit{TypeId} & \\
\mathit{univV}(\mathit{obj}(L)) = U & \Rightarrow \mathit{guard}(L,U) =_{def} \mathit{dtype}(\mathit{fid}(L)) \\
\mathit{univV}(\mathit{obj}(L)) \trianglelefteq \mathit{typeU}(T,U) & \Rightarrow \mathit{guard}(L,U) =_{def} T \\
\mathit{univV}(\mathit{obj}(L)) \trianglelefteq \mathit{objU}(\mathit{OID},C,U) & \Rightarrow \mathit{ctid?}(\mathit{guard}(L,U)) \wedge \\
 & \quad \mathit{ctid}(C) \preceq_M \mathit{guard}(L,U) \wedge \\
\multicolumn{2}{r}{(\forall T : \mathit{ctid?}(T) \wedge \mathit{guard}(L,U) \prec_M T \Rightarrow T = \mathit{ctid}(\mathrm{Object}))}
\end{array}$$

5.2.4.2 Locality. The locality rule requires that a location belonging to universe U may only depend on locations belonging to U or U's descendants. This is enforced by the following proof obligation.

Proof Obligation 5.2 (Locality Rule) *Every depends-clause* d *leads to the following proof obligation that has to be met in well-formed specifications:*

$$\mathit{dc}(\mathrm{d}, X, Y, \mathit{OS}) \wedge \mathit{wt}(\mathit{OS}) \Rightarrow \mathit{univV}(Y) \trianglelefteq \mathit{univV}(X)$$

Lemma 5.2.3. *For all open or closed programs with well-formed interface specifications, the following property holds:*

$$L \xrightarrow{OS} K \wedge \mathit{wt}(\mathit{OS}) \Rightarrow \mathit{univV}(\mathit{obj}(K)) \trianglelefteq \mathit{univV}(\mathit{obj}(L))$$

The proof can be found in App. D.2.

5.2.4.3 Authenticity. If location X.f depends on location Y.g then the authenticity rule requires that the declaration of f must be accessible in the guard of Y.g w.r.t. the universe to which X belongs. This is achieved by the following proof obligation.

Proof Obligation 5.3 (Authenticity Rule) *Every depends-clause* d $\equiv$ *mode* `depends f on` $\{Y.\mathrm{g} \mid P\}$; *declared in a class or interface with TypeId* T *leads to the following proof obligation that has to be met in well-formed specifications:*

$$dc(\mathrm{d}, X, Y, OS) \wedge wt(OS) \Rightarrow accessibleL(X.\mathrm{f}, guard(Y.\mathrm{g}, univV(X)))$$

Lemma 5.2.4. *For all open or closed programs with well-formed interface specifications, the following property holds:*

$$L \xrightarrow{OS} K \wedge wt(OS) \Rightarrow accessibleL(L, guard(K, univV(obj(L))))$$

The proof can be found in App. D.2.

5.2.4.4 Visibility. The declaration of a dependency of X.f on Y.g must be contained in every scope that contains the declarations of f and the guard G of Y.g w.r.t. the universe to which X belongs. Therefore, the depends-clause for a direct dependency of X.f on Y.g must be declared in the module of the declaration type of f or of G. According to the authenticity rule, the declaration type of f is in the scope of G. Thus, we can require that the depends-clause is declared in the module of G. This is enforced by the following proof obligation.

Proof Obligation 5.4 (Visibility Rule) *Every depends-clause* d $\equiv$ *mode* `depends f on` $\{Y.\mathrm{g} \mid P\}$; *declared in a class or interface with TypeId* T *leads to the following proof obligation that has to be met in well-formed specifications:*

$$dc(\mathrm{d}, X, Y, OS) \wedge wt(OS) \Rightarrow module(guard(Y.\mathrm{g}, univV(X))) = module(\mathrm{T})$$

5.2.5 Axiomatization of the Notdepends-Relation

If two fields f and g are declared in a scope S then we can conclude that X.f cannot depend on Y.g if

1. the dependency cannot be derived from the depends-clauses declared in S and
2. extensions of S cannot declare such a dependency, which is controlled by the visibility rule.

In the following, we formalize these two requirements.

5.2.5.1 Absence of Declared Dependencies. Since the depends-relation is transitive, its axiomatization is fairly simple: It is sufficient to introduce axioms for reflexivity, transitivity, and all directly declared dependencies. However, the situation is a lot more complicated for the notdepends-relations since it requires a closed formula that specifies the conditions under which two locations do not depend on each other. To illustrate the complexity of this problem, we consider the following example:

Example 5.2.1.

```
module M;
public class C {
  C next;
  abstract public AbsSort f;
  depends f on {Y.f | Y = $(this.next)};
}
```

From this depends-clause, we can conclude that X.f depends on Y.f if Y is reachable from X by following a chain of `next`-locations (besides some conditions about liveness, typing, etc.)[5] Since this depends-clause is the only depends-clause in the scope of M, we also know that — according to the declarations in the scope of M — X.f does not depend on Y.f if there is no such reference chain from X to Y. The step from the above depends-clause to an axiom using reachability is already a nontrivial abstraction. One can imagine that the conditions for the absence of a dependency get quite complex if they are automatically generated by a tool that cannot perform such abstractions, and if several depends-clauses for each location, transitive dependencies, and, in particular, more complex depends-clauses are involved. To handle this complexity, we take the following approach which is explained in detail below:

1. We build equivalence classes of locations where an equivalence class contains exactly the locations with a given simple field id.
2. For a given set of modules S, we determine the condition under which a location with field f depends on a location with field g, according to the declarations in S. This condition is expressed in one closed formula.
3. The negation of this condition is a closed formula that describes under which condition a location with field f does not depend on a location with field g, according to the declarations in S.

Let S be the set of modules of a closed program $\mathcal{P}$. The depends-relation in a store OS during execution of $\mathcal{P}$ can be described by a directed graph $G(OS, S)$ with locations as nodes. $G(OS, S)$ contains an edge from L to K if L depends directly on K in OS (i.e., this dependency is declared in one depends-clause or is due to reflexivity). To be able to describe these graphs statically, we introduce a graph $G'(S)$ that unifies the graphs $G(OS, S)$ for all stores OS. In $G'(S)$, we identify all nodes for locations with the same simple field id. That is, $G'(S)$ has equivalence classes of locations as nodes, characterized by the simple field ids declared in S. There is an edge from f to g in $G'(S)$ if S contains a depends-clause d where f and g are the fields of the dependent and the dependee, resp. There can be several edges from f to g in $G'(S)$. To capture the dynamic aspects of the depends-relation, we mark the edge from f to g with the identifier of the corresponding depends-clause.

[5] In most cases, X.f would also depend on the `next`-locations of the reachable objects. We omit these dependencies for simplicity.

These marks are used to determine under which conditions the depends-clause declares X.f to depend on Y.g in a store OS (see definition of dc in Subsection 5.2.2).

For a closed program $\mathcal{P}$ consisting of a set of modules S, we know that X.f might depend on Y.g in any store if there is at least one path from f to g in $G'(S)$. In an open program with core S, we know that X.f might depend on Y.g in any store *according to the dependencies declared in* S if there is at least one path from f to g in $G'(S)$. In both cases, the condition under which X.f depends on Y.g is described by a predicate that is obtained from the marks of the edges of all paths from f to g. Since these paths can contain alternatives and cycles, this transformation is not straightforward. It is performed in three steps[6]:

(a) We define a finite automaton for S [HU79, Per90]. The states, transitions, and input symbols correspond to the nodes, edges, and marks of $G'(S)$.
(b) We characterize all paths from the state for f to the state for g by a regular expression.
(c) We transform this regular expression into a predicate that expresses the conditions under which X.f depends on Y.g in some OS — according to the dep-clauses in S.

We explain these steps and illustrate their application to Example 5.2.1 in the following.

Finite Automaton. For each set of modules S (in particular, for each core of an open program and each closed program), we define a finite automaton $\mathfrak{A}(S)$ as follows:

1. *States:* For each simple field id declared in S, $\mathfrak{A}(S)$ has one state. The states are numbered by cardinal numbers $1, \ldots, H(S)$. That is, there is a bijection σ_S from the simple field ids declared in S to the set $\{1, \ldots, H(S)\}$. For simplicity, we use the numbers to refer to the states in the following.
2. *Alphabet:* The set of identifiers, $DepId$, for the depends-clauses declared in S is the alphabet of $\mathfrak{A}(S)$.
3. *Transitions:* The transitions of $\mathfrak{A}(S)$ are a set $T_S \subseteq Nat \times DepId \times Nat$. For each depends-clause with id d declared in S, T_S contains a transition $(\sigma_S(\mathrm{f}), d, \sigma_S(\mathrm{g}))$, where f and g are the fields of the dependent and the dependee, resp.
4. *Initial and accepting states:* As explained below, we use the automaton to compute the regular expression that brings the automaton from one state into another. However, we are not interested in the language accepted by $\mathfrak{A}(S)$. Therefore, the initial and accepting states are arbitrary states in $\{1, \ldots, H(S)\}$.

[6] [BRS99] uses a similar technique to describe reference chains in linked data structures.

Since the automaton $\mathfrak{A}(S)$ contains exactly one transition for each symbol of its alphabet and no ϵ-transitions, $\mathfrak{A}(S)$ is deterministic. The automaton for Example 5.2.1 is illustrated by Figure 5.7. d is the identifier for the depends-clause in this example.

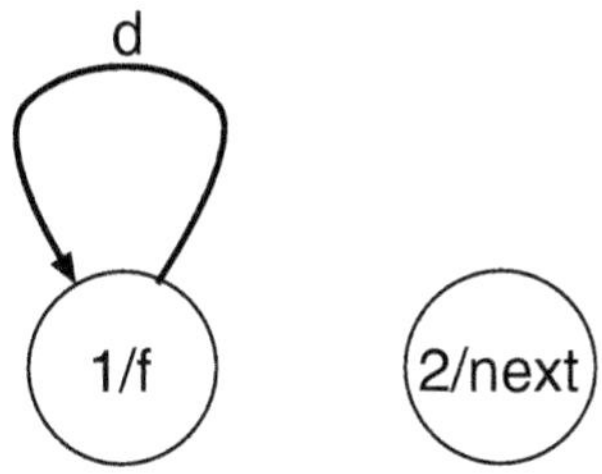

Fig. 5.7. Automaton for Example 5.2.1

Regular Expressions. As explained in [HU79], the paths from state A to state B in a deterministic automaton $\mathfrak{A}(S)$ are characterized by the words that bring $\mathfrak{A}(S)$ from state A to state B. These words can be described by a regular expression $R_{A,B}(S)$. It is defined as follows:

$$R_{A,B}(S) =_{def} R^{H(S)}_{A,B}(S)$$
$$R^0_{A,B}(S) =_{def} \begin{cases} \sum_{\mathrm{d}_i:(A,\mathrm{d}_i,B)\in T_S} \mathrm{d}_i & \text{if } A \neq B \\ \epsilon + \sum_{\mathrm{d}_i:(A,\mathrm{d}_i,B)\in T_S} \mathrm{d}_i & \text{if } A = B \end{cases}$$
$$R^N_{A,B}(S) =_{def} R^{N-1}_{A,B}(S) + R^{N-1}_{A,N}(S)(R^{N-1}_{N,N}(S))^* R^{N-1}_{N,B}(S)$$

$R^N_{A,B}(S)$ describes the set of words (i.e., sequences of *DepId*) that bring $\mathfrak{A}(S)$ from state A to state B without going through states with numbers greater than N. The sub- and superscripts of R range over natural numbers. Note that the initial and accepting states of $\mathfrak{A}(S)$ are irrelevant for the definition of $R_{A,B}(S)$. Since the definitions above are constructive, the regular expressions can be computed automatically by a verification tool. The paths in $\mathfrak{A}(S)$ from the state for field f to the state for field g are characterized by $R_{\sigma_S(\mathrm{f}),\sigma_S(\mathrm{g})}(S)$.

From Regular Expressions to Predicates. We define a function *rc* that yields for a regular expression $R_{\sigma_S(\mathrm{f}),\sigma_S(\mathrm{g})}(S)$, objects X and Y, and store OS whether X.f depends on Y.g in OS, according to the depends-clauses declared in S. The definition of this function is rather intuitive. In its description, we use the numbers of states and the corresponding field ids synonymously:

1. $\varnothing$: If there is no path from f to g then X.f does not depend on Y.g in any state. That is, *rc* yields false.
2. ϵ: Since there are no ϵ-transitions in $\mathfrak{A}(S)$, this regular expression indicates that f and g are identical and that the dependency is not declared in the program. Therefore, it is due to reflexivity, and *rc* yields whether X and Y denote the same object.

3. d: A single symbol indicates that the dependency is declared in depends-clause d. According to the axiomatization of $\longrightarrow$, dc describes the conditions under which this depends-clause leads to the dependency $X.\mathrm{f} \xrightarrow{OS} Y.\mathrm{g}$. Thus, rc yields the same result as dc in this case.
4. R_1R_2: This product describes an indirect dependency. That is, rc yields true if there is an intermediate location L such that $X.\mathrm{f}$ depends on L and L depends on $Y.\mathrm{g}$ in OS. That is, rc is defined recursively in terms of the predicates for R_1 and R_2.
5. $R_1 + R_2$: The union indicates that there are alternative paths from f to g. Consequently, rc yields true for $R_1 + R_2$ if it yields true for R_1 or R_2.
6. R^*: The Kleene operator specifies cyclic paths. Thus, rc yields true if there is a (possibly empty) sequence of locations $L_1, \ldots, L_n$ such that $X.\mathrm{f}$ depends on L_1, L_i depends on L_{i+1}, and L_n depends in $Y.\mathrm{g}$. Depending on the length of the sequence, this case is analogous to case 2, 3, or 4.

We formalize this definition by the following function. *regExpr* is the sort of regular expressions. Its definition as abstract data type is straightforward. We use the common syntax for regular expressions to improve readability.

$$
\begin{array}{lll}
\multicolumn{3}{l}{rc : regExpr \times Value \times Value \times Store \rightarrow Bool} \\
rc(\varnothing, X, Y, OS) & \Leftrightarrow_{def} & false \\
rc(\epsilon, X, Y, OS) & \Leftrightarrow_{def} & (X = Y) \\
rc(\mathrm{d}, X, Y, OS) & \Leftrightarrow_{def} & dc(\mathrm{d}, X, Y, OS) \\
rc(R_1R_2, X, Y, OS) & \Leftrightarrow_{def} & \exists Z : rc(R_1, X, Z, OS) \wedge rc(R_2, Z, Y, OS) \\
rc(R_1 + R_2, X, Y, OS) & \Leftrightarrow_{def} & rc(R_1, X, Y, OS) \vee rc(R_2, X, Y, OS) \\
rc(R^*, X, Y, OS) & \Leftrightarrow_{def} & \exists N : \exists Z_0, \ldots, Z_N : Z_0 = X \wedge Z_N = Y \wedge \\
 & & \bigwedge_{i=1}^{N} rc(R, Z_{i-1}, Z_i, OS)
\end{array}
$$

Note that rc is defined over the structure of regular expressions. Therefore, we have to distinguish between a regular expression and the regular set it describes. According to Lemma D.2.5, $rc(R_1, X, Y, OS)$ and $rc(R_2, X, Y, OS)$ are equal if R_1 and R_2 describe the same regular set. This property allows one to simplify the regular expressions coming from an automaton before applying rc.

By the above definitions, we can formalize the exact conditions under which a location $X.\mathrm{f}$ depends on location $Y.\mathrm{g}$ in store OS — according to the declarations in a set of modules S — by the following expression. We use such expressions for the axiomatization of the notdepends-relation in Paragraph 5.2.5.3.

$$rc(R_{\sigma(\mathrm{f}),\sigma(\mathrm{g})}(S), X, Y, OS)$$

In Example 5.2.1, we simplify the regular expression $R_{1,1}$ to d^* and get the following three equivalent predicates for the dependency $X.\mathrm{f} \xrightarrow{OS} Y.\mathrm{f}$:

$$
\begin{array}{l}
rc(R_{1,1}(S), X, Y, OS) \qquad \text{or} \qquad rc(\mathrm{d}^*, X, Y, OS) \qquad \text{or} \\
\exists N : \exists Z_0, \ldots, Z_N : Z_0 = X \wedge Z_N = Y \wedge \bigwedge_{i=1}^{N} rc(\mathrm{d}, Z_{i-1}, Z_i, OS)
\end{array}
$$

One can prove by induction on N that the last predicate implies that X reaches Y in OS via a chain of `next`-locations, which corresponds to our intuition for the depends-clause d.

As presented above, the technique seems fairly complicated. However, a verification tool can automatically generate the automata, determine the regular expressions, and simplify them by appropriate heuristics. Therefore, the user is not faced with this complexity. It is worth noting that part of the complexity is due to the flexibility of our depends-clauses. If the user could only declare simple static and dynamic dependencies (see [LN00]) instead of using arbitrary predicates in depends-clauses, we could replace rc by a slightly simpler function that expresses reachability via paths described by regular expressions over field names. We sketched this idea in [MPH00b].

5.2.5.2 Consistency with Program Extensions. For two locations L and K with fields declared in a set of modules S, the technique described in the previous paragraphs provides us with a predicate that specifies under which conditions L does not depend on K in a store OS, according to the declarations in S. For an open program $\mathcal{P}$, we know that L does not depend on K if this predicate is false and if extensions of $\mathcal{P}$ cannot introduce such a dependency. In the following, we formalize the second requirement.

Due to the visibility rule (see Obligation 5.4), we know that a direct dependency can only be declared in the module that contains the declaration of the guard of the dependee w.r.t. the universe to which the dependent belongs. That is, if f and g are declared in a set of modules S then extensions of S can introduce a direct dependency $X.\mathrm{f} \stackrel{OS}{\longrightarrow} Y.\mathrm{g}$ only if the guard of $Y.\mathrm{g}$ w.r.t. the universe to which X belongs is not in S. If we take transitive dependencies into account, a dependency $X.\mathrm{f} \stackrel{OS}{\longrightarrow} Y.\mathrm{g}$ can be declared only if one of the guards of $Y.\mathrm{g}$ w.r.t. the universes "between" the universes to which X and Y belong is not declared in S. That is, we can formalize the condition under which an extension of S cannot introduce such a dependency as follows ($wt(OS)$ is required since the visibility rule makes only statements about well-typed stores):

$$wt(OS) \wedge (\forall U : univV(Y) \lhd U \unlhd univV(X) \Rightarrow module(guard(Y.\mathrm{g}, U)) \in S)$$

This requirement is trivially true if $X.\mathrm{f}$ and $Y.\mathrm{g}$ belong to the same universe or if X is the owner of the universe to which Y belongs.

5.2.5.3 Axioms for the Notdepends-Relation. We are now equipped to specify the notdepends-relation. Let M be a module and $S = \{N \mid imports(\mathrm{M}, N)\}$ be the scope of M. For each pair of simple field ids f, g declared in S, we generate an axiom of the following form (we omit the application of σ in the following):

$$\begin{array}{l} wt(OS) \wedge (\ \forall U : univV(Y) \lhd U \unlhd univV(X) \Rightarrow module(guard(Y.\mathrm{g}, U)) \in S\ ) \wedge \\ \neg rc(R_{\mathrm{f},\mathrm{g}}(S), X, Y, OS) \Rightarrow \neg(X.\mathrm{f} \stackrel{OS}{\longrightarrow} Y.\mathrm{g}) \end{array}$$

The axiom is placed in the theory where all identifiers of depends-clauses occurring in $R_{f,g}(S)$ are present. If no such theory exists, the axiom is not generated. Omitting certain axioms weakens the specification, but does not lead to serious problems in most realistic programs for three reasons:

- A verification tool can generate weaker axioms. For instance, if the axiom for $R_{f,g}(S) = $ de cannot be generated since there is no theory for which the declarations of d and e are present, it is still possible to generate a weaker axiom for the notdepends-relation in the theory that contains the declaration of d (and analogously for e):

  $$wt(OS) \wedge (\ \forall U : univV(Y) \lhd U \unlhd univV(X) \Rightarrow module(guard(Y.\mathrm{g}, U)) \in S\ ) \wedge$$
  $$\neg \exists Z : rc(\mathrm{d}, X, Z, OS) \Rightarrow \neg (X.\mathrm{f} \stackrel{OS}{\longrightarrow} Y.\mathrm{g})$$

  The regular expression de describes a transitive dependency. This transitive dependency does not exist if one of the single dependencies described by d and e is not there. We strengthen the assumption of the initial axiom by requiring that the dependency described by d does not exist and by saying nothing about e. More formally, we use the definition of *rc* for concatenated regular expressions: $rc(\mathrm{de}, X, Y, OS)$ holds if and only if there exists an object Z such that $rc(\mathrm{d}, X, Z, OS)$ and $rc(\mathrm{e}, Z, Y, OS)$ hold. That is, if there is no Z such that $rc(\mathrm{d}, X, Z, OS)$ holds, then $rc(\mathrm{de}, X, Y, OS)$ does not hold.
  Such weakenings are helpful in many situations: Consider a string object with abstract location L, and a list structure, where the abstraction of the list depends on a private location K of the list. Due to information hiding, there is in general no axiom that specifies that L does not depend on K. However, this property can be derived from an axiom like the one above if (according to the depends-clauses in a given scope) string abstractions do not depend on the abstract value of a list, which is usually the case.
- In most applications, dependencies follow the reference structure of the object store. In these cases, the more fields involved in the reference chain from the dependent to the dependee the more likely it is that an axiom for the notdepends-relation cannot be generated. Since the authenticity and visibility rules force the programmer to structure his implementations in different universes, the reference chains between objects that belong to one universe contain usually a rather small number of different fields. Due to the locality provided by universes (see Paragraph 5.1.3.1), verification of a method is mainly concerned with objects belonging to the current universe and its child universes. Thus, the axioms for the interesting locations are usually available.
- To be able to make depends-clauses accessible for clients, the specifier can apply the "readonly by specification" pattern (see Paragraph 4.2.1.3) to loosen information hiding without giving up encapsulation.

Modular Soundness and Consistency. This concludes the formalization of the depends-relation. As already explained in Subsection 5.1.2, modular soundness of our technique is guaranteed by using underspecification. However, we have to show that the axiomatization of the depends-relation and its negation is consistent. That is, for each open or closed program, there must be a model satisfying all axioms described above[7]. We present such a model in App. D.4.

5.2.6 Example

To demonstrate how to declare dependencies and how to prove that they meet the modularity requirements, we revisit the list example (see App. C.1 and Paragraph 4.2.1.3). The automaton for module `LIST` is illustrated in Figure 5.8. The identifiers for the depends-clauses can be found as comments in App. C.1.

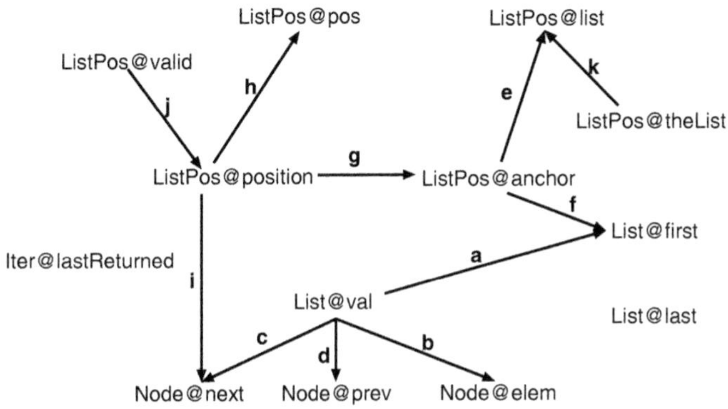

Fig. 5.8. Automaton for Module `LIST`

5.2.6.1 Lists. As presented in Paragraph 4.2.1.3, our list implementation has only one abstract field `val`. According to its representation, X.val depends on X.first as well as all `elem`- and `next`-locations of X's node structure. These dependencies are sufficient to prove consistency with representation (Obligation 5.1) for `val`. However, it is convenient to introduce additional dependencies: A method that modifies the abstract value of a list (e.g., `appFront`) in general re-arranges the node structure. This involves modification of `next`- and `prev`-locations. To keep the modifies-clauses of such methods simple, we

[7] More precisely, a model for all axioms of the formal data and state model is required. However, since there is a model for the axiomatization of the object store [PH97b], and since the axiomatization of the depends-relation is almost independent of the rest of the data and state model, we consider only the axioms presented in this section.

declare X.val to also depend on the prev-locations of X's node structure. That is, we declare the following dependencies in class List:

$$\texttt{protected depends val on } \{Y.\text{first} \mid Y = \text{this}\};$$
$$\texttt{protected depends val on } \{Y.\text{elem} \mid \rho(\$(\text{this.first}), Y, \$, \text{next})\};$$
$$\texttt{protected depends val on } \{Y.\text{next} \mid \rho(\$(\text{this.first}), Y, \$, \text{next})\};$$
$$\texttt{protected depends val on } \{Y.\text{prev} \mid \rho(\$(\text{this.first}), Y, \$, \text{next})\};$$

To show that the specification of List is well-formed, we prove Obligations 5.1 to 5.4 for val and the above depends-clauses in the following.

Consistency with Representation. To prove Obligation 5.1, we first show the following property for *col*:

Lemma 5.2.5. *If all* elem- *and* next*-location of a node structure hold the same values in two stores then the list of references stored in the node structure is equal in these stores.*

$$\Big(\rho(X, Y, OS, \text{next}) \wedge Y \neq null \Rightarrow OS(Y.\text{elem}) = OS'(Y.\text{elem}) \wedge$$
$$OS(Y.\text{next}) = OS'(Y.\text{next})\Big) \Rightarrow col(X, OS) = col(X, OS')$$

The proof of the lemma runs by case distinction: If X does not reach *null* via next-locations, the lemma follows from the definition of *col* and Lemma 3.1.10 (ii). If X reaches *null* via next-locations, the lemma is proved by induction on the length of this reference chain and uses Lemma 3.1.10 (ii). Based on this lemma, we prove Obligation 5.1:

$$X \neq null \wedge tidD(typeof(X)) \preceq_M ctid(\text{List}) \wedge alive(X, OS) \wedge alive(X, OS') \wedge$$
$$wt(OS) \wedge wt(OS') \wedge (\forall K_C : X.\text{val} \xrightarrow{OS} mklc(K_C) \Rightarrow OS(K_C) = OS'(K_C))$$
$$\Rightarrow \quad [\![\ \text{Declared dependencies of } X.\text{val}\ ]\!]$$
$$X \neq null \wedge tidD(typeof(X)) \preceq_M ctid(\text{List}) \wedge alive(X, OS) \wedge alive(X, OS') \wedge$$
$$OS(X.\text{first}) = OS'(X.\text{first}) \wedge (\rho(OS(X.\text{first}), Y, OS, \text{next}) \wedge Y \neq null \Rightarrow$$
$$OS(Y.\text{elem}) = OS'(Y.\text{elem}) \wedge OS(Y.\text{next}) = OS'(Y.\text{next}))$$
$$\Rightarrow \quad [\![\ \text{Lemma 5.2.5}\ ]\!]$$
$$X \neq null \wedge tidD(typeof(X)) \preceq_M ctid(\text{List}) \wedge alive(X, OS) \wedge alive(X, OS') \wedge$$
$$col(OS(X.\text{first}), OS) = col(OS'(X.\text{first}), OS')$$
$$\Rightarrow$$
$$X \neq null \wedge tidD(typeof(X)) \preceq_M ctid(\text{List}) \wedge alive(X, OS) \wedge alive(X, OS') \wedge$$
$$cut(col(OS(X.\text{first}), OS)) = cut(col(OS'(X.\text{first}), OS'))$$
$$\Rightarrow \quad [\![\ \text{Definition of } rep_{\text{val}}\ ]\!]$$
$$OS \equiv_{X.\text{val}} OS'$$

Locality. To prove that a dependee belongs to the same universe to which the dependent belongs or to a descendant thereof, we can exploit type information as in the following lemma:

Lemma 5.2.6. *If an object Y is reachable from object X via locations the fields of which have ground types then X and Y belong to the same universe.*

$$X \neq null \wedge Y \neq null \wedge wt(OS) \wedge grndT?([f]) \wedge \rho(X, Y, OS, f) \Rightarrow$$
$$univV(X) = univV(Y)$$

The proof of the lemma runs by induction on the length of the reference chain.

By this lemma, the proof of Obligation 5.2 is trivial for the depends-clauses for `val`. Note that we use static type information and well-typedness of object stores to show this obligation. In particular, we exploit that readwrite references point from an object belonging to universe U to an object belonging to U or a child universe of U. An abstract location must not depend on locations that are only reachable via readonly references and can therefore belong to arbitrary universes. The locality requirement cannot be proved for such dependencies.

Authenticity. In the above depends-clauses, the guard of each dependee of X.val w.r.t. the universe to which X belongs is *ctid*(List) (this is obvious for X.first and easy to show by Lemma 5.2.6 for the other dependees). Thus, Obligation 5.3 is trivially met by the above depends-clauses.

Visibility. Since the guard of the dependees of X.val w.r.t. $univV(X)$ (i.e., *ctid*(List)) is declared in module `LIST`, Obligation 5.4 is met.

5.2.6.2 List Positions. For the abstract fields of class `ListPos`, we declare the following depends-clauses:

`protected depends anchor on` $\{Y.\text{list} \mid Y = \text{this}\}$;
`depends anchor on` $\{Y.\text{first} \mid Y = \$(\text{this.list})\}$;

`public depends position on` $\{Y.\text{anchor} \mid Y = \text{this}\}$;
`protected depends position on` $\{Y.\text{pos} \mid Y = \text{this}\}$;
`public depends position on` $\{Y.\text{next} \mid \rho(\$(\text{this.anchor}), Y, \$, \text{next})\}$;

`public depends valid on` $\{Y.\text{position} \mid Y = \text{this}\}$;

The depends-clauses for `anchor` show that a dynamic dependency such as $Y.\text{anchor} \xrightarrow{OS} \$(Y.\text{list}).\text{first}$ requires at least the declaration of two dependencies: the actual dependency of Y.anchor on $\$(Y.\text{list})$.first and a dependency on the *pivot location* Y.list. The latter declaration is necessary to prove Obligation 5.1: Obviously, a modification of Y.list can change the value held by an abstract location since it might redirect the reference path from Y to another `first`-location.

The `position`- and `valid`-locations of a `ListPos`-object both depend on the `anchor`- and the `pos`-location of this object as well as all `next`-locations of all nodes in the object structure. Instead of declaring these dependencies separately for `position` and `valid`, we declare X.valid to depend on X.position since methods that may affect validity are, in general, allowed to modify the position. The proofs of Obligations 5.1 to 5.4 are very similar to the proofs for List@val. We omit them for brevity.

5.2.7 Discussion

Explicit dependencies allow us to formulate modularity requirements. These requirements are used to restrict the representations of abstract fields in a way that makes modular verification of frame properties possible (see Section 5.4). On the other hand, these restrictions limit the class of programs to which our technique can be applied. We discuss the restrictions imposed by Obligation 5.1, the syntax of depends-clauses, and the modularity rules in the following. A detailed comparison to the treatment of dependencies in Leino's and Nelson's work can be found in Subsection 5.5.1.

5.2.7.1 Consistency of Representations and Dependencies. In Subsection 5.2.3, we have explained that Obligation 5.1 requires that if all dependees of an abstract location L in store OS hold the same values in stores OS and OS' then each dependee of L in OS' is also a dependee of L in OS. This requirement has the following implications:

1. The set of dependees of L must not be changed by modifying a location that is not a dependee of L. This implies for dependees that are reachable from the object of L that every location on the path from L's object to the dependee must in general also be a dependee of L. We illustrated this for the `anchor`-field of class `ListPos` in Paragraph 5.2.6.2.
2. In OS', L must in general not depend on locations of objects that are alive in OS', but not in OS. Such dependencies can for instance occur if L is declared to depend on the `first`-locations of all `List`-objects. In this case, allocation of a new `List`-object introduces a new dependee for L. To avoid such situations, the objects of L's dependees in any store must be alive in every store in which L's object is alive. This is guaranteed if in any store each dependee is reachable from the object of the dependent (see [PH97b, Lemma 3.2viii]).

The former aspect increases the number of depends-clauses, but does not affect expressiveness of our technique. A more restricted syntax for depends-clauses (like in [LN00]) would allow a verification tool to automatically add certain dependencies and thus reduce the syntactic overhead for the specifier.

The latter aspect requires dependees to be reachable from the object of the dependent. Whereas this requirement is usually met by abstract fields that express data abstraction of object structures (such as `List`'s `val`-field, see Subsection 5.2.6), it is too restrictive to express certain aliasing patterns, in particular if these patterns involve all objects of a type (see Example 6.4.1).

Although requirement 2 restricts expressiveness of abstract fields, the limitations are endurable in our framework for two reasons: (1) For modular verification, the most interesting aliasing property is the absence of aliasing (see Subsection 1.3.5). In many cases, this property can be expressed and enforced by the universe type system. (2) In Subsection 6.4.1, we discuss an approach to relieve invariants of the reachability restriction. So-called *module invariants* allow one to express aliasing patterns beyond the capabilities of the universe type system.

5.2.7.2 Depends-Clauses. By our semantic treatment of dependencies, we can provide very general depends-clauses: Basically, an abstract location X.f can depend on arbitrary locations with a given field name. Although Obligation 5.1 requires dependees to be reachable from the object of the dependent (see Paragraph 5.2.7.1), our depends-clauses provide more flexibility than dependencies of other approaches [Lei95b, LN00]:

- Predicates such as ρ can be used to specify the dependees of a location, which simplifies for instance the specification of recursive data structures (see for example the depends-clauses for `List`'s `val`-field in Subsection 5.2.6).
- Since our depends-clauses do not syntactically enforce that dependees are reachable from the corresponding dependent, they provide a basis for a generalization of our techniques such as the module invariants sketched in Subsection 6.4.1. Such invariants are useful to express sharing properties, which cannot be handled by the restricted depends-clauses of [Lei95b, LN00].

For the axiomatization of the notdepends-relation (see Subsection 5.2.5), we have to require a fixed field name for each depends-clause. Thus, we can for instance not specify that an abstract location $X.\mathrm{f}$ depends on all locations reachable from X. That would be nice to express disjointness of object structures, but was not necessary in the examples we have looked at so far.

The generality of our depends-clauses provides flexibility, but requires, on the other hand, to prove modularity requirements. The restrictive depends-clauses used in [Lei95b, LN00] would allow a verification tool to check the modularity requirements statically and therefore simplify verification. In this book, we want to achieve a maximum of flexibility to show the expressiveness of our technique. For practical applications, it will be important to find the right balance between expressiveness and static checkability. However, such a decision should be based on major case studies which are considered future work.

5.2.7.3 Locality Rule. The locality rule is fairly natural: Usually, abstractions of dynamic components abstract from the states of their interface and representation objects. As long as these objects are reachable from an interface object via readwrite references, such abstractions meet the locality requirement. Objects that are only reachable via readonly references can be seen as *arguments* of a dynamic component (e.g., the elements in a container). It seems widely accepted that abstractions of a dynamic component must not depend on the states of its arguments (see e.g., the arg mode in [CPN98]).

Although the locality rule provides enough flexibility for most programs, there are applications that cannot be handled due to this requirement. For instance the validity of a hash table depends on the states of its elements, since these states are used to compute the hash values[8]. However, the elements are in general not part of the hash table's representation and can therefore belong to arbitrary universes. Consequently the validity property cannot be handled in a modular way.

[8] Thanks to John Boyland for a discussion of this example.

5.2.7.4 Authenticity Rule. Of all modularity rules, the authenticity rule imposes the most restrictive requirement: If the field of a dependee of location L is declared in a different module than the field of L, this dependee must belong to a descendant of the universe to which L belongs. This has three major implications that are explained in the following.

Must Use Universes. The authenticity rule forces programmers to use object and type universes whenever a type declaration declares a dependency where the field of the dependee is declared in an imported module. In such situations, all restrictions of the universe type system (see Subsection 2.2.6) apply.

Static Dependencies on Locations with Inherited Fields. Let L be a location with a field declared in module M. L must not depend on a location K of the same object, if K's field is declared in a module imported by M. We illustrate this restriction in Example 5.2.2.

Example 5.2.2. We assume that `Component` is a very simple AWT component that stores the width of the screen area that is reserved for a component. It is declared in module `COMPONENT` (see below). `Circle` (declared in module `CIRCLE`) is a special component to display circles. A `Circle`-object stores its radius. Such a circle-object is valid if the circle fits into the reserved area. We express validity by an abstract field `valid`. X.valid depends on X.width. Since `width` is declared outside the module `CIRCLE`, this dependency violates the authenticity rule. If the dependency was allowed, methods that have access to `width` (such as `resize`) could modify `valid` without being able to detect this modification.

```
module COMPONENT;

public class Component {
  protected int width;
  public int resize(...) {
    modifies {this.width};
    {...}
}

module CIRCLE imports COMPONENT;

public class Circle extends Component {
  int radius;
  public abstract Bool valid
  def valid by 2 * $(this.radius) ≤ $(this.width);
  depends valid on {Y.radius | Y = X};
  depends valid on {Y.width | Y = X}; // illegal
}
```

Non-authentic abstract locations like the `valid`-location in the example occur when a subtype declares a static dependency on a location the field of which is inherited. We have investigated four approaches that would allow us to use non-authentic abstract locations:

1. We could weaken the semantics of modifies-clauses such that methods are allowed to modify non-authentic locations. If methods could only modify non-authentic locations of the `this`-object as in the example above, this approach would be feasible. However, Mojave's access modes allow methods to modify non-authentic locations of other objects than `this`: If the fields of the dependees have public, protected, or default access, methods of various classes can modify non-authentic locations via their dependees. But even if these fields have private or private protected access, a method of class C can modify non-authentic locations of C-objects different from `this` since access modes control access on the class- rather than on the object-level.
   Therefore, allowing methods to modify non-authentic locations leads to a much weaker semantics of modifies-clauses that is not suitable to verify method invocations. More fine-grained access modes that control access on the object-level could help to remedy the shortcomings of this approach. However, the development of alternative access modes is a non-trivial task that is beyond the scope of this book.
2. An alternative approach to providing non-authentic locations is to keep the strong semantics of modifies-clauses and to guarantee that every method that might modify a non-authentic location L automatically covers L by its modifies-clause. This could be achieved by introducing additional dependencies: For every dependency of L on K that does not meet the authenticity requirement, we could introduce a dependency of K on L. Therefore, methods that are allowed to modify K may also modify L. In Example 5.2.2, this would mean to introduce a dependency of X.width on X.valid, which allows `resize` to modify this.valid. This approach has several severe shortcomings:
   - It does not work properly for transitive dependencies. Assume that a method modifies a dependee of K in a way that leaves the value of K unchanged, but affects the value of L. This method does not have to cover K by its modifies-clause. Therefore, it modifies the non-authentic location L without permission. To avoid this problem, all dependees of K must also depend on L.
   - It leads to a large number of additional dependencies that weaken the specification of frame properties and make verification more difficult.
   - Concrete locations depend only on themselves. Therefore, to introduce the cyclic dependencies described above, we have to introduce an abstract location for each concrete location (i.e., apply the "readonly by specification" pattern) and enforce that the abstract locations are used in modifies-clauses. However, since we only provide public abstract fields, this approach is not compatible with information hiding.
   - Automatically adding locations to the set of modifiable locations might be a solution for ordinary abstract fields, but nor for invariants. As explained in Chapter 6 we regard invariants as abstract locations that

must not be modified by nonprivate methods. Therefore, non-authentic invariants are not supported by this approach since they would be allowed to be modified.

3. We could enforce subclasses that introduce non-authentic locations to override all methods of their superclasses that might modify the non-authentic locations (for instance, based on specifications such as the callable-clauses in [RL00]). However, this approach does not work in the presence of public, protected, or default access fields since in this case, other methods than those of superclasses can modify the non-authentic locations via their dependees. The same argument applies when transitive dependencies are involved.
4. The fourth approach is a work-around for the problem. Multiple inheritance can be simulated by single inheritance: Instead of inheriting from class C, a class D can declare a field of type C and wrapper methods of the C-methods that forward invocations to the C-object. By the same pattern, one can replace single inheritance by a uses-relation and forwarding. Thereby, static dependencies on locations with inherited fields are turned into dynamic dependencies which allows one to apply universes to achieve authenticity. Although this pattern can help in some situations, it is not a general solution to the problem since it forbids inheritance.

To sum up, all four approaches are not satisfactory. Therefore, the problem of static dependencies on locations with inherited fields remains an open problem. It also occurs in Leino's and Nelson's work. In the future, we plan to investigate whether more fine-grained access modes allow us to find a satisfying solution.

Guards of Object Universes. Object universes can lead to problems in the context of inheritance and extended state: A class C that is not a direct subclass of `Object` can in general not use object universes for its representation: C cannot introduce an abstract location $X.\mathrm{f}$ that depends on locations belonging to the object universe owned by X. The guard of the dependees w.r.t. the universe to which X belongs is a superclass D of C. If C and D are not declared in the same module, f is not accessible in D, which violates authenticity. Despite this limitation, object universes can be used in numerous applications:

- In particular in class libraries, subclassing is often used only among classes of the same modules (see e.g., the Java API, especially the AWT [Gea97]). In these cases, object universes can be used for the extended state of subclasses without limitations.
- Subclasses can use type universes for their extended state whenever the inherited state and the extended state do not need to share objects. This work-around provides enough expressiveness for most implementation patterns for the price of weaker alias control for the extended state. However,

appropriate invariants and verification can compensate for the weaker alias control (see Subsection 6.4.1).

That is, despite the restrictive definition of guards, object universes can be used in many implementations, in particular in class libraries, which contain the most frequently reused code.

5.2.7.5 Visibility Rule. Due to the authenticity rule, dependencies between locations belonging to the same universe are usually declared together with the field of the dependee, which is supported by the visibility rule. When the dependee belongs to a descendant of the universe to which the dependent belongs, the visibility rule requires the depends-clause to be placed in the same module as the guard of the dependee w.r.t. the universe to which the dependent belongs. This requirement can in general be met if type universes are used since they allow the programmer to choose between several universes and thus several guards. However, like with the authenticity rule, the visibility requirement is often too strong when object universes in combination with inheritance are used as illustrated by the following example:

Example 5.2.3.

```
module SUPER;

public class Super extends Object {
  public abstract AbsSort f;
}

module SUB imports SUPER, LIST;

public class Sub extends Super {
  rep < this > List l;
  depends f on {Y.val | Y = $(this.l)};
}
```

The depends-clause in class `Sub` does not meet the visibility requirement since the relevant guard is `Super` which is declared in a different module. To avoid this problem, we can use the methodologies we have suggested in the above discussion of the authenticity rule: The problem does not occur if the list was stored in the type universe for `Sub` or if `Super` and `Sub` were declared in the same module.

The main application of abstract fields is the specification of abstract values for dynamic components. In most cases, the dependencies of such abstractions meet all requirements of our techniques and are not affected by the limitations discussed above. In particular, the dependees are reachable from the interface objects via readwrite references, and the representations of the dynamic components are encapsulated by means of universes. Therefore, our modularity requirements are weak enough to handle such abstractions and, hence, support a wide range of Mojave programs. The main restriction — static dependencies on locations with inherited fields — remains as open problem for future research.

5.3 Formalization of Modifies-Clauses

In this section, we explain the syntax of modifies-clauses and formalize the meaning presented in Subsection 5.1.1.

Syntax. Since modifies-clauses specify the absence of modifications, it is difficult to define a reasonable meaning if one method specification contains several modifies-clauses, especially if some of the modifies-clauses are inherited from supertypes. To avoid this complexity, we provide only one modifies-clause for each method. It can occur wherever a req-clause is allowed (see Subsection 4.2.2). Modifies-clauses have the form

$$\texttt{modifies}\ M;$$

where M is a Γ_{pre}-term of sort *set of Location*. Like with req-clauses, the access mode of a modifies-clause is identical to the access mode of the method. We use `modifies ∅;` as default when a modifies-clause is omitted.

Formal Meaning. According to the informal semantics presented in Subsection 5.1.1, a method with modifies-clause M is allowed to modify locations that are mentioned in the modifies-clause and their dependees. We call this set of modifiable locations the *downward closure* of M ("down to more concrete locations", see [Lei95b]). It is defined by a function δ:

$$\delta : \textit{set of Location} \times \textit{Store} \rightarrow \textit{set of Location}$$
$$\delta(M, OS) =_{def} \{L \mid \exists K \in M : K \xrightarrow{OS} L\}$$

Since the depends-relation is a function of stores, the downward-closure is store-dependent.

Based on this function, we define the semantics of a modifies-clause by translating it into a pre-post-pair (such a translation is often called *desugaring*). The formal meaning in terms of Hoare triples is then defined by the semantics of the pre-post-pair. A modifies-clause of the above form is desugared into the following pre-post-pair, where *mode* is the access mode of the corresponding method:

$$\begin{aligned} \textit{mode}\ \texttt{pre}\ & \$ = OS \wedge \textit{alive}(\textit{obj}(L), \$) \wedge \textit{univV}(\textit{obj}(L)) \trianglelefteq \mathcal{U} \wedge D = \delta(M, \$); \\ \texttt{post}\ & L \in D \vee \$ \equiv_L OS; \end{aligned}$$

This semantics reveals four interesting aspects of modifies-clauses:

- Since the semantics is defined in terms of pre- and postconditions, it does not constrain temporary modifications. That is, a method can modify a location and re-establish the initial value without specifying the modification in the modifies-clause (see Paragraph 5.5.1.5 for a discussion of temporary modifications).
- A method can modify locations of newly created objects without declaring these modifications. We regard initialization of new objects as functional property that has to be specified by pre-post-pairs.

- Since modifies-clauses are desugared into pre-post-pairs, the semantics for pre-post-specifications (see Paragraph 4.2.2.2) applies to modifies-clauses as well. In particular, we can assume the requires-clause, type and liveness annotations, and invariants to hold in the prestate.
  Furthermore, inheritance of pre-post-pairs leads to inheritance of modifies-clauses, and thus to behavioral subtyping. The proof obligations for inherited modifies-clauses can in general easily be proved by showing that the modifies-clause of the subtype method is a subset of the modifies-clause of the supertype method. The semantics of modifies-clauses is weak enough to allow subtypes to gain the right to modify the extended state by introducing additional dependencies. This way, locations of the extended state can be added to the downward-closure of inherited modifies-clauses.
- The semantics of modifies-clauses supports the locality concept described in Paragraph 5.1.3.1: Locations that do not belong to the current universe or its descendants may be modified without declaration. Note that modifies-clauses do not constrain the modification of formal parameters and local variables.

Example. In the following, we present the modifies-clauses of two methods of the list example. Method List:setAtPos modifies the abstract value of the list. Since n belongs to the node structure of the list (this is guaranteed by the req-clause) and this.val depends on all `elem`-locations of the node structure, the method is allowed to modify n.elem.

```
protected int setAtPos(readonly Node n, readonly Object v)
 req      n ≠ null ∧ index($(this.first), n, $) = N ∧ N > 0;
 modifies {this.val};
```

The flexibility of our modifies-clauses is illustrated by method List:appFront. Since the method adds a new node at the front of the list, the abstract values of all valid list positions for that list are changed. Furthermore, adding a new element to the list affects the abstract value of the list. These two properties are expressed by the following modifies-clause.

```
public int appFront(readonly Object v)
 modifies {this.val} ∪ {Y.position | tidD(typeof(Y)) ≼_M ctid(ListPos)∧
          $(Y.theList) = this ∧ $(Y.valid)};
```

Note that this modifies-clause requires one to refer to the list of a list position in public specifications. This is achieved by the the abstract field `theList`. Besides list positions, the abstract values of `ListProperty`-objects are affected by the execution of `appFront`. However, the affected `ListProperty`-objects belong to the parent universe of the current universe (see Fig. 2.8) and must therefore not be declared in the modifies-clause. We verify the frame properties of List:setAtPos and another method in Subsection 5.4.5.

5.4 Verification of Frame Properties

The most important contribution of this section is a modularity theorem that enables modular verification of frame properties. In particular, this theorem shows that the modularity requirements presented in Subsection 5.2.4 are sufficiently strong for this task.

Similar to functional behavior, frame properties can be verified by (1) verifying method bodies under the assumption that all virtual methods behave according to their specifications, and (2) applying the proof strategy of Lemma 3.3.2 to show the proof obligations for virtual methods and to discard the assumptions. As presented above, our specification technique for frame properties meets the requirements for the application of the proof strategy:

1. All context conditions for depends-clauses and modifies-clauses can be checked locally in a type declaration and the declarations of its supertypes. The modularity requirements (Proof Obligations 5.1 to 5.4) are concerned with single def- or depends-clauses and can be proved locally in the scope of these clauses. The proofs carry over to extended programs. Thus, the composition of well-formed specifications consisting of depends- and modifies-clauses yields a well-formed specification.

2.–4. The semantics of modifies-clauses is defined by desugaring them into pre-post-pairs. Since pre-post-specifications meet the requirements 2 to 4, they are also met by the proof obligations generated for modifies-clauses.

The proof strategy allows us to focus on the verification of method bodies. In the following, we explain why frame properties of method bodies can be verified modularly, present important lemmas about the possible modifications caused by field updates and method executions, and illustrate the verification of frame properties by an example.

5.4.1 Verification of Method Bodies

Frame properties are concerned with modifications of the object store. The body of a method can modify the store by object creation, field updates, and method invocations. In the following, we explain why the effects of each of these operations can be handled in a modular way. Thereby, we use two *accessibility properties* that are guaranteed by the locality and authenticity rules (see Subsection 5.1.3). Both properties require that the specification of the program to be verified is well-formed.

Accessibility Property 1: If a method T@m modifies a location K that belongs to a descendant of the current universe (either by field update or by method invocation) then the fields of all locations belonging to the current universe that depend on K are accessible in T.

Accessibility Property 2: The fields of all relevant locations (i.e., locations belonging to the current universe or its descendants) that might be affected by a field update in method T@m are accessible in T.

Based on these properties, the following proof methodology can be used to verify frame properties of method bodies.

Object Creation. Object creation does not affect the value held by concrete or abstract locations (Lemma 5.2.2). Therefore, new-statements are trivial for the verification of frame properties.

Field Update. Since a field update in method T@m cannot affect relevant locations with fields that are not accessible in T (Accessibility Property 2), one can use a case distinction over all fields accessible in T to reason about the effects of a field update[9]. Based on the corresponding def-clauses and the axioms for the depends-relation and its negation, one can prove for each accessible field that the corresponding relevant locations are either covered by T@m's modifies-clause or not affected by the field update. We illustrate such a proof in Subsection 5.4.5.

Method Invocation. Let T@m invoke a method n. Due to our proof strategy, we can assume that n behaves according to its specification. If T@m and n are executed in the same universe, it is sufficient to show that the modifies-clause of n is a subset of the downward-closure of T@m's modifies-clause. If n is executed in a child universe U of the current universe of T@m's execution, we have to consider three cases: (1) If a relevant abstract location L belongs to U or a descendant thereof, it can only be modified by n if it is covered by n's modifies-clause. Again, it suffices to prove that n's modifies-clause is a subset of the downward-closure of T@m's modifies-clause. (2) If L belongs to a descendant of T@m's current universe, but not to U or a descendant thereof, the locality rule and the local update property guarantee that L is left unchanged by execution of n. (3) If L belongs to T@m's current universe, Accessibility Property 1 guarantees that the field of L is accessible in T. As with field updates, we can use a case distinction over all accessible abstract fields and Lemma 5.2.1 to reason about the method invocation.

The methodology sketched above is based on the accessibility properties and the local update property. We formalize and prove these properties in the following subsections. Based on these properties, we prove the *modularity theorem for frame properties*: A method T@m can only modify relevant abstract locations the fields of which are accessible in T@m. An example that illustrates the methodology for the verification of frame properties and the application of the modularity theorem can be found in Subsection 5.4.5.

[9] Such a case distinction is only possible if the formal framework allows one to reason about all fields declared in a scope. In our framework, this is enabled (1) by encoding abstraction functions by abstract fields, (2) by using closed modules instead of open packages, and (3) by the axioms generated for modules and type declarations (see Subsection 3.1.1).

5.4.2 Local Update Property

Due to the universe invariant, a method m can update concrete locations only if they belong to the current universe or its descendants. We formalize this *local update property* as language property (see Definition 3.2.1). Analogously to the type annotations of Definition 3.2.3, we use an operator *lu* to add local update annotations to a triple:

Definition 5.4.1 (Local Update Annotations). *The definition of $lu(\mathbf{A})$ depends on the kind of* $\mathbf{A}$*:*

- *Let* m *be a virtual method* T:m *or a method implementation* T@m. *For method annotations of the form* $\{\, \mathbf{P} \,\}$ m $\{\, \mathbf{Q} \,\}$, $lu(\mathbf{A})$ *is defined as follows:*

  $$\{\, \mathbf{P} \wedge \$ = OS \wedge \mathcal{U} = U \wedge \bigwedge_{i=0}^{k} typeof(\mathrm{v}_i) \preceq \tau([\mathrm{v}_i]) \wedge wt(\$) \,\}$$
  m
  $$\{\, \mathbf{Q} \wedge (\neg univV(obj(mklc(K_C))) \trianglelefteq U \Rightarrow \$(K_C) = OS(K_C)) \,\}$$

  where $\mathrm{v}_0, \ldots, \mathrm{v}_k$ *are the formal parameters of* m. OS, U, *and* K_C *are fresh logical variables that neither occur in any specification nor in any proof.*
- *For statement annotations of the form* $\{\, \mathbf{P} \,\}$ STMT $\{\, \mathbf{Q} \,\}$, $lu(\mathbf{A})$ *is defined as follows:*

  $$\{\, \mathbf{P} \wedge \$ = OS \wedge \mathcal{U} = U \wedge \bigwedge_{i=0}^{n} typeof(\mathrm{v}_i) \preceq \tau([\mathrm{v}_i]) \wedge wt(\$) \wedge$$
  $$(static(\mathrm{T@m}) \Leftrightarrow \mathrm{this} = null) \,\}$$
  STMT
  $$\{\, \mathbf{Q} \wedge (\neg univV(obj(mklc(K_C))) \trianglelefteq U \Rightarrow \$(K_C) = OS(K_C)) \,\}$$

  where T@m *is the method implementation enclosing* STMT, $\mathrm{v}_0, \ldots, \mathrm{v}_k$ *are the formal parameters, and* $\mathrm{v}_{k+1}, \ldots, \mathrm{v}_n$ *are the local variables of* T@m. *Again,* OS, U, *and* K_C *are fresh logical variables.*

Lemma 5.4.1 (Local Update Property). *If the specification of an open or closed program* $\mathcal{P}$ *is well-formed and if there is a proof for* $\mathcal{A} \rhd \mathbf{A}$ *in* $\mathcal{P}$ *then there is a proof for* $lu(\mathcal{A}), ro(\mathcal{A}), typed(\mathcal{A}) \rhd lu(\mathbf{A})$.

According to Definition 3.2.1, the local update property is a language property. *lu* is greater than *ro* and *typed* in the ordering of operators for language properties. The proof of Lemma 5.4.1 can be found in App. D.2.

Similarly to the local update property, the universe type system guarantees that a method can create only objects that belong to the current universe or its descendants. Since this *local creation property* is not used in the sequel of this book, we omit a formalization here.

5.4.3 Accessibility Properties

In the following, we formalize and prove the accessibility properties described in Subsection 5.4.1. Both properties hold for programs with well-formed specifications only.

Accessibility Property 1. The first accessibility property guarantees that if a method T@m modifies a location K that belongs to a descendant of the current universe (either by field update or by method invocation) then all locations belonging to the current universe that depend on K are accessible in T. For the proof, we can assume the following properties that are guaranteed by the context conditions of Mojave and the well-formedness conditions for specifications:

1. T@m is an implementation of a readwrite method. Therefore, T denotes a class that is different from `Object`.
2. Since Mojave is type safe, we can assume well-typedness of the object store.
3. Since K belongs to a descendant of the current universe, there exists a child universe V of the current universe such that K belongs to V or a descendant thereof. The locality rule guarantees that T@m can only modify K by updating a location belonging to V or invoking a method in V. If V is the type universe associated with dynamic type S, we know that the type declaration of S is present in T. If V is the type universe owned by `this`, the class of `this` must be a subclass of T.

These considerations are formalized by the following lemma:

Lemma 5.4.2 (Accessibility Property 1). *For all open or closed programs with well-formed interface specifications, the following property holds:*

$$\begin{array}{l} ctid?(T) \wedge T \neq ctid(\text{Object}) \wedge L \xrightarrow{OS} K \wedge wt(OS) \wedge \\ \Big(univV(obj(K)) \trianglelefteq typeU(S,U) \wedge imports(module(T), module(S)) \vee \\ univV(obj(K)) \trianglelefteq objU(OID,C,U) \wedge ctid(C) \preceq_M T \Big) \wedge \\ univV(obj(L)) = U \Rightarrow accessibleL(L,T) \end{array}$$

Proof of Lemma 5.4.2:

Case 1: $mklc?(L)$

$$\begin{array}{l} L \xrightarrow{OS} K \wedge univV(obj(L)) = U \wedge \\ (univV(obj(K)) \trianglelefteq typeU(S,U) \vee univV(obj(K)) \trianglelefteq objU(OID,C,U)) \wedge \\ \Rightarrow \;[\![\text{ Axiom } \mathbf{dep3}, \text{ definition of } \trianglelefteq]\!] \\ K = L \wedge univV(obj(L)) \neq univV(obj(K)) \\ \Rightarrow \;[\![\text{ Contradiction }]\!] \\ accessibleL(L,T) \end{array}$$

Case 2: *mkla?*(L)

$accessMode(fid(L)) = public \wedge ctid?(T) \wedge T \neq ctid(\text{Object}) \wedge L \xrightarrow{OS} K \wedge wt(OS) \wedge$
$(univV(obj(K)) \trianglelefteq typeU(S,U) \wedge imports(module(T), module(S)) \vee$
$univV(obj(K)) \trianglelefteq objU(OID,C,U) \wedge ctid(C) \preceq_M T) \wedge univV(obj(L)) = U$

$\Rightarrow$ ⟦ Lemma 5.2.4 ⟧

$accessMode(fid(L)) = public \wedge ctid?(T) \wedge T \neq ctid(\text{Object}) \wedge$
$(univV(obj(K)) \trianglelefteq typeU(S,U) \wedge imports(module(T), module(S)) \vee$
$univV(obj(K)) \trianglelefteq objU(OID,C,U) \wedge ctid(C) \preceq_M T) \wedge$
$univV(obj(L)) = U \wedge accessibleL(L, guard(K, univV(obj(L))))$

$\Rightarrow$

$ctid?(T) \wedge T \neq ctid(\text{Object}) \wedge accessMode(fid(L)) = public \wedge$
$(univV(obj(K)) \trianglelefteq typeU(S,U) \wedge imports(module(T), module(S)) \vee$
$univV(obj(K)) \trianglelefteq objU(OID,C,U) \wedge ctid(C) \preceq_M T) \wedge$
$accessibleL(L, guard(K,U))$

$\Rightarrow$ ⟦ Definition of *guard* ⟧

$ctid?(T) \wedge T \neq ctid(\text{Object}) \wedge accessMode(fid(L)) = public \wedge$
$accessibleL(L, guard(K,U)) \wedge (guard(K,U) = S \wedge$
$imports(module(T), module(S)) \vee ctid?(guard(K,U)) \wedge ctid(C) \preceq_M guard(K,U) \wedge$
$(\forall T' : ctid?(T') \wedge guard(K,U) \prec_M T' \Rightarrow T' = ctid(\text{Object})) \wedge ctid(C) \preceq_M T)$

$\Rightarrow$ ⟦ Single inheritance (Axiom **subM2**) ⟧

$T \neq ctid(\text{Object}) \wedge accessMode(fid(L)) = public \wedge accessibleL(L, guard(K,U)) \wedge$
$(guard(K,U) = S \wedge imports(module(T), module(S)) \vee (T \preceq_M guard(K,U) \vee$
$guard(K,U) \prec_M T) \wedge (\forall T' : ctid?(T') \wedge guard(K,U) \prec_M T' \Rightarrow T' = ctid(\text{Object})))$

$\Rightarrow$ ⟦ Definitions of *accessible*, *accessibleL*; Axiom **import2** ⟧

$accessibleL(L,T)$

□

The proof of Lemma 5.4.2 gives insight to the necessity of two important restrictions of our specification framework:

- The key idea of the proof is that if L is accessible in $guard(K,U)$, and $guard(K,U)$ is present in T then L is accessible in T. This consequence requires that abstract locations are public. As soon as other access modes are used, this "transitive accessibility" does not hold in general[10].
- T is an arbitrary superclass of the class of the `this`-object different from `Object`. To guarantee that the guard of K w.r.t. U is present in T, we have to use the restrictive definition of guards for object universes (see Subsection 5.2.4).

[10] Transitive accessibility can also be achieved by omitting friend mechanisms. That is, if type universes and concrete fields can only have private or private protected access, and abstract fields have private protected or public access then the transitivity of the subtype relation guarantees transitive accessibility. However, we consider protected and default access as important means for efficient implementations. Therefore, we did not follow this approach.

Accessibility Property 2. The second accessibility property states that the fields of all relevant locations that might be affected by a field update in method T@m are accessible in T. Again, Mojave's context conditions provide us with several properties:

1. As with the first accessibility property, we know that T@m is an implementation of a readwrite method and T must denote a class that is different from `Object`.
2. T@m can only update locations with fields accessible in T.
3. Again, we can assume welltypedness of the object store.
4. The updated location belongs to the current universe or one of its child universes. In the latter case, we get the same assumptions as in point 3 of Accessibility Property 1.

We can formalize Accessibility Property 2 as follows:

Lemma 5.4.3 (Accessibility Property 2). *For all open or closed programs with well-formed interface specifications, the following property holds:*

$$\begin{array}{l} \mathit{ctid?}(T) \wedge T \neq \mathit{ctid}(\mathrm{Object}) \wedge L \xrightarrow{OS} K \wedge \mathit{accessibleL}(K,T) \wedge \\ \mathit{univV}(\mathit{obj}(L)) \trianglelefteq U \wedge \mathit{wt}(OS) \wedge (\mathit{univV}(\mathit{obj}(K)) = U \vee \\ \mathit{univV}(\mathit{obj}(K)) = \mathit{typeU}(S,U) \wedge \mathit{imports}(\mathit{module}(T), \mathit{module}(S)) \vee \\ \mathit{univV}(\mathit{obj}(K)) = \mathit{objU}(OID,C,U) \wedge \mathit{ctid}(C) \preceq_M T) \Rightarrow \mathit{accessibleL}(L,T) \end{array}$$

The proof of this lemma is based on the locality and authenticity requirements. It can be found in App. D.2.

5.4.4 Modularity Theorem for Frame Properties

The simple methodology for the verification of frame properties described in Subsection 5.4.1 requires to apply the local update property resp. the accessibility properties for each field update statement and each method invocation. These properties are used to prove that a method implementation T@m cannot modify relevant locations with fields that are not declared in the scope of T. To get rid of the recurring proof steps, we can formalize this property as theorem and prove it once for all programs.

Definition 5.4.2 (Unchanged-Annotations). *We use an operator uc to add unchanged-annotations to a triple* $\mathbf{A}$. *The definition of* $uc(\mathbf{A})$ *depends on the kind of* $\mathbf{A}$*:*

– *Let* m *be a virtual method* T:m *or a method implementation* T@m. *For method annotation of the form* $\{\ \mathbf{P}\ \}\ \mathrm{m}\ \{\ \mathbf{Q}\ \}$, $uc(\mathbf{A})$ *is defined as follows:*

$$\begin{array}{l} \{\ \mathbf{P} \wedge \$ = OS \wedge \mathit{alive}(\mathit{obj}(L),\$) \wedge \mathit{univV}(\mathit{obj}(L)) \trianglelefteq \mathcal{U} \wedge \neg \mathit{presentL}(L,\mathrm{T}) \wedge \\ \bigwedge_{i=0}^{k} \mathit{typeof}(\mathrm{v}_i) \preceq \tau([\mathrm{v}_i]) \wedge \mathit{wt}(\$)\ \} \\ \mathrm{m} \\ \{\ \mathbf{Q} \wedge OS \equiv_L \$\ \} \end{array}$$

– *For statement annotation of the form* { **P** } STMT { **Q** }, $uc(\mathbf{A})$ *is defined as follows, where* T@m *is the method implementation enclosing* STMT*:*

$$\{\ \mathbf{P} \wedge \$ = OS \wedge alive(obj(L), \$) \wedge univV(obj(L)) \trianglelefteq \mathcal{U} \wedge \neg presentL(L, \mathrm{T}) \wedge$$
$$\bigwedge_{i=0}^{n} typeof(\mathrm{v}_i) \preceq \tau([\mathrm{v}_i]) \wedge wt(\$) \wedge (static(\mathrm{T@m}) \Leftrightarrow \mathrm{this} = null)\ \}$$
STMT
$$\{\ \mathbf{Q} \wedge OS \equiv_L \$\ \}$$

L is a fresh logical variable that neither occurs in any specification nor in any proof.

Unchanged-annotations have one unlovely shortcoming: They do not carry over from subtype methods to corresponding supertype methods since the scope of the supertype is a subset of the scope of the subtype. Therefore, a location that is not present in the supertype can be present in the subtype. As a consequence of this shortcoming, we cannot prove that *uc* is a language property operator. However, the following property holds (see App. D.2 for the proof):

Theorem 5.4.1 (Modularity Theorem for Frame Properties). *If the specification of an open or closed program* $\mathcal{P}$ *is well-formed and if there is a proof for* $\mathcal{A} \,\triangleright\, \mathbf{A}$ *in* $\mathcal{P}$ *that does not contain applications of the subtype-rule then there is a proof for* $uc(\mathcal{A}), lu(\mathcal{A}), ro(\mathcal{A}), oal(\mathcal{A}), typed(\mathcal{A}) \,\triangleright\, uc(\mathbf{A})$

Although unchanged-annotations do not describe a language property, *uc* can be used like a language property operator if it is applied to proofs that do not contain applications of the subtype-rule. Recall that we assume that programs are proved using the proof strategy of Lemma 3.3.2. The strategy is based on proofs of method bodies and method implementations. As we have explained in Subsection 4.3.2, we can assume that these proofs are constructed without using the subtype-rule. A verification tool can check or enforce this restriction and therefore use *uc* like a language property operator when it executes the proof strategy. In particular, we can treat *uc* as language property operator in the definition of modular correctness (Definition 3.3.2). Consequently, the shortcoming of unchanged-annotations is not critical in practice as we will illustrate in the following subsection.

5.4.5 Example

To illustrate the methodology presented in Subsection 5.4.1 and the application of the modularity theorem, we prove the frame properties of List:setAtPos and ListPos:setValue.

According to Lemma 3.3.2, modular correctness requires to verify the bodies of the implementations of virtual methods based on appropriate assumptions. We do that for List:setAtPos and ListPos:setValue in the following.

5.4.5.1 Body of List@setAtPos. We verify the frame properties of List@setAtPos to illustrate how one can reason about the effects of field updates in a modular way. The relevant parts of the method specification are as follows:

```
protected int setAtPos(readonly Node n, readonly Object v)
  req      n ≠ null ∧ index($(this.first), n, $) = N ∧ N > 0;
  modifies {this.val};
```

In the following, we use **R** to abbreviate the conjunction of List@setAtPos's requires-clause, the type and liveness annotations for List@setAtPos's body, and the invariants that can be assumed in the prestate of List@setAtPos. That is, we have to prove the following sequent:

$$\rhd \ \{\ \mathbf{R} \wedge \$ = OS \wedge alive(obj(L), \$) \wedge univV(obj(L)) \trianglelefteq \mathcal{U} \wedge D = \delta(\{\text{this.val}\}, \$)\ \}$$
$$body(\text{List@setAtPos})$$
$$\{\ L \in D \vee \$ \equiv_L OS\ \}$$

First, we prove that the frame properties hold for all locations that are present in `List`:

$$\begin{array}{l} \rhd \ \{\ \mathbf{R} \wedge presentL(L, ctid(\text{List})) \wedge \$ = OS \wedge alive(obj(L), \$) \wedge \\ \quad univV(obj(L)) \trianglelefteq \mathcal{U} \wedge D = \delta(\{\text{this.val}\}, \$)\ \} \\ \qquad body(\text{List@setAtPos}) \\ \quad \{\ L \in D \vee \$ \equiv_L OS\ \} \end{array} \qquad (5.1)$$

We prove this sequent as follows:

$\{\ \mathbf{R} \wedge presentL(L, ctid(\text{List})) \wedge \$ = OS \wedge alive(obj(L), \$) \wedge univV(obj(L)) \trianglelefteq \mathcal{U} \wedge$
$D = \delta(\{\text{this.val}\}, \$)\ \}$

$\Rightarrow\ [\![$ Definition of $\mathbf{R}$ $]\!]$

$\{\ \text{n} \neq null \wedge typeof(\text{n}) \preceq \tau(orepT(ctid(\text{Node}))) \wedge wt(\$) \wedge presentL(L, ctid(\text{List})) \wedge$
$\$ = OS \wedge \rho(\$(\text{this.first}), \text{n}, \$, \text{next}) \wedge alive(obj(L), \$) \wedge univV(obj(L)) \trianglelefteq \mathcal{U} \wedge$
$D = \delta(\{\text{this.val}\}, \$)\ \}$

```
nn = (rep<this> Node) n;
```

$\{\ \text{nn} \neq null \wedge typeof(\text{nn}) \preceq \tau(orepT(ctid(\text{Node}))) \wedge wt(\$) \wedge$
$presentL(L, ctid(\text{List})) \wedge \$ = OS \wedge \rho(\$(\text{this.first}), \text{nn}, \$, \text{next}) \wedge alive(obj(L), \$) \wedge$
$univV(obj(L)) \trianglelefteq \mathcal{U} \wedge D = \delta(\{\text{this.val}\}, \$)\ \}$

$\Rightarrow\ [\![\ * \ ]\!]$

$\{\ \text{nn} \neq null \wedge (L \in D \vee \$\langle \text{nn.elem} := \text{v} \rangle \equiv_L OS)\ \}$

```
nn.elem = v;
```

$\{\ L \in D \vee \$ \equiv_L OS\ \}$

The implication marked with $*$ can be proved by a case distinction over the field of L. In this example, all fields that are present in `List` are also accessible in `List`, which simplifies verification. If this would not be the case, we could use Lemma 5.4.3 to derive the desired property for locations with fields that are present but not accessible in `List`.

Case 1: elem. If the field of L is `elem`, L only depends on nn.elem if L = nn.elem, since `elem` is a concrete field (Axiom **dep3**). From the depends-clauses for `val` and $\rho(\$(\text{this.first}), \text{nn}, \$, \text{next})$, we can conclude this.val $\xrightarrow{\$} L$ and therefore $L \in D$ in this case. If L does not depend on nn.elem, Axiom **store1** and Lemma 5.2.1 imply $\$\langle \text{nn.elem} := \text{v}\rangle \equiv_L OS$.

Case 2: val. The regular expression for a dependency $L \xrightarrow{\$}$ nn.elem in the automaton for module `LIST` (see Fig. 5.8) is b. Furthermore, the locality rule guarantees that L can only depend on nn.elem if L belongs to the current universe or the object universe owned by `this`. In both cases, the guard of nn.elem w.r.t. the universe to which L belongs is declared in module `LIST`. Thus, we can conclude from the axioms for the notdepends-relation and the definition of rc that $L \xrightarrow{\$}$ nn.elem only holds if $dc(\text{b}, obj(L), \text{nn}, \$)$ holds. Since `this` is the only owner of the node structure that contains nn, $\rho(\$(obj(L).\text{first}), \text{nn}, \$, \text{next})$ only holds if $obj(L) = \text{this}$, which implies $L \in D$. If L does not depend on nn.elem, we can again apply Lemma 5.2.1.

Case 3: other fields. For all other fields that are present in List, the regular expression describing a dependency $L \xrightarrow{\$}$ nn.elem is $\varnothing$ (see Fig. 5.8). Like in case 2, the guard of nn.elem w.r.t. the universe to which L belongs is declared in module `LIST`. Therefore, the axioms for the notdepends-relation imply $\neg(L \xrightarrow{\$} \text{nn.elem})$ and thus $\$\langle \text{nn.elem} := \text{v}\rangle \equiv_L OS$ (Axiom **store1** and Lemma 5.2.1).

From the above proof, one can easily see that there is also a proof for

$$\rhd \{ \mathbf{R} \} \; body(\text{List@setAtPos}) \; \{ \, true \, \}$$

By applying Theorem 5.4.1 to this sequent and using the strength-rule, we get:

$$\begin{array}{l} \rhd \; \{ \mathbf{R} \wedge \neg presentL(L, ctid(\text{List})) \wedge \$ = OS \wedge alive(obj(L), \$) \wedge \\ \quad univV(obj(L)) \trianglelefteq \mathcal{U} \wedge D = \delta(\{\text{this.val}\}, \$) \; \} \\ \quad\; body(\text{List@setAtPos}) \\ \quad \{ \; OS \equiv_L \$ \; \} \end{array}$$

Applying the disjunct-rule to sequent 5.1 and the above sequent yields the desired property for the body of List@setAtPos.

5.4.5.2 Body of ListPos@setValue. ListPos:setValue is specified as follows:

```
public int setValue(readonly Object v)
  req       $(this.valid);
  modifies {$(this.theList).val};
```

By the verification of ListPos@setValue's body, we show how method invocations can be handled. Below, **A** abbreviates the frame properties of method List:setAtPos:

$$\{\ \mathbf{R}' \wedge \$ = OS \wedge alive(obj(L), \$) \wedge univV(obj(L)) \trianglelefteq \mathcal{U} \wedge D = \delta(\{\text{this.val}\}, \$)\ \}$$
List:setAtPos
$$\{\ L \in D \vee \$ \equiv_L OS\ \}$$

That is, we have to prove the following sequent. Again, we use **R** to abbreviate the conjunction of the requires-clause of ListPos@setValue, the type and liveness annotations, and the relevant invariants.

$$\mathbf{A} \triangleright \{\ \mathbf{R} \wedge \$ = OS \wedge alive(obj(L), \$) \wedge univV(obj(L)) \trianglelefteq \mathcal{U} \wedge D = \delta(\{\$(\text{this.theList}).\text{val}\}, \$)\ \}$$
body(ListPos@setValue)
$$\{\ L \in D \vee \$ \equiv_L OS\ \}$$

We prove this sequent as follows:

$$\{\ \mathbf{R} \wedge \$ = OS \wedge alive(obj(L), \$) \wedge univV(obj(L)) \trianglelefteq \mathcal{U} \wedge D = \delta(\{\$(\text{this.theList}).\text{val}\}, \$)\ \}$$
$\Rightarrow$ ⟦ representation of this.theList ⟧
$$\{\ \text{this} \neq null \wedge \$(\text{this.list}) \neq null \wedge \mathbf{R}'[\$(\text{this.list})/\text{this}, univV(\$(\text{this.list}))/\mathcal{U}] \wedge \$ = OS \wedge alive(obj(L), \$) \wedge univV(obj(L)) \trianglelefteq univV(\$(\text{this.list})) \wedge D = \delta(\{\$(\text{this.list}).\text{val}\}, \$)\ \}$$
l = this.list;
$$\{\ \text{this} \neq null \wedge \text{l} \neq null \wedge \mathbf{R}'[\text{l}/\text{this}, univV(\text{l})/\mathcal{U}] \wedge \$ = OS \wedge alive(obj(L), \$) \wedge univV(obj(L)) \trianglelefteq univV(\text{l}) \wedge D = \delta(\{\text{l.val}\}, \$)\ \}$$
n = this.pos;
$$\{\ \text{l} \neq null \wedge \mathbf{R}'[\text{l}/\text{this}, univV(\text{l})/\mathcal{U}] \wedge \$ = OS \wedge alive(obj(L), \$) \wedge univV(obj(L)) \trianglelefteq univV(\text{l}) \wedge D = \delta(\{\text{l.val}\}, \$)\ \}$$
$\Rightarrow$
$$\{\ \text{l} \neq null \wedge (\mathbf{R}' \wedge \$ = OS \wedge alive(obj(L), \$) \wedge univV(obj(L)) \trianglelefteq \mathcal{U} \wedge D = \delta(\{\text{this.val}\}, \$))[\text{l}/\text{this}, \text{n}/\text{n}, \text{v}/\text{v}, univV(\text{l})/\mathcal{U}]\ \}$$
result = l.List:setAtPos(n,v); ⟦ assumpt-axiom, invocation-rule ⟧
$$\{\ L \in D \vee \$ \equiv_L OS\ \}$$

This concludes our discussion of modular specification and verification of frame properties. Based on explicit dependencies and the universe programming model, we have presented a semantics of modifies-clauses that is suitable for modular verification. Appropriate restrictions on dependencies allow us to provide a modularly sound axiomatization of the depends-relation and to prove the modularity theorem, which enables modular verification of frame properties. In the next chapter, we show how these techniques can be adapted for the modular verification of type invariants. Work that is related to our technique is discussed in the next section.

5.5 Related Work

The approach to the frame problem taken in this book is closely related to the treatment of frame properties in the ESC project. Therefore, we discuss the relation of our technique to the work by Leino and Nelson in detail in the next subsection. The second subsection summarizes other work related to the frame problem.

5.5.1 Leino's and Nelson's Work on Dependencies

The work by Leino and Nelson provides a basis for our work by introducing explicit dependencies and downward-closures for modifies-clauses. In the following, we compare their work to our approach in detail. This discussion is mainly based on [LN97], but also on [DLN98, Jos97, Lei95a, Lei95b, LN00, LS97b].

5.5.1.1 Static and Dynamic Dependencies. The idea of making dependencies explicit in interface specifications was first mentioned in [Lei95b]. Compared to our approach, the depends-clauses of Leino and Nelson are very restrictive: They only provide static dependencies of the form `depends this.f on this.g;` and dynamic dependencies of the form `depends this.f on this.p.g;`. These restricted forms of depends-clauses allow one to check many aspects of dependencies statically (in particular, the modularity requirements for static dependencies), but require recursive data structures to be handled by recursive depends-clauses (i.e., depends-clauses where the fields of the dependent and the dependee are identical). Our approach allows one to declare a depends-clause that hides this recursion in predicates such as reachability, which simplifies specifications and proofs (see for instance the depends-clauses for `List`'s `val`-field in Subsection 5.2.6).

In Leino's and Nelson's framework, static and dynamic dependencies are handled completely different: They are declared and formalized differently, play different roles in the desugaring of modifies-clauses, and have to meet different modularity requirements. We managed to unify static and dynamic dependencies in our approach. This unification simplifies the treatment of dependencies significantly. In particular, the universe type system and the notion of guards allow us to formulate general modularity requirements that apply to all dependencies.

5.5.1.2 Closures and the Meaning of Modifies-Clauses. Leino and Nelson handle information hiding and the extended state problem by the same rule as we do: A method may modify locations that are mentioned in its modifies-clause and their dependees. Therefore, Leino and Nelson use closures similar to our downward closure to desugar modifies-clauses.

For static dependencies, this closure is called *static closure* in [LN00] and *downward closure* in [Lei95b]. In contrast to our work, this closure is not based on an underspecified depends-relation. Instead, Leino and Nelson use a scope-dependent closure. The static closure of a set of variables M in a scope S consists of all variables in M and their dependees as far as the dependencies are static and declared in S. So-called *residues* are used to represent dependees that are not visible in S. Scope-dependent closures lead to a scope-dependent semantics of modifies-clauses. As explained in Subsection 5.1.1, such a semantics is difficult to handle by Hoare-style programming logics. Furthermore, modular soundness of the scope-dependent semantics has to be proved explicitly, whereas it follows from underspecification in our approach. Leino and Nelson have proved modular soundness of their approach for static dependencies. The advantage of scope-dependent closures is that they make an axiomatization of the notdepends-relation dispensable. This axiomatization is the most complex part of our technique.

To handle the problem that occurs when imported code is reused (see Example 5.1.1), Leino and Nelson use a different closure for dynamic dependencies called *dynamic closure*. The dynamic closure is the union of the downward closure and a portion of the upward closure. Like the static closure, it is scope-dependent and leads therefore to the same problems. In contrast to static dependencies, Leino and Nelson have not proved modular soundness of their technique for dynamic dependencies so far. The locality principle of universes allows us to restrict the semantics of modifies-clauses to relevant locations. Therefore, we can avoid upward closures.

5.5.1.3 Modularity Requirements. Leino and Nelson use different modularity rules for static and dynamic dependencies. Whereas the rules for static dependencies are well justified, the rules for dynamic dependencies seem to be rather ad-hoc for two reasons: (1) Whereas we use a restricted programming model (the universe programming model) to systematically derive the necessary modularity rules, Leino and Nelson restrict the programming model *by* modularity rules, which makes them more complex. (2) A soundness proof that would provide insight to the necessary rules for dynamic dependencies is still missing in Leino's and Nelson's work.

We used Leino's and Nelson's rules for static dependencies as a basis and generalized them to dynamic dependencies based on the universe programming model. In the following, we compare the modularity requirements of the two approaches in detail.

Visibility Requirement. Leino's and Nelson's visibility requirement and our visibility requirement are very similar. In both approaches, this requirement is used to determine that a location does not depend on another. That is, it is necessary for the soundness of the scope-dependent downward closures in Leino's and Nelson's approach, whereas it guarantees a consistent axiomatization of the depends-relation and its negation in our approach.

For static dependencies, both visibility rules are equivalent. By using universes and guards, we could generalize the visibility rule to dynamic dependencies.

Top-Down Requirement. The top-down requirement (which is called *authenticity requirement* in [Lei95b]) corresponds to our authenticity requirement. Both requirements guarantee that program extensions cannot introduce abstractions that might be modified by an imported method without being covered by its modifies-clause. Again, the top-down requirement and our authenticity rule are equivalent for static dependencies. Enforcing that abstract locations with fields declared in clients of a module M can only depend on locations with fields declared in M if the dependee belongs to a descendant of the universe to which the dependent belongs, and restricting the semantics of modifies-clauses to relevant locations allows us to generalize the top-down requirement to dynamic dependencies.

Pivot Declaration Requirement. The pivot of a dynamic dependency is the field of the location that holds the reference to the object of the dependee (the p in the depends-clause in Paragraph 5.5.1.1). The pivot declaration requirement requires that the depends-clause for a dynamic dependency is visible wherever the pivot field is. This requirement is not necessary in our approach for the following reason: Assume that an abstract location X.f depends on \$(X.p).g; then it also depends on X.p since an update of X.p might modify X.f. Therefore, our approach requires to declare a dependency of X.f on X.p[11]. The visibility rule for this depends-clause imposes the same effective requirement as the pivot declaration requirement, which makes the extra requirement dispensable.

Absence of Leaking. The absence of leaking requirement is motivated by the following problem: Assume that a class T uses class S as data representation (i.e., T contains a concrete field of range type S), where S and T are declared in different modules. Let L be an abstract location of a T-object that depends on a location of the referenced S-object X. According to Leino and Nelson, *leaking* means that a method m declared outside the scope of T can get hold of a reference to X. By using this reference, m can modify L unexpectedly. To prevent such patterns, Leino and Nelson require programs to be designed such that leaking does not occur. This is enforced by using virginity [DLN98, LS99], which is described in Section 2.3.

In our approach, the problem of leaking is addressed by the authenticity rule and the encapsulation provided by universes. In the scenarios described above, the authenticity rule enforces that X belongs to a descendant of the universe U to which the T-object belongs. Due to our semantics of modifies-clauses, L is not relevant for methods executed in a descendant of U. For all methods that are executed in other universes and that can get a readwrite reference to X, the authenticity rule guarantees that they have access to L.

Although we also prevent the kind of leaking described above, our approach provides more flexibility than the approach based on virginity taken by Detlefs, Leino, and Nelson [DLN98]: (1) Detlefs, Leino, and Nelson do not

[11] Technically, this depends-clause is necessary to prove Obligation 5.1.

allow methods to return references held by pivot locations, which they call a *somewhat drastic restriction.* Universes are less restrictive, allowing references to be passed freely around as long as the universe invariant is not violated. In particular, readonly references can be passed to any object. (2) [DLN98] requires the set of values held by pivot locations and the set of values held by non-pivot locations to be disjoint at any execution point (the restriction is called *apartheid*). There is no correspondence to this restriction in our approach. Apartheid is violated in several interesting implementations such as our list example: `Node`'s `next`-fields are pivot fields for `List`'s abstract `val`-field, but `prev`-fields are not. However, in doubly linked lists, the values held by `next`-locations are not disjoint from the values held by `prev`-locations.

Disjoint Ranges Requirement. The disjoint ranges requirement states that pivot locations with fields declared in different modules hold different references in every pre- or poststate of a method. This requirement is necessary to rule out harmful co-dependencies as described in Example 1.3.4. In our approach, such co-dependencies are prevented by the authenticity rule and the visibility rule. For instance in Example 1.3.4, `Client1` and `Client2` have to use different universes for their representations, which guarantees that the representations are disjoint.

It is interesting that both approaches require that certain aliases to not occur: Leino and Nelson require absence of leaking and disjoint ranges. It is exactly the same scenario (dependencies on locations with fields declared in imported modules) that motivate these requirements, and in which our authenticity rule forces programmers to use universes. However, the approaches are quite different. Leino and Nelson enforce absence of leaking by virginity and disjoint ranging by conjoining appropriate formulas to pre- and postconditions of all methods. In contrast, we use a type system to control aliases, which allows us to simplify the modularity requirements.

Swinging Pivots Requirement. According to the swinging pivots requirement, a method may modify a pivot location only if the new value is *null* or a newly created object. This requirement essentially guarantees that a method does not introduce new dynamic dependencies between locations of objects that exist in the prestate. The swinging pivots requirement is useful to verify method bodies that contain several method invocations. If the first method modifies the depends-relation, it is difficult to relate the modifies-clauses of all subsequent invocations to the modifies-clause of the enclosing method since the downward closures refer to different depends-relations. As admitted by Leino and Nelson, the swinging pivots requirement is extremely strong. Therefore, we do not have a corresponding requirement in our technique. Instead, we leave it to the programmer/specifier to provide sufficiently complete method specifications that allow one to verify several subsequent method invocations. A programmer can follow the swinging pivots requirement as programming discipline and thereby achieve the same results.

To sum up, most requirements in Leino's and Nelson's work have a direct correspondence in our work, and the other way round. Given the similarity of our programming languages and of our techniques, it is natural that both approaches end up with similar modularity requirements. However, the universe type system and our semantics of modifies-clauses allow us to formulate the modularity requirements in a more uniform way.

5.5.1.4 Summary. The specification technique for frame properties in Leino's and Nelson's work is tailored towards extended static checking whereas we aim at formal verification. This difference motivates most of the design decisions taken in the two approaches. Therefore, each of the two approaches has advantages for its particular application area. Our semantical treatment of dependencies gives insight to the modular specification and verification of frame properties from which the extended static checking community can benefit as well. In particular, we developed a modularly sound solution to the frame problem based on the universe type system and appropriate modularity rules. Both the type system and the modularity rules can also be applied in the context of extended static checking.

5.5.1.5 Benevolent Side-Effects. In [Lei95a], Leino points out an interesting aspect of the semantics of modifies-clauses and temporary modifications of locations. In general, our semantics of modifies-clauses allows a method to modify a location and re-establish the initial value without specifying the modification in the modifies-clause. However, such methods are usually difficult to verify.

Consider a method m that temporarily modifies an abstract location L and that is specified to modify nothing. To verify m, it does not suffice to show that the value held by L is re-established before m terminates. It is also necessary to prove this property for L's dependees. Otherwise, so-called benevolent side-effects (that is, side-effects that do not affect the value held by the abstract location L) could exist in which case m would not satisfy its modifies-clause.

One can easily prove that the values held by the dependees are re-established if m modifies L by field-write-statements only since, in this case, it is clear which modifications have to be turned back. However, if the value held by L is modified by a method invocation and re-established by another invocation, the invoked methods must guarantee that they also re-establish the values held by L's dependees, and their specifications must make this property explicit. However, for the sake of information hiding and abstraction, method specifications do usually not express the effects of a method execution on all dependees of an abstract location, which makes verification of methods that perform temporary modifications of abstract locations very difficult in practice.

5.5.2 Other Work on the Frame Problem

The frame problem has first been described in the context of artificial intelligence [MH69]. [BMR95] gives a survey of work on the frame problem in design specifications but does not discuss important issues of OO-implementations (e.g., extended state, modular verification). [BMR95] proposes to organize the permission to modify variables around variables instead around methods. However, the semantics of such specifications in terms of proof obligations is unclear and its capability to support modular verification is not addressed.

Modifies-Clauses. Modifies-clauses have first been used in the Larch project, for instance in LCL [GH93]. Aside from Larch/C++ [Lea97], the Larch ISLs do not provide abstract fields with explicit dependencies. Therefore, they do not support modular verification of frame properties. The modular specification technique for frame properties developed in [Lei95b] (see above) has been adopted by Larch/C++: Modifies-clauses contain a set of variables the abstract values of which may be changed by the method. A special construct allows one to express that the abstract values of all objects reachable from a given object may be modified. Such modifies-clauses are easy to handle, but are not sufficiently expressive for several implementation patterns. For instance, the modifies-clause of `List`'s `appFront`-method (see Section 5.3) could not be expressed in Larch/C++. Besides modifies-clauses, Larch/C++ provides so-called trashes-clauses that are used to specify the destruction of objects [CGR96]. Since Mojave does not provide object deallocation, trashes-clauses are not necessary here. Our techniques can be extended to trashes-clauses if methods can only deallocate objects belonging to the current universe and its descendants, which would allow the semantics of modifies-clauses to be adapted to trashes-clauses. The effects of a deallocation on abstract locations can be determined by allowing abstract fields to depend on the liveness of objects and by applying our modularity requirements to these dependencies.

Like Larch/C++, JML [LBR99a] applies the specification technique for frame properties developed by Leino and Nelson (*abstract fields* and *modifies-clauses* are called *model fields* and *modifiable-clauses* in JML). Our semantics of modifies-clauses is very similar to the meaning of modifiable-clauses in JML, but differs in two aspects: (1) The semantics of modifiable-clauses is not restricted to relevant locations. (2) Modifiable-clauses are interpreted as giving rights to assign to variables, and do not permit temporary modifications of variables not covered by the clause. This stronger semantics allows one to partly check modifiable-clauses statically and simplifies the treatment of concurrent programs because it guarantees that locations not covered by a modifiable-clause are unchanged when a thread is interrupted while executing a method. That is, there is more information available about the state in which a different threads becomes active. We use a weaker semantics since JML's interpretation is difficult to express in Hoare-style programming logics. In particular, it leads to preconditions for field-write-statements that refer to depends-clauses and the modifies-clause of the enclosing method, which means that the programming logic is no longer independent of interface specifications.

Both Larch/C++ and JML do not enforce modularity requirements such as authenticity for abstract fields. Therefore, they do not directly support modular verification of frame properties. However, the techniques for modular verification of frame properties presented in this book (especially the restriction to relevant dependencies and the modularity requirements) can also be applied to languages such as JML that use the stronger interpretation of modifies-clauses described above.

In this book, the extended state problem is solved by allowing subtypes to introduce additional dependencies for inherited abstract locations. The same technique is used in Larch/C++ [Lea97], JML [LBR99b], the Extended Static Checking project [DLNS98, LN00], and in [MPH00b]. An alternative approach to the extended state problem is presented in [Lei98]. Instead of abstract fields, so-called data groups are used to represent sets of concrete locations. Like abstract locations, data groups can be mentioned in modifies-clauses and provide support for information hiding and modification of extended state. They are a natural way to reflect a programmer's intention. In contrast to abstract locations, data groups do not have a value. This allows one to drop the authenticity requirement. But on the other hand, data groups cannot be used to specify functional behavior in terms of abstract values which is crucial for verification of OO-programs. Moreover, data groups can be simulated by abstract fields and dependencies.

Relations on Object Stores. [PH97b] uses relations on object stores to specify frame properties. For instance, one can express that two stores are equivalent w.r.t. all locations that are reachable from a given object X, but may differ in other locations. Relations on object stores are a very expressive way to specify frame properties, but such specifications tend to become complex and are not very intuitive. The semantics of modifies-clauses is defined by a parameterized relation on object stores. That is, modifies-clauses can be regarded as syntactic sugar for more low-level specifications based on relations on object stores.

6. Modular Specification and Verification of Type Invariants

Type invariants (invariants for short) describe well-formedness criteria of objects and object structures. Based on a discussion of an invariant semantics for nonmodular programs, we explain the problems of modular verification of invariants and our approach to their solution. By regarding invariants as boolean abstractions, we apply our techniques for alias and dependency control to invariants. Thereby, we define a meaning for type invariants that is appropriate for modular verification. We show how invariants can be verified modularly, discuss the expressiveness of our invariants, and present related work.

6.1 Motivation and Approach

Although invariants are a fundamental concept of software development [Hoa72, Dij76, Mey88], the meaning of type invariants in object-oriented programs is still discussed controversially (see Section 6.5). In this section, we explain an invariant semantics that is appropriate for verification in a nonmodular setting. We analyze and illustrate the shortcomings of this semantics for modular verification and explain our approach to their remedy.

6.1.1 Invariant Semantics for Nonmodular Programs

In this subsection, we summarize the work on the meaning of invariants in nonmodular programs, mainly [PH97b] (other invariant semantics are discussed in Section 6.5). To define the meaning of an invariant, we have to answer two questions:

1. For which objects does the invariant have to hold?
2. In which execution states does the invariant have to hold?

The invariant of a type declaration T describes properties that should hold for all living objects of T and its subtypes. To answer the second question, we have to consider the following points:

Peter Müller: Modular Specification ..., LNCS 2262, pp. 195–211, 2002.

1. Invariants cannot be required to hold in all execution states. In intermediate states during method executions, invariants often have to be violated temporarily, for instance, to rearrange object structures. Therefore, invariants can only be required to hold in pre- and poststates of method executions. The states in which invariants have to hold are often called *visible states* [Lea97].
2. In general, the implementation of a method m relies on certain invariants to work correctly. These invariants are required to hold in the prestate of executions of m. Although often suggested in the literature, it is not sufficient if only the invariant of the `this`-object or the invariants of all instances of the enclosing class hold: During execution of m, field accesses and method invocations on other objects require that the invariants of all objects reachable from m's parameters hold in the prestate of m. To simplify the semantics of invariants, [PH97b] requires the invariants of *all* living objects to hold in prestates.
3. The above requirement forces verifiers to show that the invariants of all living objects hold upon invocations of, at least, all public methods. To be able to show this property for consecutive method invocations, methods must guarantee that the invariants of all living objects hold in the poststate of method executions. In particular, methods must establish the invariants of newly created objects.
4. According to the previous two points, the pre- and poststates of all method executions are visible states. However, *helper methods* that are used to perform auxiliary operations should neither assume invariants to hold in the prestate nor be required to preserve invariants (we use the term *preserve* for both, preserving the invariant of existing objects and establishing the invariants for newly created objects). Most specification frameworks regard either private methods or all nonpublic methods as helper methods. If only private methods are used as helper methods, clients of these methods have access to their implementations which allows verifiers to prove the properties they are interested in. If all nonpublic methods are regarded as helper methods, the specifications of these methods must state which invariants might by violated by the methods to allow client code to be verified modularly. In this book, we regard only private methods as helper methods. The presented technique works as well for the other choice.

To sum up the previous paragraphs, the semantics for invariants in nonmodular programs requires the invariants of all living objects to hold in the pre- and poststates of all nonprivate methods.

6.1.2 Problems for Modular Verification of Invariants

According to the above semantics, each nonprivate method of a program must preserve the invariant of each allocated object. This semantics entails two problems for (modular) verification that are discussed in the following.

6.1.2.1 Invariants and Program Extensions. Without far-reaching restrictions, the above invariant semantics cannot be extended to modular programs: Consider a set of modules M that is extended by a set of modules N. According to the above invariant semantics, essentially[1] the following four kinds of proof obligations have to be shown for the extended program (we neglect private methods here):

1. Each method in M must preserve each invariant in M.
2. Each method in M must preserve each invariant in N.
3. Each method in N must preserve each invariant in N.
4. Each method in N must preserve each invariant in M.

Whereas obligations of kinds 1 and 3 can be proved as in a nonmodular setting, the other obligations are problematic. Obligations of kind 2 are proof obligations about imported code. Since this code is not available for verification in a modular setting, we would have to restrict the invariants that can be declared in N such that they are automatically preserved by methods in M. Although the code is available to show obligations of kind 4, such obligations cannot be proved for those invariants in M that are hidden from client modules. As explained in Section 4.1, hidden specification parts are often necessary to preserve information hiding.

6.1.2.2 Invariants of Object Structures. The second problem occurs when invariants describe properties of object structures (in particular, dynamic components) rather than single objects. It also occurs in nonmodular settings, but is aggravated by modular development. We illustrate the problem by the following example, which is similar to the example discussed in Subsection 1.3.3:

Example 6.1.1. Objects of class `MyBean` use a list to store their internal data (see App. C.2). To simplify algorithms, this list should not contain any element more than once. This property is specified as invariant of class `MyBean` (*notMTO* yields true if a list contains no element more than once).

invariant $notMTO(\$(\$(this.beanRep).val))$;

However, since `List`'s `appFront`-method allows one to add arbitrary objects to the list, it does not preserve `MyBean`'s invariant in general. Therefore, the proof obligations for this invariant cannot be shown for *all* methods of the

[1] Actually, only the conjunction of all invariants must be preserved. However, in most practical applications, that is equivalent to verifying the invariants of M and N separately.

program. That is, the specified invariant does not hold in all possible visible states.

With the above invariant semantics, MyBean's invariant can only be guaranteed by using a different list class. In general, that requires one to implement a new list class, L2, the methods of which preserve the invariant. Note that L2 cannot be implemented as a subclass of List since it has to change the behavior of appFront (i.e., it is not a behavioral subtype). Thus, inheritance cannot be exploited, and L2 has to be developed from scratch. Obviously, this work-around obstructs reuse in an unbearable way.

Situations as illustrated in Example 6.1.1 occur whenever a dynamic component wants to establish an invariant for its representation that is stronger than the invariants that are guaranteed by the classes that are (re-)used to implement the representation. Whereas this problem can be circumvented in a nonmodular setting by using very complex invariants and requires-clauses (for instance, in case the this-object is referenced by a MyBean-object, the specification of appFront could require that the element to be added is not already contained in the list), it leads to unbearable restrictions for modular development. To solve this problem, we need an invariant semantics that does not require methods of the representation of a dynamic component to preserve the invariants of the interface objects.

In the next subsection, we describe our approach to solving the two problems above.

6.1.3 Approach

Verification of invariants is closely related to verification of frame properties: Like abstract fields, invariants map the states of objects or object structures to values, in this case boolean values. Verifying invariants means to show that methods do not change these boolean values from true to false, just like verification of frame properties means to show that the value held by certain locations is not modified by a method. A closer look at the problems of invariant verification described above reveals further similarities between the verification of invariants and the verification of frame properties:

- To guarantee that methods of imported type declarations preserve the invariants declared in importing modules (proof obligations of kind 2 in Paragraph 6.1.2.1), invariants have to be restricted such that the invariants declared in importing modules are automatically preserved by the imported methods. This is analogous to the restrictions of abstract fields that are necessary to guarantee that reused methods obey their modifies-clauses in any scope they may be reused.
- To allow a dynamic component D to establish an invariant for its representation that is not preserved by all methods of the classes used to implement

D, methods executed on D's representation should not be required to preserve the invariants of D's interface objects. Analogously, methods of D's representation must be allowed to modify abstract locations of D's interface objects without covering these locations by their modifies-clauses. This is necessary to be able to use imported classes to implement the representation (see Subsection 5.1.1).

Due to the close relation between abstract fields and invariants as well as between verification of frame properties and verification of invariants, we suggest to regard invariants as special abstract fields and to apply the technique developed for the verification of frame properties to invariant verification. We explain this approach in the following.

6.1.3.1 Invariants with Explicit Dependencies. Regarding invariants as special abstract fields with representations and explicit dependencies allows us to restrict the dependencies of invariants such that methods automatically preserve invariants declared outside their scope. Recall that the modularity rules for abstract fields presented in Subsection 5.1.3 guarantee that methods do not modify abstract locations declared outside their scope. The same rules enable us to apply the modularity theorem for frame properties (Theorem 5.4.1) to automatically discard proof obligations of kind 2.

Furthermore, explicit dependencies (in particular, the axiomatization of the notdepends-relation) can be used to show that methods preserve the invariants of imported type declarations (obligations of kind 4) even if the actual representations of the invariants are hidden from the clients. Therefore, treating invariants as abstract fields with explicit dependencies solves the problem described in Paragraph 6.1.2.1.

Despite the far-reaching correspondence between invariants and abstract fields, they differ in one important aspect: Invariants have a semantics that leads to proof obligations for methods whereas ordinary abstract fields don't. We describe this semantics in the next paragraph.

6.1.3.2 The Meaning of Type Invariants. As explained in Subsection 6.1.1, invariants are used for two purposes in the context of formal specification and verification:

1. Invariants can be assumed in the prestate of method executions. Thus, they serve as abbreviation to avoid the recurring specification of requirements.
2. To be able to verify consecutive method invocations, invariants must be preserved by all nonprivate methods of a program.

In the following, we discuss three possible invariant semantics w.r.t. these purposes and the problems described in Subsection 6.1.2.

Semantics 1. The invariant semantics for nonmodular programs (see Subsection 6.1.1), which is essentially used in [PH97b, Lea97, HK00], would serve both of the above purposes, but entails the two problems described in Subsection 6.1.2. In particular, to solve the problem of program extensions (see Paragraph 6.1.2.1), dependencies of invariants would have to be restricted such that any nonprivate method m would preserve all invariants declared outside m's scope. To accomplish that, we would need much stronger restrictions than the ones used for the verification of frame properties since the semantics of modifies-clauses covers *relevant* locations only, whereas this invariant semantics would cover the invariants of *all* living objects. As discussed for the semantics of modifies-clauses in Subsection 5.1.1, the restrictions necessary to cover all objects would prevent effective reuse and would therefore not be appropriate for modular development.

Semantics 2. An alternative approach would realize invariants by ordinary abstract fields that in particular would not lead to proof obligations. Purpose 1 would be able to be served by appropriate conventions; for instance, all abstract locations with fields named *valid* could be required to hold *true* in method prestates. Whether a method preserves an invariant would be specified by frame axioms: Violated invariants would be abstract locations that are modified by the method and must therefore be covered by its modifies-clause. Thus, consecutive method invocations would be able to be verified by using frame properties (purpose 2).

This treatment of invariants would rest upon the semantics of modifies-clauses. In our framework, that would mean that methods must declare whether invariants of objects in the current universe or its descendants (*relevant invariants*) are violated, but must not specify violation of other invariants. That would (1) allow us to apply the restrictions for dependencies used for the verification of frame properties to solve the problem of program extensions (see Paragraph 6.1.2.1), and (2) solve the problem of invariants for object structures (see Paragraph 6.1.2.2) since invariants of interface objects of a dynamic component D are not relevant for methods executed on D's representation.

The disadvantage of this approach would be that it is not obvious in which execution states an invariant holds. One would have to refer to the single modifies-clauses (and possibly the declared dependencies) to deduce the states in which an invariant holds. Invariants alone would not be very meaningful.

A Hybrid Approach. To remedy the deficiencies of the above semantics, we combine the notion of visible states from semantics 1 with the notion of relevant invariants from semantics 2: The visible states are defined as in semantics 1 (i.e., the pre- and poststates of nonprivate methods[2]). In each visible

[2] more precisely, of nonprivate methods except of readonly instance methods (see below)

state, the relevant invariants have to hold. That is, each nonprivate method must preserve the relevant invariants. Relevant invariants that are violated by private methods have to be covered by the modifies-clauses of these methods. This hybrid semantics solves the problems described in Subsection 6.1.2 in the same way as semantics 2.

Since only relevant invariants have to hold in visible states, the caller of a method can only guarantee that those invariants hold upon a method invocation that are relevant for the caller. According to the universe programming model, readwrite methods and static readonly methods can only be invoked in the current universe or its descendants. Therefore, each invariant that is relevant for the execution of such a method is also relevant for its caller. However, the situation is different for readonly instance methods: Since readonly references can refer to arbitrary universes, we cannot assume that all relevant invariants hold in the prestate of readonly instance methods since callers are in general not able to guarantee this condition upon invocation. Thus, the pre- and poststates of readonly instance methods are not visible states. Consequently, this invariant semantics serves purpose 1 in a limited way only. Invariants that are necessary to guarantee the correctness of readonly instance methods have to be repeated in requires-clauses or preconditions[3]. Since all nonprivate methods are required to preserve relevant invariants (which is trivially met by readonly methods), verification of consecutive method invocations (purpose 2) can be handled by this semantics.

6.2 Specification of Type Invariants

In this section, we formalize the ideas described above. We explain how invariants as well as their representations and dependencies are declared, present the axiomatization of invariants, and describe their formal meaning. Furthermore, we illustrate the specification of invariants by an example.

6.2.1 Declaration of Type Invariants

Although invariants are treated as abstract fields, they have to be declared differently such that the appropriate proof obligations can be generated. An invariant `inv` is introduced by a declaration of the following form:

```
public invariant inv;
```

Besides the fact that we axiomatize that inv is an invariant (see below), such a declaration is synonymous to the following declaration of an abstract field:

public abstract *Bool* inv;

That means that for invariants,

[3] This limitation is due to the notion of relevant invariants and therefore also occurs in semantics 2.

- the same context conditions apply as for ordinary abstract fields (see Subsection 4.2.1). In particular, there can be several invariants for each type declaration, which is for instance necessary if some well-formedness criteria (that is, the representations of some invariants) should be exposed whereas others should be hidden from clients.
- the corresponding constants of sorts *SimpleAFieldId* and *AFieldId* are introduced.
- the signature of the representation function rep_{inv} and the corresponding axiom for L-equivalence are generated (see Paragraph 4.2.1.1).
- representations and dependencies can be declared by def-clauses and depends-clauses exactly as for ordinary abstract fields. In particular, these clauses have to meet the same well-formedness conditions (Obligations 5.1–5.4).

To be able to discern between invariants and ordinary abstract fields, we introduce the following function:

$$invSF : SimpleAFieldId \rightarrow Bool$$

For each invariant resp. ordinary abstract field T@f declared in a program, we add an axiom of the form $invSF(\mathrm{T@f})$ resp. $\neg invSF(\mathrm{T@f})$ to the theory that contains the declaration of the constant T@f. To simplify notations, we introduce a function *invL* that yields whether a location is an instance of an invariant:

$$\begin{array}{l} invL : Location \rightarrow Bool \\ L = aloc(locA(X,F)) \Rightarrow (invL(L) \Leftrightarrow_{def} invSF(F)) \\ L = cloc(locC(X,F)) \Rightarrow \neg invL(L) \end{array}$$

To be able to quantify over all invariants of a program, we introduce a function signature:

$$invrep : Location \times Store \rightarrow Bool$$

For each invariant T@f declared in a program, we add the following axiom to the theory that contains the declaration of the constant T@f:

$$L = aloc(locA(X, \mathrm{T@f})) \Rightarrow (invrep(L, OS) \Leftrightarrow rep_{\mathrm{T@f}}(X, OS))$$

Relevant invariants of living objects must not be violated by nonprivate methods. That is, their value must not be changed during execution of such methods. To simplify the application of the verification technique for frame properties to the verification of invariants (see Paragraph 6.3.1.2), we check statically that invariants do not occur as dependee in any depends-clause. Thereby, we ensure that invariants cannot "slip" into the downward-closure of a modifies-clause. That is, we can prove locally in the scope of a method m that an invariant is not covered by m's modifies-clause without having to care about the dependencies that might be introduced by program extensions. The syntax checks guarantee the following lemma (the proof is analogous to Proof 5.2.3):

Lemma 6.2.1. *In each program with well-formed interface specification, the following property holds:*

$$invL(L) \wedge K \neq L \Rightarrow \neg(K \xrightarrow{OS} L)$$

6.2.2 Example

To illustrate the declaration of type invariants, we specify the well-formedness criteria for class `List` (see App. C.1 for the implementation of `List`). A list object is well-formed if

1. the `first`- and `last`-locations reference different `Node`-objects (we have one dummy node at each end of the list);
2. the last node can be reached from the first by following a sequence of `next`-references;
3. the last node has no successor (this is required for the function *col* to work correctly, see Paragraph 4.2.1.3).

These properties are formalized as type invariant of `List`:

protected def inv by $\$(\text{this.first}) \neq null \wedge \$(\text{this.last}) \neq null \wedge$
$\rho(\$(\text{this.first}), \$(\text{this.last}), \$, \text{next}) \wedge$
$\$(\$(\text{this.last}).\text{next})) = null \wedge$
$\$(\text{this.first}) \neq \$(\text{this.last});$

protected depends inv on $\{Y.\text{first} \mid Y = \text{this}\};$
protected depends inv on $\{Y.\text{last} \mid Y = \text{this}\};$
protected depends inv on $\{Y.\text{next} \mid \rho(\$(\text{this.first}), Y, \$, \text{next}) \vee$
$Y = \$(\text{this.last})\};$

It is easy to see that this invariant is well-formed:

Obligation 5.1: X.inv depends on the `first`- and `last`-locations of X and the `next`-locations of all nodes of the list. That is, all dependees are reachable from X. The proof obligation can easily be shown by using Lemma 3.1.10.

Obligation 5.2: X.inv depends only on locations of objects belonging to the same universe as X (X.first and X.last) and a child universe thereof (dependees of the form Y.next).

Obligation 5.3: The guard of all dependees of X.inv w.r.t. the universe to which X belongs is `List`. Since the invariant inv is declared in this class, the authenticity requirement is met.

Obligation 5.4: The depends-clauses are declared in the class that is the guard of the dependees (class `List`).

The above example illustrates that invariants as well as their representations and dependencies can be declared like abstract fields. In particular, representations and dependencies can be hidden from clients by using access modes. In Subsection 6.3.2, we prove that `List`'s `createList`-method preserves the above invariant.

6.2.3 Formal Meaning of Invariants

In this subsection, we formalize the invariant semantics explained in Paragraph 6.1.3.2. The relevant invariants of living objects have to hold in all visible states. That is,

1. they have to hold in the initial state in which program execution begins.
2. they can be assumed in the prestate of every nonprivate method except readonly instance methods and must be preserved by each nonprivate method.

Whereas the former condition is trivially true since there are no living objects in the initial state, we have to generate proof obligations to guarantee the latter property. To do that, we introduce the following function:

$$\begin{aligned}&\mathit{inv} : \mathit{Store} \times \mathit{Universe} \rightarrow \mathit{Bool}\\ &\mathit{inv}(OS, U) \Leftrightarrow_{def} \forall L : \mathit{univV}(\mathit{obj}(L)) \trianglelefteq U \wedge \mathit{alive}(\mathit{obj}(L), OS) \wedge\\ &\qquad\qquad\qquad\quad \mathit{invL}(L) \Rightarrow \mathit{invrep}(L, OS)\end{aligned}$$

$\mathit{inv}(OS, U)$ yields whether all invariants of living objects that belong to U or one of U's descendants hold in store OS. Based on this function, we express the proof obligations for invariants by a pre-post-pair. The formal meaning in terms of Hoare triples is therefore defined by the semantics of the pre-post-pair (see Paragraph 4.2.2.2). Each nonprivate readwrite method implicitly contains the following pre-post-pair, where *mode* is the access mode of the method:

mode `pre` $\mathcal{U} = U$;
    `post` $\mathit{inv}(\$, U)$;

Recall from the semantics of pre-post-pairs that for nonprivate readwrite methods, $\mathit{inv}(\$, \mathcal{U})$ is added to the precondition when the pre-post-pair is translated into a Hoare triple. That is, the above pre-post-pair expresses that every nonprivate readwrite method m must preserve the relevant invariants of objects that are alive in m's prestate and must establish the invariants of objects that are created during execution of m. Since readonly methods do not modify the object store, we do not need proof obligations for these methods.

6.3 Verification of Type Invariants

The meaning of type invariants leads to proof obligations for all nonprivate readwrite methods of a program. In this section, we show how these obligations can be proved modularly by reducing invariant verification to verification of frame properties.

6.3.1 Verification Methodology

In analogy to the verification of frame properties, invariants can be verified by applying the proof strategy of Lemma 3.3.2. That is, it suffices to verify method bodies based on the assumption that all virtual methods behave according to their specifications. In this subsection, we show that invariants meet the requirements of Lemma 3.3.2 and explain how method bodies can be verified modularly.

6.3.1.1 Using the Proof Strategy for Program Composition. Like frame properties, invariants meet the requirements of the proof strategy of Lemma 3.3.2. Due to the similarity to ordinary abstract fields, invariants meet requirements 1, 3, and 4 in the same way (see Section 5.4). Requirement 2 is fulfilled for the following reason: By defining the invariant semantics based on *inv* (which universally quantifies over all invariants of a program), we achieve that the declaration of invariants does not lead to new proof obligations for imported methods. Instead, each nonprivate method has to preserve *all* relevant invariants of living objects, independent of the scope the method is declared in.

Therefore, we can verify invariants by (1) verifying method bodies under the assumption that all virtual methods behave according to their specifications, and (2) applying the proof strategy of Lemma 3.3.2 to show the proof obligations for virtual methods and to discard the assumptions. Consequently, we focus on the verification of method bodies in the following.

6.3.1.2 Verification of Method Bodies. Conceptually, the proof obligation stemming from invariants for the body *b* of a nonprivate readwrite method m can be split into two parts:

1. *b establishes the invariants of all objects that are created during execution of b.* *b* can create new objects (1) by the new-statement or (2) by method invocations. In the former case, the type declaration of the newly created object and thus its invariants are present in m's scope, which allows one to prove that the invariants are established. In the latter case, the invoked method n belongs to one of the following groups:
   - n *is private.* In this case, the code of n is available for verification and can be used to show that the invariants are established.
   - n *is readonly.* Readonly methods must not create objects.
   - n *is nonprivate and readwrite.* In this case, n must establish the invariants of the objects it creates. It remains to show that *b* does not violate the invariants after they have been established by n. This is analogous to the verification of frame properties, which allows us to apply the same methodology.
2. *b preserves the relevant invariants of all objects that are allocated in m's prestate.* To show this obligation, we use the frame properties of *b* and prove that no relevant invariant is covered by m's modifies-clause. To

prove that, we (1) show that no invariant is contained in the location set M mentioned in m's modifies-clause, and (2) apply Lemma 6.2.1 to show that M's downward-closure does also not contain invariants.

Both parts can be verified modularly. In the general case (i.e., when new-statements are followed by method invocations in a method body), both parts have to be proved in an interweaved way to guarantee that the invariants of new objects are established before methods are invoked. However, most method bodies (especially method bodies that do not create objects) allow one to prove the two parts separately. To simplify verification of such method bodies, we formalize this methodology by the following lemma:

Lemma 6.3.1 (Modularity Lemma for Invariants). *If the specification of an open or closed program $\mathcal{P}$ is well-formed and if there is a proof in $\mathcal{P}$ for the sequents*

$$\begin{array}{l} \mathcal{A} \triangleright \{\, \mathbf{P} \wedge inv(\$,\mathcal{U}) \wedge invL(L) \wedge alive(obj(L),\$) \wedge univV(obj(L)) \trianglelefteq \mathcal{U} \wedge \\ \quad \$ = OS \wedge D = \delta(M,\$) \,\} \\ \quad \mathrm{COMP} \\ \{\, L \in D \vee \$ \equiv_L OS \,\} \end{array} \tag{6.1}$$

and

$$\begin{array}{l} \mathcal{A} \triangleright \{\, \mathbf{P} \wedge inv(\$,\mathcal{U}) \wedge invL(L) \wedge \neg alive(obj(L),\$) \wedge univV(obj(L)) \trianglelefteq \mathcal{U} \,\} \\ \quad \mathrm{COMP} \\ \{\, alive(obj(L),\$) \Rightarrow invrep(L,\$) \,\} \end{array} \tag{6.2}$$

and if $invL(L) \Rightarrow L \notin M$ holds, then there is a proof for

$$\mathcal{A} \triangleright \{\, \mathbf{P} \wedge inv(\$,\mathcal{U}) \wedge \mathcal{U} = U \,\}\ \mathrm{COMP}\ \{\, inv(\$,U) \,\}$$

where M is the location set mentioned in the modifies-clause of the method that contains COMP (resp. of COMP in case COMP is a method), and D, L, OS, and U are logical variables that do not occur in **P**.

Sequent 6.1 can be obtained by applying the strength-rule to the sequent for COMP's frame properties. For method bodies, this sequent is usually proved during verification of frame properties. The proof of this lemma is rather straightforward and can be found in App. D.3.

6.3.2 Example

In this subsection, we prove that the body of List@createList preserves all relevant invariants. The example demonstrates how method bodies that contain both method invocations and object creation can be verified. In particular, the example illustrates the application of Lemma 6.3.1.

To prove that List@createList preserves all relevant invariants, we have to show the following sequent

$$\mathcal{A} \triangleright \{\ inv(\$,\mathcal{U}) \wedge \mathcal{U} = U \wedge \mathrm{TA}\ \}\ body(\text{List@createList})\ \{\ inv(\$,U)\ \} \tag{6.3}$$

where $\mathcal{A}$ contains the triples for the two pre-post-pairs and the frame properties of List@init (see App. C.1), and TA abbreviates the type and liveness annotations for the body of List@createList. Since List@createList's modifies-clause is empty, it suffices to show the following two sequents (see App. D.3 for the proofs) to apply Lemma 6.3.1 which yields Sequent 6.3 and completes the proof.

$$\begin{array}{l} \mathcal{A} \triangleright \{\ invL(L) \wedge alive(obj(L),\$) \wedge \$ = OS \wedge \mathrm{TA} \wedge univV(obj(L)) \trianglelefteq \mathcal{U} \wedge \\ \qquad D = \delta(\varnothing,\$)\ \} \\ \qquad body(\text{List@createList}) \\ \quad \{\ \$ \equiv_L OS \vee L \in D\ \} \end{array} \tag{6.4}$$

$$\begin{array}{l} \mathcal{A} \triangleright \{\ \mathrm{TA} \wedge inv(\$,\mathcal{U}) \wedge invL(L) \wedge \neg alive(obj(L),\$) \wedge univV(obj(L)) \trianglelefteq \mathcal{U}\ \} \\ \qquad body(\text{List@createList}) \\ \quad \{\ alive(obj(L),\$) \Rightarrow invrep(L,\$)\ \} \end{array} \tag{6.5}$$

This example concludes our discussion of modular specification and verification of type invariants. We have shown that type invariants can be regarded as abstract fields which allows us to apply the specification and verification technique for frame properties to type invariants. In particular, a novel semantics of type invariants and appropriate restrictions on the permissible dependencies of invariants enable us to show the proof obligations stemming from invariants modularly.

6.4 Discussion

In this section, we discuss the expressiveness of our type invariants and explain how the presented specification and verification technique can be adapted for the treatment of history constraints.

6.4.1 Module Invariants

Applying the modularity requirements for abstract fields to type invariants allows us to verify invariants modularly. We have discussed the limitations imposed by these requirements in Subsection 5.2.7. In particular, we pointed out that Obligation 5.1 requires that the abstraction or the invariant of an object X may only depend on locations reachable from X. Whereas this restriction is natural for data abstraction of object structures and can also be found for type invariants in the literature [PH97b], it is a more severe limitation for general invariants: For some implementations, it is useful to specify the relation between different object structures (such as disjointness) or properties of whole *object configurations* (i.e., sets of objects that are not necessarily linked by references). If the objects of such configurations are not reachable from a single object, we cannot express properties of the configurations as type invariants. We illustrate that in Example 6.4.1.

Example 6.4.1. Different `MyBean`-objects are supposed to have disjoint lists as representations. Since `MyBean` is implemented using type universes (see App. C.2), this property is not guaranteed by the type system. Therefore, we would like to specify it as invariant of class `MyBean`:

def inv by $\$(\text{this.beanRep}) \neq \mathit{null} \wedge$
$\forall Y : Y \neq \text{this} \wedge Y \neq \mathit{null} \Rightarrow \$(Y.\text{beanRep}) \neq \$(\text{this.beanRep});$
depends inv on $\{Y.\text{beanRep} \mid \mathit{univV}(Y) = \mathit{univV}(\text{this})\};$

However, this invariant does not satisfy Obligation 5.1 since Y.beanRep is in general not reachable from `this`. Thus, the invariant is not well-formed.

Example 6.4.1 demonstrates that our framework does in general not allow one to specify properties of object configurations as type invariants. However, such properties are interesting, in particular, to achieve stronger alias control than provided by type universes. As explained in [LN00] certain kinds of properties of object configurations can be expressed by so-called *program invariants* or *module invariants*. Module invariants are invariants that are tailored towards the particular purpose of specifying object configurations. Therefore, they must be more expressive than type invariants in this aspect, but can be more restrictive in other areas.

A simple approach to providing module invariants is as follows: Module invariants are specified as part of a module interface. A module invariant in module M may only depend on concrete locations with fields declared in M. Thus, it is present in any scope in which one of its dependees is accessible. This allows one to generate and show proof obligations for all methods that might violate the module invariant, since each of these methods has M in its scope. Therefore, such invariants can be verified modularly. Although they are very restrictive, such module invariants enable one to specify properties like the one illustrated in Example 6.4.1 (the invariant depends only on `beanRep`-locations).

The focus of this chapter is on demonstrating that the techniques for the modular specification and verification of frame properties carry over to type invariants. Therefore, we do not discuss module invariants in more detail. A formalization of module invariants is considered future work.

6.4.2 History Constraints

History constraints are used to specify a property of the history of values which a location may take [LW93, LW94]. More precisely, a history constraint describes a reflexive, transitive relation on object stores. Specification frameworks that have history constraints use a semantics for history constraints that is similar to the semantics of invariants (see e.g., [Lea97]): (1) History constraints are associated with type declarations. The history constraint of type declaration T expresses properties of the history of the values held by the locations of T-objects and objects reachable from T-objects. (2) The pre-

and poststates of all nonprivate methods have to fulfill the history constraints for all objects that are allocated in the prestate. That is, each ordered pair of visible states in the execution of a program must fulfill the history constraints for all objects allocated in the earlier state.

Because of their similar semantics, history constraints lead to the same problems for modular specification and verification as type invariants (see Subsection 6.1.2). However, we can apply the same techniques to solve these problems:

1. History constraints can be regarded as abstract fields that map the states of an object structure in two stores to a boolean value.
2. Like invariants, history constraints have dependencies. If all dependees of a history constraint c hold the same values in two stores then these stores must fulfill c.
3. Dependencies of history constraints have to be explicitly declared. The same modularity requirements as for abstract fields and invariants apply.
4. The semantics of history constraints has to be weakened. Nonprivate methods have to fulfill the history constraints of objects belonging to the current universe and its descendants only (relevant history constraints).

By these properties, we can verify history constraints modularly: In analogy to the modularity theorem for frame properties (Theorem 5.4.1), the modularity rules guarantee that the pre- and poststates of each method m fulfill all relevant history constraints declared outside m's scope. For all other relevant history constraints, we can use their definitions to show that they are fulfilled by m's pre- and poststate.

We do not elaborate on history constraints here. However, the sketch above indicates that our techniques can by extended to handle modular specification and verification of history constraints.

6.5 Related Work

Although invariants are a fundamental concept for formal reasoning and can be found in almost all specification frameworks, many approaches treat invariants rather superficially: For instance, Anna [Luc90] keeps invariants implicit which does not allow one to use them for formal reasoning; Eiffel [Mey92b] uses a semantics that does not guarantee that invariants hold in all visible states and that is thus not appropriate for formal verification. In the following, we discuss related work on the semantics and on modular verification of type invariants.

Meaning of Invariants. The basic idea that invariants must hold in all visible states is widely accepted [Hoa72, LG86, Mey88]. However, the proof obligations used to guarantee this property differ significantly.

Many frameworks require the invariant of a type T to be preserved by T's exported methods only (see for instance LM3 [Jon91a, Lar, FAQ 4.14], Eiffel [Mey92b, Sections 9.12 and 9.17], other work by Meyer [Mey88, Mey92a], and [LW94]). These proof obligations guarantee that invariants hold in all visible states if (1) the internal state of an object of type T can only be modified by T's methods (in particular, there are no protected or public fields) and (2) invariants express properties of single objects rather than object structures only (otherwise, modification of any object of the object structure could violate the invariant [Szy98, HK00]).

In a more general setting, the stronger proof obligations described in Subsection 6.1.1 are required. This semantics is formalized in [PH97b]. We explained the problems of this semantics for modular verification in Subsection 6.1.2 and solved them by using explicit dependencies for invariants and by introducing the notion of relevant invariants.

Larch/C++ [Lea97] adapted Poetzsch-Heffter's invariant semantics. In contrast to our work, Larch/C++ requires only public methods to preserve invariants.

[HK00] presents a proof system that guarantees that invariants hold in all visible states. The basic idea of this proof system is to syntactically analyze invariants to determine which methods of a program could violate which invariants. Thus, appropriate proof obligations for these methods can be generated. The presented approach is sound, but has two major drawbacks: (1) It requires that a method can only update fields of the `this`-object. (2) Without appropriate restrictions, the syntactic analysis of invariants does not work for modular programs.

Like in this book, [Lei95b] regards invariants as abstract fields. However, Leino's invariants do not lead to proof obligations. Thus, invariants that are required for the verification of a method implementation must be mentioned in the method's precondition, and preservation of invariants is handled by modifies-clauses. The same approach is taken in the ESC project [DLNS98]. As we have explained in Paragraph 6.1.3.2, this treatment of invariants is not based on the notion of visible states. Therefore, one has to refer to the single modifies-clauses (and possibly the declared dependencies) to deduce the states in which an invariant holds.

Modular Verification of Invariants. In frameworks, where invariants of a type T lead to proof obligations for T's methods only (see above), modularity does not cause problems for verification since each method must only preserve invariants that are present in its scope. However, this approach is too restrictive for realistic OO-programs since it forbids invariants over object structures.

Replacing invariants by ordinary boolean abstractions that do not lead to proof obligations (as in [Lei95b]) circumvents the problem of modular verification of invariants. Techniques for the modular verification of frame properties can be used to show that invariants hold in certain execution states.

[LS97a] investigates the modular verification of object invariants, that is, invariants that depend only on the locations of a single object. To prove modularly that each method of a program preserves all object invariants, Leino and Stata use their modularity requirements for static dependencies (see Paragraph 5.5.1.3) to restrict the dependencies of invariants. To tackle the problem of dependencies on inherited locations (see Paragraph 5.2.7.4), they use so-called *write protected* fields that allow them to relax their modularity requirements.

Leino and Nelson [LN00, Section 9.3] mention the need for program invariants that allow one to specify properties of several objects or object structures such as injectivity of certain locations. The modularity requirements that are necessary to verify program invariants modularly are extremely restrictive. In particular, Leino and Nelson do not allow invariants to depend on abstract locations. Furthermore, an invariant must be present in each scope in which the field of one of its dependees is accessible. This requirement essentially forbids dynamic dependencies on locations with fields declared in imported modules, and thus most program invariants about object structures. However, they are capable of expressing properties like the invariant discussed in Subsection 6.4.1. Therefore, designated program invariants are no substitute for type invariants, but they complement type invariants for more expressive specifications. Rüping [Rüp94] presents a notion of module invariants that is similar to Leino's and Nelson's program invariants. He uses the same modularity requirements to make modular verification possible.

7. Conclusion

> *"Normal science [...] is a highly cumulative enterprise, eminently successful in its aim, the steady extension of the scope and precision of scientific knowledge."* Thomas S. Kuhn [Kuh70, p. 52]

In the previous chapters, we presented techniques for the modular specification and verification of object-oriented programs. For the first time, modular sound techniques for the treatment of frame properties and type invariants in modular OO-programs were developed. The key to this achievement is the combination of specification and verification techniques with a type system for alias control. Their formal integration allowed us to define novel semantics for modifies-clauses and type invariants as well as to provide modularity requirements for explicit dependencies that make the modular verification of frame properties and invariants possible.

In this chapter, we summarize the technical contributions of this book, sketch the research project in which the work for this book was carried out, and explain how the presented techniques can be implemented in verification tools. Besides the development of new techniques, our investigation of formal specification and verification provided insights to the nature of modular OO-programming and the language features used for this task. Thereby, we identified promising directions for future research in these and related areas. Their description concludes this book.

7.1 Summary and Contributions

In this section, we summarize the main contributions of this book.

Summary. Modular program development is driven by four objectives: Explicit structure, separate development, information hiding, and reuse. To be suitable for modular development, specification and verification techniques must be capable of handling language features for modular programming and support these objectives, that is, enable modular development of specifications and proofs. This book presented modular specification and verification

Peter Müller: Modular Specification ..., LNCS 2262, pp. 213–222, 2002.

techniques for functional behavior, frame properties, and invariants of object-oriented programs written in a Java-like language. The presented techniques are based on the hierarchical universe programming model that restricts aliasing. A sophisticated type system is used to enforce this programming model.

The universe programming model divides the object store into dynamic components. Readwrite references between objects of different dynamic components — and thus aliases — are restricted. Readonly references can connect arbitrary objects, but may not be used to modify the states of referenced objects. The universe type system can be used to statically check whether a program respects this programming model. For this purpose, the type system uses different universes for the representations of different dynamic components. In each universe, there is a dynamic type for each type declaration of a program. Although structurally identical, the dynamic types in different universes are distinct. Therefore, objects of one dynamic type cannot be assigned to variables expecting another, which allows one to control reference passing between different dynamic components. The types for readonly references are supertypes of the corresponding readwrite types. Thus, variables of readonly types can hold references to objects that belong to arbitrary universes. By providing object universes, type universes, and readonly types, the universe type system supports implementation patterns such as dynamic components with several interface objects, iterators, and binary methods that cannot be handled by related approaches.

Whereas aliasing is expressed and controlled by a type system, we specify other program properties by declarative interface specifications and prove them by a Hoare-style programming logic. This programming logic ensures that properties that can be proved for an open program also hold in all well-formed extensions of this program. That is, the logic guarantees modular soundness of our verification technique. Our interface specification technique supports information hiding (1) by describing the different interfaces of a type declaration in different theories of the data and state model and (2) by providing access modes for the specification primitives. Thereby, we guarantee that interface specifications do not reveal implementation details that are supposed to be hidden.

We presented an interface specification language that provides abstract fields with explicit dependencies, pre-post-specifications, modifies-clauses, and type invariants. Abstract fields are used to map objects or object structures to values of the abstract domain. Functional method behavior can be expressed by pre-post-specifications.

Modifies-clauses and explicit dependencies are used to specify frame properties. To make modular verification of frame properties possible, we use the universe programming model (1) to define the notion of relevant locations of a method execution, (2) to formalize a novel semantics for modifies-clauses that is limited to relevant locations, and (3) to restrict the permissible dependencies of an abstract location by modularity rules. These rules enable us to axiomatize the depends-relation in a consistent way and to prove a modularity theorem for frame properties. In the formalizations and rules, static and dynamic dependencies are treated in a uniform way, which leads to a leaner formal model and simplifies proofs.

Regarding type invariants as special abstract fields enables us to apply the specification and verification technique for frame properties to invariants. In particular, we define a novel semantics for invariants that makes modular verification of invariants possible.

Contributions. In the following, we summarize the main contributions of this book for researchers in the area of formal specification and verification, for programming language designers, for interface specification language designers, and for programmers.

Researchers in Formal Specification and Verification. We already mentioned the main contributions for our main audience in Subsection 1.5.3. We revisit them here to point out which contributions are specific to OO-programming and which can be applied as well to procedural languages that provide abstract data types (for instance, based on records). In general, subtyping and inheritance lead to additional complexity for most of the presented problems, techniques, and formalizations. On the other hand, classes and objects provide a clear structure of programs and object stores which simplified the development of the universe programming model and of modular specification and verification techniques.

- *Universe programming model and type system:* We introduced the universe type system since alias control is difficult to achieve in the presence of subtyping and inheritance (see Subsection 1.3.5). Although some problems of alias control do not occur in procedural languages, the universe programming model is still useful to structure the heap memory. Most concepts of the universe type system can be adapted to procedural programming. However, readonly types are realized as supertypes of readwrite types and rely on subtyping and cast-statements which are typical OO-features.
- *Definition of modular correctness:* Our definition of modular correctness is specifically tailored towards languages that provide subtyping and dynamic method binding. For procedural programs, a simpler notion of modular correctness would suffice. Moreover, the composition of proofs for procedural programs is simpler since the effects of dynamic binding that are described in Paragraph 3.3.4.1 do not occur.
- *Modular specification and verification of frame properties:* Besides the extended state problem (see Subsection 1.3.4) which is caused by inheritance and thus specific to OO-programs, modular specification and verification of frame properties in object-oriented and procedural settings entail similar problems, especially the need to reason about abstractions that are declared outside the scope of the module to be verified. Therefore, our explicit dependencies, modularity requirements, and the refined semantics of modifies-clauses can be applied to procedural programs as well.

– *Modular specification and verification of type invariants:* Modular verification of invariants in procedural programs leads to the same problems as in OO-programs (see Subsection 6.1.2). The specification and verification technique described in Chapter 6 can also be applied to procedural programs.

Programming Language Designers. The most interesting contribution for this group is the statically-checkable universe type system for alias control. Aside from its benefit for formal verification, the type system can be applied to structure object stores, to prevent unwanted side-effects due to aliasing, to simplify thread synchronization, and to support distributed programming. Readonly references and methods are useful language features in general, not only in the context of modular verification.

The discussion of module concepts, information hiding, and encapsulation in Subsection 2.1.2 revealed several problems in these areas and sketched solutions. Furthermore, this book suggested several directions for future research that are presented below.

Interface Specification Language Designers. This book explained which features should be provided by an interface specification language to support modular verification. It clarified the semantics of interface specifications that is necessary to enable modular verification, which helps specification language designers to define precise semantics for their languages. Moreover, we explained the need for information hiding in interface specifications and showed how it can be achieved. Aside from classical interface specifications, the universe type system is an interesting supplement for interface specification languages to express and check sharing properties.

Programmers. Although most techniques presented here are too complex to be directly applied in industrial software development, programmers can learn from this book. We claim that implementations that are difficult to verify are also difficult to maintain. Therefore, also programmers that do not want to apply our verification techniques should aim at developing implementations that respect our universe programming model and the modularity requirements for abstractions and invariants. Even without the support of language features such as the universe type system, programmers should structure their programs and apply alias control by convention. Our treatment of modular correctness showed what kind of properties have to be described in informal specifications to enable safe subclassing of reused implementations. Although most programmers do not use formal interface specification languages, the specification techniques presented in this book can guide programmers to comprehensive documentation.

7.2 The Lopex Project

Most of the techniques presented in this book have been developed in the research project Lopex at the University of Hagen, Germany. Lopex stands for "logic-based programming environments constructed from formal language specifications". Such programming environments are software development tools that support formal specification and verification. As part of the project, we have developed a prototype of a logic-based programming environment for a subset of Java: The Java Interactive Verification Environment JIVE.

The JIVE system supports formal specification and verification of nonmodular programs written in the Java subset SVENJA [MMPH97]. The specification and verification technique used in JIVE is based on Poetzsch-Heffter's work [PH97b]: Declarative interface specifications and Hoare logic are used to specify and verify programs.

When a specified SVENJA program is fed into JIVE, the system syntax and type checks the program and its specification and generates a set of proof obligations in terms of Hoare triples from the interface specification. Users can then interactively develop proofs for these obligations by (1) applying rules of the programming logic, (2) using control operations such as copy and paste of proof parts, or (3) invoking so-called proof strategies that automate recurring proof steps. For the individual proof steps, users are supported by the general-purpose theorem prover PVS [COR+95]. The current proof state is visualized by a graphical user interface. Different views to a proof session help users not to get lost in complex proofs.

In the next section, we explain how the modular specification and verification technique presented in this book can be implemented in the JIVE system.

7.3 Tool Support

As becomes clear from this book, specifications and correctness proofs for OO-programs tend to be rather complex. To keep this complexity manageable, developers of specifications and proofs should be supported by sophisticated software tools that perform three important tasks:

1. They prevent or detect flaws by checking programs, specifications, and proofs for syntactical correctness. For instance, they guarantee that the rules of the programming logic are applied correctly.
2. They automate recurring proof steps by strategies. Thereby, they reduce the effort of verification and allow users to focus on the interesting proof parts.
3. They allow users to visualize programs, specifications, and proofs. Different views present only those parts of a project that are relevant at a certain stage. This way, much of the complexity can be hidden from the user.

The JIVE system performs these tasks for the formal specification and verification of nonmodular OO-programs. Due to its smart architecture [MPH00a], JIVE can be enhanced to support modular specification and verification without fundamentally changing the system. In this section, we sketch the adaptions that are necessary to handle the techniques described in this book.

Support for modular specification and verification requires adaption of the parser, the data and state model, the generation of proof obligations, and the verification support. We sketch the required modifications in these areas in the following. An implementation description of JIVE can be found in [MMPH00].

Frontend. The frontend parses and checks specified programs. It must be enhanced in three ways: (1) It must handle the new specification primitives described in this book, namely abstract fields, def- and depends-clauses, and modifies-clauses. (2) We have to implement the universe type system. To do that, we have to adjust the parser and implement the additional context conditions (see Subsection 2.2.5). (3) The frontend must be capable of reading and analyzing single modules instead of complete programs. For all of these modifications, we can apply standard techniques from compiler construction.

Data and State Model. In the JIVE system, the PVS language is used to formalize the data and state model. In its current version, this formalization works only for closed programs since it contains inclusive axioms (see Paragraph 3.1.1.4) for types, etc. To support open programs, we have to use the data and state model described in Subsection 3.1.1. Since the formal language used in this book is essentially a subset of the PVS language, the translation is straightforward. Furthermore, we have to adapt the generation of program-dependent theories in order to support information hiding. We have explained the resulting theory structure in Paragraph 3.1.1.1.

Proof Obligations. The generation of proof obligations has to be adapted in three ways: (1) To guarantee well-formedness, interface specifications lead to proof obligations in predicate logic. The JIVE system must be enhanced to permit program-independent lemmas as proof obligations and to generate these obligations. Since such lemmas are already supported as parts of proofs, these modifications are straightforward. (2) Whereas JIVE already provides requires-clauses, pre-post-pairs, and invariants, we have to add the generation of proof obligations for modifies-clauses. (3) We have to implement specification inheritance.

Verification Support. To support the presented verification technique, we have to modify JIVE w.r.t. three aspects: (1) To provide universes, the programming logic of JIVE has to be slightly changed. (2) Modularity requires the specifications of imported modules to be available for verification as Hoare lemmas (see Paragraph 1.4.4.3). (3) Application of language properties (see Section 3.2) requires to automatically generate new proofs from existing ones. These generation steps as well as the strategy for the composition of open programs (see Paragraph 3.3.4.2) can be implemented as proof strategies in the system. Besides these necessary changes, a variety of features can be added to facilitate modular verification and, in particular, the handling of dependencies. Dealing with dependencies should be simplified by (partial) visualizations of the depends-relation like in Figure 5.7. The automaton used to generate the axioms for the notdepends-relation (see Subsection 5.2.5) allows the system to provide powerful strategies that automate parts of the verification of frame properties. In particular, parts of the case distinctions described in Subsection 5.4.1 can be generated automatically.

For our current research project *Verificard* on "tool-assisted specification and verification of Java Card programs" [Ver01], we will develop the next release of JIVE. In particular, we plan to implement at least parts of the modifications suggested above.

7.4 Directions for Future Work

The extensive treatment of modular specification and verification in this book illustrates the complexity of this topic. Although we solved several open problems in this area, a lot of work is still to be done in order to develop languages and techniques that are easy to apply, supported by sophisticated tools, and sufficiently powerful to find their way to becoming common software development practice. In this section, we briefly discuss the tasks that we consider the next steps towards this goal.

Language Design. In this book, we investigated modular specification and verification based on the limited language support provided by most OO-languages. We presume that more refined language features can help to make the presented techniques more expressive, easier to apply, and partly statically-checkable, which would bring us closer to the goal of component-based programming. Especially the following areas seem promising to us:

- *Information hiding and encapsulation:* In current OO-languages, access modes support information hiding and encapsulation based on classes and modules only. With more fine-grained access control, weaker modularity requirements for abstract fields might suffice for modular verification of frame properties and invariants. Therefore, we suggest to investigate (1) access modes that control access on the object level, (2) encapsulation techniques for whole object structures, (3) better friend mechanisms, (4) write-protected fields, (5) access modes that specifically support hierarchical classes and modules, and (6) combinations of the first five approaches. For instance, fields that are readable and writable for a class and its subclasses, but only readable for friends might help to solve the problem described in Example 5.2.2.

- *Inheritance:* Due to inheritance and information hiding, subclasses can contain inherited methods without even knowing of their existence. However, these methods can modify the state of subclass objects and, thus, their abstract value. This problem becomes manifest at two points of this book: the definition of guards for object universes and the problem of dependencies on locations with inherited fields. Alternative inheritance mechanisms (see e.g., Sather [SOM94] and Beta [MMPN93]) might be helpful to simplify the structure and, thus, modular specification and verification of programs.
- *Module concepts:* To keep the results of this book applicable to a wide range of languages, we used a very simple module concept. Whereas module concepts for functional programming languages have been studied intensely, modularization features in OO-languages are often neglected [Szy92]. However, sophisticated module concepts can help to control aliasing and to simplify verification. In particular, access modes for type declarations, hierarchical classes and modules, composition techniques that support both combination and synthesis of classes and modules, and even a unification of classes and modules are interesting topics for future research.

Type Systems for Alias Control. The universe type system plays a vital role for our specification and verification technique. In this book, we presented the core of a type system for alias control. For practical applications, a variety of extensions could make the type system more expressive. In particular, genericity is an important feature that is not supported yet. Parameterization over universes (similar to context parameters in ownership types [CPN98]) would allow the universe type system to support role separation. Besides its well-known applications, parameterization over type declarations would improve reusability of implementations that use type universes (see Paragraph 2.2.4.2). Furthermore, support for static fields should be provided.

Techniques for alias analysis could be used to infer alias information and thus universe type information from ordinary Java programs. This is interesting to generate universe type annotations automatically for existing class libraries.

In subsection 2.2.6, we have mentioned several applications for the universe type system: Optimization, synchronization in concurrent programs, object migration in distributed programs, and implementation of operational interface specifications. Each of them is an interesting research area that has not been explored yet.

Programming Logics. To our knowledge, the problem of modular completeness of programming logics (see Paragraph 3.3.4.1) has not been addressed so far. We expect both the development of modular complete programming logics for OO-languages and research on modular completeness and its relation to the common notion of relative completeness to provide new insights to the semantics of modular OO-programs.

Dependencies. Explicit dependencies and appropriate modularity rules make modular verification of frame properties and invariants possible. However, for practical applications, the solution presented in this book must be improved in various ways:

- *Expressiveness:* Although we already managed to generalize the depends-clauses and modularity rules of Leino's and Nelson's approach, we are still not able to handle certain implementation patterns (see for instance Example 5.2.2) and to express certain sharing properties. For the latter application, requiring that dependees must be reachable from the corresponding dependents is too restrictive. To solve this problem, we suggest to explore two approaches: (1) By providing modifies-clauses that also describe the modification of newly created objects, we could use a weaker consistency obligation (Obligation 5.1) that does not require reachability of dependees. (2) Module invariants could be used to specify those patterns of aliasing that are particularly interesting for modular verification based on the universe type system (see Subsection 6.4.1).
- *Static checkability:* Syntactically restricted depends-clauses could allow a verification tool to check at least some of the proof obligations for well-formed interface specifications statically. Furthermore, they could simplify the axiomatization of the notdepends-relation. However, restricting depends-clauses will in general affect expressiveness of the technique. Therefore, major case studies should be carried out to determine the right balance between expressiveness and static checkability.

Implementation and Case Studies. In this book, we focused on *techniques* for modular specification and verification. To evaluate these techniques and to develop *methods* for specification and verification, extensive case studies should be carried out. Such case studies will provide insights to (1) strengths and shortcomings of our techniques, (2) proof methods that are necessary to develop sophisticated verification tools and proof strategies, (3) the scalability of our techniques, and (4) possible simplifications of the whole framework.

To make case studies feasible, the universe type system and support for our specification and verification technique have to be implemented in a verification tool such as JIVE. As mentioned in Section 7.3, we plan to do at least parts of this work in the Verificard project. In this project, our techniques will also be used to specify the Java Card API. That is, we can apply the techniques to a class library and thus evaluate their usefulness for this interesting application area (see introduction).

According to Thomas S. Kuhn, "normal science" is a steady accumulation of knowledge that eventually leads to a scientific revolution — radically new ideas, theories, and techniques (see quote at the beginning of this chapter). In the area of software development, such a revolution could lead to a breakthrough of component-based development. We envision that prefabricated components with precisely documented behavior and certified quality could be bought from different vendors and combined to new programs. Sophisticated techniques and highly automated tools could be applied by programmers to show correctness of the composite program based on the correctness of its constituents. In the tradition of normal science, this book aims at bringing us closer to that revolution and, thus, to the efficient development of reliable software.

A. Formal Background and Notations

In this appendix, we explain the formal background of our techniques and explain notations and naming conventions.

A.1 Formal Background

The techniques presented in this book can be formulated in different formal systems. We use multisorted first-order logic and recursive data type definitions since (1) such specifications are expressive enough for our purposes and simple enough to be handled by most computer scientists; (2) the programming logic used in this book was developed for a similar framework [PH97b]; (3) such specifications are supported by most of the available proof checkers and theorem provers such as PVS [OSR93], Isabelle [Pau94], and LP (the Larch Prover [GG91]) which allows us to use any of those as reasoning aids.

Formulas. A *multisorted signature* Σ is a tuple $\langle S, F\rangle$ where S is a set of *sorts* and F is a set of *functions* equipped with a mapping $fsig : F \rightarrow (S^* \times S)$. *fsig* maps each function to its *function signature.* Function signatures are written in the form $(s_1 \times \ldots \times s_n \rightarrow s_0)$. Functions with signatures of the form $\rightarrow s_0$ are called *constants* of sort s_0.

All multisorted signatures contain a sort *Bool* and for each sort s the function $=_s$ with function signature $(s \times s \rightarrow \mathit{Bool})$ denoting equality on sort s; we drop the subscript if sort s is clear from the context.

Let $\Sigma = \langle S, F\rangle$ be a signature, *VAR* be an S-sorted set of *logical variables*, and let the set of *Σ-terms* of sort s, denoted by $T(\Sigma, \mathit{VAR})_s$, be defined as usual (see e.g. [Wir90, Section 2.1]). The set of *Σ-formulas* $\mathit{WFF}(\Sigma)$ is the least set satisfying the following properties:

1. every term of sort *Bool* is in $\mathit{WFF}(\Sigma)$;
2. if $G, H \in \mathit{WFF}(\Sigma)$, then $\neg G, (G \wedge H), (G \vee H), (G \Rightarrow H)$, and $(G \Leftrightarrow H)$ are in $\mathit{WFF}(\Sigma)$;
3. if $X_s \in \mathit{VAR}_s$ and $G \in \mathit{WFF}(\Sigma)$, then $(\forall X_s : G)$ and $(\exists X_s : G)$ are in $\mathit{WFF}(\Sigma)$.

Σ-formulas are denoted by bold capital letters **P**, **Q**, etc. The logical operators have the usual precedences: $\neg, \wedge, \vee, \Rightarrow, \Leftrightarrow, \forall, \exists$ with $\neg$ having the highest precedence.

Peter Müller: Modular Specification ..., LNCS 2262, pp. 223–226, 2002.

Substitution of all free occurrences of a variable X or a constant c by a term t in formula $\mathbf{P}$ is denoted by $\mathbf{P}[t/X]$ resp. $\mathbf{P}[t/c]$. In both cases, the sort of the term and the sort of the variable or constant have to be identical.

Data Types. Sorts can be introduced by *uninterpreted sort declarations* of the form $s : Sort$ or by abstract data type definitions (see below).

We assume the following four basic data types with the usual operations: data type Boolean with sort *Bool* and constants *true* and *false*; data type Nat of nonnegative integers with sort *Nat*, the usual operations, and the canonical total ordering; data type Integer with infinite sort *Integer*, finite sort *Int*, and the usual integer operations[1]. The sort *Int* is used to model the finite integer range of our programming language. A formalization of *Integer*, *Int*, and appropriate mappings can be found in [PH97b].

Recursive data types play an important role in specification and programming. Accordingly, almost every specification framework provides a special construct for their definition (see e.g., [OSR93, Pau94, GH93]). We use the following notation to define recursive data types:

$$
\begin{array}{l}
\textbf{data type} \\
\begin{array}{rcl}
DSrt_1 & = & constr_{1,1}\ (sel^1_{1,1} : USrt^1_{1,1},\ \ldots,\ sel^{m_{1,1}}_{1,1} : USrt^{m_{1,1}}_{1,1}) \\
& | & \ldots \\
& | & constr_{1,c_1}\ (sel^1_{1,c_1} : USrt^1_{1,c_1},\ \ldots,\ sel^{m_{1,c_1}}_{1,c_1} : USrt^{m_{1,c_1}}_{1,c_1}) \\
\ldots & & \\
DSrt_n & = & constr_{n,1}\ (sel^1_{n,1} : USrt^1_{n,1},\ \ldots,\ sel^{m_{n,1}}_{n,1} : USrt^{m_{n,1}}_{n,1}) \\
& | & \ldots \\
& | & constr_{n,c_n}\ (sel^1_{n,c_n} : USrt^1_{n,c_n},\ \ldots,\ sel^{m_{n,c_n}}_{n,c_n} : USrt^{m_{n,c_n}}_{n,c_n})
\end{array} \\
\textbf{end data type}
\end{array}
$$

Such a definition introduces

- the sorts $DSrt_i$;
- the constructor functions $constr_{i,j}$; the sorts $USrt^k_{i,j}$ have to be either previously defined or in $\{DSrt_1, \ldots, DSrt_n\}$.
- a discriminator function $constr_{i,j}? : DSrt_i \rightarrow Bool$. $constr_{i,j}?(t)$ yields *true* if t is constructed by $constr_{i,j}$ and *false* otherwise.
- the selector functions $sel^k_{i,j}$; selector functions are optional.
- the usual set of axioms for abstract data types (e.g., for structural induction, extensionality, etc. See e.g., [OSR93] for details.)

To keep the framework simple, we do not provide parameterized sorts. However, we assume a set of list and set data types with elements of various sorts. We write *list/set of S* to abbreviate the sort of lists resp. sets with elements of sort S. These data types provide the usual constructors and operations.

[1] see [PH97b] for a formalization of Integer.

Theories. Universal specifications are grouped into theories. Each definition, axiom, lemma, etc. belongs to exactly one theory. To refer to specification parts of other theories in a theory T, these theories have to be imported explicitly by T. We assume that each theory imports the *prelude theory* that contains the predefined data types (see above). The import relation on theories has to be acyclic.

A.2 Notations

Formulas. In formulas, we use roman font for constants and italic fonts for variables. In axioms and lemmas, all free variables are universally quantified at the outermost level, where the quantification ranges over all values of the sort of the quantified variable. For instance, an axiom $imports(\mathrm{M}, N)$ is equivalent to $\forall (N : \mathit{ModId}) : imports(\mathrm{M}, N)$ (note that M is a constant). For brevity, we keep the sorts of variables and constants implicit where possible, but use the naming conventions described in the next paragraph.

Naming Conventions for Variables. We use certain names for variables and constants of different sorts. The connection of names and sorts is summarized in the following table. Unless otherwise stated, the names in the left column are used for variables and constants of the sorts in the right column (if there are several sorts for one name, the correct sort becomes clear from the context). Except for the indices A and C, primed or indexed variables have the same sort as the corresponding plain variables.

Names	Sorts	Names	Sorts
M	*AccessMode*	$\mathcal{M}$, $\mathcal{S}$	*set of ModId*
F_A	*AFieldId*	i, j, k, l, n, N, M	*Nat*
K_A, L_A	*ALocation*	O, *OID*	*ObjId*
F_C	*CFieldId*	R	*regExpr*
C,D, E	*ClassId*	f, g, f_A, g_A, T@f, S@g	*SimpleAFieldId*
K_C, L_C	*CLocation*	f, g, f_C, g_C, T@f, S@g	*SimpleCFieldId*
d	*DepId*	*OS*	*Store*
F, G	*FieldId*	R, S, T	*TypeId*, *DynType*, *Type*
T@m, S@n	*ImplId*	U, V, W	*Universe*
K, L	*Location*	X, Y, Z	*Value*
M, N	*ModId*	T:m, S:n	*VirtualMethodId*

Notations for Proofs and Proof Outlines. In proofs, we mention the properties used in a proof step (formulas, axioms, lemmas, rules, etc.) in comments, which are enclosed in double brackets ($[\![\ ]\!]$). If several properties are used in one step, we enumerate them separated by commas meaning "and". A formula followed by axioms or lemmas in parentheses means that the formula can be derived by the mentioned axioms and lemmas.

Proofs in programming logic are mostly presented as so-called *proof outlines.* In proof outlines, proofs are displayed as programs annotated with formulas and rule applications. A rule application is displayed by two horizontal lines with arrows pointing at each other. The antecedent and the program part of the succedent are printed between the lines whereas the pre- and the postcondition of the succedent are displayed above the upper and below the lower line, resp. For applications of the strength- and the weak-rule, only an implication is displayed. Assumptions are not presented in proof outlines. This notation is very intuitive and therefore not explained in detail here (see [PH97b, Owi75] for further information).

We use double horizontal lines to display the application of a language property operator (see Def. 3.2.1). That is, a double horizontal line can be read as "if there is a proof for the sequent above the double line, then there is a proof for the sequent below." In proof outlines, the application of language property operators is displayed analogously by a pair of double horizontal lines with arrows at the end.

B. Predefined Type Declarations

Each Mojave program contains three predefined type declarations: Like in Java, `Object` is the root of the class hierarchy. `Interface` is used as a default if a class does not implement any other interface. `Operator` contains a set of static methods for the usual unary and binary operations. Since these methods cannot be implemented in Mojave, they are marked as `native` to indicate that their behavior is predefined. For brevity, we present only the methods that are needed in this book. The full set of operator methods (in particular, methods for arithmetic operations) can be found in [MMPH97].

```
public class Object {
 public boolean native equals(readonly Object p) readonly
  public pre  p = O ∧ this = T ∧ tidD(typeof(this)) = ctid(Object) ∧ $ = OS;
  public post result = bool(O = T) ∧ $ = OS;
}

public interface Interface {}

public class Operator {
 public static native boolean equalO
                        (readonly Object a, readonly Object b) readonly
  public pre  a = X ∧ b = Y ∧ $ = OS;
  public post result = bool(X = Y) ∧ $ = OS;

 public static native boolean equalB (boolean a, boolean b) readonly
  public pre  aB(a) = A ∧ aB(b) = B ∧ $ = OS;
  public post result = bool(A = B) ∧ $ = OS;

 public static native boolean condAnd (boolean a, boolean b) readonly
  public pre  aB(a) = A ∧ aB(b) = B ∧ $ = OS;
  public post result = bool(A ∧ B) ∧ $ = OS;

 public static native boolean condOr (boolean a, boolean b) readonly
  public pre  aB(a) = A ∧ aB(b) = B ∧ $ = OS;
  public post result = bool(A ∨ B) ∧ $ = OS;

 public static native boolean not (boolean a) readonly
  public pre  aB(a) = A ∧ $ = OS;
  public post result = bool(¬A) ∧ $ = OS;

 ...
}
```

Peter Müller: Modular Specification ..., LNCS 2262, p. 227, 2002.

C. Examples

The following two sections contain the example used throughout this book: a doubly linked list with positions and iterators (module `LIST`), and a dynamic component with properties (module `PROPERTY`). To illustrate the concrete syntax of Mojave and to demonstrate the application of the universe type system, we present the implementation of both modules in the following. The classes `Node`, `List`, `ListPos`, and `ListProperty` also contain specifications. For these classes, we present the abstract fields and type invariants with def- and depends-clauses, the requires- and modifies-clauses of their methods, and some pre-post-pairs. In the example, we use *true* as default formula if req-clauses or single pre- or postconditions are omitted.

C.1 Doubly Linked List

```
module LIST;

public class Node {
 public Node prev, next;
 public readonly Object elem;
 public invariant inv;

 public def inv by     ($(this.next) ≠ null⇒$($(this.next).prev) = this)∧
                       ($(this.prev) ≠ null⇒$($(this.prev).next) = this)∧
                       ρ(this, null, $, next) ∧ ρ(this, null, $, prev);

 public depends inv on {Y.next | ρ(this, Y, $, next) ∨ Y = $(this.prev)};
 public depends inv on {Y.prev | ρ(this, Y, $, prev) ∨ Y = $(this.next)};
}


public class List {
 protected rep<this> Node first, last;

 public abstract list of Value val;
 protected def val by      cut(col($(this.first), $));

 protected depends val on {Y.first | Y = this};                    // a
 protected depends val on {Y.elem | ρ($(this.first), Y, $, next)}; // b
 protected depends val on {Y.next | ρ($(this.first), Y, $, next)}; // c
 protected depends val on {Y.prev | ρ($(this.first), Y, $, next)}; // d
```

Peter Müller: Modular Specification ..., LNCS 2262, pp. 229–235, 2002.

`public invariant inv;`

`protected def inv by` $\$(\text{this.first}) \neq \mathit{null} \wedge \$(\text{this.last}) \neq \mathit{null} \wedge$
$\rho(\$(\text{this.first}), \$(\text{this.last}), \$, \text{next}) \wedge$
$\$(\$(\text{this.last}).\text{next}) = \mathit{null} \wedge$
$\$(\text{this.first}) \neq \$(\text{this.last});$

`protected depends inv on` $\{Y.\text{first} \mid Y = \text{this}\};$
`protected depends inv on` $\{Y.\text{last} \mid Y = \text{this}\};$
`protected depends inv on` $\{Y.\text{next} \mid \rho(\$(\text{this.first}), Y, \$, \text{next}) \vee$
$Y = \$(\text{this.last})\};$

`private int init()`
`req` $\forall K_C : \$(K_C) \neq \text{this};$
`private pre` $\text{this} = X$
`post` $\mathit{invrep}(X.\text{inv}, \$)$
`private pre` $\mathit{invL}(L) \wedge \neg \mathit{alive}(\mathit{obj}(L), \$)$
`post` $\mathit{alive}(\mathit{obj}(L), \$) \Rightarrow \mathit{invrep}(L, \$)$
`modifies` $\{\text{this.val}, \text{this.inv}\};$

```
{
    rep<this> Node f,l;

    f = new rep<this> Node();   l = new rep<this> Node();
    f.next = l;                 l.prev = f;
    this.first = f;             this.last  = l;
}
```

```
public static List createList()
{
    int dummy;
    result = new List();
    dummy = result.init();
}
```

`public boolean isEmpty() readonly`
`req` $\mathit{inv}(\$, \mathcal{U});$

```
{
    readonly Node f,l;

    f = this.first;   l = this.last;
    f = f.next;       result = Operator.equalO(f,l);
}
```

`public int appFront(readonly Object v)`
`modifies` $\{\text{this.val}\} \cup \{Y.\text{position} \mid \$(Y.\text{theList}) = \text{this} \wedge \$(Y.\text{valid})\};$

```
{
    rep<this> Node f,nn,n;

    f = this.first;   nn = new rep<this> Node();
    nn.elem = v;      nn.prev = f;
    n = f.next;       nn.next = n;
    f.next = nn;      n.prev = nn;
}
```

```
protected int remove(readonly Node n)
```

req $n \neq \mathit{null} \wedge \rho(\$(\text{this.first}), \text{n}, \$, \text{next}) \wedge \text{n} \neq \$(\text{this.first}) \wedge$
$\text{n} \neq \$(\text{this.last})$;

modifies $\{\text{this.val}\} \cup$
$\{Y.\text{position} \mid \$(Y.\text{theList}) = \text{this} \wedge$
$\$(Y.\mathit{position}) \geq \mathit{index}(\$(\text{this.first}), \text{n}, \$)\} \cup$
$\{Y.\text{valid} \mid \$(Y.\text{theList}) = \text{this} \wedge$
$\$(Y.\mathit{position}) = \mathit{index}(\$(\text{this.first}), \text{n}, \$)\}$;

```
{
    rep<this> Node nn,pr,ne;

    nn = (rep<this> Node) n;
    pr = nn.prev;
    ne = nn.next;
    pr.next = ne;
    ne.prev = pr;
    // this is needed to preserve the invariant for nn
    nn.prev = null;
    nn.next = null;
}
```

```
public readonly Object getFirst() readonly
```

req $\mathit{inv}(\$, \mathcal{U})$;

```
{
    readonly Node n;

    n = this.first;
    n = n.next;
    result = n.elem;
}
```

```
public ListPos getPos(int index)
```

req $\mathit{aI}(\text{index}) > 0 \wedge \mathit{aI}(\text{index}) \leq \mathit{length}(\$(\text{this.val}))$;

```
{
    rep<this> Node n;
    boolean b1;

    n = this.first;
    b1 = true;
    while(b1) {
        n = n.next;
        index = Operator.plus(index,-1);
        b1 = Operator.greater(index,0);
    }
    result = new ListPos();
    result.list = this;
    result.pos = n;
}
```

```
protected int setAtPos(readonly Node n, readonly Object v)
           req       n ≠ null ∧ index($(this.first), n, $) = N ∧ N > 0;
 protected pre       $(n.next) ≠ null ∧ v = V ∧ this = L ∧ $(L.val) = S;
           post      $(L.val) = update(S, N, V);
           modifies  {this.val};

 {
     rep<this> Node nn;

     nn = (rep<this> Node) n;
     nn.elem = v;
 }

public boolean equalsList(readonly List l) readonly
 req l ≠ null ∧ inv($, U);
 {
     readonly Node n1,n2,l1,l2;
     boolean  b, b1, b2, e;
     readonly Object o1,o2;

     result = true;
     n1 = this.first;
     n2 = l.first;
     n1 = n1.next;   // skip dummy node
     n2 = n2.next;   // skip dummy node
     l1 = this.last;
     l2 = l.last;
     b = true;
     b1 = true;

     while(b) {
         o1 = n1.elem;
         o2 = n2.elem;
         e  = Operator.equalO(o1,o2);
         if (e) {                          // elements are equal
             n1 = n1.next;
             n2 = n2.next;
             b1 = Operator.equalO(n1,l1);
             b2 = Operator.equalO(n2,l2);
             b1 = Operator.not(b1);
             b2 = Operator.not(b2);
             b  = Operator.condAnd(b1,b2);
         } else {
             result = false;
             b = false;
         }
     }
     b = Operator.condOr(b1,b2);
     if (b) result = false; else ;
 }
}
```

```
public class ListPos {
 protected List list;
 protected readonly Node pos;

 public    abstract Value anchor;
           def anchor by         $($(this.list).first);
 protected depends anchor on     {Y.list | Y = this};                          // e
           depends anchor on     {Y.first | Y = $(this.list)};                 // f

 public    abstract Nat position;
 protected def position by       index($(this.anchor), $(this.pos), $);
 public    depends position on   {Y.anchor | Y = this};                        // g
 protected depends position on   {Y.pos | Y = this};                           // h
 public    depends position on   {Y.next | ρ($(this.anchor), Y, $, next};      // i

 public    abstract Bool valid;
 protected def valid by          ρ($(this.anchor), $(this.pos), $, next)∧
                                 $(this.anchor) ≠ $(this.pos)∧
                                 $($(this.pos).next) ≠ null;
 public    depends valid on      {Y.position | Y = this};                      // j

 public    abstract Value theList;
 protected def theList by        $(this.list);
 protected depends theList on    {Y.list | Y = this};                          // k

 public invariant inv;
 protected def inv by            $(this.list) ≠ null ∧ $(this.pos) ≠ null
 protected depends inv on        {Y.list | Y = this};
 protected depends inv on        {Y.pos | Y = this};


 public int setValue(readonly Object v)
        req      $(this.valid);
  public pre     $(this.theList) = L ∧ $(L.val) = S ∧ v = V∧
                 $(this.position) = N;
        post     $(L.val) = update(S, N, V);
        modifies {$(this.theList).val};

  {
     List l;
     readonly Node n;
     l = this.list;
     n = this.pos;
     result = l.setAtPos(n,v);
  }


 public readonly Object getValue() readonly
  req $(this.valid) ∧ inv($, U);

   {
      readonly Node n;
      n = this.pos;
      result = n.elem;
   }

}
```

```
public class Iter extends ListPos {
    protected readonly Node lastReturned;

    public static Iter createIter(List l) {
      readonly Node f;
      readonly List rol;

      result = new Iter();
      rol = l;
      f = rol.first;
      result.list = l;
      f = f.next;
      result.pos = f;
    }

    public boolean hasNext() readonly {
      readonly Node p,ln;
      readonly List l;

      p = this.pos;
      l = this.list;
      ln = l.last;
      result = Operator.notequalO(p,ln);
    }

    public readonly Object next() {
      readonly Node p;

      p = this.pos;
      result = p.elem;
      this.lastReturned = p;
      p = p.next;
      this.pos = p;
    }

    public int remove() {
      List l;
      readonly Node n;

      l = this.list;
      n = this.lastReturned;
      result = l.remove(n);
    }
}
```

C.2 Property Editor

```
module PROPERTY imports LIST;

public class MyBean {
    rep<MyBean> List beanRep;

    public static MyBean createMyBean() {
      rep<MyBean> List l;
      l = rep<MyBean> List.createList();
      result = new MyBean();    result.beanRep = l;
    }

    public Property getProperty(int i) {
      rep<MyBean> List l;       rep<MyBean> ListPos pos;

      l = this.beanRep;         pos = l.getPos(i);
      result = ListProperty.createListProperty(pos);
    }
}

public interface Property {
    public int setValue(readonly Object v);
    public readonly Object getValue() readonly;
}

public class ListProperty implements Property {
 protected rep<MyBean> ListPos lp;

 public    abstract Nat propPos;
 protected def propPos by       $($(this.lp).position);
 protected depends propPos on   {Y.lp | Y = this};                    // l
 protected depends propPos on   {Y.position | Y = $(this.lp)};        // m

 public    abstract Value propList;
 protected def propList by      $($(this.lp).theList);
 protected depends propList on {Y.lp | Y = this};                     // n
 protected depends propList on {Y.theList | Y = $(this.lp)};          // o

 public invariant inv;
 protected def inv by           $(this.lp) ≠ null ∧ $($(this.lp).valid);
 protected depends inv on       {Y.lp | Y = this};
 protected depends inv on       {Y.valid | Y = $(this.lp)};

 public static ListProperty createListProperty(rep<MyBean> ListPos p)
  req p ≠ null ∧ $(p.valid);

  { result = new ListProperty(); result.lp = p; }

 public int setValue(readonly Object v)
  modifies {$(this.propList).val};

  { rep<MyBean> ListPos p; p = this.lp; result = p.setValue(v); }

 public readonly Object getValue() readonly
  req inv($,𝒰);
  { readonly ListPos p; p = this.lp; result = p.getValue(); }
```

D. Auxiliary Lemmas, Proofs, and Models

D.1 Auxiliary Lemmas and Proofs from Chapter 3

Proof of Lemma 3.1.1:

$\preceq_T$ is reflexive and transitive by definition. It remains to show antisymmetry:

$$S \preceq_T T \wedge T \preceq_T S \Rightarrow S = T$$

This proof runs by case distinction on the forms of S and T.

Case 1: $S = grndT(S')$
$S \preceq_T T \wedge T \preceq_T S \wedge S = grndT(S')$
$\Rightarrow$ [Axiomatization of $\preceq_T$]
$T = grndT(T') \wedge S = grndT(S') \wedge S' \preceq_M T' \wedge T' \preceq_M S'$ for some T'
$\Rightarrow$ [Antisymmetry of $\preceq_M$ (Axiom **subM1**)]
$T = grndT(T') \wedge S = grndT(S') \wedge S' = T'$
$\Rightarrow$
$S = T$

The cases for rep, readonly, and primitive types are analogous or trivial. □

For a more convenient handling of universes, we introduce an auxiliary function h that yields the depth of a universe in the universe hierarchy:

$$\begin{array}{ll} h : Universe \rightarrow Nat & \\ h(stdU) & = 0 \\ h(typeU(T,U)) & = 1 + h(U) \\ h(objU(OID,C,U)) & = 1 + h(U) \end{array}$$

The following two auxiliary lemmas about h are used in the proof of Lemma 3.1.3. Basically, both lemmas express that the natural number N used in the universe order $\trianglelefteq_N$ is the difference between the depths of the two compared universes.

Lemma D.1.1.

$$U \trianglelefteq_N V \Rightarrow h(U) - h(V) = N$$

Proof of Lemma D.1.1:

We prove this lemma by induction on N:

Peter Müller: Modular Specification ..., LNCS 2262, pp. 237–269, 2002.

Induction Basis: $N = 0$
$U \trianglelefteq_0 V \Rightarrow U = V \Rightarrow h(U) - h(V) = 0$
Induction Step: $N \geq 0$
$U \trianglelefteq_{N+1} V$
$\Rightarrow$ $[\![$ Definition of $\trianglelefteq_N$ $]\!]$
$\exists W, T, OID, C : (U = typeU(T, W) \vee U = objU(OID, C, W)) \wedge W \trianglelefteq_N V$
$\Rightarrow$ $[\![$ Induction hypothesis $]\!]$
$\exists W, T, OID, C : (U = typeU(T, W) \vee U = objU(OID, C, W)) \wedge h(W) - h(V) = N$
$\Rightarrow$ $[\![$ Definition of h $]\!]$
$\exists W : h(U) = 1 + h(W) \wedge h(W) - h(V) = N$
$\Rightarrow$
$h(U) - h(V) = N + 1$

□

Lemma D.1.2.

$$U \trianglelefteq_N V \wedge V \trianglelefteq_M W \Rightarrow U \trianglelefteq_{N+M} W$$

Proof of Lemma D.1.2:

We prove the lemma by induction on N:

Induction Basis: $N = 0$
$U \trianglelefteq_0 V \wedge V \trianglelefteq_M W$
$\Rightarrow$ $[\![$ Definition of $\trianglelefteq_N$ $]\!]$
$U = V \wedge V \trianglelefteq_M W$
$\Rightarrow$
$U \trianglelefteq_{0+M} W$

Induction Step: $N \geq 0$
$U \trianglelefteq_{N+1} V \wedge V \trianglelefteq_M W$
$\Rightarrow$ $[\![$ Definition of $\trianglelefteq_N$ $]\!]$
$\exists U', T, OID, C : (U = typeU(T, U') \vee U = objU(OID, C, U')) \wedge U' \trianglelefteq_N V \wedge$
$V \trianglelefteq_M W$
$\Rightarrow$ $[\![$ Induction hypothesis $]\!]$
$\exists U', T, OID, C : (U = typeU(T, U') \vee U = objU(OID, C, U')) \wedge U' \trianglelefteq_{N+M} W$
$\Rightarrow$ $[\![$ Definition of $\trianglelefteq_N$ $]\!]$
$U \trianglelefteq_{N+M+1} W$

□

Proof of Lemma 3.1.3:

1. Reflexivity
$U \trianglelefteq_0 U \Rightarrow \exists N : U \trianglelefteq_N U \Rightarrow U \trianglelefteq U$

2. Transitivity
$U \trianglelefteq V \wedge V \trianglelefteq W$
$\Rightarrow$ $[\![$ Definition of $\trianglelefteq$ $]\!]$
$\exists N, M : U \trianglelefteq_N V \wedge V \trianglelefteq_M W$
$\Rightarrow$ $[\![$ Lemma D.1.2 $]\!]$
$\exists N, M : U \trianglelefteq_{N+M} W$
$\Rightarrow$ $[\![$ Definition of $\trianglelefteq$ $]\!]$
$U \trianglelefteq W$

3. Antisymmetry
$U \trianglelefteq V \wedge V \trianglelefteq U$
$\Rightarrow$ $[\![$ Definition of $\trianglelefteq$ $]\!]$
$\exists N, M : U \trianglelefteq_N V \wedge V \trianglelefteq_M U$
$\Rightarrow$ $[\![$ Lemma D.1.1 $]\!]$
$\exists N, M : U \trianglelefteq_N V \wedge h(U) - h(V) = N \wedge h(V) - h(U) = M$
$\Rightarrow$ $[\![$ N and M are natural numbers $\Rightarrow N = M = 0$ $]\!]$
$U = V$

□

Proof of Lemma 3.1.5:

$\preceq$ is reflexive and transitive by definition. The proof of antisymmetry

$$S \preceq T \wedge T \preceq S \Rightarrow S = T$$

runs by case distinction on the forms of S and T.

Case 1: $S = \mathit{refDT}(S', U)$
$S \preceq T \wedge T \preceq S \wedge S = \mathit{refDT}(S', U)$
$\Rightarrow$ [Axiomatization of $\preceq$]
$T = \mathit{refDT}(T', U) \wedge S = \mathit{refDT}(S', U) \wedge S' \preceq_M T' \wedge T' \preceq_M S'$ for some T'
$\Rightarrow$ [Antisymmetry of $\preceq_M$ (Axiom **subM1**)]
$T = \mathit{refDT}(T', U) \wedge S = \mathit{refDT}(S', U) \wedge S' = T'$
$\Rightarrow$
$S = T$

The case for dynamic readonly types is analogous. The cases for primitive dynamic types are trivial. □

Proof of Lemma 3.1.7:

The proof runs by case distinction on the forms of S and T.

Case 1: $S = \mathit{grndT}(S')$
$S \preceq_T T \wedge S = \mathit{grndT}(S')$
$\Rightarrow$ [Axiomatization of $\preceq_T$]
$S = \mathit{grndT}(S') \wedge$
$(T = \mathit{grndT}(T') \wedge S' \preceq_M T' \vee T = \mathit{roT}(T') \wedge S' \preceq_M T')$ for some T'
$\Rightarrow$ [Definition of dyn]
$(\mathit{dyn}(T, X, U) = \mathit{refDT}(T', U) \vee \mathit{dyn}(T, X, U) = \mathit{roDT}(T')) \wedge$
$\mathit{dyn}(S, X, U) = \mathit{refDT}(S', U) \wedge S' \preceq_M T'$
$\Rightarrow$ [Axiomatization of $\preceq$]
$\mathit{dyn}(S, X, U) \preceq \mathit{dyn}(T, X, U)$

Case 2 ($S = \mathit{trepT}(S', R)$) is analogous to Case 1.

Case 3:. $S = \mathit{orepT}(S')$
$S \preceq_T T \wedge S = \mathit{orepT}(S') \wedge \mathit{ref?}(X)$
$\Rightarrow$ [Axiomatization of $\preceq_T$]
$S = \mathit{orepT}(S') \wedge (T = \mathit{orepT}(T') \wedge S' \preceq_M T' \vee T = \mathit{roT}(T') \wedge S' \preceq_M T') \wedge$
$X = \mathit{ref}(C, \mathit{OID}, V)$ for some T', C, OID, V
$\Rightarrow$ [Definition of dyn]
$\mathit{dyn}(S, X, U) = \mathit{refDT}(S', \mathit{objU}(\mathit{OID}, C, U)) \wedge S' \preceq_M T' \wedge$
$(\mathit{dyn}(T, X, U) = \mathit{refDT}(T', \mathit{objU}(\mathit{OID}, C, U)) \vee \mathit{dyn}(T, X, U) = \mathit{roDT}(T'))$
$\Rightarrow$ [Axiomatization of $\preceq$]
$\mathit{dyn}(S, X, U) \preceq \mathit{dyn}(T, X, U)$

Case 4 ($S = roT(S')$) is analogous to Case 1. Cases 5 and 6 ($S = booleanT$ and $S = intT$) are trivial.

Case 7: $S = nullT$
$S \preceq_T T \wedge S = nullT$
$\Rightarrow$ [Axiomatization of $\preceq_T$]
$(T = grndT(T') \vee T = trepT(T', R) \vee T = orepT(T') \vee T = roT(T') \vee$
$T = nullT) \wedge S = nullT$ for some T', R
$\Rightarrow$ [Definition of dyn]
$dyn(T, X, U) = refDT(T', V) \vee dyn(T, X, U) = roDT(T') \vee$
$dyn(T, X, U) = nullDT \wedge dyn(S, X, U) = nullDT$ for some V
$\Rightarrow$ [Axiomatization of $\preceq$]
$dyn(S, X, U) \preceq dyn(T, X, U)$

□

Proof of Lemma 3.1.8:

$presentL(L, S) \wedge imports(module(T), module(S))$
$\Rightarrow$ ⟦ Definition of $presentL$ ⟧
$imports(module(S), module(dtype(fid(L)))) \wedge imports(module(T), module(S))$
$\Rightarrow$ ⟦ Transitivity of $imports$ (Axiom **import1**) ⟧
$imports(module(T), module(dtype(fid(L))))$
$\Rightarrow$ ⟦ Definition of $presentL$ ⟧
$presentL(L, T)$

□

Proof of Lemma 3.1.9:

$accessibleL(L, T)$
$\Rightarrow$ ⟦ Definition of $accessibleL$ ⟧
$accessible(accessMode(fid(L)), dtype(fid(L)), T)$
$\Rightarrow$ ⟦ Lemma 3.1.2 ⟧
$imports(module(T), module(dtype(fid(L))))$
$\Rightarrow$ ⟦ Definition of $presentL$ ⟧
$presentL(L, T)$

□

Proof of Lemma 3.2.2:
The proof runs by case distinction on the forms of S and T.

Case 1: $grndT?(S)$
$dyn(S * T, X, U)$
$=$ ⟦ Definition of $*$ ⟧
$dyn(T, X, U)$
$=$ ⟦ $orepT?(T) \Rightarrow X = Y$, definitions of dyn and $univ$ ⟧
$dyn(T, Y, univ(dyn(S, X, U)))$

Case 2: $S = trepT(S', R)$
$univ(dyn(S, X, U)) = univ(refDT(S', typeU(R, U))) = typeU(R, U)$

Case 2.1: $T = grndT(T')$
$dyn(S * T, X, U) =$ ⟦ Definition of $*$ ⟧
$dyn(trepT(T', R), X, U) =$ ⟦ Definition of dyn ⟧
$refDT(T', typeU(R, U)) = refDT(T', univ(dyn(S, X, U)))$
$=$ ⟦ Definition of dyn ⟧
$dyn(grndT(T'), Y, univ(dyn(S, X, U))) = dyn(T, Y, univ(dyn(S, X, U)))$

Case 2.2: $trepT?(T)$
The combination $S * T$ is undefined.

Case 2.3: $orepT?(T)$
The combination $S * T$ is undefined.

Case 2.4: $T = roT(T')$
$dyn(S * T, X, U) =$ ⟦ Definition of $*$ ⟧
$dyn(roT(T'), X, U) =$ ⟦ Definition of dyn ⟧
$dyn(roT(T'), Y, univ(dyn(S, X, U))) = dyn(T, Y, univ(dyn(S, X, U)))$

Case 2.5: $T = booleanT \vee T = intT \vee T = nullT$
$S * T = T \wedge (T = booleanT \vee T = intT \vee T = nullT)$
$\Rightarrow$ ⟦ Definition of dyn ⟧
$dyn(T, Y, univ(dyn(S, X, U))) = dyn(S * T, X, U)$

Case 3: $S = orepT(S')$
$univ(dyn(S, X, U)) = univ(refDT(S', objU(oid(X), cidV(X), U))) =$
$objU(oid(X), cidV(X), U)$

Case 3 is analogous to Case 2.

Case 4: $roT?(S)$
$roT?(S) \wedge \neg roT?(S)$
$\Rightarrow$
$false$
$\Rightarrow$
$dyn(T, Y, univ(dyn(S, X, U))) = dyn(S * T, X, U)$

Case 5: $booleanT?(S) \vee intT?(S) \vee nullT?(S)$
The combination $S * T$ is undefined.

□

Proof of Lemma 3.2.3:

The proof runs by case distinction on the form of T.

Case 1: $T = grndT(T')$
$dyn(T, Y, V) = dyn(grndT(T'), Y, V)$
$=$ ⟦ Definition of dyn ⟧
$refDT(T', V)$
$\preceq$ ⟦ Axiomatization of $\preceq$ ⟧
$roDT(T')$
$=$ ⟦ Definition of dyn ⟧
$dyn(roT(T'), X, U)$
$=$ ⟦ Definition of $*$ ⟧
$dyn(S * T, X, U)$

Case 2 ($T = trepT(T', R)$) and Case 3 ($T = orepT(T')$) are analogous to Case 1.

Case 4: $T = roT(T')$
$dyn(T, Y, V) = dyn(roT(T'), Y, V)$
$=$ ⟦ Definition of dyn ⟧
$roDT(T')$
$=$ ⟦ Definition of dyn ⟧
$dyn(roT(T'), X, U)$
$=$ ⟦ Definition of $*$ ⟧
$dyn(S * T, X, U)$
$\Rightarrow$ ⟦ Reflexivity of $\preceq$ (Lemma 3.1.5) ⟧
$dyn(T, Y, V) \preceq dyn(S * T, X, U)$

Case 5: $T = booleanT \vee T = intT \vee T = nullT$
$S * T = T \wedge (T = booleanT \vee T = intT \vee T = nullT)$
$\Rightarrow$ ⟦ Definition of dyn ⟧
$dyn(T, Y, V) = dyn(S * T, X, U)$
$\Rightarrow$ ⟦ Reflexivity of $\preceq$ (Lemma 3.1.5) ⟧
$dyn(T, Y, V) \preceq dyn(S * T, X, U)$

□

For the proof of Lemma 3.2.5, we show that the readonly annotations can be removed from a sequent:

Lemma D.1.3.

$$\frac{\mathcal{A} \triangleright \{\, \mathbf{P} \wedge \$ = OS \,\} \text{ COMP } \{\, \mathbf{Q} \wedge \$ = OS \,\}}{\mathcal{A} \triangleright \{\, \mathbf{P} \,\} \text{ COMP } \{\, \mathbf{Q} \,\}}$$

Proof of Lemma D.1.3:

$$\cfrac{\cfrac{\cfrac{\mathcal{A} \triangleright \{\, \mathbf{P} \wedge \$ = OS \,\} \text{ COMP } \{\, \mathbf{Q} \wedge \$ = OS \,\}}{\mathcal{A} \triangleright \{\, \mathbf{P} \wedge \$ = OS \,\} \text{ COMP } \{\, \mathbf{Q} \,\}} \; [\![\text{weak-rule}]\!]}{\mathcal{A} \triangleright \{\, \exists OS : \mathbf{P} \wedge \$ = OS \,\} \text{ COMP } \{\, \mathbf{Q} \,\}} \; [\![\text{ex-rule}]\!]}{\mathcal{A} \triangleright \{\, \mathbf{P} \,\} \text{ COMP } \{\, \mathbf{Q} \,\}} \; [\![\text{strength-rule}]\!]$$

□

Proof of Lemma 3.2.5:

We use the same proof technique as for the type safety proof (Proof 3.2.1). We omit all cases that are trivial or analogous to the corresponding cases in the type safety proof. The derivations are trivial for readwrite methods and statements in readwrite methods. Thus, we show only the cases for readonly methods and statements in readonly methods.

Induction Basis.

New-axiom: new-statements are not allowed in readonly methods.

Field-write-axiom: field-write-statements are not allowed in readonly methods.

Predefined method implementations: Since all predefined methods have $\$ = OS$ in their pre- and postconditions, the proofs for that methods are trivial and therefore omitted.

Induction Step.

Invocation-rule: For method invocations, we have to look at both cases: (1) the invocation statement occurs in a readwrite method; (2) the invocation statement occurs in a readonly method. Case (1) is trivial if the invoked method is readwrite. Otherwise, we derive

$$\frac{\dfrac{ro(\mathcal{A}) \rhd \{ \mathbf{P} \wedge \$ = OS \} \text{ S:n } \{ \mathbf{Q} \wedge \$ = OS \}}{ro(\mathcal{A}) \rhd \{ \mathbf{P} \} \text{ S:n } \{ \mathbf{Q} \}} [\![\text{Lemma D.1.3}]\!]}{\begin{array}{l} ro(\mathcal{A}) \rhd \{ \text{w} \neq \mathit{null} \wedge \mathbf{P}[\text{w/this}, \text{e}_1/\text{p}_1, \ldots, \text{e}_n/\text{p}_n, \mathit{univV}(\text{w})/\mathcal{U}] \} \\ \qquad \text{v} = \text{w.S:n}(\text{e}_1, \ldots, \text{e}_n); \\ \qquad \{ \mathbf{Q}[\text{v/result}] \} \end{array}} [\![\text{invocation-rule}]\!]$$

If the invocation-statement occurs in a readonly method, the invoked method must be readonly (context-condition). Thus, we derive:

$\{ \text{w} \neq \mathit{null} \wedge \mathbf{P}[\text{w/this}, \text{e}_1/\text{p}_1, \ldots, \text{e}_n/\text{p}_n, \mathit{univV}(\text{w})/\mathcal{U}] \wedge \$ = OS \}$

$\Rightarrow$

$\{ \text{w} \neq \mathit{null} \wedge (\mathbf{P} \wedge \$ = OS)[\text{w/this}, \text{e}_1/\text{p}_1, \ldots, \text{e}_n/\text{p}_n, \mathit{univV}(\text{w})/\mathcal{U}] \}$

$\text{v} = \text{w.S:n}(\text{e}_1, \ldots, \text{e}_n);$ $[\![$ applying the invocation-rule to the ind. hypothesis $]\!]$

$\{ (\mathbf{Q} \wedge \$ = OS)[\text{v/result}] \}$

$\Rightarrow$

$\{ \mathbf{Q}[\text{v/result}] \wedge \$ = OS \}$

Subtype-rule: We assume that S:m overrides T:m. If T:m is readonly, S:m has to be readonly (context condition); the proof for this case is trivial. The proof is also trivial if both methods are readwrite. If T:m is readwrite and S:m is readonly, we prove the consequent by applying Lemma D.1.3 and the subtype-rule.

Class-rule: A virtual method for a non-abstract method is readonly if and only if the corresponding implementation is readonly. Thus, the proof is trivial. □

D.2 Auxiliary Lemmas and Proofs from Chapter 5

Before we prove Lemmas 5.2.1 and 5.2.2, we introduce three auxiliary lemmas:

Lemma D.2.1. *Each location can be composed by applying the appropriate constructor to its object and its field id:*

(i) $mklc(L) \Rightarrow L = mklc(locC(obj(L), scfid(cfid(fid(L)))))$
(ii) $mkla(L) \Rightarrow L = mkla(locA(obj(L), safid(afid(fid(L)))))$

Proof of Lemma D.2.1:

(i) $L = mklc(cloc(F_C, OID, U))$ for some F_C, OID, U $[\![$ Definition of *Location* $]\!]$
$mklc(locC(obj(L), scfid(cfid(fid(L)))))$
$=$ $[\![$ Definitions of *fid*, *obj* $]\!]$
$mklc(locC(ref(otype(cfield(F_C)), OID, U), scfid(cfid(cfield(F_C)))))$
$=$ $[\![$ Definition of $locC$ $]\!]$
$mklc(cloc(mkCFieldId(scfid(cfid(cfield(F_C))), otype(cfield(F_C))), OID, U))$
$=$ $[\![$ $cfid(cfield(F_C)) = F_C$, Axiom **field8** $]\!]$
$mklc(cloc(F_C, OID, U)) = L$

(ii) analogously.

□

Lemma D.2.2. *The type of the object of a location L is a subtype of the declaration type of L's field:*

$$tidD(typeof(obj(L))) \preceq_M dtype(fid(L))$$

Proof of Lemma D.2.2:
Case 1: $L = mklc(cloc(F_C, OID, U))$ for some F_C, OID, U

$$\begin{array}{lcl} tidD(typeof(obj(L))) & = & [\![\text{ Def. of } obj]\!] \\ tidD(typeof(ref(otype(cfield(F_C)), OID, U))) & = & [\![\text{ Def. of } typeof \text{ and } fid]\!] \\ tidD(refDT(ctid(otype(fid(L))), U)) & = & [\![\text{ Def. of } tidD]\!] \\ cid(otype(fid(L))) & \preceq_M & [\![\text{ Axiom } \mathbf{field3}]\!] \\ dtype(fid(L)) & & \end{array}$$

Case 2 ($L = mkla(aloc(F_A, OID, U))$ for some F_A, OID, U) is analogous.

□

Lemma D.2.3. *For each dependency $L \xrightarrow{OS} K$, the object of the dependee is alive in OS if the object of the dependent in alive in OS:*

$$alive(obj(L), OS) \wedge L \xrightarrow{OS} K \Rightarrow alive(obj(K), OS)$$

Proof of Lemma D.2.3:
For closed programs $\mathcal{P}$, $\_ \xrightarrow{OS} \_$ is the smallest relation satisfying **dep1**, **dep2**, and the axioms generated for the depends-clauses declared in $\mathcal{P}$. Therefore, from $L \xrightarrow{OS} K$ we can conclude that there is a sequence of locations $L_0, \ldots, L_n$ such that $L_0 = L$, $L_n = K$, and $L_{i-1} \xrightarrow{OS} L_i (i = 1, \ldots, n)$, where each of these dependencies stems either from **dep1** or from a depends-clause with id d_i. In the former case, we have $L_{i-1} = L_i$, and thus

$$alive(obj(L_{i-1}), OS) \Rightarrow alive(obj(L_i), OS)$$

In the latter case, we know from the axioms generated for the depends-clause d_i that $dc(d_i, obj(L_{i-1}), obj(L_i), OS)$ and, thus, $alive(obj(L_i), OS)$ holds. From the transitivity of implication, we conclude $alive(obj(L_0), OS) \Rightarrow alive(obj(L_n), OS)$. Since the property holds for all closed programs, it also holds for all open programs. □

Proof of Lemma 5.2.1:
For closed programs $\mathcal{P}$, we prove the lemma by case distinction: (1) For concrete locations, the lemma is a direct consequence of Axiom **dep3**. (2) For abstract locations, we prove the lemma as follows: We abbreviate $tidD(typeof(obj(L)))$ by S_L. From Lemma D.2.2, we know $S_L \preceq_M dtype(fid(L))$. Since S_L is the *TypeId* of a class, the representation of $safid(afid(fid(L)))$ must be defined for objects of type S_L (context condition 3 for def-clauses). That is, there is a class T in $\mathcal{P}$ that is a superclass of S_L ($S_L \preceq_M$ T) and that contains a def-clause for $safid(afid(fid(L)))$. Since the specification of $\mathcal{P}$ is well-formed, we can use Obligation 5.1 for this def-clause to conclude:

$(obj(L) \neq null \wedge tidD(typeof(obj(L))) \preceq_M \mathrm{T} \wedge alive(obj(L), OS) \wedge$
$alive(obj(L), OS') \wedge wt(OS) \wedge wt(OS') \wedge$
$(\forall K_C : mkla(locA(obj(L), \mathrm{f})) \xrightarrow{OS} mklc(K_C) \Rightarrow OS(K_C) = OS'(K_C)) \Rightarrow$
$OS \equiv_{mkla(locA(obj(L),\mathrm{f}))} OS')$
$\Rightarrow$ $[\![$ $obj(L) \neq null$, $\mathrm{S}_L \preceq_M \mathrm{T}$, Lemma D.2.1 $]\!]$
$(alive(obj(L), OS) \wedge alive(obj(L), OS') \wedge wt(OS) \wedge wt(OS') \wedge$
$(\forall K_C : L \xrightarrow{OS} mklc(K_C) \Rightarrow OS(K_C) = OS'(K_C)) \Rightarrow OS \equiv_L OS')$
$\Rightarrow$ $[\![$ Lemma D.2.3 $]\!]$
$(alive(obj(L), OS) \wedge alive(obj(L), OS') \wedge wt(OS) \wedge wt(OS') \wedge$
$(\forall K_C : L \xrightarrow{OS} mklc(K_C) \wedge alive(obj(mklc(K_C)), OS) \Rightarrow OS(K_C) = OS'(K_C)) \Rightarrow$
$OS \equiv_L OS')$

Since the property holds for all closed programs, it also holds for all open programs. □

Proof of Lemma 5.2.2:

The proof of this lemma is analogous to Proof 5.2.1. Essentially, we have to show

$$alive(obj(L), OS) \wedge wt(OS) \Rightarrow wt(OS\langle S, U\rangle) \wedge \forall K_C : OS(K_C) = OS\langle S, U\rangle(K_C)$$

which follows from Axiom **store5**. □

Proof of Lemma 5.2.3:

We prove that the lemma holds for all closed programs $\mathcal{P}$. Analogously to Proof D.2.3, we conclude that there is a sequence of locations $L_0, \ldots, L_n$ such that $L_0 = L$, $L_n = K$, and $L_{i-1} \xrightarrow{OS} L_i (i = 1, \ldots, n)$, where each of these dependencies stems either from **dep1** or from a depends-clause with id d_i.

In the former case, we have $L_{i-1} = L_i$, and thus

$$univV(obj(L_{i-1})) = univV(obj(L_i)) \ .$$

In the latter case, we know from the axioms generated for the depends-clause d_i that $dc(\mathrm{d}_i, obj(L_{i-1}), obj(L_i), OS)$ holds. Since $\mathcal{P}$'s specification is well-formed, we conclude from Obligation 5.2 for d_i:

$$dc(\mathrm{d}_i, obj(L_{i-1}), obj(L_i), OS) \wedge wt(OS) \Rightarrow univV(obj(L_i)) \trianglelefteq univV(obj(L_{i-1}))$$

Since $\trianglelefteq$ is reflexive and transitive, we get

$$univV(obj(L_i)) \trianglelefteq univV(obj(L_{i-1})) \ \text{ for } \ i = 1, \ldots, n$$

in both cases, and thus $univV(obj(K)) \trianglelefteq univV(obj(L))$. The property holds for all closed programs and, thus, for all open programs. □

The following lemma is used in Proof 5.2.4.

Lemma D.2.4.

$$\begin{array}{l} univV(obj(J)) \trianglelefteq univV(obj(K)) \wedge univV(obj(K)) \trianglelefteq univV(obj(L)) \wedge \\ accessMode(fid(L)) = public \wedge accessibleL(L, guard(K, univV(obj(L)))) \wedge \\ accessibleL(K, guard(J, univV(obj(K)))) \Rightarrow accessibleL(L, guard(J, univV(obj(L)))) \end{array}$$

Proof of Lemma D.2.4:

Case 1: $univV(obj(K)) = univV(obj(L))$

$$\begin{array}{l} univV(obj(K)) = univV(obj(L)) \wedge accessMode(fid(L)) = public \wedge \\ accessibleL(L, guard(K, univV(obj(L)))) \wedge accessibleL(K, guard(J, univV(obj(K)))) \\ \Rightarrow \ [\![\text{ Definition of } guard]\!] \\ accessMode(fid(L)) = public \wedge \\ accessibleL(L, dtype(fid(K))) \wedge accessibleL(K, guard(J, univV(obj(L)))) \\ \Rightarrow \ [\![\text{ Definition of } accessibleL]\!] \\ accessMode(fid(L)) = public \wedge \\ accessible(accessMode(fid(L)), dtype(fid(L)), dtype(fid(K))) \wedge \\ accessible(accessMode(fid(K)), dtype(fid(K)), guard(J, univV(obj(L)))) \\ \Rightarrow \ [\![\text{ Lemma 3.1.2 }]\!] \\ accessMode(fid(L)) = public \wedge \\ imports(module(dtype(fid(K))), module(dtype(fid(L)))) \wedge \\ imports(module(guard(J, univV(obj(L)))), module(dtype(fid(K)))) \\ \Rightarrow \ [\![\text{ Transitivity of } imports \text{ (Axiom } \mathbf{import1})]\!] \\ accessMode(fid(L)) = public \wedge \\ imports(module(guard(J, univV(obj(L)))), module(dtype(fid(L)))) \\ \Rightarrow \ [\![\text{ Definitions of } accessible, \ accessibleL]\!] \\ accessibleL(L, guard(J, univV(obj(L)))) \end{array}$$

Case 2: $univV(obj(K)) \lhd univV(obj(L))$

$$\begin{array}{l} univV(obj(J)) \trianglelefteq univV(obj(K)) \wedge univV(obj(K)) \lhd univV(obj(L)) \wedge \\ accessibleL(L, guard(K, univV(obj(L)))) \\ \Rightarrow \ [\![\text{ Definitions of } guard, \trianglelefteq, \text{ and } \lhd]\!] \\ guard(K, univV(obj(L))) = guard(J, univV(obj(L))) \wedge \\ accessibleL(L, guard(K, univV(obj(L)))) \\ \Rightarrow \\ accessibleL(L, guard(J, univV(obj(L)))) \end{array}$$

□

Proof of Lemma 5.2.4:

We prove that the lemma holds for all closed programs $\mathcal{P}$. Analogously to Proof D.2.3, we conclude that there is a sequence of locations $L_0, \ldots, L_n$ such that $L_0 = L$, $L_n = K$, and $L_{i-1} \xrightarrow{OS} L_i (i = 1, \ldots, n)$, where each of these dependencies stems either from **dep1** or from a depends-clause with id d_i. We show by induction on N:

$$\begin{array}{l} N \geq 1 \wedge N \leq n \wedge \\ \bigwedge_{i=1}^{N} L_{i-1} \xrightarrow{OS} L_i \wedge wt(OS) \Rightarrow accessibleL(L_0, guard(L_N, univV(obj(L_0)))) \end{array} \quad \text{(D.1)}$$

Induction Basis: $N = 1$
Case 1: $L_0 = L_1$
$L_0 = L_1$
$\Rightarrow$ [[Definitions of *guard* and *accessibleL*]]
$accessibleL(L_0, guard(L_N, univV(obj(L_0))))$

Case 2: $L_0 \neq L_1$
$dc(\mathrm{d}_1, obj(L_0), obj(L_1), OS) \wedge wt(OS) \wedge 1 \leq n$ [[axiom for the dep-clause d_1]]
$\Rightarrow$ [[$\mathcal{P}$'s specification is well-formed, Obligation 5.3 for d_1]]
$accessibleL(L_0, guard(L_N, univV(obj(L_0))))$

Induction Step: $N \geq 1$
Case 1: $L_0 = L_{N+1}$
analogously to induction basis

Case 2: $L_0 \neq L_{N+1}$
$\bigwedge_{i=1}^{N+1} L_{i-1} \xrightarrow{OS} L_i \wedge wt(OS) \wedge N+1 \leq n$
$\Rightarrow$
$\bigwedge_{i=1}^{N} L_{i-1} \xrightarrow{OS} L_i \wedge L_N \xrightarrow{OS} L_{N+1} \wedge wt(OS) \wedge N \leq n$
$\Rightarrow$ [[Induction hypothesis, analogously to induction basis, analogously to Proof 5.2.3, L_0 is abstract (**dep3**) $\Rightarrow accessMode(fid(L_0)) = public$]]
$univV(obj(L_{N+1})) \trianglelefteq univV(obj(L_N)) \wedge univV(obj(L_N)) \trianglelefteq univV(obj(L_0)) \wedge$
$accessibleL(L_0, guard(L_N, univV(obj(L_0)))) \wedge$
$accessibleL(L_N, guard(L_{N+1}, univV(obj(L_N)))) \wedge accessMode(fid(L_0)) = public$
$\Rightarrow$ [[Lemma D.2.4]]
$accessibleL(L_0, guard(L_{N+1}, univV(obj(L_0))))$

For closed programs, Lemma 5.2.4 is trivial if $L = K$ (see induction basis). Otherwise, it is a direct consequence of Formula D.1. Since the property holds for all closed programs, it also holds for all open programs. □

For a more convenient handling of regular expressions and *rc*, we define the following function that corresponds to *rc* but takes sets of words (i.e., sequences of *DepId*) as argument. $\mathcal{L}$: *regExpr* $\rightarrow$ *set of list of DepId* maps regular expressions R to the set of words described by R. We use the standard definition of $\mathcal{L}$ [HU79].

$$\begin{aligned} &l : \textit{set of list of DepId} \times \textit{Value} \times \textit{Value} \times \textit{Store} \rightarrow \textit{Bool} \\ &l(M, X, Y, OS) \Leftrightarrow_{def} \exists w \in M : w = a_1 \ldots a_k \wedge \exists Z_0, \ldots, Z_k : \\ &\qquad Z_0 = X \wedge Z_k = Y \wedge \bigwedge_{i=1}^{k} dc(a_i, Z_{i-1}, Z_i, OS) \end{aligned}$$

Lemma D.2.5. *Applying rc to a regular expression R is equivalent to applying l to $\mathcal{L}(R)$:*
$rc(R, X, Y, OS) \Leftrightarrow l(\mathcal{L}(R), X, Y, OS)$

Proof of Lemma D.2.5:

We prove this lemma by induction over the structure of R.

Induction Basis:
Case 1: $R = \varnothing$
$rc(\varnothing, X, Y, OS) \Leftrightarrow \mathit{false} \Leftrightarrow l(\varnothing, X, Y, OS)$

Case 2: $R = \epsilon$
$rc(\epsilon, X, Y, OS) \Leftrightarrow X = Y$
$l(\mathcal{L}(\epsilon), X, Y, OS) \Leftrightarrow \exists w \in \mathcal{L}(\epsilon) : w = a_1 \dots a_0 \wedge \exists Z_0 : Z_0 = X \wedge Z_0 = Y \Leftrightarrow$
$X = Y$

Case 3: $R = d$
$rc(d, X, Y, OS) \Leftrightarrow dc(d, X, Y, OS) \Leftrightarrow$
$\exists w \in \mathcal{L}(d) : w = d \wedge \exists Z_0, Z_1 : Z_0 = X \wedge Z_1 = Y \wedge dc(d, Z_0, Z_1, OS) \Leftrightarrow$
$l(\mathcal{L}(d), X, Y, OS)$

Induction Step:
Case 1: $R = R_1 R_2$
$rc(R_1 R_2, X, Y, OS)$
$\Leftrightarrow$ [[Definition of rc]]
$\exists Z : rc(R_1, X, Z, OS) \wedge rc(R_2, Z, Y, OS)$
$\Leftrightarrow$ [[Induction hypothesis]]
$\exists Z : l(\mathcal{L}(R_1), X, Z, OS) \wedge l(\mathcal{L}(R_2), Z, Y, OS)$
$\Leftrightarrow$ [[Definition of l]]
$\exists Z : \exists w_1 \in \mathcal{L}(R_1), w_2 \in \mathcal{L}(R_2) : w_1 = a_1 \dots a_k \wedge w_2 = a_{k+1} \dots a_l \wedge \exists Z_0, \dots, Z_l :$
$$Z_0 = X \wedge Z_k = Z \wedge Z_{k+1} = Z \wedge Z_l = Y \wedge \bigwedge_{i=1}^{l} dc(a_i, Z_{i-1}, Z_i, OS)$$
$\Leftrightarrow$ [[Definition of $\mathcal{L}$]]
$\exists w \in \mathcal{L}(R_1 R_2) : w = a_1 \dots a_l \wedge \exists Z_0, \dots, Z_l : Z_0 = X \wedge Z_l = Y \wedge$
$\bigwedge_{i=1}^{l} dc(a_i, Z_{i-1}, Z_i, OS)$
$\Leftrightarrow$ [[Definition of l]]
$l(\mathcal{L}(R_1 R_2), X, Y, OS)$

Case 2: $R = R_1 + R_2$
$rc(R_1 + R_2, X, Y, OS)$
$\Leftrightarrow$ [[Definition of rc]]
$rc(R_1, X, Y, OS) \vee rc(R_2, X, Y, OS)$
$\Leftrightarrow$ [[Induction hypothesis]]
$l(\mathcal{L}(R_1), X, Y, OS) \vee l(\mathcal{L}(R_2), X, Y, OS)$
$\Leftrightarrow$ [[Definition of l]]
$(\exists w_1 \in \mathcal{L}(R_1) : w_1 = a_1 \dots a_k \wedge \exists Z_0, \dots, Z_k : Z_0 = X \wedge Z_k = Y \wedge$
$\bigwedge_{i=1}^{k} dc(a_i, Z_{i-1}, Z_i, OS)) \quad \vee$
$(\exists w_2 \in \mathcal{L}(R_2) : w_2 = a_1 \dots a_n \wedge \exists Z_0, \dots, Z_n : Z_0 = X \wedge Z_n = Y \wedge$
$\bigwedge_{i=1}^{n} dc(a_i, Z_{i-1}, Z_i, OS))$
$\Leftrightarrow$ [[Definition of $\mathcal{L}$]]
$\exists w \in \mathcal{L}(R_1 + R_2) : w = a_1 \dots a_m \wedge \exists Z_0, \dots, Z_m : Z_0 = X \wedge Z_m = Y \wedge$
$\bigwedge_{i=1}^{m} dc(a_i, Z_{i-1}, Z_i, OS)$
$\Leftrightarrow$ [[Definition of l]]
$l(\mathcal{L}(R_1 + R_2), X, Y, OS)$

Case 3: $R = R_1^*$

$rc(R_1^*, X, Y, OS)$

$\Leftrightarrow$ ⟦ Definition of rc ⟧

$\exists N : \exists Z_0, \ldots, Z_N : Z_0 = X \wedge Z_N = Y \wedge \bigwedge_{i=1}^{N} rc(R_1, Z_{i-1}, Z_i, OS)$

$\Leftrightarrow$ ⟦ Induction hypothesis ⟧

$\exists N : \exists Z_0, \ldots, Z_N : Z_0 = X \wedge Z_N = Y \wedge \bigwedge_{i=1}^{N} l(\mathcal{L}(R_1), Z_{i-1}, Z_i, OS)$

$\Leftrightarrow$ ⟦ Definition of l ⟧

$\exists N : \exists Z_0, \ldots, Z_N : Z_0 = X \wedge Z_N = Y \wedge \bigwedge_{i=1}^{N} \Big[\exists w \in \mathcal{L}(R_1) : w = a_1 \ldots a_k \wedge$

$\exists A_0, \ldots, A_k : A_0 = Z_{i-1} \wedge A_k = Z_i \wedge \bigwedge_{j=1}^{k} dc(a_j, A_{j-1}, A_j, OS) \Big]$

$\Leftrightarrow$

$\exists N : \exists w \in \mathcal{L}(R_1) : w = a_1 \ldots a_k \wedge \exists Z_0, \ldots, Z_{N \times k} :$

$\bigwedge_{i=1}^{N} \bigwedge_{j=1}^{k} dc(a_j, Z_{i \times j-1}, Z_{i \times j}, OS) \wedge Z_0 = X \wedge Z_{N \times k} = Y$

$\Leftrightarrow$ ⟦ Definition of $\mathcal{L}$ ⟧

$\exists N : \exists w \in \mathcal{L}(R_1^*) : w = (a_1 \ldots a_k)^N \wedge \exists Z_0, \ldots, Z_{N \times k} :$

$\bigwedge_{i=1}^{N} \bigwedge_{j=1}^{k} dc(a_j, Z_{i \times j-1}, Z_{i \times j}, OS) \wedge Z_0 = X \wedge Z_{N \times k} = Y$

$\Leftrightarrow$ ⟦ $p := N \times k$ ⟧

$\exists p : \exists w \in \mathcal{L}(R_1^*) : w = a_1 \ldots a_p \wedge \exists Z_0, \ldots, Z_p : Z_0 = X \wedge Z_p = Y \wedge$

$\bigwedge_{i=1}^{p} dc(a_i, Z_{i-1}, Z_i, OS)$

$\Leftrightarrow$ ⟦ Definition of l ⟧

$l(\mathcal{L}(R_1^*), X, Y, OS)$

□

Proof of Lemma 5.4.1:

Like the other program properties, we prove Lemma 5.4.1 by induction on the depth of the proof for $\mathcal{A} \rhd \mathbf{A}$. Since many cases are trivial (e.g., the cases for statements that do not modify the object store) or analogous to the proofs for other language properties (e.g., the cases for the assumpt- and false-axiom), we show only the interesting cases here.

Induction Basis.

New-axiom:

$\{ \mathbf{P}[new(\$, cid(tid(\mathrm{T})), univ(\tau(\mathrm{T})))/\mathrm{v}, \$\langle cid(tid(\mathrm{T}), univ(\tau(\mathrm{T})))\rangle/\$] \wedge \$ = OS \wedge$
$\mathcal{U} = U \wedge \bigwedge_{i=0}^{n} typeof(\mathrm{v}_i) \preceq \tau([\mathrm{v}_i]) \wedge wt(\$) \wedge (static(\mathrm{T@m}) \Leftrightarrow \mathrm{this} = null) \}$

$\Rightarrow$ ⟦ Axiom **store5** ⟧

$\{ \mathbf{P}[new(\$, cid(tid(\mathrm{T})), univ(\tau(\mathrm{T})))/\mathrm{v}, \$\langle cid(tid(\mathrm{T}), univ(\tau(\mathrm{T})))\rangle/\$] \wedge$
$(\neg univV(obj(mklc(K_C))) \trianglelefteq U \Rightarrow \$\langle cid(tid(\mathrm{T}), univ(\tau(\mathrm{T})))\rangle(K_C) = OS(K_C)) \}$

$\Rightarrow$

$\{ (\mathbf{P} \wedge (\neg univV(obj(mklc(K_C))) \trianglelefteq U \Rightarrow \$(K_C) =$
$OS(K_C)))[new(\$, cid(tid(\mathrm{T})), univ(\tau(\mathrm{T})))/\mathrm{v}, \$\langle cid(tid(\mathrm{T}), univ(\tau(\mathrm{T})))\rangle/\$] \}$

v = new T(); ⟦ new-axiom ⟧

$\{ \mathbf{P} \wedge (\neg univV(obj(mklc(K_C))) \trianglelefteq U \Rightarrow \$(K_C) = OS(K_C)) \}$

Field-write-axiom:

$\{ \mathrm{w} \neq \mathit{null} \wedge \mathbf{P}[\$\langle locC(\mathrm{w}, \mathrm{S@f}) := \mathrm{e}\rangle/\$] \wedge \$ = OS \wedge \mathcal{U} = U \wedge$
$\bigwedge_{i=0}^{n} \mathit{typeof}(\mathrm{v}_i) \preceq \tau([\mathrm{v}_i]) \wedge wt(\$) \wedge (\mathit{static}(\mathrm{T@m}) \Leftrightarrow \mathrm{this} = \mathit{null}) \}$
$\Rightarrow$ $[\![\neg roT?([\mathtt{w}])$, Lemmas 3.1.6 and 3.1.4, Definition of $dyn]\!]$
$\{ \mathrm{w} \neq \mathit{null} \wedge \mathbf{P}[\$\langle locC(\mathrm{w}, \mathrm{S@f}) := \mathrm{e}\rangle/\$] \wedge \$ = OS \wedge univV(\mathrm{w}) \trianglelefteq U \}$
$\Rightarrow$ $[\![$ Axiom **store1** $]\!]$
$\{ \mathrm{w} \neq \mathit{null} \wedge \mathbf{P}[\$\langle locC(\mathrm{w}, \mathrm{S@f}) := \mathrm{e}\rangle/\$] \wedge$
$(\neg univV(obj(mklc(K_C))) \trianglelefteq U \Rightarrow \$\langle locC(\mathrm{w}, \mathrm{S@f}) := \mathrm{e}\rangle(K_C) = OS(K_C)) \}$
$\Rightarrow$

$\{ \mathrm{w} \neq \mathit{null} \wedge (\mathbf{P} \wedge (\neg univV(obj(mklc(K_C))) \trianglelefteq U \Rightarrow$
$\$(K_C) = OS(K_C)))[\$\langle locC(\mathrm{w}, \mathrm{S@f}) := \mathrm{e}\rangle/\$] \}$
w.S@f= e; $[\![$ field-write-axiom $]\!]$
$\{ \mathbf{P} \wedge (\neg univV(obj(mklc(K_C))) \trianglelefteq U \Rightarrow \$(K_C) = OS(K_C)) \}$

Predefined method implementations: Since all predefined methods have $\$ = OS$ in their pre- and postconditions, the local update property is a trivial consequence.

Induction Step.
Invocation-rule: If the invoked method S:n is readonly, we derive[1]:

$$\cfrac{\cfrac{\mathcal{A} \triangleright \{ \mathbf{P} \}\ \mathrm{S{:}n}\ \{ \mathbf{Q} \}}{ro(\mathcal{A}) \triangleright \{ \mathbf{P} \wedge \$ = OS \}\ \mathrm{S{:}n}\ \{ \mathbf{Q} \wedge \$ = OS \}}\ [\![\text{Lemma 3.2.5}]\!]}{lu(\mathcal{A}), ro(\mathcal{A}), typed(\mathcal{A}) \triangleright \{ \mathbf{P} \wedge \$ = OS \}\ \mathrm{S{:}n}\ \{ \mathbf{Q} \wedge \$ = OS \}}\ [\![\text{assumpt-intro-rule}]\!]$$

By this sequent, we derive the desired property. We omit the assumptions for brevity. In the following, we assume that $\mathrm{p}_0, \ldots, \mathrm{p}_l$ are the formal parameters of S:n.

$\{ \mathrm{w} \neq \mathit{null} \wedge \mathbf{P}[\mathrm{w}/\mathrm{this}, e_1/p_1, \ldots, e_l/p_l, univV(\mathrm{w})/\mathcal{U}] \wedge \$ = OS \wedge \mathcal{U} = U \wedge$
$\bigwedge_{i=0}^{n} \mathit{typeof}(\mathrm{v}_i) \preceq \tau([\mathrm{v}_i]) \wedge wt(\$) \wedge (\mathit{static}(\mathrm{T@m}) \Leftrightarrow \mathrm{this} = \mathit{null}) \}$
$\Rightarrow$

$\{ \mathrm{w} \neq \mathit{null} \wedge (\mathbf{P} \wedge \$ = OS)[\mathrm{w}/\mathrm{this}, \mathrm{e}_1/\mathrm{p}_1, \ldots, \mathrm{e}_l/\mathrm{p}_l, univV(\mathrm{w})/\mathcal{U}] \}$
$\mathrm{v} = \mathrm{w.S{:}n}(\mathrm{e}_1, \ldots, \mathrm{e}_l)$; $[\![$ applying the invocation-rule to the above sequent $]\!]$
$\{ (\mathbf{Q} \wedge \$ = OS)[\mathrm{v}/\mathrm{result}] \}$
$\Rightarrow$

$\{ \mathbf{Q}[\mathrm{v}/\mathrm{result}] \wedge (\neg univV(obj(mklc(K_C))) \trianglelefteq U \Rightarrow \$(K_C) = OS(K_C)) \}$

[1] We use the double line to indicate the application of a language property operator.

For invocations of readwrite methods, we derive:

$\{$ w $\neq$ *null* $\wedge$ $\mathbf{P}$[w/this, $e_1/p_1, \ldots, e_l/p_l$, *univV*(w)/$\mathcal{U}$] $\wedge$ \$ = *OS* $\wedge$ $\mathcal{U} = U \wedge$
$\bigwedge_{i=0}^{n}$ *typeof*(v_i) $\preceq \tau([\mathrm{v}_i])$ $\wedge$ *wt*(\$) $\wedge$ (*static*(T@m) $\Leftrightarrow$ this = *null*) $\}$

$\Rightarrow$ ⟦ S:n is readwrite $\Rightarrow \neg roT?([\mathtt{w}])$, Lemmas 3.1.6 and 3.1.4, Definition of *dyn* ⟧

$\{$ w $\neq$ *null* $\wedge$ $\mathbf{P}$[w/this, $e_1/p_1, \ldots, e_l/p_l$, *univV*(w)/$\mathcal{U}$] $\wedge$ *univV*(w) $\trianglelefteq U \wedge$
\$ = *OS* $\wedge$ $\bigwedge_{i=0}^{n}$ *typeof*(v_i) $\preceq \tau([\mathrm{v}_i])$ $\wedge$ *wt*(\$) $\wedge$ (*static*(T@m) $\Leftrightarrow$ this = *null*) $\}$

$\Rightarrow$ ⟦ analogous to Proof 3.2.1 ⟧

$\{ \exists U'$: w $\neq$ *null* $\wedge$ ($\mathbf{P}$ $\wedge$ \$ = *OS* $\wedge$ $\mathcal{U} = U'$ $\wedge$ $\bigwedge_{i=0}^{l}$ *typeof*(p_i) $\preceq \tau([\mathrm{p}_i])\wedge$
wt(\$))[w/this, $e_1/p_1, \ldots, e_l/p_l$, *univV*(w)/$\mathcal{U}$] $\wedge\, U' \trianglelefteq U$ $\}$

———————————————————————— $\downarrow$ ⟦ ex-rule ⟧

$\{$ w $\neq$ *null* $\wedge$ ($\mathbf{P}$ $\wedge$ \$ = *OS* $\wedge$ $\mathcal{U} = U'$ $\wedge$ $\bigwedge_{i=0}^{l}$ *typeof*(p_i) $\preceq \tau([\mathrm{p}_i])\wedge$
wt(\$))[w/this, $e_1/p_1, \ldots, e_l/p_l$, *univV*(w)/$\mathcal{U}$] $\wedge\, U' \trianglelefteq U$ $\}$

———————————————————————— $\downarrow$ ⟦ inv-rule ⟧

$\{$ w $\neq$ *null* $\wedge$ ($\mathbf{P}$ $\wedge$ \$ = *OS* $\wedge$ $\mathcal{U} = U'$ $\wedge$ $\bigwedge_{i=0}^{l}$ *typeof*(p_i) $\preceq \tau([\mathrm{p}_i])\wedge$
wt(\$))[w/this, $e_1/p_1, \ldots, e_l/p_l$, *univV*(w)/$\mathcal{U}$] $\}$

v = w.S:n($\mathrm{e}_1, \ldots, \mathrm{e}_l$); ⟦ applying the invocation-rule to the ind. hypothesis ⟧

$\{ (\mathbf{Q} \wedge (\neg univV(obj(mklc(K_C))) \trianglelefteq U' \Rightarrow \$(K_C) = OS(K_C)))[\mathrm{v/result}] \}$

———————————————————————— $\uparrow$ ⟦ inv-rule ⟧

$\{ (\mathbf{Q} \wedge (\neg univV(obj(mklc(K_C))) \trianglelefteq U' \Rightarrow \$(K_C) = OS(K_C)))[\mathrm{v/result}] \wedge U' \trianglelefteq U \}$

$\Rightarrow$ ⟦ Transitivity of $\trianglelefteq$ (Lemma 3.1.3) ⟧

$\{ \mathbf{Q}[\mathrm{v/result}] \wedge (\neg univV(obj(mklc(K_C))) \trianglelefteq U \Rightarrow \$(K_C) = OS(K_C)) \}$

———————————————————————— $\uparrow$ ⟦ ex-rule ⟧

$\{ \mathbf{Q}[\mathrm{v/result}] \wedge (\neg univV(obj(mklc(K_C))) \trianglelefteq U \Rightarrow \$(K_C) = OS(K_C)) \}$

Invocation-var-rule:

$\{ \mathbf{P}[\mathrm{x}/Z]$ $\wedge$ \$ = *OS* $\wedge$ $\mathcal{U} = U$ $\wedge$ $\bigwedge_{i=0}^{n}$ *typeof*(v_i) $\preceq \tau([\mathrm{v}_i])$ $\wedge$ *wt*(\$)$\wedge$
(*static*(T@m) $\Leftrightarrow$ this = *null*) $\}$

$\Rightarrow$ ⟦ *OS* and U are fresh logical variables, i.e., are different from Z ⟧

$\{$ ($\mathbf{P}$ $\wedge$ \$ = *OS* $\wedge$ $\mathcal{U} = U$ $\wedge$ $\bigwedge_{i=0}^{n}$ *typeof*(v_i) $\preceq \tau([\mathrm{v}_i])$ $\wedge$ *wt*(\$)$\wedge$
(*static*(T@m) $\Leftrightarrow$ this = *null*))[x/Z] $\}$

v = w.S:n($\mathrm{e}_1, \ldots, \mathrm{e}_l$); ⟦ applying the invocation-var-rule to the ind. hypothesis ⟧

$\{ (\mathbf{Q} \wedge (\neg univV(obj(mklc(K_C))) \trianglelefteq U \Rightarrow \$(K_C) = OS(K_C)))[\mathrm{x}/Z] \}$

$\Rightarrow$ ⟦ U, K_C, OS are fresh logical variables, i.e., are different from Z ⟧

$\{ \mathbf{Q}[\mathrm{x}/Z] \wedge (\neg univV(obj(mklc(K_C))) \trianglelefteq U \Rightarrow \$(K_C) = OS(K_C)) \}$

Implementation-rule: We abbreviate the triple $\{\, \mathbf{P} \,\}$ T@m $\{\, \mathbf{Q} \,\}$ by $\mathbf{A}$.

$$\dfrac{\begin{array}{l} \dfrac{\begin{array}{l} \dfrac{\begin{array}{l} \dfrac{\begin{array}{l} lu(\mathcal{A}), ro(\mathcal{A}), typed(\mathcal{A}), lu(\mathbf{A}), ro(\mathbf{A}), typed(\mathbf{A}) \rhd \\ \{\, \mathbf{P} \wedge \$ = OS \wedge \mathcal{U} = U \wedge \bigwedge_{i=0}^{n} typeof(\mathrm{v}_i) \preceq \tau([\mathrm{v}_i]) \wedge wt(\$) \wedge \\ (static(\mathrm{T@m}) \Leftrightarrow \mathrm{this} = null) \wedge (static(\mathrm{T@m}) \Leftrightarrow \mathrm{this} = null) \wedge \\ \bigwedge_{i=k+1}^{n} \mathrm{v}_i = init(\tau([\mathrm{v}_i])) \,\} \\ \quad body(\mathrm{T@m}) \\ \{\, \mathbf{Q} \wedge (\neg univV(obj(mklc(K_C))) \trianglelefteq U \Rightarrow \$(K_C) = OS(K_C)) \,\} \end{array}}{\begin{array}{l} lu(\mathcal{A}), ro(\mathcal{A}), typed(\mathcal{A}), lu(\mathbf{A}), ro(\mathbf{A}), typed(\mathbf{A}) \rhd \\ \{\, \mathbf{P} \wedge \$ = OS \wedge \mathcal{U} = U \wedge \bigwedge_{i=0}^{k} typeof(\mathrm{v}_i) \preceq \tau([\mathrm{v}_i]) \wedge wt(\$) \wedge \\ (static(\mathrm{T@m}) \Leftrightarrow \mathrm{this} = null) \wedge \bigwedge_{i=k+1}^{n} \mathrm{v}_i = init(\tau([\mathrm{v}_i])) \,\} \\ \quad body(\mathrm{T@m}) \\ \{\, \mathbf{Q} \wedge (\neg univV(obj(mklc(K_C))) \trianglelefteq U \Rightarrow \$(K_C) = OS(K_C)) \,\} \end{array}} [\![\text{ strength-rule }]\!] }{\begin{array}{l} lu(\mathcal{A}), ro(\mathcal{A}), typed(\mathcal{A}), ro(\mathbf{A}), typed(\mathbf{A}) \rhd \\ \{\, \mathbf{P} \wedge \$ = OS \wedge \mathcal{U} = U \wedge \bigwedge_{i=0}^{k} typeof(\mathrm{v}_i) \preceq \tau([\mathrm{v}_i]) \wedge wt(\$) \,\} \\ \quad \mathrm{T@m} \\ \{\, \mathbf{Q} \wedge (\neg univV(obj(mklc(K_C))) \trianglelefteq U \Rightarrow \$(K_C) = OS(K_C)) \,\} \end{array}} [\![\text{ implementation-rule }]\!] \\ ro(\mathcal{A}) \rhd ro(\mathbf{A}) \quad [\![\text{ Lemma 3.2.5 }]\!] \end{array}}{\begin{array}{l} lu(\mathcal{A}), ro(\mathcal{A}), typed(\mathcal{A}), typed(\mathbf{A}) \rhd \\ \{\, \mathbf{P} \wedge \$ = OS \wedge \mathcal{U} = U \wedge \bigwedge_{i=0}^{k} typeof(\mathrm{v}_i) \preceq \tau([\mathrm{v}_i]) \wedge wt(\$) \,\} \\ \quad \mathrm{T@m} \\ \{\, \mathbf{Q} \wedge (\neg univV(obj(mklc(K_C))) \trianglelefteq U \Rightarrow \$(K_C) = OS(K_C)) \,\} \end{array}} [\![\text{ assumpt-elim-rule }]\!] \\ typed(\mathcal{A}) \rhd typed(\mathbf{A}) \quad [\![\text{ Lemma 3.2.1 }]\!] \end{array}}{\begin{array}{l} lu(\mathcal{A}), ro(\mathcal{A}), typed(\mathcal{A}) \rhd \\ \{\, \mathbf{P} \wedge \$ = OS \wedge \mathcal{U} = U \wedge \bigwedge_{i=0}^{k} typeof(\mathrm{v}_i) \preceq \tau([\mathrm{v}_i]) \wedge wt(\$) \,\} \\ \quad \mathrm{T@m} \\ \{\, \mathbf{Q} \wedge (\neg univV(obj(mklc(K_C))) \trianglelefteq U \Rightarrow \$(K_C) = OS(K_C)) \,\} \end{array}} [\![\text{ assumpt-elim-rule }]\!]$$

□

Proof of Lemma 5.4.3:

Case 1: $mklc?(L)$
$L \xrightarrow{OS} K \wedge accessibleL(K,T)$
$\Rightarrow$ ⟦ Axiom **dep3** ⟧
$accessibleL(L,T)$

Case 2: $mkla?(L)$
Case 2.1: $univV(obj(L)) = univV(obj(K))$
$accessMode(fid(L)) = public \wedge L \xrightarrow{OS} K \wedge wt(OS) \wedge accessibleL(K,T)$
$\Rightarrow$ ⟦ Lemma 5.2.4 ⟧
$accessMode(fid(L)) = public \wedge accessibleL(L, guard(K, univV(obj(K))))\wedge$
$accessibleL(K,T)$
$\Rightarrow$ ⟦ Definition of *guard* ⟧
$accessibleL(L, dtype(fid(K))) \wedge accessMode(fid(L)) = public \wedge accessibleL(K,T)$
$\Rightarrow$ ⟦ Lemma 3.1.2 ⟧
$accessMode(fid(L)) = public\wedge$
$imports(module(dtype(fid(K))), module(dtype(fid(L))))\wedge$
$imports(module(T), module(dtype(fid(K))))$
$\Rightarrow$ ⟦ Transitivity of *imports* (Axiom **import1**) ⟧
$accessMode(fid(L)) = public \wedge imports(module(T), module(dtype(fid(L))))$
$\Rightarrow$ ⟦ Definition of *accessible*, *accessibleL* ⟧
$accessibleL(L,T)$

Case 2.2: $univV(obj(L)) \neq univV(obj(K))$
$ctid?(T) \wedge T \neq ctid(\text{Object}) \wedge L \xrightarrow{OS} K \wedge wt(OS) \wedge univV(obj(L)) \trianglelefteq U\wedge$
$(univV(obj(K)) = U\vee$
$univV(obj(K)) = typeU(S,U) \wedge imports(module(T), module(S))\vee$
$univV(obj(K)) = objU(OID,C,U) \wedge ctid(C) \preceq_M T)$
$\Rightarrow$ ⟦ $univV(obj(K)) \neq U$ (Lemma 5.2.3 and antisymmetry of $\trianglelefteq$); Lemma D.1.1 ⟧
$ctid?(T) \wedge T \neq ctid(\text{Object}) \wedge L \xrightarrow{OS} K \wedge wt(OS) \wedge univV(obj(L)) = U\wedge$
$(univV(obj(K)) = typeU(S,U) \wedge imports(module(T), module(S))\vee$
$univV(obj(K)) = objU(OID,C,U) \wedge ctid(C) \preceq_M T)$
$\Rightarrow$ ⟦ Lemma 5.4.2 ⟧
$accessibleL(L,T)$

□

Proof of Lemma 5.4.1:

Like the proofs for language properties, this proof runs by induction on the depth of the proof for $\mathcal{A} \triangleright \mathbf{A}$. In the following, we present the interesting cases of this proof: The cases for statements that modify the object store and the case for the class-rule.

Induction Basis.
New-axiom:

$$\{\ \mathbf{P}[new(\$, cid(tid(\mathrm{S})), univ(\tau(\mathrm{S})))/\mathrm{v}, \$\langle cid(tid(\mathrm{S}), univ(\tau(\mathrm{S})))\rangle/\$] \wedge \$ = OS \wedge$$
$$alive(obj(L), \$) \wedge univV(obj(L)) \trianglelefteq \mathcal{U} \wedge \neg presentL(L, \mathrm{T}) \wedge$$
$$\textstyle\bigwedge_{i=0}^{n} typeof(\mathrm{v}_i) \preceq \tau([\mathrm{v}_i]) \wedge wt(\$) \wedge (static(\mathrm{T@m}) \Leftrightarrow \mathrm{this} = null)\ \}$$
$$\Rightarrow$$
$$\{\ \mathbf{P}[new(\$, cid(tid(\mathrm{S})), univ(\tau(\mathrm{S})))/\mathrm{v}, \$\langle cid(tid(\mathrm{S}), univ(\tau(\mathrm{S})))\rangle/\$] \wedge$$
$$OS = \$ \wedge alive(obj(L), \$) \wedge wt(\$)\ \}$$
$$\Rightarrow \quad [\![\ \text{Lemma 5.2.2}\ ]\!]$$
$$\{\ (\mathbf{P} \wedge OS \equiv_L \$)[new(\$, cid(tid(\mathrm{S})), univ(\tau(\mathrm{S})))/\mathrm{v}, \$\langle cid(tid(\mathrm{S}), univ(\tau(\mathrm{S})))\rangle/\$]\ \}$$
$$\mathrm{v} = \mathrm{new\ S}(); \quad [\![\ \text{new-axiom}\ ]\!]$$
$$\{\ \mathbf{P} \wedge OS \equiv_L \$\ \}$$

Field-write-axiom:

$$\{\ \mathrm{v} \neq null \wedge \mathbf{P}[\$\langle locC(\mathrm{v}, \mathrm{S@f}) := \mathrm{e}\rangle/\$] \wedge \$ = OS \wedge alive(obj(L), \$) \wedge$$
$$univV(obj(L)) \trianglelefteq \mathcal{U} \wedge \neg presentL(L, \mathrm{T}) \wedge$$
$$\textstyle\bigwedge_{i=0}^{n} typeof(\mathrm{v}_i) \preceq \tau([\mathrm{v}_i]) \wedge wt(\$) \wedge (static(\mathrm{T@m}) \Leftrightarrow \mathrm{this} = null)\ \}$$
$$\Rightarrow \quad [\![\ \text{Lemma 3.1.9, analogously to Proof 3.2.1}\ ]\!]$$
$$\{\ \mathrm{v} \neq null \wedge \mathbf{P}[\$\langle locC(\mathrm{v}, \mathrm{S@f}) := \mathrm{e}\rangle/\$] \wedge typeof(\mathrm{v}) \preceq dyn([\mathrm{v}], \mathrm{this}, \mathcal{U}) \wedge$$
$$typeof(\mathrm{this}) \preceq \tau([\mathtt{this}]) \wedge (static(\mathrm{T@m}) \Leftrightarrow \mathrm{this} = null) \wedge \$ = OS \wedge$$
$$alive(obj(L), \$) \wedge univV(obj(L)) \trianglelefteq \mathcal{U} \wedge \neg accessibleL(L, \mathrm{T}) \wedge wt(\$) \wedge$$
$$wt(\$\langle locC(\mathrm{v}, \mathrm{S@f}) := \mathrm{e}\rangle)\ \}$$
$$\Rightarrow \quad \left[\!\!\left[\begin{array}{l}\text{Context conditions of Mojave;}\\ \text{definition of } dyn, \text{axiom } \mathbf{import5},\ orepT?([\mathrm{v}]) \Rightarrow \neg static(\mathrm{T@m})\end{array}\right]\!\!\right]$$
$$\{\ \mathrm{v} \neq null \wedge \mathbf{P}[\$\langle locC(\mathrm{v}, \mathrm{S@f}) := \mathrm{e}\rangle/\$] \wedge accessibleL(locC(\mathrm{v}, \mathrm{S@f}), \mathrm{T}) \wedge$$
$$univV(obj(L)) \trianglelefteq \mathcal{U} \wedge (univV(\mathrm{v}) = \mathcal{U} \vee univV(\mathrm{v}) = typeU(S', \mathcal{U}) \wedge$$
$$imports(module(\mathrm{T}), module(S')) \vee univV(\mathrm{v}) = objU(oid(\mathrm{this}), cidV(\mathrm{this}), \mathcal{U}) \wedge$$
$$ctid(cidV(\mathrm{this})) \preceq_M \mathrm{T} \wedge \mathrm{this} \neq null) \wedge \$ = OS \wedge alive(obj(L), \$) \wedge$$
$$\neg accessibleL(L, \mathrm{T}) \wedge wt(\$) \wedge wt(\$\langle locC(\mathrm{v}, \mathrm{S@f}) := \mathrm{e}\rangle)\ \}$$
$$\Rightarrow \quad \left[\!\!\left[\begin{array}{l}\text{Case 1: } L \stackrel{\$}{\longrightarrow} locC(\mathrm{v}, \mathrm{S@f}) \Rightarrow false\\ \qquad\quad (ctid?(\mathrm{T}) \wedge \mathrm{T} \neq ctid(\mathrm{Object}), \text{Lemma 5.4.3})\\ \text{Case 2: } \neg L \stackrel{\$}{\longrightarrow} locC(\mathrm{v}, \mathrm{S@f}) \Rightarrow OS \equiv_L \$\langle locC(\mathrm{v}, \mathrm{S@f}) := \mathrm{e}\rangle\\ \qquad\quad (\text{Lemma 5.2.1})\end{array}\right]\!\!\right]$$
$$\{\ \mathrm{v} \neq null \wedge \mathbf{P}[\$\langle locC(\mathrm{v}, \mathrm{S@f}) := \mathrm{e}\rangle/\$] \wedge \$\langle locC(\mathrm{v}, \mathrm{S@f}) := \mathrm{e}\rangle \equiv_L OS\ \}$$
$$\Rightarrow$$
$$\{\ \mathrm{v} \neq null \wedge (\mathbf{P} \wedge \$ \equiv_L OS)[\$\langle locC(\mathrm{v}, \mathrm{S@f}) := \mathrm{e}\rangle/\$]\ \}$$
$$\mathrm{v.S@f} = \mathrm{e}; \quad [\![\ \text{field-write-axiom}\ ]\!]$$
$$\{\ \mathbf{P} \wedge \$ \equiv_L OS\ \}$$

Predefined method implementations: Since all predefined methods have $\$ = OS$ in their pre- and postconditions, the local update property follows from the reflexivity of $\_ \equiv_{\_} \_$ (Lemma 4.2.1).

Induction Step.

Invocation-rule: If the invoked method is readonly, we derive:

$$\dfrac{\dfrac{\dfrac{\mathcal{A} \triangleright \{\ \mathbf{P}\ \}\ \mathrm{S{:}n}\ \{\ \mathbf{Q}\ \}}{ro(\mathcal{A}) \triangleright \{\ \mathbf{P} \wedge \$ = OS'\ \}\ \mathrm{S{:}n}\ \{\ \mathbf{Q} \wedge \$ = OS'\ \}}\ [\![\text{ Lemma 3.2.5 }]\!]}{ro(\mathcal{A}) \triangleright \{\ \mathbf{P} \wedge \$ = OS\ \}\ \mathrm{S{:}n}\ \{\ \mathbf{Q} \wedge \$ = OS\ \}}\ [\![\text{ subst-rule }]\!]}{uc(\mathcal{A}), lu(\mathcal{A}), ro(\mathcal{A}), oal(\mathcal{A}), typed(\mathcal{A}) \triangleright \{\ \mathbf{P} \wedge \$ = OS\ \}\ \mathrm{S{:}n}\ \{\ \mathbf{Q} \wedge \$ = OS\ \}}\ [\![\text{ assumpt-intro-rule }]\!]$$

By this sequent, we derive the desired property. We omit the assumptions for brevity.

$$\begin{array}{l}
\{\ \mathrm{w} \neq null \wedge \mathbf{P}[\mathrm{w/this}, e_1/p_1, \ldots, e_l/p_l, univV(\mathrm{w})/\mathcal{U}] \wedge \$ = OS \wedge \\
alive(obj(L), \$) \wedge univV(obj(L)) \trianglelefteq \mathcal{U} \wedge \neg presentL(L, \mathrm{T}) \wedge \\
\bigwedge_{i=0}^{n} typeof(\mathrm{v}_i) \preceq \tau([\mathrm{v}_i]) \wedge wt(\$) \wedge (static(\mathrm{T@m}) \Leftrightarrow \mathrm{this} = null)\ \} \\
\Rightarrow \\
\{\ \mathrm{w} \neq null \wedge (\mathbf{P} \wedge \$ = OS)[\mathrm{w/this}, \mathrm{e}_1/\mathrm{p}_1, \ldots, \mathrm{e}_l/\mathrm{p}_l, univV(\mathrm{w})/\mathcal{U}]\ \} \\
\mathrm{v} = \mathrm{w.S{:}n}(\mathrm{e}_1, \ldots, \mathrm{e}_l);\ \ [\![\text{ applying the invocation-rule to the above sequent }]\!] \\
\{\ (\mathbf{Q} \wedge \$ = OS)[\mathrm{v/result}]\ \} \\
\Rightarrow\ \ [\![\text{ Reflexivity of } \equiv_{_} \text{ (Lemma 4.2.1) }]\!] \\
\{\ \mathbf{Q}[\mathrm{v/result}] \wedge OS \equiv_L \$\ \}
\end{array}$$

For readwrite methods, we derive the desired property by case distinction.

Case 1:
$univV(obj(L)) \trianglelefteq univV(\mathrm{w}) \wedge$
$\exists K_C : L \xrightarrow{OS} mklc(K_C) \wedge univV(obj(mklc(K_C))) \trianglelefteq univV(\mathrm{w})$

$$\begin{array}{l}
\{\ \mathrm{w} \neq null \wedge \mathbf{P}[\mathrm{w/this}, e_1/p_1, \ldots, e_l/p_l, univV(\mathrm{w})/\mathcal{U}] \wedge \$ = OS \wedge \\
alive(obj(L), \$) \wedge univV(obj(L)) \trianglelefteq \mathcal{U} \wedge \neg presentL(L, \mathrm{T}) \wedge \\
\bigwedge_{i=0}^{n} typeof(\mathrm{v}_i) \preceq \tau([\mathrm{v}_i]) \wedge wt(\$) \wedge (static(\mathrm{T@m}) \Leftrightarrow \mathrm{this} = null) \wedge \\
univV(obj(L)) \trianglelefteq univV(\mathrm{w}) \wedge \\
\exists K_C : L \xrightarrow{OS} mklc(K_C) \wedge univV(obj(mklc(K_C))) \trianglelefteq univV(\mathrm{w})\ \} \\
\Rightarrow\ \ [\![\text{ Axiom } \mathbf{import3}\text{, Lemma 3.1.8; analogously to Proof 3.2.1 }]\!] \\
\{\ \mathrm{w} \neq null \wedge (\mathbf{P} \wedge \$ = OS \wedge alive(obj(L), \$) \wedge univV(obj(L)) \trianglelefteq \mathcal{U} \wedge \\
\neg presentL(L, \mathrm{S}) \wedge \bigwedge_{i=0}^{l} typeof(\mathrm{p}_i) \preceq \tau([\mathrm{p}_i]) \wedge \\
wt(\$))[\mathrm{w/this}, \mathrm{e}_1/\mathrm{p}_1, \ldots, \mathrm{e}_l/\mathrm{p}_l, univV(\mathrm{w})/\mathcal{U}]\ \} \\
\mathrm{v} = \mathrm{w.S{:}n}(\mathrm{e}_1, \ldots, \mathrm{e}_l);\ \ [\![\text{ applying the invocation-rule to the ind. hyp. }]\!] \\
\{\ (\mathbf{Q} \wedge OS \equiv_L \$)[\mathrm{v/result}]\ \} \\
\Rightarrow \\
\{\ \mathbf{Q}[\mathrm{v/result}] \wedge OS \equiv_L \$\ \}
\end{array} \tag{D.2}$$

Case 2:
$univV(obj(L)) = \mathcal{U} \wedge \neg univV(obj(L)) \trianglelefteq univV(\mathrm{w}) \wedge$
$\exists K_C : L \xrightarrow{OS} mklc(K_C) \wedge univV(obj(mklc(K_C))) \trianglelefteq univV(\mathrm{w})$

$$\begin{array}{l}
\{\ \mathrm{w} \neq null \wedge \mathbf{P}[\mathrm{w}/\mathrm{this}, e_1/p_1, \ldots, e_l/p_l, univV(\mathrm{w})/\mathcal{U}] \wedge \$ = OS \wedge \\
alive(obj(L), \$) \wedge univV(obj(L)) = \mathcal{U} \wedge \neg univV(obj(L)) \trianglelefteq univV(\mathrm{w}) \wedge \\
\neg presentL(L, \mathrm{T}) \wedge \bigwedge_{i=0}^{n} typeof(\mathrm{v}_i) \preceq \tau([\mathrm{v}_i]) \wedge wt(\$) \wedge \\
(static(\mathrm{T@m}) \Leftrightarrow \mathrm{this} = null) \wedge \\
\exists K_C : L \xrightarrow{OS} mklc(K_C) \wedge univV(obj(mklc(K_C))) \trianglelefteq univV(\mathrm{w})\ \} \\
\Rightarrow \quad \left[\!\left[\begin{array}{l} \neg roT?([\mathtt{w}]), \text{Definition of } dyn, \text{ axiom } \mathbf{import5}, \\ orepT?([\mathtt{w}]) \Rightarrow \neg static(\mathrm{T@m}) \end{array} \right]\!\right] \\
\{\ \exists K_C : univV(obj(L)) = \mathcal{U} \wedge univV(\mathrm{w}) \neq \mathcal{U} \wedge \neg presentL(L, \mathrm{T}) \wedge \\
L \xrightarrow{OS} mklc(K_C) \wedge univV(obj(mklc(K_C))) \trianglelefteq univV(\mathrm{w}) \wedge wt(OS) \wedge \\
(univV(\mathrm{w}) = \mathcal{U} \vee \\
univV(\mathrm{w}) = typeU(S', \mathcal{U}) \wedge imports(module(\mathrm{T}), module(S')) \vee \\
univV(\mathrm{w}) = objU(oid(\mathrm{this}), cidV(\mathrm{this}), \mathcal{U}) \wedge \\
ctid(cidV(\mathrm{this})) \preceq_M \mathrm{T} \wedge \mathrm{this} \neq null)\ \} \\
\Rightarrow \quad [\![\ ctid?(\mathrm{T}) \wedge \mathrm{T} \neq ctid(\mathrm{Object}), \text{ Lemma 5.4.2}\ ]\!] \\
\{\ \neg presentL(L, \mathrm{T}) \wedge accessibleL(L, \mathrm{T})\ \} \\
\Rightarrow \quad [\![\ \text{Contradiction (Lemma 3.1.9)}\ ]\!] \\
\{\ false\ \} \\
\mathrm{v} = \mathrm{w.S{:}n}(\mathrm{e}_1, \ldots, \mathrm{e}_l); \quad [\![\ \text{false-axiom}\ ]\!] \\
\{\ false\ \} \\
\Rightarrow \\
\{\ \mathbf{Q}[\mathrm{v}/\mathrm{result}] \wedge OS \equiv_L \$\ \}
\end{array} \tag{D.3}$$

Case 3:
$univV(obj(L)) \lhd \mathcal{U} \wedge \neg univV(obj(L)) \trianglelefteq univV(\mathrm{w}) \wedge$
$\exists K_C : L \xrightarrow{OS} mklc(K_C) \wedge univV(obj(mklc(K_C))) \trianglelefteq univV(\mathrm{w})$

$$\begin{array}{l}
\{\ \mathrm{w} \neq null \wedge \mathbf{P}[\mathrm{w}/\mathrm{this}, e_1/p_1, \ldots, e_l/p_l, univV(\mathrm{w})/\mathcal{U}] \wedge \$ = OS \wedge \\
alive(obj(L), \$) \wedge univV(obj(L)) \lhd \mathcal{U} \wedge \neg univV(obj(L)) \trianglelefteq univV(\mathrm{w}) \wedge \\
\neg presentL(L, \mathrm{T}) \wedge \bigwedge_{i=0}^{n} typeof(\mathrm{v}_i) \preceq \tau([\mathrm{v}_i]) \wedge wt(\$) \wedge \\
(static(\mathrm{T@m}) \Leftrightarrow \mathrm{this} = null) \wedge \\
\exists K_C : L \xrightarrow{OS} mklc(K_C) \wedge univV(obj(mklc(K_C))) \trianglelefteq univV(\mathrm{w})\ \} \\
\Rightarrow \quad [\![\ \text{Lemma 5.2.3, definition of } dyn\ ]\!] \\
(\forall K : L \xrightarrow{OS} K \wedge wt(OS) \Rightarrow univV(obj(K)) \trianglelefteq univV(obj(L))) \wedge \\
univV(obj(L)) \lhd \mathcal{U} \wedge univV(\mathrm{w}) \trianglelefteq_1 \mathcal{U} \wedge \neg univV(obj(L)) \trianglelefteq univV(\mathrm{w}) \wedge \\
wt(OS) \wedge \exists K_C : L \xrightarrow{OS} mklc(K_C) \wedge univV(obj(mklc(K_C))) \trianglelefteq univV(\mathrm{w})\ \} \\
\Rightarrow \quad [\![\ \text{Contradiction } (mklc(K_C) \text{ for } K, \text{ Lemmas D.1.1 and D.1.2})\ ]\!] \\
\{\ false\ \} \\
\mathrm{v} = \mathrm{w.S{:}n}(\mathrm{e}_1, \ldots, \mathrm{e}_l); \quad [\![\ \text{false-axiom}\ ]\!] \\
\{\ false\ \} \\
\Rightarrow \\
\{\ \mathbf{Q}[\mathrm{v}/\mathrm{result}] \wedge OS \equiv_L \$\ \}
\end{array} \tag{D.4}$$

Case 4:

$\neg\exists K_C : L \stackrel{OS}{\longrightarrow} mklc(K_C) \wedge univV(obj(mklc(K_C))) \trianglelefteq univV(\mathrm{w})$

First, we apply several language property operators. We omit the assumptions in the following for brevity.

$$\{\, \mathbf{P} \wedge \bigwedge_{i=0}^{l} typeof(\mathrm{p}_i) \preceq \tau([\mathrm{p}_i]) \wedge wt(\$) \wedge R = \tau(ret(\mathrm{S{:}n})) \wedge alive(X,\$) \wedge \$ = OS \wedge \mathcal{U} = U \,\}$$

$$\uparrow \quad [\![\text{ all-rule }]\!]$$

$$\{\, \mathbf{P} \wedge \bigwedge_{i=0}^{l} typeof(\mathrm{p}_i) \preceq \tau([\mathrm{p}_i]) \wedge wt(\$) \wedge R = \tau(ret(\mathrm{S{:}n})) \wedge alive(X,\$) \wedge \$ = OS \wedge \mathcal{U} = U \,\}$$

$$\Rightarrow$$

$$\{\, \mathbf{P} \wedge \bigwedge_{i=0}^{l} typeof(\mathrm{p}_i) \preceq \tau([\mathrm{p}_i]) \wedge wt(\$) \wedge R = \tau(ret(\mathrm{S{:}n})) \wedge alive(X,\$) \wedge \$ = OS \wedge \mathcal{U} = U \wedge \bigwedge_{i=0}^{l} typeof(\mathrm{p}_i) \preceq \tau([\mathrm{p}_i]) \wedge wt(\$) \,\}$$

$$\downarrow \quad [\![\text{ Lemma 5.4.1 }]\!]$$

$$\{\, \mathbf{P} \wedge \bigwedge_{i=0}^{l} typeof(\mathrm{p}_i) \preceq \tau([\mathrm{p}_i]) \wedge wt(\$) \wedge R = \tau(ret(\mathrm{S{:}n})) \wedge alive(X,\$) \,\}$$

$$\downarrow \quad [\![\text{ Lemma 3.2.4 }]\!]$$

$$\{\, \mathbf{P} \wedge \bigwedge_{i=0}^{l} typeof(\mathrm{p}_i) \preceq \tau([\mathrm{p}_i]) \wedge wt(\$) \wedge R = \tau(ret(\mathrm{S{:}n})) \,\}$$

$$\downarrow \quad [\![\text{ Lemma 3.2.1 }]\!]$$

$$\{\, \mathbf{P} \,\}$$

S:n

$$\{\, \mathbf{Q} \,\}$$

$$\uparrow \quad [\![\text{ Lemma 3.2.1 }]\!]$$

$$\{\, \mathbf{Q} \wedge typeof(\text{result}) \preceq R \wedge wt(\$) \,\}$$

$$\uparrow \quad [\![\text{ Lemma 3.2.4 }]\!]$$

$$\{\, \mathbf{Q} \wedge typeof(\text{result}) \preceq R \wedge wt(\$) \wedge alive(X,\$) \,\}$$

$$\uparrow \quad [\![\text{ Lemma 5.4.1 }]\!]$$

$$\{\, \mathbf{Q} \wedge typeof(\text{result}) \preceq R \wedge wt(\$) \wedge alive(X,\$) \wedge (\neg univV(obj(mklc(K_C))) \trianglelefteq U \Rightarrow \$(K_C) = OS(K_C)) \,\}$$

$$\uparrow \quad [\![\text{ all-rule }]\!]$$

$$\{\, \forall K_C : \mathbf{Q} \wedge typeof(\text{result}) \preceq R \wedge wt(\$) \wedge alive(X,\$) \wedge (\neg univV(obj(mklc(K_C))) \trianglelefteq U \Rightarrow \$(K_C) = OS(K_C)) \,\}$$

$$\Rightarrow$$

$$\{\, \mathbf{Q} \wedge wt(\$) \wedge alive(X,\$) \wedge \forall K_C : (\neg univV(obj(mklc(K_C))) \trianglelefteq U \Rightarrow \$(K_C) = OS(K_C)) \,\}$$

By this sequent, we derive (we omit the assumptions for brevity):

$$\begin{array}{l}
\{\, \mathrm{w} \neq \mathit{null} \wedge \mathbf{P}[\mathrm{w}/\mathrm{this}, \mathrm{e}_1/p_1, \ldots, e_l/p_l, \mathit{univV}(\mathrm{w})/\mathcal{U}] \wedge \$ = \mathit{OS} \wedge \\
\mathit{alive}(\mathit{obj}(L), \$) \wedge \mathit{univV}(\mathit{obj}(L)) \trianglelefteq \mathcal{U} \wedge \neg \mathit{presentL}(L, \mathrm{T}) \wedge \\
\bigwedge_{i=0}^{n} \mathit{typeof}(\mathrm{v}_i) \preceq \tau([\mathrm{v}_i]) \wedge \mathit{wt}(\$) \wedge (\mathit{static}(\mathrm{T@m}) \Leftrightarrow \mathrm{this} = \mathit{null}) \wedge \\
\neg(\exists K_C : L \xrightarrow{OS} \mathit{mklc}(K_C) \wedge \mathit{univV}(\mathit{obj}(\mathit{mklc}(K_C))) \trianglelefteq \mathit{univV}(\mathrm{w}))\, \}
\end{array}$$

$\Rightarrow$ ⟦ use $\mathit{univV}(\mathrm{w})$ for U; analogously to Proof 3.2.1 ⟧

$$\begin{array}{l}
\{\, \exists U, R : \mathrm{w} \neq \mathit{null} \wedge (\mathbf{P} \wedge \bigwedge_{i=0}^{l} \mathit{typeof}(\mathrm{p}_i) \preceq \tau([\mathrm{p}_i]) \wedge \mathit{wt}(\$) \wedge \\
R = \tau(\mathit{ret}(\mathrm{S{:}n})) \wedge \mathit{alive}(\mathit{obj}(L), \$) \wedge \$ = \mathit{OS} \wedge \\
\mathcal{U} = U)[\mathrm{w}/\mathrm{this}, \mathrm{e}_1/\mathrm{p}_1, \ldots, \mathrm{e}_l/\mathrm{p}_l, \mathit{univV}(\mathrm{w})/\mathcal{U}] \wedge \mathit{alive}(\mathit{obj}(L), \mathit{OS}) \wedge \\
\mathit{wt}(\mathit{OS}) \wedge \neg(\exists K_C : L \xrightarrow{OS} \mathit{mklc}(K_C) \wedge \mathit{univV}(\mathit{obj}(\mathit{mklc}(K_C))) \trianglelefteq U)\, \}
\end{array}$$

———————————————————— $\downarrow$ ⟦ ex-rule ⟧

$$\begin{array}{l}
\{\, \mathrm{w} \neq \mathit{null} \wedge (\mathbf{P} \wedge \bigwedge_{i=0}^{l} \mathit{typeof}(\mathrm{p}_i) \preceq \tau([\mathrm{p}_i]) \wedge \mathit{wt}(\$) \wedge R = \tau(\mathit{ret}(\mathrm{S{:}n})) \wedge \\
\mathit{alive}(\mathit{obj}(L), \$) \wedge \$ = \mathit{OS} \wedge \mathcal{U} = U)[\mathrm{w}/\mathrm{this}, \mathrm{e}_1/\mathrm{p}_1, \ldots, \mathrm{e}_l/\mathrm{p}_l, \mathit{univV}(\mathrm{w})/\mathcal{U}] \wedge \\
\mathit{alive}(\mathit{obj}(L), \mathit{OS}) \wedge \mathit{wt}(\mathit{OS}) \wedge \\
\neg(\exists K_C : L \xrightarrow{OS} \mathit{mklc}(K_C) \wedge \mathit{univV}(\mathit{obj}(\mathit{mklc}(K_C))) \trianglelefteq U)\, \}
\end{array}$$

———————————————————— $\downarrow$ ⟦ inv-rule ⟧

$$\begin{array}{l}
\{\, \mathrm{w} \neq \mathit{null} \wedge (\mathbf{P} \wedge \bigwedge_{i=0}^{l} \mathit{typeof}(\mathrm{p}_i) \preceq \tau([\mathrm{p}_i]) \wedge \mathit{wt}(\$) \wedge R = \tau(\mathit{ret}(\mathrm{S{:}n})) \wedge \\
\mathit{alive}(\mathit{obj}(L), \$) \wedge \$ = \mathit{OS} \wedge \mathcal{U} = U)[\mathrm{w}/\mathrm{this}, \mathrm{e}_1/\mathrm{p}_1, \ldots, \mathrm{e}_l/\mathrm{p}_l, \mathit{univV}(\mathrm{w})/\mathcal{U}]\, \}
\end{array} \quad (D.5)$$

———————————————————— $\downarrow$ ⟦ subst-rule ⟧

$$\begin{array}{l}
\{\, \mathrm{w} \neq \mathit{null} \wedge (\mathbf{P} \wedge \bigwedge_{i=0}^{l} \mathit{typeof}(\mathrm{p}_i) \preceq \tau([\mathrm{p}_i]) \wedge \mathit{wt}(\$) \wedge R = \tau(\mathit{ret}(\mathrm{S{:}n})) \wedge \\
\mathit{alive}(X, \$) \wedge \$ = \mathit{OS} \wedge \mathcal{U} = U)[\mathrm{w}/\mathrm{this}, \mathrm{e}_1/\mathrm{p}_1, \ldots, \mathrm{e}_l/\mathrm{p}_l, \mathit{univV}(\mathrm{w})/\mathcal{U}]\, \}
\end{array}$$

$\mathrm{v} = \mathrm{w.S{:}n}(\mathrm{e}_1, \ldots, \mathrm{e}_l);$

$$\begin{array}{l}
\{\, (\mathbf{Q} \wedge \mathit{wt}(\$) \wedge \mathit{alive}(X, \$) \wedge \\
\forall K_C : (\neg \mathit{univV}(\mathit{obj}(\mathit{mklc}(K_C))) \trianglelefteq U \Rightarrow \$(K_C) = \mathit{OS}(K_C)))[\mathrm{v}/\mathrm{result}]\, \}
\end{array}$$

———————————————————— $\uparrow$ ⟦ subst-rule ⟧

$$\begin{array}{l}
\{\, (\mathbf{Q} \wedge \mathit{wt}(\$) \wedge \mathit{alive}(\mathit{obj}(L), \$) \wedge \\
\forall K_C : (\neg \mathit{univV}(\mathit{obj}(\mathit{mklc}(K_C))) \trianglelefteq U \Rightarrow \$(K_C) = \mathit{OS}(K_C)))[\mathrm{v}/\mathrm{result}]\, \}
\end{array}$$

———————————————————— $\uparrow$ ⟦ inv-rule ⟧

$$\begin{array}{l}
\{\, (\mathbf{Q} \wedge \mathit{wt}(\$) \wedge \mathit{alive}(\mathit{obj}(L), \$) \wedge \mathit{alive}(\mathit{obj}(L), \mathit{OS}) \wedge \mathit{wt}(\mathit{OS}) \wedge \\
\forall K_C : (\neg \mathit{univV}(\mathit{obj}(\mathit{mklc}(K_C))) \trianglelefteq U \Rightarrow \$(K_C) = \mathit{OS}(K_C)))[\mathrm{v}/\mathrm{result}] \wedge \\
\neg(\exists K_C : L \xrightarrow{OS} \mathit{mklc}(K_C) \wedge \mathit{univV}(\mathit{obj}(\mathit{mklc}(K_C))) \trianglelefteq U)\, \}
\end{array}$$

$\Rightarrow$ ⟦ Lemma 5.2.1 ⟧

$$\{\, \mathbf{Q}[\mathrm{v}/\mathrm{result}] \wedge \mathit{OS} \equiv_L \$\, \}$$

———————————————————— $\uparrow$ ⟦ ex-rule ⟧

$$\{\, \mathbf{Q}[\mathrm{v}/\mathrm{result}] \wedge \mathit{OS} \equiv_L \$\, \}$$

Now, we combine the four cases by the disjunct-rule, which yields the desired property. In the following, we abbreviate

$$\begin{array}{l} \mathrm{w} \neq \mathit{null} \wedge \mathbf{P}[\mathrm{w}/\mathrm{this}, e_1/p_1, \ldots, e_l/p_l, \mathit{univV}(\mathrm{w})/\mathcal{U}] \wedge \$ = \mathit{OS} \wedge \\ \mathit{alive}(\mathit{obj}(L), \$) \wedge \neg \mathit{presentL}(L, \mathrm{T}) \wedge \bigwedge_{i=0}^{n} \mathit{typeof}(\mathrm{v}_i) \preceq \tau([\mathrm{v}_i]) \wedge \mathit{wt}(\$) \wedge \\ (\mathit{static}(\mathrm{T@m}) \Leftrightarrow \mathrm{this} = \mathit{null}) \end{array}$$

by $\mathbf{P}'$, $\mathbf{Q}[\mathrm{v}/\mathrm{result}] \wedge OS \equiv_L \$$ by $\mathbf{Q}'$, and $uc(\mathcal{A})$, $lu(\mathcal{A})$, $ro(\mathcal{A})$, $oal(\mathcal{A})$, $typed(\mathcal{A})$ by $\mathcal{S}$. We derive:

$$\begin{array}{ll}
\mathcal{S} \triangleright \; \{ \mathbf{P}' \wedge \mathit{univV}(\mathit{obj}(L)) = \mathcal{U} \wedge \neg \mathit{univV}(\mathit{obj}(L)) \trianglelefteq \mathit{univV}(\mathrm{w}) \wedge & \\
\quad \exists K_C : L \xrightarrow{OS} \mathit{mklc}(K_C) \wedge \mathit{univV}(\mathit{obj}(\mathit{mklc}(K_C))) \trianglelefteq \mathit{univV}(\mathrm{w}) \; \} & \\
\quad \mathrm{v} = \mathrm{w.S{:}n}(\mathrm{e}_1, \ldots, \mathrm{e}_l); & \\
\quad \{ \mathbf{Q}' \} \quad [\![\mathrm{D.3}]\!] & \\
\mathcal{S} \triangleright \; \{ \mathbf{P}' \wedge \mathit{univV}(\mathit{obj}(L)) \triangleleft \mathcal{U} \wedge \neg \mathit{univV}(\mathit{obj}(L)) \trianglelefteq \mathit{univV}(\mathrm{w}) \wedge & \\
\quad \exists K_C : L \xrightarrow{OS} \mathit{mklc}(K_C) \wedge \mathit{univV}(\mathit{obj}(\mathit{mklc}(K_C))) \trianglelefteq \mathit{univV}(\mathrm{w}) \; \} & \\
\quad \mathrm{v} = \mathrm{w.S{:}n}(\mathrm{e}_1, \ldots, \mathrm{e}_l); & \\
\quad \{ \mathbf{Q}' \} \quad [\![\mathrm{D.4}]\!] & \\
\hline
\mathcal{S} \triangleright \; \{ \mathbf{P}' \wedge \mathit{univV}(\mathit{obj}(L)) \trianglelefteq \mathcal{U} \wedge \neg \mathit{univV}(\mathit{obj}(L)) \trianglelefteq \mathit{univV}(\mathrm{w}) \wedge & [\![\text{disjunct-rule}]\!] \\
\quad \exists K_C : L \xrightarrow{OS} \mathit{mklc}(K_C) \wedge \mathit{univV}(\mathit{obj}(\mathit{mklc}(K_C))) \trianglelefteq \mathit{univV}(\mathrm{w}) \; \} & \\
\quad \mathrm{v} = \mathrm{w.S{:}n}(\mathrm{e}_1, \ldots, \mathrm{e}_l); & \\
\quad \{ \mathbf{Q}' \} & \\
\mathcal{S} \triangleright \; \{ \mathbf{P}' \wedge \mathit{univV}(\mathit{obj}(L)) \trianglelefteq \mathcal{U} \wedge \mathit{univV}(\mathit{obj}(L)) \trianglelefteq \mathit{univV}(\mathrm{w}) \wedge & \\
\quad \exists K_C : L \xrightarrow{OS} \mathit{mklc}(K_C) \wedge \mathit{univV}(\mathit{obj}(\mathit{mklc}(K_C))) \trianglelefteq \mathit{univV}(\mathrm{w}) \; \} & \\
\quad \mathrm{v} = \mathrm{w.S{:}n}(\mathrm{e}_1, \ldots, \mathrm{e}_l); & \\
\quad \{ \mathbf{Q}' \} \quad [\![\mathrm{D.2}]\!] & \\
\hline
\mathcal{S} \triangleright \; \{ \mathbf{P}' \wedge \mathit{univV}(\mathit{obj}(L)) \trianglelefteq \mathcal{U} \wedge & [\![\text{disjunct-rule}]\!] \\
\quad \exists K_C : L \xrightarrow{OS} \mathit{mklc}(K_C) \wedge \mathit{univV}(\mathit{obj}(\mathit{mklc}(K_C))) \trianglelefteq \mathit{univV}(\mathrm{w}) \; \} & \\
\quad \mathrm{v} = \mathrm{w.S{:}n}(\mathrm{e}_1, \ldots, \mathrm{e}_l); & \\
\quad \{ \mathbf{Q}' \} & \\
\mathcal{S} \triangleright \; \{ \mathbf{P}' \wedge \mathit{univV}(\mathit{obj}(L)) \trianglelefteq \mathcal{U} \wedge \neg \exists K_C : L \xrightarrow{OS} \mathit{mklc}(K_C) \wedge & \\
\quad \mathit{univV}(\mathit{obj}(\mathit{mklc}(K_C))) \trianglelefteq \mathit{univV}(\mathrm{w}) \; \} & \\
\quad \mathrm{v} = \mathrm{w.S{:}n}(\mathrm{e}_1, \ldots, \mathrm{e}_l); & \\
\quad \{ \mathbf{Q}' \} \quad [\![\mathrm{D.5}]\!] & \\
\hline
\mathcal{S} \triangleright \; \{ \mathbf{P}' \wedge \mathit{univV}(\mathit{obj}(L)) \trianglelefteq \mathcal{U} \; \} \; \mathrm{v} = \mathrm{w.S{:}n}(\mathrm{e}_1, \ldots, \mathrm{e}_l); \; \{ \mathbf{Q}' \} & [\![\text{disjunct-rule}]\!]
\end{array}$$

Implementation-rule: We abbreviate the triple $\{\,\mathbf{P}\,\}$ T@m $\{\,\mathbf{Q}\,\}$ by $\mathbf{A}$.

$$\dfrac{\dfrac{\begin{array}{l} uc(\mathcal{A}), lu(\mathcal{A}), ro(\mathcal{A}), oal(\mathcal{A}), typed(\mathcal{A}), uc(\mathbf{A}), lu(\mathbf{A}), ro(\mathbf{A}), oal(\mathbf{A}), typed(\mathbf{A}) \rhd \\ \{\,\mathbf{P} \wedge \$ = OS \wedge alive(obj(L),\$) \wedge univV(obj(L)) \trianglelefteq \mathcal{U} \wedge \neg presentL(L,\mathrm{T}) \wedge \\ \bigwedge_{i=0}^{n} typeof(\mathrm{v}_i) \preceq \tau([\mathrm{v}_i]) \wedge wt(\$) \wedge (static(\mathrm{T@m}) \Leftrightarrow \mathrm{this} = null) \wedge \\ (static(\mathrm{T@m}) \Leftrightarrow \mathrm{this} = null) \wedge \bigwedge_{i=k+1}^{n} \mathrm{v}_i = init(\tau([\mathrm{v}_i]))\,\} \\ \; body(\mathrm{T@m})\ \{\,\mathbf{Q} \wedge OS \equiv_L \$\,\} \end{array}}{\begin{array}{l} uc(\mathcal{A}), lu(\mathcal{A}), ro(\mathcal{A}), oal(\mathcal{A}), typed(\mathcal{A}), uc(\mathbf{A}), lu(\mathbf{A}), ro(\mathbf{A}), oal(\mathbf{A}), typed(\mathbf{A}) \rhd \\ \{\,\mathbf{P} \wedge \$ = OS \wedge alive(obj(L),\$) \wedge univV(obj(L)) \trianglelefteq \mathcal{U} \wedge \neg presentL(L,\mathrm{T}) \wedge \\ \bigwedge_{i=0}^{k} typeof(\mathrm{v}_i) \preceq \tau([\mathrm{v}_i]) \wedge wt(\$) \wedge \\ (static(\mathrm{T@m}) \Leftrightarrow \mathrm{this} = null) \wedge \bigwedge_{i=k+1}^{n} \mathrm{v}_i = init(\tau([\mathrm{v}_i]))\,\} \\ \; body(\mathrm{T@m})\ \{\,\mathbf{Q} \wedge OS \equiv_L \$\,\} \end{array}}\ [\![\text{ strength-rule }]\!]}{\begin{array}{l} uc(\mathcal{A}), lu(\mathcal{A}), ro(\mathcal{A}), oal(\mathcal{A}), typed(\mathcal{A}), lu(\mathbf{A}), ro(\mathbf{A}), oal(\mathbf{A}), typed(\mathbf{A}) \rhd \\ \{\,\mathbf{P} \wedge \$ = OS \wedge alive(obj(L),\$) \wedge univV(obj(L)) \trianglelefteq \mathcal{U} \wedge \neg presentL(L,\mathrm{T}) \wedge \\ \bigwedge_{i=0}^{k} typeof(\mathrm{v}_i) \preceq \tau([\mathrm{v}_i]) \wedge wt(\$)\,\} \\ \; \mathrm{T@m}\ \{\,\mathbf{Q} \wedge OS \equiv_L \$\,\} \end{array}}\ [\![\text{ implementation-rule }]\!]$$

$$\dfrac{\begin{array}{l} \ldots \\ typed(\mathcal{A}) \rhd typed(\mathbf{A}) \quad [\![\text{ Lemma 3.2.1 }]\!] \\ oal(\mathcal{A}) \rhd oal(\mathbf{A}) \quad [\![\text{ Lemma 3.2.4 }]\!] \\ ro(\mathcal{A}) \rhd ro(\mathbf{A}) \quad [\![\text{ Lemma 3.2.5 }]\!] \\ lu(\mathcal{A}), ro(\mathcal{A}), typed(\mathcal{A}) \rhd lu(\mathbf{A}) \quad [\![\text{ Lemma 5.4.1 }]\!] \end{array}}{\begin{array}{l} uc(\mathcal{A}), lu(\mathcal{A}), ro(\mathcal{A}), oal(\mathcal{A}), typed(\mathcal{A}) \rhd \\ \{\,\mathbf{P} \wedge \$ = OS \wedge alive(obj(L),\$) \wedge univV(obj(L)) \trianglelefteq \mathcal{U} \wedge \neg presentL(L,\mathrm{T}) \wedge \\ \bigwedge_{i=0}^{k} typeof(\mathrm{v}_i) \preceq \tau([\mathrm{v}_i]) \wedge wt(\$)\,\} \\ \; \mathrm{T@m}\ \{\,\mathbf{Q} \wedge OS \equiv_L \$\,\} \end{array}}\ [\![\text{ assumpt-elim-rule }]\!]$$

Subtype-rule: According to the requirements of Theorem 5.4.1, applications of the subtype-rule do not occur in the proof for $\mathcal{A} \rhd \mathbf{A}$.

Class-rule: Let S@m = *impl*(T:m). We derive from the induction hypothesis ($\mathcal{S}$ abbreviates $uc(\mathcal{A}), lu(\mathcal{A}), ro(\mathcal{A}), oal(\mathcal{A}), typed(\mathcal{A})$):

$$\dfrac{\begin{array}{l} \mathcal{S} \rhd \{\, typeof(\mathrm{this}) = refDT(\mathrm{T},\mathcal{U}) \wedge \mathbf{P} \wedge \$ = OS \wedge alive(obj(L),\$) \wedge \\ \quad univV(obj(L)) \trianglelefteq \mathcal{U} \wedge \neg presentL(L,\mathrm{S}) \wedge \bigwedge_{i=0}^{k} typeof(\mathrm{v}_i) \preceq \tau([\mathrm{v}_i]) \wedge wt(\$)\,\} \\ \quad \mathrm{S@m} \\ \quad \{\,\mathbf{Q} \wedge OS \equiv_L \$\,\} \\ \neg presentL(L,\mathrm{T}) \Rightarrow \neg presentL(L,\mathrm{S}) \quad [\![\ \mathrm{T} \preceq_M \mathrm{S}, \text{ axiom } \mathbf{import2}, \text{ Lemma 3.1.8 }]\!] \end{array}}{\begin{array}{l} \mathcal{S} \rhd \{\, typeof(\mathrm{this}) = refDT(\mathrm{T},\mathcal{U}) \wedge \mathbf{P} \wedge \$ = OS \wedge alive(obj(L),\$) \wedge \\ \quad univV(obj(L)) \trianglelefteq \mathcal{U} \wedge \neg presentL(L,\mathrm{T}) \wedge \bigwedge_{i=0}^{k} typeof(\mathrm{v}_i) \preceq \tau([\mathrm{v}_i]) \wedge wt(\$)\,\} \\ \quad \mathrm{S@m} \\ \quad \{\,\mathbf{Q} \wedge OS \equiv_L \$\,\} \end{array}}\ [\![\text{ strength-rule }]\!]$$

By this sequent and the induction hypothesis, we prove:

$$\mathcal{S} \triangleright \{\ \mathit{typeof}(\text{this}) = \mathit{refDT}(\text{T},\mathcal{U}) \wedge \mathbf{P} \wedge \$ = \mathit{OS} \wedge \mathit{alive}(\mathit{obj}(L),\$) \wedge \mathit{univV}(\mathit{obj}(L)) \trianglelefteq \mathcal{U} \wedge \neg \mathit{presentL}(L,\text{T}) \wedge \bigwedge_{i=0}^{k} \mathit{typeof}(\text{v}_i) \preceq \tau([\text{v}_i]) \wedge \mathit{wt}(\$)\ \}\ \text{S@m}\ \{\ \mathbf{Q} \wedge \mathit{OS} \equiv_L \$\ \}$$

$$\mathcal{S} \triangleright \{\ \mathit{typeof}(\text{this}) \prec \mathit{refDT}(\text{T},\mathcal{U}) \wedge \mathbf{P} \wedge \$ = \mathit{OS} \wedge \mathit{alive}(\mathit{obj}(L),\$) \wedge \mathit{univV}(\mathit{obj}(L)) \trianglelefteq \mathcal{U} \wedge \neg \mathit{presentL}(L,\text{T}) \wedge \bigwedge_{i=0}^{k} \mathit{typeof}(\text{v}_i) \preceq \tau([\text{v}_i]) \wedge \mathit{wt}(\$)\ \}\ \text{T:m}\ \{\ \mathbf{Q} \wedge \mathit{OS} \equiv_L \$\ \}$$

[[class-rule]]

$$\mathcal{S} \triangleright \{\ \mathit{typeof}(\text{this}) \preceq \mathit{refDT}(\text{T},\mathcal{U}) \wedge \mathbf{P} \wedge \$ = \mathit{OS} \wedge \mathit{alive}(\mathit{obj}(L),\$) \wedge \mathit{univV}(\mathit{obj}(L)) \trianglelefteq \mathcal{U} \wedge \neg \mathit{presentL}(L,\text{T}) \wedge \bigwedge_{i=0}^{k} \mathit{typeof}(\text{v}_i) \preceq \tau([\text{v}_i]) \wedge \mathit{wt}(\$)\ \}\ \text{T:m}\ \{\ \mathbf{Q} \wedge \mathit{OS} \equiv_L \$\ \}$$

□

D.3 Auxiliary Lemmas and Proofs from Chapter 6

Lemma D.3.1. *In all programs with well-formed interface specifications, the following property holds: If L is the location for an invariant and two stores are L-equivalent then invrep yields the same value for L in both stores.*

$$\mathit{invL}(L) \wedge \mathit{OS} \equiv_L \mathit{OS}' \wedge \mathit{invrep}(L, \mathit{OS}) \Rightarrow \mathit{invrep}(L, \mathit{OS}')$$

Proof of Lemma D.3.1:

We prove that the lemma holds in all closed programs and thus in all open programs as well. In closed programs with well-formed interface specifications, we can assume that the appropriate axioms about L-equivalence and *invrep* are generated for L and the simple field id of L.

$\mathit{invL}(L) \wedge \mathit{OS} \equiv_L \mathit{OS}' \wedge \mathit{invrep}(L, \mathit{OS})$

$\Rightarrow$ [[Definition of *invL*, $L = \mathit{aloc}(\mathit{locA}(X,\text{f}))$ for suitable X and f]]

$L = \mathit{aloc}(\mathit{locA}(X,\text{f})) \wedge \mathit{OS} \equiv_{X.\text{f}} \mathit{OS}' \wedge \mathit{invrep}(L, \mathit{OS})$

$\Rightarrow$ [[Axioms generated for *invrep*]]

$L = \mathit{aloc}(\mathit{locA}(X,\text{f})) \wedge \mathit{OS} \equiv_{X.\text{f}} \mathit{OS}' \wedge \mathit{rep}_{\text{f}}(X, \mathit{OS})$

$\Rightarrow$ [[Axioms generated for $\_ \equiv_{\_} \_$]]

$L = \mathit{aloc}(\mathit{locA}(X,\text{f})) \wedge \mathit{rep}_{\text{f}}(X, \mathit{OS}')$

$\Rightarrow$ [[Axioms generated for *invrep*]]

$\mathit{invrep}(L, \mathit{OS}')$

□

Proof of Lemma 6.3.1:

We prove the sequent in several steps. We omit the assumption set $\mathcal{A}$ for brevity.

$$\{\, \mathbf{P} \wedge \mathit{inv}(\$,\mathcal{U}) \wedge \mathit{invL}(L) \wedge \mathit{alive}(\mathit{obj}(L),\$) \wedge \mathit{univV}(\mathit{obj}(L)) \trianglelefteq \mathcal{U} \,\}$$

$$\Rightarrow \quad \llbracket \text{ Definition of } \mathit{inv};\ \mathit{invL}(L) \Rightarrow L \notin M, \text{ Lemma 6.2.1 } \rrbracket$$

$$\{\, \exists D, OS : \mathbf{P} \wedge \mathit{inv}(\$,\mathcal{U}) \wedge \mathit{invL}(L) \wedge \mathit{alive}(\mathit{obj}(L),\$) \wedge \$ = OS \wedge$$
$$\mathit{univV}(\mathit{obj}(L)) \trianglelefteq \mathcal{U} \wedge D = \delta(M,\$) \wedge L \notin D \wedge \mathit{invL}(L) \wedge \mathit{invrep}(L, OS) \,\}$$

$\overline{\qquad\qquad\qquad\qquad\qquad\qquad\qquad\qquad\qquad\qquad}$ $\downarrow$ $\llbracket$ ex-rule $\rrbracket$

$$\{\, \mathbf{P} \wedge \mathit{inv}(\$,\mathcal{U}) \wedge \mathit{invL}(L) \wedge \mathit{alive}(\mathit{obj}(L),\$) \wedge \mathit{univV}(\mathit{obj}(L)) \trianglelefteq \mathcal{U} \wedge$$
$$\$ = OS \wedge D = \delta(M,\$) \wedge L \notin D \wedge \mathit{invL}(L) \wedge \mathit{invrep}(L, OS) \,\}$$

$\overline{\qquad\qquad\qquad\qquad\qquad\qquad\qquad\qquad\qquad\qquad}$ $\downarrow$ $\llbracket$ inv-rule $\rrbracket$

$$\{\, \mathbf{P} \wedge \mathit{inv}(\$,\mathcal{U}) \wedge \mathit{invL}(L) \wedge \mathit{alive}(\mathit{obj}(L),\$) \wedge$$
$$\mathit{univV}(\mathit{obj}(L)) \trianglelefteq \mathcal{U} \wedge \$ = OS \wedge D = \delta(M,\$) \,\}$$
$$\text{COMP} \quad \llbracket \text{ Sequent 6.1 } \rrbracket \tag{D.6}$$
$$\{\, L \in D \vee \$ \equiv_L OS \,\}$$

$\overline{\qquad\qquad\qquad\qquad\qquad\qquad\qquad\qquad\qquad\qquad}$ $\uparrow$ $\llbracket$ inv-rule $\rrbracket$

$$\{\, (L \in D \vee \$ \equiv_L OS) \wedge L \notin D \wedge \mathit{invL}(L) \wedge \mathit{invrep}(L, OS) \,\}$$
$$\Rightarrow$$
$$\{\, \$ \equiv_L OS \wedge \mathit{invL}(L) \wedge \mathit{invrep}(L, OS) \,\}$$
$$\Rightarrow \quad \llbracket \text{ Lemma D.3.1 } \rrbracket$$
$$\{\, \mathit{alive}(\mathit{obj}(L),\$) \Rightarrow \mathit{invrep}(L,\$) \,\}$$

$\overline{\qquad\qquad\qquad\qquad\qquad\qquad\qquad\qquad\qquad\qquad}$ $\uparrow$ $\llbracket$ ex-rule $\rrbracket$

$$\{\, \mathit{alive}(\mathit{obj}(L),\$) \Rightarrow \mathit{invrep}(L,\$) \,\}$$

Applying the disjunct-rule to Sequents 6.2 and D.6 yields:

$$\{\, \mathbf{P} \wedge \mathit{inv}(\$,\mathcal{U}) \wedge \mathit{invL}(L) \wedge \mathit{univV}(\mathit{obj}(L)) \trianglelefteq \mathcal{U} \,\}$$
$$\text{COMP}$$
$$\{\, \mathit{alive}(\mathit{obj}(L),\$) \Rightarrow \mathit{invrep}(L,\$) \,\}$$

By this sequent, we derive:

$$\{\, \mathbf{P} \wedge \mathit{inv}(\$,\mathcal{U}) \wedge \mathcal{U} = U \wedge \mathit{univV}(\mathit{obj}(L)) \trianglelefteq U \wedge \mathit{invL}(L) \,\}$$
$$\Rightarrow$$
$$\{\, \mathbf{P} \wedge \mathit{inv}(\$,\mathcal{U}) \wedge \mathit{univV}(\mathit{obj}(L)) \trianglelefteq \mathcal{U} \wedge \mathit{invL}(L) \wedge$$
$$(\mathit{univV}(\mathit{obj}(L)) \trianglelefteq U \wedge \mathit{invL}(L)) \,\}$$

$\overline{\qquad\qquad\qquad\qquad\qquad\qquad\qquad\qquad\qquad\qquad}$ $\downarrow$ $\llbracket$ inv-rule $\rrbracket$

$$\{\, \mathbf{P} \wedge \mathit{inv}(\$,\mathcal{U}) \wedge \mathit{univV}(\mathit{obj}(L)) \trianglelefteq \mathcal{U} \wedge \mathit{invL}(L) \,\}$$
$$\text{COMP} \tag{D.7}$$
$$\{\, \mathit{alive}(\mathit{obj}(L),\$) \Rightarrow \mathit{invrep}(L,\$) \,\}$$
$$\Rightarrow$$
$$\{\, \mathit{alive}(\mathit{obj}(L),\$) \wedge \mathit{univV}(\mathit{obj}(L)) \trianglelefteq U \wedge \mathit{invL}(L) \Rightarrow \mathit{invrep}(L,\$) \,\}$$

$\overline{\qquad\qquad\qquad\qquad\qquad\qquad\qquad\qquad\qquad\qquad}$ $\uparrow$ $\llbracket$ inv-rule $\rrbracket$

$$\{\, (\mathit{alive}(\mathit{obj}(L),\$) \wedge \mathit{univV}(\mathit{obj}(L)) \trianglelefteq U \wedge \mathit{invL}(L) \Rightarrow \mathit{invrep}(L,\$)) \wedge$$
$$(\mathit{univV}(\mathit{obj}(L)) \trianglelefteq U \wedge \mathit{invL}(L)) \,\}$$

From Sequent 6.2, we get:

$$
\begin{array}{ll}
\{\, \mathbf{P} \wedge inv(\$,\mathcal{U}) \wedge \mathcal{U} = U \wedge \neg(univV(obj(L)) \trianglelefteq U \wedge invL(L)) \,\} & \\
\hline
 & \downarrow \quad [\![\text{ inv-rule }]\!] \\
\{\, \mathbf{P} \wedge inv(\$,\mathcal{U}) \wedge \mathcal{U} = U \,\} & \\
\Rightarrow \quad [\![\text{ We can assume that there is at least one invariant, e.g., in } \texttt{Object}]\!] & \\
\{\, \exists L : \mathbf{P} \wedge inv(\$,\mathcal{U}) \wedge invL(L) \wedge \neg alive(obj(L),\$) \wedge univV(obj(L)) \trianglelefteq \mathcal{U} \,\} & \\
\hline
 & \downarrow \quad [\![\text{ ex-rule }]\!] \\
\{\, \mathbf{P} \wedge inv(\$,\mathcal{U}) \wedge invL(L) \wedge \neg alive(obj(L),\$) \wedge univV(obj(L)) \trianglelefteq \mathcal{U} \,\} & \\
\text{COMP} \quad [\![\text{ Sequent 6.2 }]\!] & \\
\{\, alive(obj(L),\$) \Rightarrow invrep(L,\$) \,\} & \\
\Rightarrow & \\
\{\, true \,\} & \\
\hline
 & \uparrow \quad [\![\text{ ex-rule }]\!] \\
\{\, true \,\} & \\
\hline
 & \uparrow \quad [\![\text{ inv-rule }]\!] \\
\{\, \neg(univV(obj(L)) \trianglelefteq U \wedge invL(L)) \,\} & \\
\Rightarrow & \\
\{\, (alive(obj(L),\$) \wedge univV(obj(L)) \trianglelefteq U \wedge invL(L) \Rightarrow invrep(L,\$)) \wedge & \\
\neg(univV(obj(L)) \trianglelefteq U \wedge invL(L)) \,\} &
\end{array}
\tag{D.8}
$$

We apply the disjunct-rule to Sequents D.7 and D.8 and derive the desired sequent:

$$
\begin{array}{ll}
\{\, \mathbf{P} \wedge inv(\$,\mathcal{U}) \wedge \mathcal{U} = U \,\} & \\
\hline
 & \downarrow \quad [\![\text{ all-rule }]\!] \\
\{\, \mathbf{P} \wedge inv(\$,\mathcal{U}) \wedge \mathcal{U} = U \,\} & \\
\text{COMP} \quad [\![\text{ Disjunction of Sequents D.7 and D.8 }]\!] & \\
\{\, alive(obj(L),\$) \wedge univV(obj(L)) \trianglelefteq U \wedge invL(L) \Rightarrow invrep(L,\$) \,\} & \\
\hline
 & \uparrow \quad [\![\text{ all-rule }]\!] \\
\{\, \forall L : alive(obj(L),\$) \wedge univV(obj(L)) \trianglelefteq U \wedge invL(L) \Rightarrow invrep(L,\$) \,\} & \\
\Rightarrow \quad [\![\text{ Definition of } inv]\!] & \\
\{\, inv(\$,U) \,\} &
\end{array}
$$

□

Proof of Sequent 6.4. In the following proofs, TA′ abbreviates the type and liveness annotations for List@init. Sequent 6.4 is obtained by applying the assumpt-intro-rule to the following sequent:

$\{ \; invL(L) \wedge alive(obj(L), \$) \wedge \$ = OS \wedge \mathrm{TA} \wedge univV(obj(L)) \trianglelefteq \mathcal{U} \wedge$
$D = \delta(\varnothing, \$) \; \}$
$\Rightarrow$ ⟦ Axioms **store11**, **store7**, **store5**, **store8** and **store10**, Lemma 5.2.2 ⟧
$\{ \; new(\$, \mathrm{List}, \mathcal{U}) \neq null \wedge \forall K_C : \$\langle \mathrm{List}, \mathcal{U}\rangle(K_C) \neq new(\$, \mathrm{List}, \mathcal{U}) \wedge invL(L) \wedge$
$alive(obj(L), \$\langle \mathrm{List}, \mathcal{U}\rangle) \wedge \mathrm{TA} \wedge univV(obj(L)) \trianglelefteq \mathcal{U} \wedge \$\langle \mathrm{List}, \mathcal{U}\rangle \equiv_L OS \wedge$
$obj(L) \neq new(\$, \mathrm{List}, \mathcal{U}) \; \}$
result = new List();
$\{ \; \mathrm{result} \neq null \wedge \forall K_C : \$(K_C) \neq \mathrm{result} \wedge invL(L) \wedge alive(obj(L), \$) \wedge \mathrm{TA} \wedge$
$univV(obj(L)) \trianglelefteq \mathcal{U} \wedge \$ \equiv_L OS \wedge obj(L) \neq \mathrm{result} \; \}$
$\Rightarrow$ ⟦ Lemmas 3.1.6, 3.1.4, and 6.2.1 ⟧
$\{ \; \exists D', OS' : \mathrm{result} \neq null \wedge \forall K_C : \$(K_C) \neq \mathrm{result} \wedge alive(obj(L), \$) \wedge \$ = OS' \wedge$
$\mathrm{TA} \wedge univV(obj(L)) \trianglelefteq univV(\mathrm{result}) \wedge D' = \delta(\{\mathrm{result.val}, \mathrm{result.inv}\}, \$) \wedge$
$L \notin D' \wedge OS' \equiv_L OS \; \}$
———————————————————— ↓ ⟦ ex-rule ⟧
$\{ \; \mathrm{result} \neq null \wedge \forall K_C : \$(K_C) \neq \mathrm{result} \wedge alive(obj(L), \$) \wedge \$ = OS' \wedge \mathrm{TA} \wedge$
$univV(obj(L)) \trianglelefteq univV(\mathrm{result}) \wedge D' = \delta(\{\mathrm{result.val}, \mathrm{result.inv}\}, \$) \wedge L \notin D' \wedge$
$OS' \equiv_L OS \; \}$
———————————————————— ↓ ⟦ inv-rule ⟧
$\{ \; \mathrm{result} \neq null \wedge \forall K_C : \$(K_C) \neq \mathrm{result} \wedge alive(obj(L), \$) \wedge \$ = OS' \wedge \mathrm{TA} \wedge$
$univV(obj(L)) \trianglelefteq univV(\mathrm{result}) \wedge D' = \delta(\{\mathrm{result.val}, \mathrm{result.inv}\}, \$) \; \}$
$\Rightarrow$
$\{ \; \mathrm{result} \neq null \wedge (\forall K_C : \$(K_C) \neq \mathrm{this} \wedge alive(obj(L), \$) \wedge \$ = OS' \wedge \mathrm{TA}' \wedge$
$univV(obj(L)) \trianglelefteq \mathcal{U} \wedge$
$D' = \delta(\{\mathrm{this.val}, \mathrm{this.inv}\}, \$))[\mathrm{result}/\mathrm{this}, univV(\mathrm{result})/\mathcal{U}] \; \}$
dummy=result.List@init(); ⟦ assumpt-axiom, invocation-rule ⟧
$\{ \; \$ \equiv_L OS' \vee L \in D' \; \}$
———————————————————— ↑ ⟦ inv-rule ⟧
$\{ \; (\$ \equiv_L OS' \vee L \in D') \wedge L \notin D' \wedge OS' \equiv_L OS \; \}$
$\Rightarrow$ ⟦ Lemma 4.2.1 ⟧
$\{ \; \$ \equiv_L OS \vee L \in D \; \}$
———————————————————— ↑ ⟦ ex-rule ⟧
$\{ \; \$ \equiv_L OS \vee L \in D \; \}$

Proof of Sequent 6.5. We prove the sequent in three steps: (1) We prove that List@createList preserves the invariants of the objects List@init creates (Sequent D.9); (2) We show that List@createList establishes the invariant of the new `List`-object (Sequent D.10); (3) We build the disjunction of Sequents D.9 and D.10 which yields Sequent 6.5.

$\{ \; \mathrm{TA} \wedge invL(L) \wedge \neg alive(obj(L), \$\langle \mathrm{List}, \mathcal{U}\rangle) \; \}$
$\Rightarrow$ ⟦ Axioms **store11**, **store5**, **store8** and **store10** ⟧
$\{ \; new(\$, \mathrm{List}, \mathcal{U}) \neq null \wedge \forall K_C : \$\langle \mathrm{List}, \mathcal{U}\rangle(K_C) \neq new(\$, \mathrm{List}, \mathcal{U}) \wedge \mathrm{TA} \wedge$
$invL(L) \wedge \neg alive(obj(L), \$\langle \mathrm{List}, \mathcal{U}\rangle) \; \}$
result = new List();
$\{ \; \mathrm{result} \neq null \wedge \forall K_C : \$(K_C) \neq \mathrm{result} \wedge \mathrm{TA} \wedge$ (D.9)
$invL(L) \wedge \neg alive(obj(L), \$) \; \}$
$\Rightarrow$
$\{ \; \mathrm{result} \neq null \wedge (\forall K_C : \$(K_C) \neq \mathrm{this} \wedge \mathrm{TA}' \wedge invL(L) \wedge$
$\neg alive(obj(L), \$))[\mathrm{result}/\mathrm{this}, univV(result)/\mathcal{U}] \; \}$
dummy=result.List@init(); ⟦ assumpt-axiom, invocation-rule ⟧
$\{ \; alive(obj(L), \$) \Rightarrow invrep(L, \$) \; \}$

$\{ \text{TA} \wedge invL(L) \wedge obj(L) = new(\$, \text{List}, \mathcal{U}) \}$

$\Rightarrow$ [[Axioms **store11**, **store5**, **store8** and **store10**]]

$\{ new(\$, \text{List}, \mathcal{U}) \neq null \wedge \forall K_C : \$\langle \text{List}, \mathcal{U} \rangle (K_C) \neq new(\$, \text{List}, \mathcal{U}) \wedge \text{TA} \wedge$
$typeof(new(\$, \text{List}, \mathcal{U})) = refDT(ctid(\text{List}), \mathcal{U}) \wedge invL(L) \wedge$
$obj(L) = new(\$, \text{List}, \mathcal{U}) \}$

result = new List();

$\{ \text{result} \neq null \wedge \forall K_C : \$(K_C) \neq \text{result} \wedge \text{TA} \wedge$
$typeof(\text{result}) = refDT(ctid(\text{List}), \mathcal{U}) \wedge invL(L) \wedge obj(L) = \text{result} \}$

$\Rightarrow$

$\{ \exists X : \text{result} \neq null \wedge \forall K_C : \$(K_C) \neq \text{result} \wedge \text{TA} \wedge \text{result} = X \wedge$
$typeof(X) = refDT(ctid(\text{List}), \mathcal{U}) \wedge invL(L) \wedge obj(L) = X \}$

———————————————————— $\downarrow$ [[ex-rule]]

$\{ \text{result} \neq null \wedge \forall K_C : \$(K_C) \neq \text{result} \wedge \text{TA} \wedge \text{result} = X \wedge$
$typeof(X) = refDT(ctid(\text{List}), \mathcal{U}) \wedge invL(L) \wedge obj(L) = X \}$

———————————————————— $\downarrow$ [[inv-rule]]

$\{ \text{result} \neq null \wedge \forall K_C : \$(K_C) \neq \text{result} \wedge \text{TA} \wedge \text{result} = X \}$ (D.10)

$\Rightarrow$

$\{ \text{result} \neq null \wedge$
$(\forall K_C : \$(K_C) \neq \text{this} \wedge \text{TA}' \wedge \text{this} = X)[\text{result}/\text{this}, univV(result)/\mathcal{U}] \}$

dummy=result.List@init(); [[assumpt-axiom, invocation-rule]]

$\{ invrep(X.\text{inv}, \$)[\text{dummy}/\text{result}] \}$

$\Rightarrow$

$\{ invrep(X.\text{inv}, \$) \}$

———————————————————— $\uparrow$ [[inv-rule]]

$\{ invrep(X.\text{inv}, \$) \wedge typeof(X) = refDT(ctid(\text{List}), \mathcal{U}) \wedge$
$invL(L) \wedge obj(L) = X \}$

$\Rightarrow$ [[Lemma D.2.2]]

$\{ alive(obj(L), \$) \Rightarrow invrep(L, \$) \}$

———————————————————— $\uparrow$ [[ex-rule]]

$\{ alive(obj(L), \$) \Rightarrow invrep(L, \$) \}$

Finally, we build the disjunction of Sequents D.9 and D.10 which yields Sequent 6.5:

$\{ \text{TA} \wedge inv(\$, \mathcal{U}) \wedge invL(L) \wedge \neg alive(obj(L), \$) \wedge univV(obj(L)) \trianglelefteq \mathcal{U} \}$

$\Rightarrow$ [[Axiom **store7**]]

$\{ \text{TA} \wedge invL(L) \wedge (obj(L) = new(\$, \text{List}, \mathcal{U}) \vee \neg alive(obj(L), \$\langle \text{List}, \mathcal{U} \rangle)) \}$

body(List@createList) [[disjunct-rule]]

$\{ alive(obj(L), \$) \Rightarrow invrep(L, \$) \}$

D.4 A Model for the Axiomatization of the Depends-Relation

As explained in Subsection 5.1.2, the notdepends-relation in an open program $\mathcal{P}$ can only be axiomatized in a reasonable way if $\mathcal{P}$ has a well-formed interface specification. Otherwise, extensions of $\mathcal{P}$ could introduce dependencies that are inconsistent with the axiomatization of the notdepends-relation. Consequently, we show in the following that there is a model for the axiomatization of the depends-relation and its negation for each program that has a well-formed interface specification. To show that, we prove two properties: (1) There is a model for each closed program. (2) Each model for a closed program $\mathcal{P}$ is also a model for the cores of all open programs that contain $\mathcal{P}$.

Lemma D.4.1. *Let $\mathcal{P}$ be a closed program with set of modules S. If $\mathcal{P}$ has a well-formed interface specification, then the function*

$$\begin{array}{l} dep : Location \times Location \times Store \rightarrow Bool \\ dep(X.\mathrm{f}, Y.\mathrm{g}, OS) \Leftrightarrow_{def} rc(R_{\mathrm{f},\mathrm{g}}(S), X, Y, OS) \end{array}$$

is a model for $\_ \stackrel{-}{\rightarrow} \_$.

For the proof of the above lemma, we need the following auxiliary lemma. It relates the automaton for a set of modules S to the automaton for a subset S' of S. Essentially, it says that program extensions cannot introduce dependencies between locations if (1) the fields of the locations and (2) the guards of the dependee w.r.t. all universes between the universe to which the dependee belongs and the universe to which the dependent belongs are declared in S'. This property is guaranteed by the visibility rule. The lemma is needed to show that the axiomatization of the notdepends-relation is consistent.

Lemma D.4.2.

$$\begin{array}{l} a_1 \ldots a_N \in \mathcal{L}(R_{f,g}(S)) \wedge \bigwedge_{i=1}^{N} dc(a_i, Z_{i-1}, Z_i, OS) \wedge wt(OS) \wedge S' \subseteq S \wedge \\ module(dtype(fid(Z_0.f))) \in S' \wedge module(dtype(fid(Z_N.g))) \in S' \wedge \\ \left(\forall U : univV(Z_N) \lhd U \unlhd univV(Z_0) \Rightarrow module(guard(Z_N.g, U)) \in S' \right) \Rightarrow \\ a_1 \ldots a_N \in \mathcal{L}(R_{f,g}(S')) \end{array}$$

Proof of Lemma D.4.2:

We prove the lemma by induction on N:

Induction Basis: $N = 0$

$\epsilon \in \mathcal{L}(R_{f,g}(S)) \wedge module(dtype(fid(Z_0.f))) \in S'$
$\Rightarrow$ ⟦ Automaton does not contain ϵ-transitions ⟧
$f = g \wedge module(dtype(fid(Z_0.f))) \in S'$
$\Rightarrow$
$\epsilon \in \mathcal{L}(R_{f,g}(S'))$

Induction Step: $N \geq 0$

$a_1 \ldots a_{N+1} \in \mathcal{L}(R_{f,g}(S)) \wedge \bigwedge_{i=1}^{N+1} dc(a_i, Z_{i-1}, Z_i, OS) \wedge wt(OS) \wedge S' \subseteq S \wedge$
$module(dtype(fid(Z_0.f))) \in S' \wedge module(dtype(fid(Z_{N+1}.g))) \in S' \wedge$
$(\ \forall U : univV(Z_{N+1}) \lhd U \unlhd univV(Z_0) \Rightarrow module(guard(Z_{N+1}.g, U)) \in S'\ )$
$\Rightarrow$ ⟦ the transition labeled with a_{N+1} leads from the state for h to the state for g; Obligations 5.2 and 5.3 for a_{N+1} ⟧
$univV(Z_{N+1}) \unlhd univV(Z_N) \wedge accessibleL(Z_N.\mathrm{h}, guard(Z_{N+1}.g, univV(Z_N))) \wedge$
$module(dtype(fid(Z_{N+1}.g))) \in S' \wedge$
$(\ \forall U : univV(Z_N) \lhd U \Rightarrow guard(Z_N.\mathrm{h}, U) = guard(Z_{N+1}.g, U)\ ) \wedge$
$a_1 \ldots a_N \in \mathcal{L}(R_{f,\mathrm{h}}(S)) \wedge \bigwedge_{i=1}^{N+1} dc(a_i, Z_{i-1}, Z_i, OS) \wedge wt(OS) \wedge S' \subseteq S \wedge$
$module(dtype(fid(Z_0.f))) \in S' \wedge module(guard(Z_{N+1}.g, univV(Z_N))) \in S'$
$(\ \forall U : univV(Z_{N+1}) \lhd U \unlhd univV(Z_0) \Rightarrow module(guard(Z_{N+1}.g, U)) \in S'\ ) \wedge$
$\Rightarrow$ ⟦ Definition of $accessibleL$ ⟧

$a_1 \ldots a_N \in \mathcal{L}(R_{f,\mathrm{h}}(S)) \wedge \bigwedge_{i=1}^{N} dc(a_i, Z_{i-1}, Z_i, OS) \wedge wt(OS) \wedge S' \subseteq S \wedge$
$module(dtype(fid(Z_0.f))) \in S' \wedge module(dtype(fid(Z_N.\mathrm{h}))) \in S' \wedge$
$(\ \forall U : univV(Z_N) \lhd U \unlhd univV(Z_0) \Rightarrow module(guard(Z_N.\mathrm{h}, U)) \in S'\ ) \wedge$
$module(guard(Z_{N+1}.g, univV(Z_N))) \in S'$
$\Rightarrow$ ⟦ Induction hypothesis, Obligation 5.4 for a_{N+1}; T is the declaration type of dep-clause a_{N+1} ⟧
$a_1 \ldots a_N \in \mathcal{L}(R_{f,\mathrm{h}}(S')) \wedge module(dtype(fid(Z_N.\mathrm{h}))) \in S' \wedge$
$module(guard(Z_{N+1}.g, univV(Z_N))) = module(\mathrm{T}) \wedge$
$module(guard(Z_{N+1}.g, univV(Z_N))) \in S'$
$\Rightarrow$ ⟦ the declarations of h and a_{N+1} are in S' ⟧
$a_1 \ldots a_{N+1} \in \mathcal{L}(R_{f,g}(S'))$

□

Based on Lemma D.4.2, we can now prove Lemma D.4.1.

Proof of Lemma D.4.1:

1. Reflexivity (Axiom **dep1**):

   $\epsilon \in \mathcal{L}(R_{\mathrm{f,f}})$ ⟦ Definition of $R^0_{A,B}$ ⟧
   $\Rightarrow$
   $\exists w \in \mathcal{L}(R_{\mathrm{f,f}}) : w = a_1 \ldots a_0 \wedge \exists Z_0 : Z_0 = X \wedge Z_0 = X$
   $\Rightarrow$ ⟦ Definition of l ⟧
   $l(\mathcal{L}(R_{\mathrm{f,f}}), X, X, OS)$
   $\Rightarrow$ ⟦ Lemma D.2.5 ⟧
   $rc(R_{\mathrm{f,f}}, X, X, OS)$
   $\Rightarrow$ ⟦ Definition of dep ⟧
   $dep(X.\mathrm{f}, X.\mathrm{f}, OS)$

2. Transitivity (Axiom **dep2**):

$$\begin{aligned}
&dep(X.\mathrm{f}, Y.\mathrm{g}, OS) \wedge dep(Y.\mathrm{g}, Z.\mathrm{h}, OS) \\
&\Rightarrow \quad [\![\text{ Definition of } dep\text{, Lemma D.2.5 }]\!] \\
&l(\mathcal{L}(R_{\mathrm{f,g}}), X, Y, OS) \wedge l(\mathcal{L}(R_{\mathrm{g,h}}), Y, Z, OS) \\
&\Rightarrow \quad [\![\text{ Definition of } l \text{ }]\!] \\
&\exists v \in \mathcal{L}(R_{\mathrm{f,g}}) : v = a_1 \ldots a_m \wedge \exists Z_0, \ldots, Z_m : \\
&Z_0 = X \wedge Z_m = Y \wedge \bigwedge_{i=1}^{m} dc(a_i, Z_{i-1}, Z_i, OS) \wedge \\
&\exists w \in \mathcal{L}(R_{\mathrm{g,h}}) : w = b_1 \ldots b_n \wedge \exists Z_0, \ldots, Z_n : \\
&Z_0 = Y \wedge Z_m = Z \wedge \bigwedge_{i=1}^{n} dc(b_i, Z_{i-1}, Z_i, OS) \\
&\Rightarrow \quad [\![\text{ shifting indices: } a_{m+i} := b_i \text{ }]\!] \\
&\exists v \in \mathcal{L}(R_{\mathrm{f,g}}), w \in \mathcal{L}(R_{\mathrm{g,h}}) : v = a_1 \ldots a_m \wedge w = a_{m+1} \ldots a_{m+n} \wedge \\
&\exists Z_0, \ldots, Z_{m+n} : Z_0 = X \wedge Z_m = Y \wedge Z_m = Y \wedge Z_{m+n} = Z \wedge \\
&\bigwedge_{i=1}^{m+n} dc(a_i, Z_{i-1}, Z_i, OS) \\
&\Rightarrow \quad [\![\text{ Definition of } \mathcal{L} \text{ [HU79, p. 28], } k := m + n \text{ }]\!] \\
&\exists w \in \mathcal{L}(R_{\mathrm{f,g}} R_{\mathrm{g,h}}) : w = a_1 \ldots a_k \wedge \exists Z_0, \ldots, Z_k : Z_0 = X \wedge Z_k = Z \wedge \\
&\bigwedge_{i=1}^{k} dc(a_i, Z_{i-1}, Z_i, OS) \\
&\Rightarrow \quad [\![\text{ Definition of } l \text{ }]\!] \\
&l(\mathcal{L}(R_{\mathrm{f,g}} R_{\mathrm{g,h}}), X, Z, OS) \\
&\Rightarrow \quad [\![\ \mathcal{L}(R_{\mathrm{f,g}} R_{\mathrm{g,h}}) \subseteq \mathcal{L}(R_{\mathrm{f,h}}) \ ]\!] \\
&l(\mathcal{L}(R_{\mathrm{f,h}}), X, Z, OS) \\
&\Rightarrow \quad [\![\text{ Lemma D.2.5, Definition of } dep \text{ }]\!] \\
&dep(X.\mathrm{f}, Z.\mathrm{h}, OS)
\end{aligned}$$

3. Concrete locations (Axiom **dep3**): For concrete locations $X.\mathrm{f}$, we get

$$\begin{aligned}
&dep(X.\mathrm{f}, Y.\mathrm{g}, OS) \\
&\Rightarrow \quad [\![\text{ Definition of } dep\text{, Lemma D.2.5 }]\!] \\
&l(\mathcal{L}(R_{\mathrm{f,g}}), X, Y, OS) \\
&\Rightarrow \quad [\![\ \mathrm{f} = \mathrm{g} \Rightarrow R_{\mathrm{f,g}} = \epsilon, \ \mathrm{f} \neq \mathrm{g} \Rightarrow R_{\mathrm{f,g}} = \varnothing \ ]\!] \\
&X.\mathrm{f} = Y.\mathrm{g}
\end{aligned}$$

4. Axioms for depends-clauses: Consider the axiom that is generated for a depends-clause d: $dc(d, X, Y, OS) \Rightarrow X.\mathrm{f} \stackrel{OS}{\longrightarrow} Y.\mathrm{g}$. For such an axiom, we derive:

$$\begin{aligned}
&dc(d, X, Y, OS) \\
&\Rightarrow \quad [\![\text{ Definition of } rc \text{ }]\!] \\
&rc(d, X, Y, OS) \\
&\Rightarrow \quad [\![\text{ Lemma D.2.5 }]\!] \\
&l(\{d\}, X, Y, OS) \\
&\Rightarrow \quad [\![\ \{d\} \subseteq \mathcal{L}(R_{\mathrm{f,g}}) \ ]\!] \\
&l(\mathcal{L}(R_{\mathrm{f,g}}), X, Y, OS) \\
&\Rightarrow \quad [\![\text{ Lemma D.2.5, Definition of } dep \text{ }]\!] \\
&dep(X.\mathrm{f}, Y.\mathrm{g}, OS)
\end{aligned}$$

5. Axioms for the negation of $\longrightarrow$:
Axioms for f and g are generated for scopes $S', S' \subseteq S$ that contain the declaration of both fields. The set of states, transitions, and the alphabet

of $\mathfrak{A}(S')$ are subsets of the states, transitions, and the alphabet of $\mathfrak{A}(S)$. We assume that the states are consistently renumbered when a program is extended. Therefore, we can omit σ_S and $\sigma_{S'}$ in the following.

$$
\begin{array}{l}
dep(X.\mathrm{f}, Y.\mathrm{g}, OS) \wedge wt(OS) \wedge S' \subseteq S \wedge \\
module(dtype(fid(X.\mathrm{f}))) \in S' \wedge module(dtype(fid(Y.\mathrm{g}))) \in S' \wedge \\
(\, \forall U : univV(Y) \lhd U \unlhd univV(X) \Rightarrow module(guard(Y.\mathrm{g}, U)) \in S' \,) \\
\Rightarrow \quad [\![\text{ Definition of } dep\text{, Lemma D.2.5 }]\!] \\
l(\mathcal{L}(R_{\mathrm{f,g}}(S)), X, Y, OS) \wedge wt(OS) \wedge S' \subseteq S \wedge \\
module(dtype(fid(X.\mathrm{f}))) \in S' \wedge module(dtype(fid(Y.\mathrm{g}))) \in S' \wedge \\
(\, \forall U : univV(Y) \lhd U \unlhd univV(X) \Rightarrow module(guard(Y.\mathrm{g}, U)) \in S' \,) \\
\Rightarrow \quad [\![\text{ Definition of } l \text{ }]\!] \\
\exists w \in \mathcal{L}(R_{\mathrm{f,g}}(S)) : w = a_1 \ldots a_k \wedge \exists Z_0, \ldots, Z_k : Z_0 = X \wedge Z_k = Y \wedge \\
\bigwedge_{i=1}^{k} dc(a_i, Z_{i-1}, Z_i, OS) \wedge wt(OS) \wedge S' \subseteq S \wedge \\
module(dtype(fid(X.\mathrm{f}))) \in S' \wedge module(dtype(fid(Y.\mathrm{g}))) \in S' \wedge \\
(\, \forall U : univV(Y) \lhd U \unlhd univV(X) \Rightarrow module(guard(Y.\mathrm{g}, U)) \in S' \,) \\
\Rightarrow \quad [\![\text{ Lemma D.4.2 }]\!] \\
\exists w \in \mathcal{L}(R_{\mathrm{f,g}}(S')) : w = a_1 \ldots a_k \wedge \exists Z_0, \ldots, Z_k : Z_0 = X \wedge Z_k = Y \wedge \\
\bigwedge_{i=1}^{k} dc(a_i, Z_{i-1}, Z_i, OS) \wedge \\
\Rightarrow \quad [\![\text{ Definition of } l \text{ }]\!] \\
l(\mathcal{L}(R_{\mathrm{f,g}}(S')), X, Y, OS) \\
\Rightarrow \quad [\![\text{ Lemma D.2.5 }]\!] \\
rc(R_{\mathrm{f,g}}(S'), X, Y, OS)
\end{array}
$$

□

Lemma D.4.3. *Let $\mathcal{P}'$ be an open program with core S', and $\mathcal{P}$ a closed program with set of modules S. If $\mathcal{P}'$ has a well-formed interface specification and $\mathcal{P}'$ contains $\mathcal{P}$ (i.e., $S' \subseteq S$), then the model for the axiomatization of the depends-relation for $\mathcal{P}$ is also a model for the axiomatization for the core of $\mathcal{P}'$.*

Proof of Lemma D.4.3:

The depends-relation and its negation are axiomatized by **dep1**, **dep2**, **dep3**, the axioms generated for the depends-relation, and the axioms generated for its negation. Each of these axioms that is contained in the universal specification for the core of $\mathcal{P}'$ is also contained in the universal specification for $\mathcal{P}$ ($S' \subseteq S$). Thus, the model for $\mathcal{P}$ is also a model for the core of $\mathcal{P}'$. □

Bibliography

[AdB94] P. America and F. de Boer. Reasoning about dynamically evolving process structures. *Formal Aspects of Computing*, 6:269–316, 1994.

[AL97] M. Abadi and K. R. M. Leino. A logic of object-oriented programs. In M. Bidoit and M. Dauchet, editors, *TAPSOFT '97: Theory and Practice of Software Development, 7th International Joint Conference CAAP/FASE, Lille, France*, volume 1214 of *Lecture Notes in Computer Science*, pages 682–696. Springer-Verlag, 1997.

[Alm97] P. S. Almeida. Balloon types: Controlling sharing of state in data types. In M. Akşit and S. Matsuoka, editors, *ECOOP '97: Object-Oriented Programming*, volume 1241 of *Lecture Notes in Computer Science*, pages 32–59. Springer-Verlag, 1997.

[Ame83] American National Standards Institute, Inc. *Ada Programming Language*, ansi/mil-std-1815a edition, January 1983.

[Ame87] P. America. Inheritance and subtyping in a parallel object-oriented language. In J. Bézivin, editor, *ECOOP '87, European Conference on Object-Oriented Programming, Paris, France*, volume 276 of *Lecture Notes in Computer Science*, pages 234–242. Springer-Verlag, 1987.

[Ame89] P. America. A behavioural approach to subtyping in object-oriented programming languages. Technical Report 443, Philips Research Laboratories, Nederlandse Philips Bedrijven B. V., 1989.

[Ame91] P. America. Designing an object-oriented programming language with behavioural subtyping. In J. W. de Bakker, W. P. de Roever, and G. Rozenberg, editors, *Foundations of Object-Oriented Languages*, volume 489 of *Lecture Notes in Computer Science*, pages 60–90. Springer-Verlag, 1991.

[Apt81] K. R. Apt. Ten years of Hoare logic: A survey — part I. *ACM Trans. on Prog. Languages and Systems*, 3:431–483, 1981.

[BA96] M. Ben-Ari. *Understanding Programming Languages*. John Wiley & Sons, 1996.

[Bac88] R. J. R. Back. A calculus of refinement for program derivations. *Acta Informatica*, 25:593–624, 1988.

[Ban95] G. S. Banavar. *An Application Framework for Compositional Modularity*. PhD thesis, The University of Utah, 1995.

[Bar97] J. Barnes. *Ada 95 Rationale*, volume 1247 of *Lecture Notes in Computer Science*. Springer, 1997.

[BC90] G. Bracha and W. Cook. Mixin-based inheritance. *ACM SIGPLAN Notices*, 25(10):303–311, October 1990. *OOPSLA ECOOP '90 Proceedings*, N. Meyrowitz (editor).

[BG77] R. M. Burstall and J. A. Goguen. Putting theories together to make specifications. In *Proc. 5th International Joint Conference on Artificial Intelligence*, pages 1045–1058. Morgan Kaufmann Publishers, 1977.

[BG94] P. Borba and J. A. Goguen. On refinement and FOOPS. Technical Report PRG-TR-17-94, Oxford University Computing Laboratory, 1994.

[Bij89] A. Bijlsma. Calculating with pointers. *Science of Computer Programming*, 12:191–205, 1989.

[BL91] G. Bracha and G. Lindstrom. Modularity meets inheritance. Technical Report UUCS-91-017, University of Utah, October 1991.

[BLO94] G. S. Banavar, G. Lindstrom, and D. Orr. Type-safe composition of object modules. In *Computer Systems and Education*, pages 188–200. McGraw Hill, 1994. Also available as University of Utah Technical Report UUCS-94-001.

[BMR95] A. Borgida, J. Mylopoulos, and R. Reiter. On the frame problem in procedure specifications. *IEEE Transactions on Software Engineering*, 21(10):785–798, October 1995.

[Boe99] F. S. de Boer. A WP-calculus for OO. In W. Thomas, editor, *Foundations of Software Science and Computation Structures*, volume 1578 of *Lecture Notes in Computer Science*, pages 135–149. Springer-Verlag, 1999.

[Bok99] B. Bokowski. Implementing "object ownership to order". Presented at the Intercontinental Workshop on Aliasing in Object-Oriented Systems at ECOOP'99), 1999. Available from `http://cuiwww.unige.ch/~ecoopws/iwaoos/papers/index.html`.

[Boo94] G. Booch. *Object oriented analysis and design with applications*. Addison-Wesley, 1994.

[BPF97] K. B. Bruce, L. Petersen, and A. Fiech. Subtyping is not a good "match" for object-oriented languages. In M. Akşit and S. Matsuoka, editors, *ECOOP '97: Object-Oriented Programming*, volume 1241 of *Lecture Notes in Computer Science*, pages 104–127. Springer-Verlag, 1997.

[BPJ00] J. van den Berg, E. Poll, and B. Jacobs. First steps in formalising JML. In S. Drossopoulou, S. Eisenbach, B. Jacobs, G. T. Leavens, P. Müller, and A. Poetzsch-Heffter, editors, *Formal Techniques for Java Programs*. Technical Report 269, Fernuniversität Hagen, 2000. Available from `www.informatik.fernuni-hagen.de/pi5/publications.html`.

[Bra92] G. Bracha. *The Programming Language Jigsaw: Mixins, Modularity and Multiple Inheritance*. PhD thesis, The University of Utah, 1992.

[BRS99] M. Benedikt, T. Reps, and M. Sagiv. A decidable logic for describing linked data structures. In S. D. Swierstra, editor, *Programming Languages and Systems (ESOP '99)*, volume 1576 of *Lecture Notes in Computer Science*, pages 2–19. Springer-Verlag, 1999.

[Bud91] T. Budd, editor. *Object-Oriented Programming*. Addison-Wesley, 1991.

[BV99] B. Bokowski and J. Vitek. Confined types. In *Proceedings of Object-Oriented Programming Systems, Languages, and Applications (OOPSLA)*, ACM SIGPLAN Notices, 1999.

[CDD$^+$89] D. Carrington, D. Duke, R. Duck, P. King, and G. Rose. *Object-Z: an object oriented extension to Z*. North-Holland, 1989.

[CFR93] T. R. Colburn, J. H. Fetzer, and T. L. Rankin. *Program Verification*. Kluwer Academic Publishers, 1993.

[CGR96] P. Chalin, P. Grogono, and T. Radhakrishnan. Identification of and solutions to shortcomings of LCL, a larch/c interface specification language. In M.-C. Gaudel and J. Woodcock, editors, *FME '96: Industrial Benefit and Advances in Formal Methods*, volume 1051 of *Lecture Notes in Computer Science*, pages 385–404. Springer-Verlag, January 1996.

[CH96] G. Cornell and C. S. Horstmann. *Java bis ins Detail*. Heise, 1996.

[CL94] Y. Cheon and G. T. Leavens. The Larch/Smalltalk interface specification language. *ACM Transactions on Software Engineering and Methodology*, 3(3):221–253, July 1994.

[Cla93] U. Claussen. *Objektorientiertes Programmieren*. Springer-Verlag, 1993.

[COR+95] J. Crow, S. Owre, J. Rushby, N. Shankar, and M. Srivas. *A Tutorial Introduction to PVS*, April 1995.

[Cou90] P. Cousot. Methods and logics for proving programs. In J. van Leeuwen, editor, *Handbook of Theoretical Computer Science*, volume B, chapter 15, pages 841–993. Elsevier Science Publishers, 1990.

[CPN98] D. G. Clarke, J. M. Potter, and J. Noble. Ownership types for flexible alias protection. In *Proceedings of Object-Oriented Programming Systems, Languages, and Applications (OOPSLA)*, volume 33(10) of *ACM SIGPLAN Notices*, October 1998.

[Dav99] M. Davis. Immutables. *Java-Report*, 4(4):70–77, April 1999.

[DGLM95] M. Day, R. Gruber, B. Liskov, and A. C. Myers. Subtypes vs. where clauses: Constraining parametric polymorphism. In *Proceedings of the 10th Annual Conference on Object-Oriented Programming, Systems, Languages, and Applications (OOPSLA '95)*, volume 30 of *ACM SIGPLAN Notices*, pages 156–168, 1995.

[Dha97] K. K. Dhara. Behavioral subtyping in object-oriented languages. Technical Report 97-09, Iowa State University, May 1997.

[Dij76] E. W. Dijkstra. *A Discipline of Programming*. Prentice-Hall, 1976.

[Dip98] P. Dippold. Logische Grundlagen einer Teilsprache von Java. Master's thesis, Fernuniversität Hagen, 1998. (in German).

[DK92] E. H. Durr and J. van Katwijk. VDM++: A formal specification language for object-oriented design. In *TOOLS Europe '92*, pages 63–77, 1992.

[DL96] K. K. Dhara and G. T. Leavens. Forcing behavioral subtyping through specification inheritance. In *Proceedings of the 18th International Conference on Software Engineering*, pages 258–267. IEEE Computer Society Press, 1996.

[DLN98] D. L. Detlefs, K. R. M. Leino, and G. Nelson. Wrestling with rep exposure. Research Report 156, Digital Systems Research Center, 1998.

[DLNS98] D. L. Detlefs, K. R. M. Leino, G. Nelson, and J. B. Saxe. Extended static checking. Research Report 159, Digital Systems Research Center, 1998. see also `www.research.digital.com/SRC/esc/Esc.html`.

[ES90] M. A. Ellis and B. Stroustrup. *The Annotated C++ Reference Manual*. Addison-Wesley, 1990.

[Fai85] R. E. Fairley. *Software Engineering Concepts*. McGraw-Hill, 1985.

[FGJM85] K. Futatsugi, J. Goguen, J.-P. Jouannaud, and J. Meseguer. Principles of OBJ2. In *Principles of Programming Languages*, pages 52–66. ACM, 1985.

[Flo67] R. W. Floyd. Assigning meanings to programs. In *Mathematical Aspects of Computer Science*, volume 19 of *Proceedings of Symposia in Applied Mathematics*, pages 19–32. American Mathematical Society, 1967.

[FM96] J. Feiler and A. Meadow. *Essential OpenDoc.* Addison-Wesley, 1996.

[FM98] C. Fischer and D. Meemken. JaWa: Java with assertions. In C. H. Cap, editor, *JIT '98 Java-Informations-Tage 1998*. Springer-Verlag, 1998.

[Gea97] D. M. Geary. *Graphic Java 1.1: Mastering the AWT.* Sun Microsystems Press, 1997.

[GG91] S. J. Garland and J. V. Guttag. A guide to LP, the Larch Prover. Technical Report 82, Digital Systems Research Center, 1991.

[GH93] J. V. Guttag and J. J. Horning. *Larch: Languages and Tools for Formal Specification.* Springer-Verlag, 1993.

[GJS96] J. Gosling, B. Joy, and G. Steele. *The Java Language Specification.* Addison-Wesley, Reading, MA, 1996.

[GMP90] D. Guaspari, C. Marceau, and W. Polak. Formal verification of Ada programs. *IEEE Transactions on Software Engineering*, 16(9):1058–1075, September 1990.

[GP82] W. D. Gillett and S. V. Pollack. *An Introduction to Engineered Software.* Holt, Rinehart and Winston, 1982.

[GTZ98] D. Genius, M. Trapp, and W. Zimmermann. An approach to improve locality using sandwich types. In X. Leroy and A. Ohori, editors, *Proceedings of the 2nd Types in Compilation Workshop*, volume 1473 of *Lecture Notes in Computer Science*, pages 194–214. Springer-Verlag, 1998.

[GWM+00] J. Goguen, T. Winkler, J. Meseguer, K. Futatsugi, and J.-P. Jouannaud. Introducing OBJ. In G. Malcolm, editor, *Software Engineering with OBJ: algebraic specification in action.* Kluwer, 2000.

[Ham97] G. Hamilton. *JavaBeans.* Sun Microsystems, Inc., 1997. Available from `http://java.sun.com/beans/docs/spec.html`

[Har92] S. P. Harbison, editor. *Modula-3.* Prentice Hall, 1992.

[HC97] C. S. Horstmann and G. Cornell. *Core Java.* Sunsoft Press, 1997.

[Heh93] E. C. R. Hehner. *A Practical Theory of Programming.* Texts and Monographs in Computer Science. Springer-Verlag, 1993.

[HJ99] M. Huisman and B. Jacobs. Java program verification via a Hoare logic with abrupt termination. Technical Report CSI-R9912, Computing Science Institute, Univ. Nijmegen, 1999.

[HJ00] M. Huisman and B. Jacobs. Java program verification via a Hoare logic with abrupt termination. In E. Maibaum, editor, *Fundamental Approaches to Software Engineering*, volume 1783 of *Lecture Notes in Computer Science*, pages 284–303. Springer-Verlag, 2000.

[HK00] K. Huizing and R. Kuiper. Verification of object-oriented programs using class invariants. In E. Maibaum, editor, *Fundamental Approaches to Software Engineering*, volume 1783 of *Lecture Notes in Computer Science*, pages 208–221. Springer-Verlag, 2000.

[HLW+92] J. Hogg, D. Lea, A. Wills, D. de Champeaux, and R. Holt. Report on ECOOP'91 workshop W3: The Geneva convention on the treatment of object aliasing. *OOPS Messenger*, 3(2):11–16, 1992.

[Hoa69] C. A. R. Hoare. An axiomatic basis for computer programming. *Communications of the ACM*, 12(10):576–580, 583, 1969.

[Hoa72] C. A. R. Hoare. Proofs of correctness of data representation. *Acta Informatica*, 1:271–281, 1972.

[Hog91] J. Hogg. Islands: Aliasing protection in object-oriented languages. In A. Paepcke, editor, *OOPSLA '91 Conference Proceedings*, pages 271–285, October 1991. SIGPLAN Notices, 26 (11).

[Hol91] I. J. Holyer. *Functional Programming with Miranda.* Pitman, 1991.

[HU79] J. E. Hopcroft and J. D. Ullman. *Introduction to Automata Theory, Languages, and Computation.* Addison-Wesley, 1979.

[HW73] C. A. R. Hoare and N. Wirth. An axiomatic definition of the programming language PASCAL. *Acta Informatica*, pages 335–355, 1973.

[IP00] A. Igarashi and B. C. Pierce. On inner classes. In E. Bertino, editor, *ECOOP 2000: Object-Oriented Programming*, volume 1850 of *Lecture Notes in Computer Science*, pages 129–153. Springer-Verlag, 2000.

[JBH+98] B. Jacobs, J. van den Berg, M. Huisman, M. van Berkum, U. Hensel, and H. Tews. Reasoning about Java classes. In *Proceedings of Object-Oriented Programming Systems, Languages and Applications (OOPSLA)*, 1998. Also available as TR CSI-R9812, University of Nijmegen.

[JLMPH99] B. Jacobs, G. T. Leavens, P. Müller, and A. Poetzsch-Heffter. Formal techniques for Java programs. In A. Moreira and D. Demeyer, editors, *Object-Oriented Technology. ECOOP'99 Workshop Reader*, volume 1743 of *Lecture Notes in Computer Science.* Springer-Verlag, 1999. Available from
`www.informatik.fernuni-hagen.de/pi5/publications.html`.

[JML] JML interest list. Archive at
`www.cs.iastate.edu/~leavens/JML.html`.

[Jon90] C. B. Jones. *Systematic Software Development using VDM.* Prentice Hall, 1990.

[Jon91a] K. D. Jones. LM3: A Larch interface language for Modula-3: A definition and introduction. Technical Report 72, Digital Equipment Corporation, Systems Research Center, 1991.

[Jon91b] H. B. M. Jonkers. Upgrading the pre- and postcondition technique. In S. Prehn and W. J. Toetenel, editors, *VDM '91: Formal Software Development Methods*, volume 551 of *Lecture Notes in Computer Science*, pages 428–456. Springer-Verlag, 1991.

[Jos97] R. Joshi. Extended static checking of programs with cyclic dependencies. Technical Note 1997-028, Digital Systems Research Center, 1997. In J. Mason, editor, *1997 SRC Intern Projects.*

[Kas90] U. Kastens. *Übersetzerbau.* Oldenburg, 1990.

[Kee89] S. E. Keene. *Object-Oriented Programming in Common Lisp.* Addison-Wesley, 1989.

[KMMPN83] B. Bruun Kristensen, O. Lehrmann Madsen, B. Møller-Pedersen, and K. Nygaard. Abstraction mechanisms in the BETA programming language. In *Tenth ACM Symposium on Principles of Programming Languages*, pages 285–298, Austin, Texas, 1983.

[KR88] B. W. Kernighan and D. M. Ritchie. *The C Programming Language.* Prentice Hall, 1988.

[Kra98] R. Kramer. iContract—the Java Design by Contract tool. In R. Ege, M. Singh, and B. Meyer, editors, *Technology of Object-Oriented Languages Tools 26.* IEEE Computer Society, 1998.

[Kru92] C. W. Krueger. Software reuse. *ACM Computing Surveys*, 24(2):131–183, June 1992.

[KT90] D. Kozen and J. Tiuryn. Logics of programs. In J. van Leeuwen, editor, *Handbook of Theoretical Computer Science*, volume B, chapter 14, pages 789–840. Elsevier Science Publishers, 1990.

[KT99] G. Kniesel and D. Theissen. JAC — Java with transitive readonly access control. Presented at the Intercontinental Workshop on Aliasing in Object-Oriented Systems at ECOOP'99, 1999. Available from `http://cuiwww.unige.ch/~ecoopws/iwaoos/papers/index.html`.

[Kuh70] T. S. Kuhn. *The Structure of Scientific Revolutions*, volume 2 of *International Encyclopedia of Unified Science*. The University of Chicago Press, 2nd edition, 1970.

[Lak96] J. Lakos. *Large-Scale C++ Software Design*. Addison-Wesley, 1996.

[Lam86] L. Lamport. *LaTeX: A document preparation system*. Addison-Wesley, 1986.

[Lar] Larch frequently asked questions. Available from `www.cs.iastate.edu/~leavens/larch-faq.html`.

[LB99] G. T. Leavens and A. L. Baker. Enhancing the pre- and postcondition technique for more expressive specifications. In J. M. Wing, J. Woodcock, and J. Davies, editors, *FM'99 – Formal Methods: World Congress on Formal Methods in Development of Computer Systems*, volume 1709 of *Lecture Notes in Computer Science*, pages 1087–1106. Springer-Verlag, 1999.

[LBR99a] G. T. Leavens, A. L. Baker, and C. Ruby. JML: A notation for detailed design. In H. Kilov, B. Rumpe, and I. Simmonds, editors, *Behavioral Specifications of Businesses and Systems*, pages 175–188. Kluwer Academic Publishers, 1999.

[LBR99b] G. T. Leavens, A. L. Baker, and C. Ruby. Preliminary design of JML: A behavioral interface specification language for Java. Technical Report 98-06c, Iowa State University, Department of Computer Science, January 1999.

[LCD+94] B. Liskov, D. Curtis, M. Day, S. Ghemawhat, R. Gruber, P. Johnson, and A. C. Myers. *Theta Reference Manual*. MIT Laboratory for Computer Science, Cambridge, MA, February 1994. Programming Methodology Group Memo 88, available from `www.pmg.lcs.mit.edu/papers/thetaref/`.

[LD00] G. T. Leavens and K. K. Dhara. Concepts of behavioral subtyping and a sketch of their extension to component-based systems. In G. T. Leavens and M. Sitaraman, editors, *Foundations of Component-Based Systems*. Cambridge University Press, 2000.

[Lea88] G. T. Leavens. *Verifying Object-Oriented Programs that use Subtypes*. PhD thesis, Massachusetts Institute of Technology, 1988. Published as MIT/LCS/TR-439 in February 1989.

[Lea96] G. T. Leavens. An overview of Larch/C++: Behavioral specifications for C++ modules. In H. Kilov and W. Harvey, editors, *Specification of Behavioral Semantics in Object-Oriented Information Modeling*, chapter 8, pages 121–142. Kluwer Academic Publishers, Boston, 1996.

[Lea97] G. T. Leavens. Larch/C++ reference manual. HTML version available from `www.cs.iastate.edu/~leavens/larchc++manual/lcpp_toc.html`, July 1997.

[Lei95a] K. R. M. Leino. A myth in the modular specification of programs. Note KRML 63-0, 1995.

[Lei95b] K. R. M. Leino. *Toward Reliable Modular Programs.* PhD thesis, California Institute of Technology, 1995.

[Lei97] K. R. M. Leino. Ecstatic: An object-oriented programming language with an axiomatic semantics. In B. Pierce, editor, *Proceedings of the Fourth International Workshop on Foundations of Object-Oriented Languages*, 1997. Available from: `www.cs.indiana.edu/hyplan/pierce/fool/`.

[Lei98] K. R. M. Leino. Data groups: Specifying the modification of extended state. In *Proceedings of the 1998 ACM SIGPLAN Conference on Object-Oriented Programming, Systems, Languages, and Applications (OOPSLA '98)*, volume 33(10) of *ACM SIGPLAN Notices*, pages 144–153, October 1998.

[LG86] B. Liskov and J. Guttag. *Abstraction and Specification in Program Development.* MIT Press, 1986.

[LH92] K. Lano and H. Haughton. Reasoning and refinement in object-oriented specification languages. In O. L. Madsen, editor, *ECOOP '92 European Conference on Object-Oriented Programming*, volume 615 of *Lecture Notes in Computer Science*, pages 78–97. Springer-Verlag, 1992.

[LMMPH00] M. Labeth, J. Meyer, P. Müller, and A. Poetzsch-Heffter. Formal verification of a doubly linked list implementation: A case study using the JIVE system. Technical Report 270, Fernuniversität Hagen, 2000.

[LN97] K. R. M. Leino and G. Nelson. Abstraction and specification revisited. A revised version of this manuscript is available as technical report [LN00], 1997.

[LN00] K. R. M. Leino and G. Nelson. Data abstraction and information hiding. Technical Report 160, Compaq Systems Research Center, 2000.

[LS97a] K. R. M. Leino and R. Stata. Checking object invariants. Technical Report 1997-007, Digital Systems Research Center, January 1997.

[LS97b] K. R. M. Leino and R. Stata. Direct dependencies and the pivot visibility rule. Note KRML 69-0, 1997.

[LS99] K. R. M. Leino and R. Stata. Virginity: A contribution to the specification of object-oriented software. *Information Processing Letters*, 70(2):99–105, April 1999.

[LSS99] K. R. M. Leino, J. B. Saxe, and R. Stata. Checking Java programs via guarded commands. In B. Jacobs, G. T. Leavens, P. Müller, and A. Poetzsch-Heffter, editors, *Formal Techniques for Java Programs.* Technical Report 251, Fernuniversität Hagen, 1999. Available from `www.informatik.fernuni-hagen.de/pi5/publications.html`.

[Luc90] D. C. Luckham. *Programming with Specifications: An Introduction to Anna. A Language for Specifying Ada Programs.* Springer-Verlag, 1990.

[LW90] G. T. Leavens and W. E. Weihl. Reasoning about object-oriented programs that use subtypes (extended abstract). In N. Meyrowitz, editor, *OOPSLA ECOOP '90 Proceedings*, volume 25(10) of *ACM SIGPLAN Notices*, pages 212–223. ACM, October 1990.

[LW93] B. Liskov and J. M. Wing. Specifications and their use in defining subtypes. In A. Paepcke, editor, *Proceedings of the 1998 ACM SIGPLAN Conference on Object-Oriented Programming, Systems, Languages, and Applications (OOPSLA '93)*, volume 28 of *ACM SIGPLAN Notices*, pages 16–28. ACM Press, 1993.

[LW94] B. Liskov and J. M. Wing. A behavioral notion of subtyping. *ACM Transactions on Programming Languages and Systems*, 16(6), 1994.

[LW97] G. T. Leavens and J. M. Wing. Protective interface specifications. In M. Bidoit and M. Dauchet, editors, *TAPSOFT '97: Theory and Practice of Software Development, 7th International Joint Conference CAAP/FASE, Lille, France*, volume 1214 of *Lecture Notes in Computer Science*, pages 520–534. Springer-Verlag, 1997. Available from `ftp://ftp.cs.iastate.edu/pub/techreports/TR96-04/TR.ps.gz`.

[Mey86] B. Meyer. Genericity is versus inheritance. In *OOPSLA '86 Conference Proceedings*, volume 21 of *ACM SIGPLAN Notices*, 1986.

[Mey88] B. Meyer. *Object-Oriented Software Construction*. Prentice Hall, 1988.

[Mey92a] B. Meyer. Design by contract. In D. Mandrioli and B. Meyer, editors, *Advances in object-oriented software engineering*. Prentice Hall, 1992.

[Mey92b] B. Meyer. *Eiffel: The Language*. Prentice Hall, 1992.

[Mey02] J. Meyer. *Design and Implementation of Interactive Program Verification Tools*. PhD thesis, Fernuniversität Hagen, 2002. (to appear).

[MH69] J. McCarthy and P. Hayes. Some philosophical problems from the standpoint of artificial intelligence. In B. Melzter and D. Michie, editors, *Machine Intelligence 4*, pages 463–502. Edinburgh University Press, 1969.

[Min96] N. Minsky. Towards alias-free pointers. In P. Cointe, editor, *ECOOP '96 European Conference on Object-Oriented Programming*, volume 1098 of *Lecture Notes in Computer Science*, pages 189–209. Springer-Verlag, 1996.

[MMPH97] P. Müller, J. Meyer, and A. Poetzsch-Heffter. Programming and interface specification language of JIVE — specification and design rationale. Technical Report 223, Fernuniversität Hagen, 1997.

[MMPH99] P. Müller, J. Meyer, and A. Poetzsch-Heffter. Making executable interface specifications more expressive. In C. H. Cap, editor, *JIT '99 Java-Informations-Tage 1999*, Informatik Aktuell. Springer-Verlag, 1999. Available from `www.informatik.fernuni-hagen.de/pi5/publications.html`.

[MMPH00] J. Meyer, P. Müller, and A. Poetzsch-Heffter. The JIVE system—implementation description. Available from `www.informatik.fernuni-hagen.de/pi5/publications.html`, 2000.

[MMPN93] O. L. Madsen, B. Møller-Pedersen, and K. Nygaard. *Object-Oriented Programming in the BETA Programming Language*. Addison-Wesley, 1993.

[Mor94] C. Morgan. *Programming from Specifications*. Prentice Hall, 1994.

[MPH97a] P. Müller and A. Poetzsch-Heffter. Formal specification techniques for object-oriented programs. In M. Jarke, K. Pasedach, and K. Pohl, editors, *Informatik 97: Informatik als Innovationsmotor*, Informatik Aktuell. Springer-Verlag, 1997.

[MPH97b] P. Müller and A. Poetzsch-Heffter. Preserving the correctness of object-oriented programs under extension. In R. Berghammer and F. Simon, editors, *Programming Languages and Fundamentals of Programming*. Christian-Albrechts-Universität Kiel, 1997. Technical Report 9717.

[MPH98] P. Müller and A. Poetzsch-Heffter. Kapselung und Methodenbindung: Javas Designprobleme und ihre Korrektur. In C. H. Cap, editor, *JIT '98 Java-Informations-Tage 1998*, Informatik Aktuell. Springer-Verlag, 1998. Available from `www.informatik.fernuni-hagen.de/pi5/publications.html` (in German).

[MPH99a] P. Müller and A. Poetzsch-Heffter. Alias control is crucial for modular verification. In A. Moreira and D. Demeyer, editors, *Object-Oriented Technology. ECOOP'99 Workshop Reader*, volume 1743 of *Lecture Notes in Computer Science*, pages 154–156. Springer-Verlag, 1999. (position paper).

[MPH99b] P. Müller and A. Poetzsch-Heffter. Universes: A type system for controlling representation exposure. In A. Poetzsch-Heffter and J. Meyer, editors, *Programming Languages and Fundamentals of Programming*. Fernuniversität Hagen, 1999. Technical Report 263, URL: `www.informatik.fernuni-hagen.de/pi5/publications.html`.

[MPH00a] J. Meyer and A. Poetzsch-Heffter. An architecture for interactive program provers. In S. Graf and M. Schwartzbach, editors, *Tools and Algorithms for the Construction and Analysis of Software (TACAS)*, volume 276 of *Lecture Notes in Computer Science*, pages 63–77, 2000.

[MPH00b] P. Müller and A. Poetzsch-Heffter. Modular specification and verification techniques for object-oriented software components. In G. T. Leavens and M. Sitaraman, editors, *Foundations of Component-Based Systems*. Cambridge University Press, 2000.

[MPH00c] P. Müller and A. Poetzsch-Heffter. A type system for controlling representation exposure in Java. In S. Drossopoulou, S. Eisenbach, B. Jacobs, G. T. Leavens, P. Müller, and A. Poetzsch-Heffter, editors, *Formal Techniques for Java Programs*. Technical Report 269, Fernuniversität Hagen, 2000. Available from `www.informatik.fernuni-hagen.de/pi5/publications.html`.

[MS96] D. R. Musser and A. Saini. *STL Tutorial and Reference Guide: C++ Programming with the Standard Template Library*. Addison-Wesley, 1996.

[MTHM97] R. Milner, M. Tofte, R. Harper, and D. MacQueen. *The Definition of Standard ML (revised)*. MIT Press, 1997.

[Mül95] P. Müller. Specification and implementation of an annotation language for an object-oriented programming language. Master's thesis, Technische Universität München, 1995. (In German).

[MZW97] A. Moormann Zaremski and J. M. Wing. Specification matching software components. *ACM Transactions on Software Engineering and Methodology*, 1997.

[Nel91] G. Nelson, editor. *Systems Programming with Modula-3*. Prentice Hall, 1991. Current version of language definition available from `www.research.digital.com/SRC/m3defn/html/m3.html`

[NO98] T. Nipkow and D. von Oheimb. Java$_{\ell ight}$ is type-safe — definitely. In *Proc. 25th ACM Symp. Principles of Programming Languages*, pages 161–170. ACM Press, New York, 1998.

[NVLA99] J. Noble, J. Vitek, D. Lea, and P. S. Almeida. Aliasing in object oriented systems. In A. Moreira and D. Demeyer, editors, *Object-Oriented Technology. ECOOP'99 Workshop Reader*, volume 1743 of *Lecture Notes in Computer Science*. Springer-Verlag, 1999.

[NVP98] J. Noble, J. Vitek, and J. M. Potter. Flexible alias protection. In E. Jul, editor, *ECOOP '98: Object-Oriented Programming*, volume 1445 of *Lecture Notes in Computer Science*. Springer-Verlag, 1998.

[OCL] OCL frequently asked questions. Archive at `www.cs.ukc.ac.uk/research/sse/oclws2k/oclfaq.txt`.

[Ohe99] D. von Oheimb. Hoare logic for mutual recursion and local variables. In C. Pandu Rangan, V. Raman, and R. Ramanujam, editors, *Foundations of Software Technology and Theoretical Computer Science*, volume 1738 of *Lecture Notes in Computer Science*. Springer-Verlag, 1999.

[Ohe00] D. von Oheimb. Axiomatic semantics for $\text{Java}_{\ell ight}$. In S. Drossopoulou, S. Eisenbach, B. Jacobs, G. T. Leavens, P. Müller, and A. Poetzsch-Heffter, editors, *Formal Techniques for Java Programs*. Technical Report 269, Fernuniversität Hagen, 2000. Available from `www.informatik.fernuni-hagen.de/pi5/publications.html`.

[OMG] OMG. UML resource page. Available from `www.omg.org/uml/`.

[Omo94] S. M. Omohundro. The Sather 1.0 specification. Technical report, International Computer Science Institute, 1994.

[ON98] D. von Oheimb and T. Nipkow. Machine-checking the Java specification: Proving type-safety. In J. Alves-Foss, editor, *Formal Syntax and Semantics of Java*, volume 1523 of *Lecture Notes in Computer Science*. Springer, 1998.

[OSR93] S. Owre, N. Shankar, and J. M. Rushby. The PVS specification language (beta release). Technical report, Computer Science Laboratory SRI International, April 1993.

[OW97] M. Odersky and P. Wadler. Pizza into Java: Translating theory into practice. In *The 24th Annual ACM SIGPLAN-SIGACT Symposium on Principles of Programming Languages*. ACM Press, 1997.

[Owi75] S. Owicki. *Axiomatic Proof Techniques for Parallel Programs*. Tr-75-251, Comp. Science Dept., Cornell University, 1975.

[Par72] D. L. Parnas. On the criteria to be used in decomposing systems into modules. *Communications of the ACM*, 5(12):1053–1058, December 1972. Reprinted in [You79].

[Pau91] L. C. Paulson. *ML for the working Programmer*. Cambridge University Press, 1991.

[Pau94] L. C. Paulson. *Isabelle: A Generic Theorem Prover*, volume 828 of *Lecture Notes in Computer Science*. Springer-Verlag, 1994.

[Per90] D. Perrin. Finite automata. In J. van Leeuwen, editor, *Handbook of Theoretical Computer Science*, volume B, chapter 1, pages 1–57. Elsevier Science Publishers, 1990.

[PH97a] A. Poetzsch-Heffter. Prototyping realistic programming languages based on formal specifications. *Acta Informatica*, 34:737–772, 1997.

[PH97b] A. Poetzsch-Heffter. Specification and verification of object-oriented programs. Habilitation thesis, Technical University of Munich, Jan. 1997. URL: `www.informatik.fernuni-hagen.de/pi5/publications.html`.

[PH00] A. Poetzsch-Heffter. *Konzepte objektorientierter Programmierung*. Springer-Verlag, 2000.

[PHM98] A. Poetzsch-Heffter and P. Müller. Logical foundations for typed object-oriented languages. In D. Gries and W. De Roever, editors, *Programming Concepts and Methods (PROCOMET)*, 1998.

[PHM99] A. Poetzsch-Heffter and P. Müller. A programming logic for sequential Java. In S. D. Swierstra, editor, *Programming Languages and Systems (ESOP '99)*, volume 1576 of *Lecture Notes in Computer Science*, pages 162–176. Springer-Verlag, 1999.

[Pre97] C. Prehofer. Feature-oriented programming: A fresh look at objects. In M. Akşit and S. Matsuoka, editors, *ECOOP '97: Object-Oriented Programming*, volume 1241 of *Lecture Notes in Computer Science*, pages 32–59. Springer-Verlag, 1997.

[Rei95] W. Reif. The KIV approach to software verification. In M. Broy and S. Jähnichen, editors, KORSO*: Methods, Languages, and Tools for the Construction of Correct Software*, volume 1009 of *Lecture Notes in Computer Science*. Springer-Verlag, 1995.

[RL00] C. Ruby and G. T. Leavens. Safely creating correct subclasses without seeing superclass code. In *OOPSLA 2000 Conference on Object-Oriented Programming, Systems, Languages, and Applications*, volume 35(10) of *ACM SIGPLAN Notices*, pages 208–228, October 2000.

[Ros97] J. Rose. *Inner Classes Specification.* Sun Microsystems, Inc., 1997. Available from `http://java.sun.com/products/jdk/1.1/docs`.

[RS92] L. Rapanotti and A. Socorro. Introducing FOOPS. Technical Report PRG-TR-28-92, Oxford University Computing Laboratory, 1992.

[RS93] W. Reif and K. Stenzel. Reuse of proofs in software verification. In R. Shyamasundar, editor, *Foundation of Software Technology and Theoretical Computer Science*, volume 761 of *Lecture Notes in Computer Science*, pages 284–293. Springer-Verlag, 1993.

[RSSB98] W. Reif, G. Schellhorn, K. Stenzel, and M. Balser. Structured specifications and interactive proofs with KIV. In W. Bibel and P. Schmitt, editors, *Automated Deduction — A Basis for Applications.* Kluwer Academic Publishers, 1998.

[Rüp94] A. Rüping. Modules in object-oriented systems. In R. Ege, M. Singh, and B. Meyer, editors, *TOOLS 14 — Technology of Object-Oriented Languages and Systems.* Prentice Hall, 1994.

[RW92] M. Reiser and N. Wirth, editors. *Programming in Oberon.* ACM Press, 1992.

[She95] D. Sheppard. *An Introduction to Formal Specification with Z and VDM.* McGraw-Hill, 1995.

[SMC74] W. Stevens, G. Myers, and L. Constantine. Structured design. *IBM Systems Journal*, 13(2):115–139, May 1974. Reprinted in [You79].

[Sny86] A. Snyder. Encapsulation and inheritance in object-oriented programming languages. In *OOPSLA '86 Conference Proceedings*, volume 21 of *ACM SIGPLAN Notices*, pages 38–45, 1986.

[Sny87] A. Snyder. Inheritance and the development of encapsulated software systems. In B. Shriver and P. Wegner, editors, *Research Directions in Object-Oriented Programming*, pages 165–188. MIT Press, 1987.

[SOM94] C. A. Szypersky, S. Omohundro, and S. Murer. Engineering a programming language: The type and class system of Sather. In J. Gutknecht, editor, *Programming Languages and System Architectures*, volume 782 of *Lecture Notes in Computer Science*, pages 208–227. Springer-Verlag, 1994.

[ST88] D. Sannella and A. Tarlecki. Specifications in an arbitrary institution. *Information and Computation*, 76:165–210, 1988.

[Ste96] B. Steensgaard. Points-to analysis in almost linear time. In *Proc. 23rd ACM Symp. Principles of Programming Languages*, pages 32–41. ACM Press, 1996.

[Str91] B. Stroustrup, editor. *The C++ Programming Language, 2nd Edition.* Addison-Wesley, 1991.

[Suz80] N. Suzuki, editor. *Automatic Verification of Programs with Complex Data Structures.* Garland Publishing, 1980.

[SWO95] M. Sitaraman, B. W. Weide, and W. F. Ogden. Using abstraction relations to verify abstract data type representations. Technical Report OSU-CISRC-9/95-TR39, Ohio State University, September 1995.

[Szy92] C. A. Szypersky. Import is not inheritance — why we need both: Modules and classes. In O. L. Madsen, editor, *ECOOP '92 European Conference on Object-Oriented Programming*, volume 615 of *Lecture Notes in Computer Science*, pages 19–32. Springer-Verlag, 1992.

[Szy98] C. A. Szypersky. *Component Software — Beyond Object-Oriented Programming.* Addison-Wesley, 1998.

[TWW82] J. W. Thatcher, E. G. Wagner, and J. B. Wright. Data type specification: parameterization and the power of specification techniques. *ACM TOPLAS*, 4:711–773, 1982.

[Ull94] J. D. Ullman. *Elements of ML Programming.* Prentice-Hall, 1994.

[UR93] M. Utting and K. Robinson. Modular reasoning in an object-oriented refinement calculus. In R. S. Bird, C. C. Morgan, and J. C. P. Woodcock, editors, *Mathematics of Program Construction*, volume 669 of *Lecture Notes in Computer Science*, pages 344–367. Springer-Verlag, 1993.

[Ver01] The Verificard project. `www.verificard.org`, 2001.

[Wad90] P. Wadler. Linear types can change the world! In M. Broy and C. B. Jones, editors, *Programming Concepts and Methods (PROCOMET)*, 1990.

[WE87] J. Welsh and J. Elder. *Introduction to Modula-2.* Prentice Hall, 1987.

[WGSD89] M. Woodman, R. Griffiths, J. Souter, and M. Davies. *Portable Modula-2 Programming.* McGraw-Hill, 1989.

[Win83] J. M. Wing. A two-tiered approach to specifying programs. Technical Report TR-299, Massachusetts Institute of Technology, Laboratory for Computer Science, 1983.

[Win87] J. M. Wing. Writing Larch interface language specifications. *ACM Transactions on Programming Languages and Systems*, 9(1):1–24, January 1987.

[Wir82] M. Wirsing. Structured algebraic specifications. In B. Robinet, editor, *Proc. AFCET Symp. on Mathematics for Computer Science*, pages 93–108, 1982.

[Wir88] N. Wirth. From Modula to Oberon. *Software Practice and Experience*, 18(7), 1988.

[Wir90] M. Wirsing. Algebraic specification. In J. van Leeuwen, editor, *Handbook of Theoretical Computer Science*, volume B, chapter 13, pages 675–788. Elsevier Science Publishers, 1990.

[Wir96] N. Wirth. *Compiler Construction.* Addison-Wesley, 1996.

[WK99] J. Warmer and A. Kleppe. *The Object Constraint Language, precise modeling with UML.* Addison-Wesley, 1999.

[WPP+83] M. Wirsing, P. Pepper, H. Partsch, W. Dosch, and M. Broy. On hierarchies of abstract data types. *Acta Informatica*, 20:1–33, 1983.

[WSR00] R. Wilhelm, M. Sagiv, and T. Reps. Shape analysis. In D. A. Watt, editor, *Compiler Construction*, volume 1781 of *Lecture Notes in Computer Science*, pages 1–17. Springer-Verlag, 2000.

[XdRH97] Q. Xu, W.-P. de Roever, and J. He. The rely-guarantee method for verifying shared variable concurrent programs. *Formal Aspects of Computing*, 9(2):149–174, 1997.

[XP99] H. Xi and F. Pfenning. Dependent types in practical programming. In *Proc. 26th ACM Symp. Principles of Programming Languages*, pages 214–227. ACM Press, New York, 1999.

[XS98] Q. Xu and M. Swarup. Compositional reasoning using the assumption-commitment paradigm. In W.-P. de Roever, H. Langmaack, and A. Pnueli, editors, *Compositionality: The Significant Difference*, volume 1536 of *Lecture Notes in Computer Science*, pages 565–583. Springer-Verlag, 1998.

[You79] E. N. Yourdon. *Classics in Software Engineering.* Yourdon Press, 1979.

List of Figures

Index

Lecture Notes in Computer Science

For information about Vols. 1–2185
please contact your bookseller or Springer-Verlag

Vol. 2186: J. Bosch (Ed.), Generative and Component-Based Software Engineering. Proceedings, 2001. VIII, 177 pages. 2001.

Vol. 2187: U. Voges (Ed.), Computer Safety, Reliability and Security. Proceedings, 2001. XVI, 249 pages. 2001.

Vol. 2188: F. Bomarius, S. Komi-Sirviö (Eds.), Product Focused Software Process Improvement. Proceedings, 2001. XI, 382 pages. 2001.

Vol. 2189: F. Hoffmann, D.J. Hand, N. Adams, D. Fisher, G. Guimaraes (Eds.), Advances in Intelligent Data Analysis. Proceedings, 2001. XII, 384 pages. 2001.

Vol. 2190: A. de Antonio, R. Aylett, D. Ballin (Eds.), Intelligent Virtual Agents. Proceedings, 2001. VIII, 245 pages. 2001. (Subseries LNAI).

Vol. 2191: B. Radig, S. Florczyk (Eds.), Pattern Recognition. Proceedings, 2001. XVI, 452 pages. 2001.

Vol. 2192: A. Yonezawa, S. Matsuoka (Eds.), Metalevel Architectures and Separation of Crosscutting Concerns. Proceedings, 2001. XI, 283 pages. 2001.

Vol. 2193: F. Casati, D. Georgakopoulos, M.-C. Shan (Eds.), Technologies for E-Services. Proceedings, 2001. X, 213 pages. 2001.

Vol. 2194: A.K. Datta, T. Herman (Eds.), Self-Stabilizing Systems. Proceedings, 2001. VII, 229 pages. 2001.

Vol. 2195: H.-Y. Shum, M. Liao, S.-F. Chang (Eds.), Advances in Multimedia Information Processing – PCM 2001. Proceedings, 2001. XX, 1149 pages. 2001.

Vol. 2196: W. Taha (Ed.), Semantics, Applications, and Implementation of Program Generation. Proceedings, 2001. X, 219 pages. 2001.

Vol. 2197: O. Balet, G. Subsol, P. Torguet (Eds.), Virtual Storytelling. Proceedings, 2001. XI, 213 pages. 2001.

Vol. 2198: N. Zhong, Y. Yao, J. Liu, S. Ohsuga (Eds.), Web Intelligence: Research and Development. Proceedings, 2001. XVI, 615 pages. 2001. (Subseries LNAI).

Vol. 2199: J. Crespo, V. Maojo, F. Martin (Eds.), Medical Data Analysis. Proceedings, 2001. X, 311 pages. 2001.

Vol. 2200: G.I. Davida, Y. Frankel (Eds.), Information Security. Proceedings, 2001. XIII, 554 pages. 2001.

Vol. 2201: G.D. Abowd, B. Brumitt, S. Shafer (Eds.), Ubicomp 2001: Ubiquitous Computing. Proceedings, 2001. XIII, 372 pages. 2001.

Vol. 2202: A. Restivo, S. Ronchi Della Rocca, L. Roversi (Eds.), Theoretical Computer Science. Proceedings, 2001. XI, 440 pages. 2001.

Vol. 2203: A. Omicini, P. Petta, R. Tolksdorf (Eds.), Engineering Societies in the Agents World II. Proceedings, 2001. XI, 195 pages. 2001. (Subseries LNAI).

Vol. 2204: A. Brandstädt, V.B. Le (Eds.), Graph-Theoretic Concepts in Computer Science. Proceedings, 2001. X, 329 pages. 2001.

Vol. 2205: D.R. Montello (Ed.), Spatial Information Theory. Proceedings, 2001. XIV, 503 pages. 2001.

Vol. 2206: B. Reusch (Ed.), Computational Intelligence. Proceedings, 2001. XVII, 1003 pages. 2001.

Vol. 2207: I.W. Marshall, S. Nettles, N. Wakamiya (Eds.), Active Networks. Proceedings, 2001. IX, 165 pages. 2001.

Vol. 2208: W.J. Niessen, M.A. Viergever (Eds.), Medical Image Computing and Computer-Assisted Intervention – MICCAI 2001. Proceedings, 2001. XXXV, 1446 pages. 2001.

Vol. 2209: W. Jonker (Ed.), Databases in Telecommunications II. Proceedings, 2001. VII, 179 pages. 2001.

Vol. 2210: Y. Liu, K. Tanaka, M. Iwata, T. Higuchi, M. Yasunaga (Eds.), Evolvable Systems: From Biology to Hardware. Proceedings, 2001. XI, 341 pages. 2001.

Vol. 2211: T.A. Henzinger, C.M. Kirsch (Eds.), Embedded Software. Proceedings, 2001. IX, 504 pages. 2001.

Vol. 2212: W. Lee, L. Mé, A. Wespi (Eds.), Recent Advances in Intrusion Detection. Proceedings, 2001. X, 205 pages. 2001.

Vol. 2213: M.J. van Sinderen, L.J.M. Nieuwenhuis (Eds.), Protocols for Multimedia Systems. Proceedings, 2001. XII, 239 pages. 2001.

Vol. 2214: O. Boldt, H. Jürgensen (Eds.), Automata Implementation. Proceedings, 1999. VIII, 183 pages. 2001.

Vol. 2215: N. Kobayashi, B.C. Pierce (Eds.), Theoretical Aspects of Computer Software. Proceedings, 2001. XV, 561 pages. 2001.

Vol. 2216: E.S. Al-Shaer, G. Pacifici (Eds.), Management of Multimedia on the Internet. Proceedings, 2001. XIV, 373 pages. 2001.

Vol. 2217: T. Gomi (Ed.), Evolutionary Robotics. Proceedings, 2001. XI, 139 pages. 2001.

Vol. 2218: R. Guerraoui (Ed.), Middleware 2001. Proceedings, 2001. XIII, 395 pages. 2001.

Vol. 2219: S.T. Taft, R.A. Duff, R.L. Brukardt, E. Ploedereder (Eds.), Consolidated Ada Reference Manual. XXV, 560 pages. 2001.

Vol. 2220: C. Johnson (Ed.), Interactive Systems. Proceedings, 2001. XII, 219 pages. 2001.

Vol. 2221: D.G. Feitelson, L. Rudolph (Eds.), Job Scheduling Strategies for Parallel Processing. Proceedings, 2001. VII, 207 pages. 2001.

Vol. 2223: P. Eades, T. Takaoka (Eds.), Algorithms and Computation. Proceedings, 2001. XIV, 780 pages. 2001.

Vol. 2224: H.S. Kunii, S. Jajodia, A. Sølvberg (Eds.), Conceptual Modeling – ER 2001. Proceedings, 2001. XIX, 614 pages. 2001.

Vol. 2225: N. Abe, R. Khardon, T. Zeugmann (Eds.), Algorithmic Learning Theory. Proceedings, 2001. XI, 379 pages. 2001. (Subseries LNAI).

Vol. 2226: K.P. Jantke, A. Shinohara (Eds.), Discovery Science. Proceedings, 2001. XII, 494 pages. 2001. (Subseries LNAI).

Vol. 2227: S. Boztaş, I.E. Shparlinski (Eds.), Applied Algebra, Algebraic Algorithms and Error-Correcting Codes. Proceedings, 2001. XII, 398 pages. 2001.

Vol. 2228: B. Monien, V.K. Prasanna, S. Vajapeyam (Eds.), High Performance Computing – HiPC 2001. Proceedings, 2001. XVIII, 438 pages. 2001.

Vol. 2229: S. Qing, T. Okamoto, J. Zhou (Eds.), Information and Communications Security. Proceedings, 2001. XIV, 504 pages. 2001.

Vol. 2230: T. Katila, I.E. Magnin, P. Clarysse, J. Montagnat, J. Nenonen (Eds.), Functional Imaging and Modeling of the Heart. Proceedings, 2001. XI, 158 pages. 2001.

Vol. 2231: A. Pasetti, Software Frameworks and Embedded Control Systems. XIV, 293 pages. 2002.

Vol. 2232: L. Fiege, G. Mühl, U. Wilhelm (Eds.), Electronic Commerce. Proceedings, 2001. X, 233 pages. 2001.

Vol. 2233: J. Crowcroft, M. Hofmann (Eds.), Networked Group Communication. Proceedings, 2001. X, 205 pages. 2001.

Vol. 2234: L. Pacholski, P. Ružička (Eds.), SOFSEM 2001: Theory and Practice of Informatics. Proceedings, 2001. XI, 347 pages. 2001.

Vol. 2235: C.S. Calude, G. Păun, G. Rozenberg, A. Salomaa (Eds.), Multiset Processing. VIII, 359 pages. 2001.

Vol. 2236: K. Drira, A. Martelli, T. Villemur (Eds.), Cooperative Environments for Distributed Systems Engineering. IX, 281 pages. 2001.

Vol. 2237: P. Codognet (Ed.), Logic Programming. Proceedings, 2001. XI, 365 pages. 2001.

Vol. 2239: T. Walsh (Ed.), Principles and Practice of Constraint Programming – CP 2001. Proceedings, 2001. XIV, 788 pages. 2001.

Vol. 2240: G.P. Picco (Ed.), Mobile Agents. Proceedings, 2001. XIII, 277 pages. 2001.

Vol. 2241: M. Jünger, D. Naddef (Eds.), Computational Combinatorial Optimization. IX, 305 pages. 2001.

Vol. 2242: C.A. Lee (Ed.), Grid Computing – GRID 2001. Proceedings, 2001. XII, 185 pages. 2001.

Vol. 2243: G. Bertrand, A. Imiya, R. Klette (Eds.), Digital and Image Geometry. VII, 455 pages. 2001.

Vol. 2244: D. Bjørner, M. Broy, A.V. Zamulin (Eds.), Perspectives of System Informatics. Proceedings, 2001. XIII, 548 pages. 2001.

Vol. 2245: R. Hariharan, M. Mukund, V. Vinay (Eds.), FST TCS 2001: Foundations of Software Technology and Theoretical Computer Science. Proceedings, 2001. XI, 347 pages. 2001.

Vol. 2246: R. Falcone, M. Singh, Y.-H. Tan (Eds.), Trust in Cyber-societies. VIII, 195 pages. 2001. (Subseries LNAI).

Vol. 2247: C. P. Rangan, C. Ding (Eds.), Progress in Cryptology – INDOCRYPT 2001. Proceedings, 2001. XIII, 351 pages. 2001.

Vol. 2248: C. Boyd (Ed.), Advances in Cryptology – ASIACRYPT 2001. Proceedings, 2001. XI, 603 pages. 2001.

Vol. 2249: K. Nagi, Transactional Agents. XVI, 205 pages. 2001.

Vol. 2250: R. Nieuwenhuis, A. Voronkov (Eds.), Logic for Programming, Artificial Intelligence, and Reasoning. Proceedings, 2001. XV, 738 pages. 2001. (Subseries LNAI).

Vol. 2251: Y.Y. Tang, V. Wickerhauser, P.C. Yuen, C.Li (Eds.), Wavelet Analysis and Its Applications. Proceedings, 2001. XIII, 450 pages. 2001.

Vol. 2252: J. Liu, P.C. Yuen, C. Li, J. Ng, T. Ishida (Eds.), Active Media Technology. Proceedings, 2001. XII, 402 pages. 2001.

Vol. 2253: T. Terano, T. Nishida, A. Namatame, S. Tsumoto, Y. Ohsawa, T. Washio (Eds.), New Frontiers in Artificial Intelligence. Proceedings, 2001. XXVII, 553 pages. 2001. (Subseries LNAI).

Vol. 2254: M.R. Little, L. Nigay (Eds.), Engineering for Human-Computer Interaction. Proceedings, 2001. XI, 359 pages. 2001.

Vol. 2255: J. Dean, A. Gravel (Eds.), COTS-Based Software Systems. Proceedings, 2002. XIV, 257 pages. 2002.

Vol. 2256: M. Stumptner, D. Corbett, M. Brooks (Eds.), AI 2001: Advances in Artificial Intelligence. Proceedings, 2001. XII, 666 pages. 2001. (Subseries LNAI).

Vol. 2257: S. Krishnamurthi, C.R. Ramakrishnan (Eds.), Practical Aspects of Declarative Languages. Proceedings, 2002. VIII, 351 pages. 2002.

Vol. 2258: P. Brazdil, A. Jorge (Eds.), Progress in Artificial Intelligence. Proceedings, 2001. XII, 418 pages. 2001. (Subseries LNAI).

Vol. 2259: S. Vaudenay, A.M. Youssef (Eds.), Selected Areas in Cryptography. Proceedings, 2001. XI, 359 pages. 2001.

Vol. 2260: B. Honary (Ed.), Cryptography and Coding. Proceedings, 2001. IX, 416 pages. 2001.

Vol. 2262: P. Müller, Modular Specification and Verification of Object-Oriented Programs. XIV, 292 pages. 2002.

Vol. 2264: K. Steinhöfel (Ed.), Stochastic Algorithms: Foundations and Applications. Proceedings, 2001. VIII, 203 pages. 2001.

Vol. 2267: M. Cerioli, G. Reggio (Eds.), Recent Trends in Algebraic Development Techniques. Proceedings, 2001. X, 345 pages. 2001.

Vol. 2272: D. Bert, J.P. Bowen, M.C. Henson, K. Robinson (Eds.), ZB 2002: Formal Specification and Development in Z and B. Proceedings, 2002. XII, 535 pages. 2002.

Vol. 2273: A.R. Coden, E.W. Brown, S. Srinivasan (Eds.), Information Retrieval Techniques for Speech Applications. XI, 109 pages. 2002.

Vol. 2274: D. Naccache, P. Paillier (Eds.), Public Key Cryptography. Proceedings, 2002. XI, 385 pages. 2002.

Vol. 2275: N.R. Pal, M. Sugeno (Eds.), Advances in Soft Computing – AFSS 2002. Proceedings, 2002. XVI, 536 pages. 2002. (Subseries LNAI).